'A fascinating and timely account of the numerous ways in which urban food shapes our lives and how a spatial understanding of food can help us understand our impact on the world and our interconnectedness. With a cross-disciplinary approach and examples from across the world bringing a rich range of perspectives, this is a must-read for anyone studying urban food systems, culture and ecology.'

—Carolyn Steel, architect, urbanist, author of *Hungry City: How Food Shapes Our Lives* (2008) and *Sitopia: How Food Can Save the World* (2020), Great Britain

'Mapping cities is centuries old, but mapping food in and for cities is recent yet fast growing and diversifying. This book offers a vital survey of the act and art of urban food mapping as a practice that is increasingly used as a participatory mechanism for bringing visibility to the place of food systems within urban systems. This rich and overdue addition to the literature on cities and food, in effect, maps urban food mapping.'

—Dr. Joe Nasr, architect, urbanist, urban agriculture pioneer, lecturer at Toronto Metropolitan University, Canada

'Food is central to our urban lives and shapes our cities and yet it often remains unseen in planning, in policy and indeed in the maps made of our urban environments. *Urban Food Mapping* creatively visualises the many roles food plays in cities around the world and invites us to see urban spaces through new lenses. This book is a methodologically innovative and thought provoking addition to urban and food studies.'

—Dr. Jane Battersby, urban and human geographer, senior lecturer at the Department of Environmental and Geographical Science, University of Cape Town, South Africa

'This book reminds us how important planning is and can be for the Great Food Transformation that science warns we need. Planning wasn't appreciated by individualised choice culture. But it's back. Not before time. It helps reconnect rural and urban realities, and unpick some crazy routes food takes. Should we be wary of top-down plans but embrace civic planning? Now read on...!'

—Tim Lang, Emeritus Professor of Food Policy, City, University of London, Great Britain

'No matter from which perspective you look: if you are interested to move towards a productive urban food future, this book is a must-have! In a refreshing way, essays outline the breadth of questions and approaches to action, focusing on the role of different mapping methods as knowledge generators and communication tools. By carefully and astutely framing these approaches, the book discloses the revelatory power of mapping methods and outlines the need for urban food mapping as an urban practice and a future interdisciplinary field of research.'

—Undine Giseke, landscape architect, partner in bgmr Landschaftsarchitekten, professor emeritus at Technische Universität Berlin, Germany

Urban Food Mapping

With cities becoming so vast, so entangled and perhaps so critically unsustainable, there is an urgent need for clarity around the subject of how we feed ourselves as an urban species. Urban food mapping becomes the tool to investigate the spatial relationships, gaps, scales and systems that underlie and generate what, where and how we eat, highlighting current and potential ways to (re)connect with our diet, ourselves and our environments.

Richly explored, using over 200 mapping images in 25 selected chapters, this book identifies urban food mapping as a distinct activity and area of research that enables a more nuanced way of understanding the multiple issues facing contemporary urbanism and the manyfold roles food spaces play within it. The authors of this multidisciplinary volume extend their approaches to place making, storytelling, in-depth observation and imagining liveable futures and engagement around food systems, thereby providing a comprehensive picture of our daily food flows and intrastructures. Their images and essays combine theoretical, methodological and practical analysis and applications to examine food through innovative map-making that empowers communities and inspires food planning authorities.

This first book to systematise urban food mapping showcases and bridges disciplinary boundaries to make theoretical concepts as well as practical experiences and issues accessible and attractive to a wide audience, from the activist to the academic, the professional and the amateur. It will be of interest to those involved in the all-important work around food cultures, food security, urban agriculture, land rights, environmental planning and design who wish to create a more beautiful, equitable and sustainable urban environment.

Katrin Bohn is an architect and urban practitioner and a principal lecturer at the University of Brighton, UK. Together with André Viljoen, she forms Bohn&Viljoen Architects, developing their food-focused urban design concept *Continuous Productive Urban Landscapes (CPUL)* in theory and practice.

Mikey Tomkins is an independent researcher and artist. He holds a PhD from the University of Brighton, UK, where he is an honorary research fellow. He is director at Edible Urban, a company that consults and implements UA projects both in the UK and abroad.

Urban Food Mapping:
Making Visible the Edible City

Edited by
Katrin Bohn and Mikey Tomkins

Routledge
Taylor & Francis Group

NEW YORK AND LONDON

The cover art is drawn from an aerial image of the city of Erbil (also known in Kurdish as "Hewlêr"), in the Kurdish region of Iraq. Erbil is often cited as one of the oldest continually inhabited cities in the world. At the centre of the city is the ancient citadel, a raised and enclosed mound that includes food production, now over 4,000 years old.

Cover art: Mikey Tomkins
Layout design: Katrin Bohn
Layouting support: Alma Bohn

First published 2024
by Routledge
605 Third Avenue, New York, NY 10158

and by Routledge
4 Park Square, Milton Park, Abingdon,
Oxon, OX14 4RN

Routledge is an imprint of the Taylor & Francis Group, an informa business

ISBN: 978-1-032-40280-2 (hbk)
ISBN: 978-1-032-40281-9 (pbk)
ISBN: 978-1-003-35228-0 (ebk)

DOI: 10.4324/9781003352280

Typeset in Chaparral Pro
by Apex CoVantage, LLC

All images by the chapter authors, unless otherwise stated.

Urban Food Mapping: Making Visible the Edible City

Editors:
Katrin Bohn and
Mikey Tomkins

Editorial board:
Mila Brill
Ferne Edwards
Howard Lee
Gundula Proksch
André Viljoen
Ivonne Weichold

Contributors:

Jacques Abelman
Amélie André
Corelia Baibarac-Duignan
Silvia Rosivalová Baučeková
Janie Bickersteth
Katrin Bohn
Mila Brill
Fabrizio D'Angelo
Marthe Derkzen
Jessica Ann Diehl
Viviana Ferrario
Joana Ferro
Patrick S. Ford
Vanessa Giolai
Natacha Quintero González
Anke Hagemann
Daina Cheyenne Harvey
Will Hughes
Maitreyi Koduganti
Asia Komarova
Marjorie Landels
George Lee
Howard Lee

Nina Yiu Lai Lei
Daniel Löschenbrand
Raphaella Mascia
Anna-Lisa Müller
Sheetal Patil
Adrian Paulsen
Matthew Potteiger
Gundula Proksch
Angelika Psenner
Paula Restrepo
Bradley Rink
Stephanie Robson
Tim Rodber
Parama Roy
Mariana Sanchez Salvador
Mikey Tomkins
Gesine Tuitjer
Leonie Tuitjer
Diana Tung
André Viljoen
Dominic Walker
Ivonne Weichold
Merel Zwarts

Contents

Preface

Katrin Bohn and Mikey Tomkins

This book, *Urban Food Mapping*, is about the future: the future of people, the future of cities and the future of urban food, as well as their relationships to the planet. It marks the beginning of a specific discussion on *making visible the Edible City*, a city that is indeed a curious character: sometimes, it does not exist, but we can imagine it; sometimes, it does exist, but we don't see it or only see its fragments; and sometimes, it used to exist, but we can't relate to the traces it left.

Urban food maps can make visible such an *Edible City*: its pasts, presents and futures. And this book makes visible urban food maps. It places them side-by-side, superimposes, compares, frames, explores, questions, dissects, orders and systematises, and by doing so, maps local urban food visions held by stakeholders from across the world.

In talking about mapping, we should confess upfront that we are not cartographers, at least not in the professional sense of the word, and neither are most of our contributors. Mapping interests us because it can spatialise the relationship between people and the urban. *Urban food* mapping does this for a very particular discourse, one that has only recently emerged and gained recognition: how do we feed our growing urban centres and enjoy the benefits that urbanisation brings without impacting negatively on the planet we inhabit with every other species? This discourse is pressing, as urgent as never before. It is not about urban space *per se*, far from it: it is about people and nature and about a fair sharing of land, activities, resources, cultures and networks – focused on food and thereby, ultimately, on the future of our cities and our globe.

This book, *Urban Food Mapping*, is about the present moment too. Its twenty-five selected chapters have been developed by forty-six contributors over the course of the last three years. Each chapter is mapping a particular urban food theme and its stakeholders, in a particular place and moment of time and with a particular purpose. All maps and mappings have then been remapped against our *Urban Food Mapping Matrix*, a diagram that visualises a key intention of the book: to initiate the definition of urban food mapping as a distinct activity and area of research.

The publication grew out of the conference panel *Mapping the Edible City: Making visible communities and food in the city* at the international conference *Anthropology and Geography: Dialogues Past, Present and Future* by the UK's Royal Geographical Society and Royal Anthropological Institute. The panel was initiated and convened by anthropologist Ferne Edwards and architect Katrin Bohn with André Viljoen acting as a co-convenor. Initially planned to be held in London, it was disrupted by the Covid-19 pandemic and went online to a large audience in the autumn of 2020. Following on from it, five of the conference panel members decided to join the co-convenors in this book project: Gundula Proksch, Howard Lee, Ivonne Weichold, Mikey Tomkins and Mila Brill. Working online through the pandemic, the editorial board collaborated closely with our contributors to create the content of this first book worldwide to systematise urban food mapping.

This book, *Urban Food Mapping*, also connects to the past and to the very beginnings of our works around designing for urban agriculture.

For Katrin, my early work with André Viljoen was all about mapping urban food, especially food spaces and spaces for food. We walked through southeast London in the early 2000s, searching quiet roads, embankments, public gardens, lawns, squares, footpaths, any open, green(ish) or leftover, underused spaces to – conceptually – create the first *Continuous Productive Urban Landscapes (CPUL)*. We drew the found spaces to scale – at the time using the paper *AtoZ* as underlay – and connected them with collaged bits of images to become food-productive green fingers, corridors, lanes. . . . In 1998, we mapped our first calculations about food in the city: *Exploded London*, a paper collage, and *ElastiCity Sheffield*, drawn with ink pens onto a series of Ordnance Survey maps. We collected and visualised yield data and created tables, often illustrated, to support 'the case for urban agriculture' by mapping its co-benefits. We collaged visions of a food-productive London onto the *Photographic Atlas* which, in 2004, had just been published, the direct and conceptual predecessor of *Google Earth*. We narrated our proposals, mapping out by writing the visions of a *CPUL City* in 10, 20, 50 years. In 2004, we created our first food opportunity map, not yet called like this, about the potential of urban food in the London Thames Gateway area. We had a vision for the city we would like to live in – green; productive; full of light, air, animals and people; a city to walk through – and we communicated it through mapping. We wrote in 2005, '*The CPUL vision of the city is one which celebrates the material and the real, one which "makes visible"'*.

For Mikey, as soon as my attention turned to researching urban agriculture, back in 2004, I embraced map making. My first maps were quantitative; I would walk around neighbourhoods for hours marking on paper the various spaces that could be utilised for food production, addressing two foundational questions: how much space is available and how much food can we grow? The answer is simple: we have plenty of space, but we just can't see it as it remains concealed in the relationship between what we expect to see and what has already been mapped and built. In 2009, my maps took a more qualitative and creative turn when I conceived the *Edible Mapping Project*. The project focuses on the lived experience of urban food spaces, how people might claim the right to use land, and what an *edible urban landscape* might look like. In pursuit of this, I incorporated walking, ceramics, costumes as well as initiating the growing of food, such as wheat in central Newcastle. In parallel, since 2014, I have worked on multiple forced-migration projects, mapping and implementing urban agriculture in refugee camps and urban locations in Iraq. Here, space can be contentious and is usually traumatised. It is always already occupied by stories and people, who are often absent or would rather be elsewhere. Maps made under post-occupation quickly expose the axioms that maps are power and that they are also redundant as soon as they are drawn, erased by the constant flow of people and resources who need to both survive the day but also escape it. Within the scope of all my work, I have witnessed how maps are centrally placed as tools to illuminate, initiate and create wonder, and how, if we don't commit to tasking ourselves to create our own food maps, no one else will do it for us.

In short, this book, *Urban Food Mapping*, is about stories which connect people, food and space. It demonstrates that urban food maps, as any maps, capture the past because their subjects, once mapped, immediately become frozen in time. Yet, simultaneously, the aim of every single chapter in this colourful collection is to alert, to challenge, to change – and to help us move towards a productive urban food future where life is about more experience and less consumption.

Mapping the Edible City:
An introduction

Katrin Bohn and Mikey Tomkins

Urban food mapping tackles a diverse range of food-focused data related to specific urban situations that makes visible issues about the feeding of cities or proposes solutions for their inclusive and sustainable development.

With this publication, we wish to initiate the definition of urban food mapping as a distinct activity and area of research that enables new ways of approaching the multiple issues facing contemporary urbanism. In *Second Nature Urban Agriculture*, Kevin Morgan writes, "*feeding the city in a sustainable fashion – that is to say in a manner that is economically efficient, socially just and ecologically sound – is one of the quintessential challenges of the 21st century*" (Morgan, 2014, p. 18). Our book seeks to contribute to this challenge by making visible – through maps and mapping – the many stakeholders, sites, activities, networks and products that are (or could be) part of the process where food is provided in sufficient quantity and quality as a contributor to the wellbeing of all.

Urban food mapping as a distinct activity and area of research

With global cities becoming so vast and entangled we agree that "*the map may be the only medium through which contemporary urbanism can achieve any sort of visual coherence*" and that "*the goal of rendering legible the complex, dynamic and living entity that is a city remains an urgent one*" (Cosgrove, 2008, p. 182). Moreover, we argue that there is a specific need regarding the mapping of urban food, because it remains underrepresented within general cartography as well as within food studies and within urban development, or it is dispersed

throughout other related research and remains unseen. Therefore, the urban food discourse – from production to harvesting, distribution, processing, consumption and disposal – provides a rich arena in which to urgently apply mapping as a tool to communicate, enabling a more nuanced way of understanding our increasingly complex urban spaces and the lives lived within them.

Developing urban food mapping as a distinct area of urban practice and research will help to articulate a more tangible approach to urban planning and design that also allows a "way in" for many practitioners, communities and individuals that would otherwise be excluded in what is traditionally a tightly regulated professional realm. This urban food mapping practice connects disciplines ranging from anthropology to urban design to urban planning and architecture, from geography to fine art, from social science to food cultures, from community studies to agronomy and economy and beyond. It brings together activists, planners, artists, researchers, residents, farmers and gardeners, cooks and food sellers, local administrators, politicians, community practitioners and many more who are all involved in the vital work around food security, land rights and witnessing the everyday pleasures and threats of the urban food environment.

The urgency in providing such equitable discussion on food and cities has become acutely evident and increasingly unavoidable: it is critical for any urban development given the multiple global crises facing humanity and the environment. With most humans now living in cities consuming food produced way beyond

DOI: 10.4324/9781003352280-1

their hinterland and assisted by resource-intensive technologies and economic models, the understanding of food-focused sustainable urban development has never been more important. For example, the alarming depletion of phosphorus as a finite resource essential for agriculture or the diminishing of drinking water quantity (IPCC, 2018) bear witness that *"a greater understanding is . . . needed of the lived reality of a modern city's ability to sustainably and equitably feed itself in a crisis situation or otherwise"* (Jensen and Orfila, 2021, p. 551). The negative environmental impact already associated with industrial, large-scale food production since the 1970s (Viljoen, 2005) has become somewhat "traditional" and "harmless" in comparison to the current realities of intensifying resource scarcities, accelerating climate change (Rockström *et al.*, 2020) and the so far unknown pressures on food security caused by a worldwide pandemic (Garnett *et al.*, 2020; Sridhar *et al.*, 2022).

In engaging to this discourse, we are encouraging food mappers to slip behind the cartographic lines and disrupt the univocal map as an impartial image, unsettle the cartographic party and expose the dynamic between mapping space and having control over space. Now is a time to play, to dream, to bring biographies and reclaim spatial imagery so that alliances between multiple stakeholders can contribute to design, planning and implementing spatially bound food systems for all. As many have proclaimed: "The map is dead! Long live the map!"

The importance of the word "urban"

"Food" is the central focus of this volume. All chapters explore space and those inhabiting it through that one lens: food's productions, consumptions, distributions, its cultures, histories, landscapes and stories. The practice of exploration is "mapping". It describes the actions of people in the urban landscape engaging in "making visible the Edible City" through a range of activities from photography to hand-drawn images to descriptive writing,

computer-generated maps and many more using mapping methods long established in cartography, such as line drawing, or using technologies, such as GIS, online platforms and various forms of social media, which more recently enabled new paths for innovative food map making.

During our research, we came across a vast array of mappings about food. They range from the origins and distribution of exotic products (Millstone and Lang, 2008) to the amount of hops needed for beer (Jensen and Roy, 2013) to food miles that add up when shipping products around the world (Paxton, 1994), to name but a few examples. The resulting maps are incredibly important to raise awareness of those food issues that contribute to the environmental and social urgencies described earlier. However, they are not necessarily *urban* food maps in the sense that we would like to discuss here. In this book's context of pressing issues around food, the benefit of semantics is in the word "urban".

We contend that *urban* food mapping is not identical with food mapping and that the former is a segment of the latter. The word "urban" grounds food mapping in an urban discourse. It highlights that its protagonists are not only interested in food *per se* – which is already complex and fascinating – but also in the interrelationships between food and urbanity. *Urban* food mapping studies the effects and demands of feeding people on the urban – especially on urban space – and it does so for small and large populations, for different geographical, political, socio-economic and environmental contexts, for vegetarian and omnivore diets. For example, an evening meal is an urban as well as spatial concern, requiring consumers to picture their shopping geographically from food production to food waste. Equally, a restaurant or street market has an environmental footprint related to food production, processing, trading, consuming or recycling, at various scales and in various locations. In short, mapping urban food also means to map urban space and those who inhabit it.

Strategically, concepts such as "urban metabolism", "productive urban landscapes" or "the edible city" already use mapping to bring together the many capacities involved in urban food systems. In the 21st century, urbanisation and the concomitant food system is everyone's concern, and as Viljoen and Bohn wrote nearly 10 years ago, *"the future of a city lies in the way its people are being fed. And the future of a desirable city lies in the way its urban space provides for food"* (Bohn and Viljoen, 2014a, p. 5).

Who maps, why maps?

In their introductory chapter to *ATLAS: Geography, Architecture and Change in an Interdependent World*, Smith *et al.* state that *"the challenge faced by architects, geographers, and researchers and practitioners in related fields [is] to respond in concrete forms and shapes to the demands of a dynamic planet and globally interdependent economy"* (Smith *et al.*, 2012, p. 5). Such *"concrete forms and shapes"* are the outcomes of processes traditionally led by design professionals, just as mapping was. Yet, this division of labour has drastically changed during recent years. Participatory and co-design processes are responding to the desire of citizens to take part in urban design and planning decisions as well as to the municipal recognition that involving neighbours in "making" their neighbourhood is the best, if not only, approach to create loved and lasting places (Antony, 2014).

In responding to this, maps have emerged as a key visual tool in the initiation, conduction and presentation of food-focused urban development processes, across all involved stakeholder groups. Often, stakeholders combine diverse map-making methods moving from the simple idea of a map to the concept of mapping as an ongoing, multi-disciplinary practice. Through maps and co-led mapping processes, the transformative power of urban design and planning becomes accessible for many, with design fulfilling one of its roles: *"to invent strategies for visualizing information that makes new interpretations possible"* (Abrams and Hall, 2006, p. 12). If utilised like this in urban planning and design, *"maps [can] structure [...] our knowledge of the landscape, affecting our perception of what is important, the relative sizes and relationships between objects and spaces and where it is possible or safe to travel"* (Firth, 2015) – keeping in mind that the destination of travel, in a metaphorical sense, is a more equitable, sound and experienceable "edible city".

Consequently, urban food mapping must embrace a multiplicity of writing and image-creation to make visible the lived experience of urban space in relation to food. In our research, we identified an expansive visual approach, applying professional and traditional cartographies to the food subject as well as "amateurism" as a radical practice that includes *"the arts of speaking, inhabiting, cooking and so on"* (Highmore, 2006, p. 157). Urban food mapping often leans towards the map as art where boundaries are blurred and transgressed between maps as objective communication and other responses, such as collaging, walking or photography. *"In pointing towards the existence of other worlds – real or imagined – map artists are claiming the power of the map to achieve ends other than the social reproduction of the status quo . . . what is at stake is the nature of the world we want to live in"* (Wood, 2006, p. 10). In this world, food is an everyday matter accepting a wide variety of opinions ranging from a single resident to large government organisations. In the UK, for example, food is defined as a "critical national infrastructure", one of *"those facilities, systems, sites, information, people, networks and processes necessary for a country to function and upon which daily life depends"* (CPNI, 2019). On the other hand, the everyday matter of food is intimate, such as the feeding of a child or the price of pasta, and only noticed when disrupted, for example by crisis or sudden change.

Food clearly emerges as too fundamental, ephemeral or subjective to be controlled by a single professional discourse alone. This does not come as a surprise given the multitude of actions and stakeholders engaged and intertwined with the urban food system. And it is not all problems, as evidenced by many of the maps in this volume which are celebratory of either food products, cultures or the potential to recreate urban space. It just is, as George Orwell commented already in 1937, "*curious how seldom the all-importance of food is recognized. You see statues everywhere to politicians, poets, bishops, but none to cooks or bacon-curers or market-gardeners*" (Orwell, 2021, p. 62).

A word on urban agriculture

Within the urban food-mapping discourse, mapping urban food production occupies a special position for us, the book editors, who have made urban agriculture a focus of study and practice for many years. Over the last two decades, urban agriculture has emerged as a key spatial practice for resilient urbanism with now wide-ranging aims. Urban agriculture was defined in 1996 as

an industry that produces and markets food and fuel, largely in response to the daily demand of consumers within a town, city, or metropolis; on land and water dispersed throughout the urban and peri-urban metropolis. Applying intensive production methods, using, and reusing natural resources and urban waste, to yield a diversity of crops and livestock.

(Smit *et al.*, 1996, p. 11)

To this definition, Perez-Vazquez included "*the non-material social needs such as relaxation, exercise, health, leisure and well being*" (Perez-Vazquez, 2002), whilst Taylor Lovell added urban agriculture's "*ecological functions (e.g., biodiversity, nutrient cycling, and micro-climate control) and cultural functions (e.g., recreation, cultural heritage, and visual quality)*" (Taylor Lovell, 2010, p. 2501).

Touching upon all these qualities and functions, Bohn&Viljoen Architects formulated *Continuous Productive Urban Landscapes (CPUL)*

in the early 2000s, an urban design concept embedding urban agriculture within the urban fabric by defining *CPULs* as "*essential elements of sustainable urban infrastructure*" (Viljoen, 2005, pp. 266–268), which they first mapped and then planned alongside other urban systems, such as transport networks, water or energy supplies. Planning and designing for urban agriculture are also linked to concepts of "spatial sovereignty", which stresses the need to participate in or have autonomy over urban space (Tomkins *et al.*, 2019, p. 105). This is a physical, creative and visual demand that can be mapped as a prerequisite for food security and therefore food sovereignty.

When considered as part of urban food mapping, urban agriculture encompasses a wide spectrum including tradition, aesthetics, ecology, cultural connection or politics, and, as an urban design tool, makes multiple spatial issues visible when being mapped. The fact that urban agriculture can pivot easily across such manifold boundaries demonstrates how it has become an all-important concept for the interrogation, design and implementation of sustainable urban space. And given that food needs spaces and spaces need to be mapped in order to be planned and later used, urban food mapping has emerged as an indispensable tool to identify and advance the argument that urban food production and urban space can beneficially coexist.

The harmonising of urban space with food production is implicit in the call for a more "*sensual, qualitative measure for the spatial success of open urban space*" made by Bohn&Viljoen (Bohn and Viljoen, 2005, p. 110). To achieve such "spatial success" demands a sensual cartography, one that encompasses the social, political, environmental and emotional too, one that includes the human and non-human when mapping and quantifying physical sites. The aim is to reduce conflict through visualisations so that urban agriculture becomes inherent in urban spatial design. Visualisations, particularly those that are spatial, as most urban food mappings are, aid our acceptance of what might happen, so that urban agriculture can be explained and accepted over the normalised parameters of "traditional" planning codes that have too often protected the economic status quo. As Caquard pointed out, "*mapping the world is as much about mapping reality as it is about mapping fiction*" (Caquard, 2013). Fiction is therefore powerful, and it has a touch of sur-realism to imagine a large sign hanging over the edge of a multistorey car park announcing, "*ceci n'est pas un car park*" because it is now a rooftop farm or a compost and worm farm or a beehive or all of these.

The Urban Food Mapping Matrix

To capture the breadth, divergence and multi-coded practices of urban food maps systematically, we have visualised them in what we call the *Urban Food Mapping Matrix* (Bohn and Edwards, 2020). As a drawing, this matrix is a map itself, a diagram clustering urban food mapping actions and outputs into three components (fig. 1). At the top of the drawing sit the five key urban food mapping **themes** that, according to our research, are usually being mapped: sites, stakeholders, activities, networks and produce (represented by coloured drop pin icons). In the centre of the matrix drawing are the four main urban food mapping **types** that we identified: purpose-based, citizen-based, place-based and time-based urban food maps (each represented by a separate colour). At the bottom, we brought together the most typical mapping **methods** embraced in urban food mapping.

This approach has contradictions, limitations and overlaps, just as any "categorisation" of thoughts and practices would have. However, "categorisation" is also a form of mapping, of bringing order into the overwhelming to make it understandable and transferable, in short: to make visible urban food maps and mapping. For example: whilst the *Urban Food Mapping Matrix* is part of the urban food mapping

theory this book aims to support, it also helps us practically to structure the volume.

The five key themes in urban food mapping

According to the editors' field notes, literature and desktop research, when questioning WHAT is being mapped, urban food mappers mainly investigate the following five themes:

FOOD GROWING SITES
FOOD SYSTEM ACTIVITIES
FOOD STAKEHOLDERS
FOOD PRODUCE AND CULTURES
FOOD NETWORKS AND RESOURCES.

There is no order to these themes, and many maps cover several themes at once. Depending on the disciplinary background of the mapper(s), we can discern certain prevalences of themes but, as argued before, the best urban food maps are multi-coded and inclusive anyway. For example, Bohn&Viljoen pointed out that, whilst food growing sites were the main mapping focus of urban agriculture for a long time, there are other important issues – namely stakeholder, mana-gerial and resource capacities – that need to be considered and mapped simultaneously for any successful urban food growing project (Bohn and Viljoen, 2014b, p. 159).

This book is split into five sections which cor-respond to the five key themes in urban food mapping as described above. Each theme is repre-sented through five chapters by selected authors providing multidisciplinary approaches to that theme. The selection of authors is based on the conference panel *Mapping the Edible City* at the 2020 international conference *Anthropology and Geography: Dialogues Past, Present and Future* (see Preface). It is not a definitive selection but

Fig. 1: The Urban Food Mapping Matrix brings together the key food mapping themes and types that urban food maps explore. It also shows the main mapping methods used.

URBAN FOOD MAPPING THEMES

Systems

Climate change

Crises

Conflicts

Animals

Soil quality

Identity

Innovation

Economies

Social justice

Food stake-holders

Food growing sites

Food networks/ resources

PEOPLE FOOD SPACE

Food system activities

Food produce/ cultures

Plants

Sense of place

Actions

Change

Water

Heat

Processes

Ecologies

Food security

Circularity

MAPPING TYPES

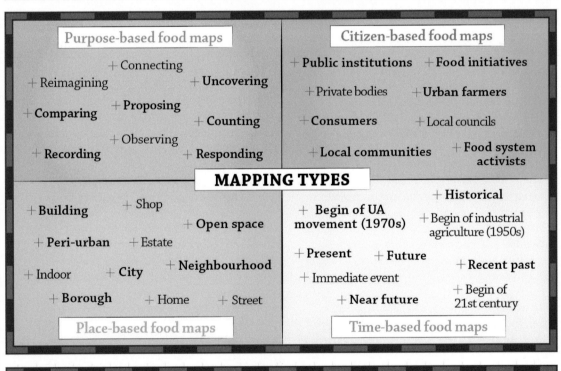

Purpose-based food maps

+ Connecting
+ Reimagining
+ Uncovering
+ Comparing
+ Proposing
+ Counting
+ Observing
+ Recording
+ Responding

Citizen-based food maps

+ **Public institutions** + **Food initiatives**
+ Private bodies + **Urban farmers**
+ **Consumers** + Local councils
+ **Local communities** + **Food system activists**

Place-based food maps

+ **Building** + **Shop**
+ **Open space**
+ **Peri-urban** + Estate
+ Indoor + **City** + **Neighbourhood**
+ **Borough** + Home + Street

Time-based food maps

+ **Historical**
+ **Begin of UA movement (1970s)** + Begin of industrial agriculture (1950s)
+ **Present** + **Future**
+ Immediate event + **Recent past**
+ Near future + Begin of 21st century

MAPPING METHODS

Counter-mapping

Drawing

Collection

Walking

Interviewing

Natural mapping

Critical cartography

Photographing

Table

Narrating

Collaging

Guerrilla mapping

Writing

List

Diagram

Audio recording

Opportunity mapping

Filming

Survey

Participatory mapping

Cartographic practices and products used in food mapping

exemplary of the millions of maps and mappings that we could have included. The content of some chapters in this book overlaps with several themes, where the emphasis we have currently placed is mutable. This observation confirms the complex nature of urban food mapping.

To visualise this complexity, we have "mapped" the 25 chapters of this volume in five breakout diagrams and texts at the start of each themed section. The diagrams act as a visual index of the chapters' contents and how they relate to the *Urban Food Mapping Matrix*. The purpose of the five themed sections is not to compartmentalise but to provide a moment of emphasis on a given theme. The breakout diagrams and texts can be used as a scaler, where the reader might read across a whole section or dive into individual chapters.

The four main urban food mapping types

Based on the editors' (design) research, the WHY, WHERE, WHOM and WHEN of urban food mapping result in the following four main mapping types:

Purpose-based urban food maps
Purpose-based urban food maps focus on visualising a particular concern that the mappers have in relation to food. Typical purpose-based urban food maps deal with uncovering, recording, counting, comparing and responding to food issues as well as with proposing change.

Our urban food maps are merely fragments from the countless stories we could have captured. As Rebecca Solnit writes, "*Every place is, if not infinite, then practically inexhaustible, and no quantity of maps will allow the distance to be completely traversed*" (Solnit *et al*., 2010, p. 2). However, accepting that territories could produce any number of stories and images has never deterred people or institutions or governments from making pictorial representations of a given location. As we enter an increasingly digital mapping age, multiple agencies are rushing to capture the city-map, whether commercial, institutional or governmental, yet, sometimes,

with a tendency to "visually flatline" the city, to render it as a single, cohesive and somewhat sedentary landscape. By contrast, the emphasis within this book is to contribute to – and maybe disrupt – this singular discourse through creative mapping responses to urban food issues from multiple communities whose purposes are to capture the unseen: the need, the care, the emotion, the emergence, character and divergence within urban food experiences in all their variety. Such an approach is described by Highmore in relation to de Certeau as the necessity "to see the object of observation outside of the frame that has already been made for it. To let the object bite back, to de-pacify the object, what is required is a disrupted and disrupting form of attention; a derailing of observation" (Highmore, 2006, p. 7).

Stating a purpose to urban food mapping allows an escape from the concept that it is objective. Within purpose-based mapping, there is an explicit intention to use maps to create arguments, present new data – or old data in a new way – to unsettle or support a new vision which will affect the lived experience of urban space. For example, one purpose that recurs throughout this book is to challenge the assumption that cities should be and are devoid of productive urban landscapes. More than half of the chapters directly relate to and map urban agriculture, either to observe, but mostly to envision an urban food abundance, where open spaces, built form and urban life support food system activities as if there never was or could be any other mode of existence for contemporary cities. Whilst addressing various themes, these purpose-based urban food mappings bring differing stories together using mapping methods which Wood also links to the writing of Debord and the Situationists, whose fictional "*maps charted social and cultural forces that were every bit as 'real' as those charted by the planners*" (Wood, 2006, p. 10). When purpose-based urban food maps reflect on a city – real or fictional – its visibility in the form of mapping moves beyond a 2D-image to include demands and actions that encompass proposing change, reimagining, uncovering, recording, in short: making visible the "edible city" as it is now and as it could be.

Place-based urban food maps

Place-based urban food maps focus on visualising food issues in relation to one or several distinct urban spaces. Typical place-based urban food maps deal with food in or on buildings, in open space, in a neighbourhood, borough or city and in the peri-urban realm.

All chapters in this volume are concerned with place-making and with the multiple agents, natures and designations that have formed and are forming urban space. If we look at our cities, we usually see space at the hands of the deliberate, the conceived. Yet, overlaying this physical space of brick – or soil – lies the visceral experience of urban inhabitants that marks their lives in the city. Place is therefore physical but also biographical, historical, under-recorded and ephemeral, and it is both qualities that urban food mapping aims to capture. Not only the seemingly static space of architecture or urban design – as shown in static, apolitical maps – but also the urban food landscapes of lives lived: the daily meal's table, a walk to the shops, or generating a social space on an urban farm crowded with possibility.

Whilst place-based urban food maps still focus on physical spaces in the city, such as neighbourhood, street, building or the peri-urban, we would like those spaces to be understood as "full of places". Place-based urban food maps should not be seen as images of borderlines marked by a series of dots on a map or an empty street, building or park. Seeing space as an arrangement of volumes or borderlines alone obscures daily lives behind cartographic iconography and could over-emphasise place as enduring and resistant, a two-dimensional façade. Consequently, we highlight place as enacted – brought alive by the human and non-human – where food is the connective agent. This invests our definition of place-based urban food maps with integrity: residents are literally "drawn" into maps and mapping

processes because this unites locations with their sensory interactions aiming towards food sovereignty and spatial sovereignty.

Place is always overlayed with time, purpose and citizens; it is never neutral but always already occupied, even in absence. This is how we deliberately visualise it in the *Urban Food Mapping Matrix* diagram. The four urban food mapping types in the centre of the diagram emphasise the connections of place-based urban food maps with those that use the place, in the times when it is being used and by considering the purpose of mapping that use. To put it another way: one cannot have access to food unless one first has space and rights over that space. Rights over space are connected to place-making and, at the same time, to mapping that place.

Time-based urban food maps

Time-based urban food maps focus on visualising food aspects over time and in relation to processes. Typical time-based urban food maps deal with urban food issues of the recent past, the present and the near future. They range from historical maps to those imagining a future far away.

Acknowledging time within mapping is important; when you mix time with space you get narratives, imagination and memories. Allowing a focus on processes, time-based food maps disrupt the notion of space as static or predicable, so that any subsequent consideration of space is already activated by social concerns (Till, 2013). And where better to start than food? Without food, as is often stated, we are "*nine meals from anarchy*" (Simms, 2022). But if a lack of food brings immediate chaos, then food itself brings a social glue to millions of humans spending their time engaged in acts of growing, processing, transporting, preparing, eating and sharing meals and produce.

Within time-based urban food maps, we understand history not as an antiquated version of a map occasionally being updated. We understand history as lived, compared and part of a future fiction and action. Temporal urban food mappings bring into focus the many absences of things that are no longer there and call into question why things are as they are. What, if the future we seek is actually the past made present? For example, if only we knew that right here, in this street, liquorice was grown, that there were cattle and that the smell of manure hung heavy in the air. Street names, squares and spaces are redolent with all sorts of food system activities, yet constantly are erased by the intensive food consumption that now occupies every urban corner. The task with time-based mapping is not a return or U-turn, but to gain ability of how we might leverage historical data and memory for a present in which there is greater equity and pleasure between foodscapes, urbanity, nature and people.

Kitchin and Dodge bring further distinction to a discussion on time with the idea that maps are processual, arguing that "*maps are never fully formed, and their work is never complete. Maps are of-the-moment, beckoned into being through practices; they are always mapping. From this perspective maps are fleeting, contingent, relational and context dependent*" (Kitchin and Dodge, 2007, p. 331). The idea of "always mapping" urban food emphasises the moment of reading and the actions it creates, such as walking and talking with people, or provokes thoughts about alternatives, rather than the assumption of an objective pictural knowledge. While an urban food map is a frame that bounds urban landscape, it is also a practice in the sense of being enacted by people in time and space, often foregrounding the user as author. Therefore, urban food maps do not pretend to be definitive, exhaustive of the data and stories available from within them but represent one moment from multiple others, within a given food-space-time nexus created by and often for a specific group of stakeholders.

Citizen-based urban food maps

Citizen-based urban food maps focus on visualising food issues in relation to people in the city. Typical citizen-based urban food maps depict urban farmers, food system activists and initiatives, *consumers and local communities as well as public institutions.*

At first sight, this type of urban food map seems to duplicate the theme *Food stakeholders*. Whilst the differences between the two are subtle indeed, we feel it is well justified to focus attention on this subject area more than once. After all, people and their actions, desires, needs and cultures, are what urban food mapping makes visible, and it is their well-being, equity and life quality that are at the centre of this book.

In our systematic, "food stakeholders" describes those humans (and non-humans) who are actively engaged in and affected by the urban food system. By contrast, "citizens" are all people in the city, including those who have no active roles in the urban food system. Here we also locate recognisable groups of people, such as public institutions or the local council which may appear in urban food mapping without being active food stakeholders. Food stakeholders are therefore a sub-group of all citizens, whereby, according to our research, it is indeed the case that they are the most mapped people in urban food mapping. Citizen-based urban food maps emphasise the importance of a holistic, inclusive approach to urban food issues where the effects of food-related urban realities and future decisions are carefully mapped across all members of society.

Additionally, it is probably no coincidence that our interest in citizen-based approaches follows a general transition where cartography has been split open as a discipline and made more accessible to a wider user group by technological advancement and opportunities, for example, widespread access to computers, the internet and social-media-based or open-source mapping software, such as *Open Street Map*. Beyond the technological, there is also an interest from spatial designers and institutions themselves to empower people by placing them on the map. Dalia Varanka discusses such advances as "*natural mapping*", a practice that "*creates personal images of places, movement, and landmarks that are highly invested with meaning*" (Varanka, 2006, p. 16). And finally, by using the word "mapping" in the book's title, we also emphasise the action of map making, asking not only who (and what, when and why) is being mapped but also who is creating the maps and who is the user.

Urban food mapping methods

This book applies a wide-ranging curatorial approach to the emerging urban food mapping discourse. Pulling in about 200 example maps and mappings in its 25 selected chapters, it showcases and transcends disciplinary boundaries, bringing together visual and textual concepts as well as practical experiences. Many of its authors exercise urban food mapping through multiple media and in several directions at once: a hand-drawn map, a GIS-generated map, a photograph, a walk, a digital diagram, a table – all sit side-by-side. Focusing on food, this volume confirms that, enabled by new technologies and a variety of mapping and especially visualisation methods, maps are no longer singular or reductive but instead are being transformed to make visible and to empower by engaging different perspectives, subjects and tempos.

Whilst urban food maps are still primarily made as drawings – as diverse as those may be – there are also numerous examples of maps being generated using photographing, filming, writing, narrating, audio recording, surveying, walking, collecting, listing and diagrammatising – or any combinations or collages of those – to name but the main urban food mapping methods that we encountered during our research. We have therefore chosen an expansive interpretation of cartography, one that bursts the parameters of a singular scientific discipline, one where urban food mappers have become free to reminisce, wander, imagine, discuss and accept the temporality of their existence and therefore their maps. Understanding urban food mappers as members of a vast heterogenous community

of citizens interested in food issues, we contend that the act of urban food map making is "omni-methodical".

This approach does not seek to disregard the scientific or academic but draws it into a relationship with the multiple makers of urban food maps and the methods they apply. It places great emphasis on who is being mapped, and why, giving prominence to people and communities, histories and visions. These mappings are not static actions and the resulting maps therefore not static objects but ones that emphasise the processes of use rather than the object in hand. To achieve such aims, key mapping methods applied in urban food mapping include counter-mapping, critical cartography, guerrilla mapping, opportunity mapping, participatory mapping, ethnocartography, eco-mapping, art mapping, indigenous mapping and natural mapping.

Using the urban food mapping matrix

Our endeavour to put urban food mapping in the spotlight as a distinct activity and area of research has four tangible outputs: (i) a definition of what it is; (ii) the identification and definition of several urban food mapping themes and types along with the identification of their typical mapping methods; (iii) a diagram, the *Urban Food Mapping Matrix*, that visualises these findings (see fig. 1); and (iv) the start of a, hopefully growing, collection of urban food maps.

Furthermore, by defining urban food *mapping* as an area of research and practice, we hope to provide a framework that can capture (design) research and multiple image-making methods, processes and outputs that would otherwise sit adrift under "other" research and practices. Within this, the *Urban Food Mapping Matrix* can add value and focus to researchers and activists who have chosen a visual approach to spatialise an argument for creating visibility and change.

The *Urban Food Mapping Matrix* can either be consulted to (i) verify whether a map is an urban food map; or to (ii) establish and compare the character and quality of a particular map or series of maps; or to (iii) be inspired and instructed to produce new urban food maps; – or, at its simplest, to (iv) raise interest in and identify gaps and new knowledge within the complex issue of urban food.

In the five breakout diagrams and texts that precede each themed section of the book, we have shown one way of using the *Urban Food Mapping Matrix* to classify existing urban food mappings. With this, the goal of our book is reached. However, it is evident how these "mappings" of the maps can be explored and assessed further to generate insights about the nature, trends or gaps of urban food mapping. Maybe, this will become another book or conference panel or an exhibition, and we will invite readers to contribute to this discussion.

Urban food mapping: A definition

Through the mappings collected in this book, we are seeking to inspire others to create further volumes of urban food maps and to further the *Urban Food Mapping Matrix*. And whilst we discuss five mapping themes and four mapping types that, we argue, bound urban food mapping, this bounding box is mutable and others will, no doubt, suggest we move the borderline, which is how it should be.

Urban food maps can be both observational and propositional tools. They are often relational with the capacity to "make visible" flows and activities that exist within the urban food system; to show connections with related resources; to illustrate infrastructures (or lack of) with regards to food access, logistics and spaces; to record food cultures and histories; and to highlight food stakeholders and their networks.

Urban food maps have power: being named and presented gives value and offers action.

Utilising this power, urban food maps can depict utopian (or dystopian) future imaginaries of what food cities could become. They develop the city map into a heterogeneous image, both in the moment but also in describing possible futures. It becomes feasible to argue that territories and maps are recursive of each other, where the physical space of the city has become so intertwined with its cartographic image that they exert an iterative power on each other. If the city and its cartographic image have indeed become co-creative, then claiming "rights to cartography" will also exert an influence on "rights to the city" and "rights to food sovereignty".

Urban food mapping enables an understanding of what is going on in a community, neighbourhood or city in terms of food. It supports independence and diversity of physical urban space through planning alternatives and therefore concomitant alternative urban food systems and urban food spaces. It also records beyond the spatial status quo to encompass the imagined, the desired, as well as the daily lived experience of space.

Urban food mapping can be used to explore and make visible any aspect of the urban food system, for any given urban site, at any given moment. Urban food maps can show local food (system) gaps and surpluses as well as local food networks thereby connecting food, urban space and residents on a visual plane. This has already proven to be a successful tool in participatory and co-design processes for many cross-sectoral urban planning issues and a prerequisite to working strategically about food in the urban realm. In short, we feel the subject of this book to be so important that we would like to conclude by offering a definition of urban food mapping as a distinct activity and area of research:

Urban food mapping tackles a diverse range of food-focused data related to specific urban situations that makes visible issues about the feeding of cities or proposes solutions for their inclusive and sustainable development.

References

Abrams, J., and Hall, P., 2006. Where/abouts. *In*: *Else/where: Mapping new cartographies of networks and territories*. Minneapolis: University of Minnesota Design Institute, 12.

Antony, S., 2014. Communal design of public spaces as a participatory goal. *In*: K. Bohn and K. Ritzmann, eds. *Playing/field urban agriculture: Ecological education and practice-based design*. Berlin: TU Berlin Publishers.

Bohn, K., and Edwards, F., 2020. *A short overview of food mapping: Developing a cross-disciplinary approach*. London: Anthropology and Geography: Dialogues Past, Present and Future International Conference [online], Royal Anthropological Institute, Royal Geographical Society, SOAS University of London, British Academy, British Museum, Great Britain.

Bohn, K., and Viljoen, A., 2005. Food in space: CPULs amongst contemporary open urban space. *In*: A. Viljoen, ed. *Continuous Productive Urban Landscape: Designing urban agriculture for sustainable cities*. London: Architectural Press, 110.

Bohn, K., and Viljoen, A., 2014a. CPUL City theory: An introduction. *In*: A. Viljoen and K. Bohn, eds. *Second Nature Urban Agriculture: Designing productive cities*. London: Routledge, 5.

Bohn, K., and Viljoen, A., 2014b. CPUL City actions: An introduction. *In*: A. Viljoen and K. Bohn, eds. *Second Nature Urban Agriculture: Designing productive cities*. London: Routledge, 159.

Caquard, S., 2013. Cartography I: Mapping narrative cartography. *Progress in Human Geography*, 37, 135–144.

Cosgrove, D.E., 2008. *Geography and vision: Seeing, imagining and representing the world*. London: I.B. Tauris.

CPNI, 2019. Critical National Infrastructure public website. [online] *Cpni.gov.uk*. Available from www.cpni.gov.uk/critical-national-infrastructure-0 [Accessed 25 Mar 2022].

Firth, R., 2015. Maps are expressions not only of power, but of desire . . . [online]. *Berfrois*. Available from www.berfrois.com/2015/05/maps-are-expressions-not-only-of-power-but-of-desire/ [Accessed 25 Mar 2022].

Garnett, P., Doherty, B., and Heron, T., 2020. Vulnerability of the United Kingdom's food supply chains exposed by COVID-19. *Nature Foods*, 1, 315–318. https://doi.org/10.1038/s43016-020-0097-7.

Highmore, B., 2006. *Michel De Certeau: Analysing culture*. London: Bloomsbury Publishing, 7, 157.

IPCC., 2018. Summary for policymakers. *In*: V. Masson-Delmotte, P. Zhai, H.O. Pörtner, D. Roberts, J. Skea, P.R. Shukla, A. Pirani, W. Moufouma-Okia, C. Péan, R. Pidcock, S. Connors, J.B.R. Matthews, Y. Chen, X. Zhou, M.I. Gomis, E. Lonnoy, T. Maycock, M. Tignor, and T. Waterfield, eds. *Global warming of 1.5°C: An IPCC special report on the impacts of global warming of 1.5°C above pre-industrial levels and related global greenhouse gas emission pathways, in the context of strengthening the global response to the threat of climate change, sustainable development, and efforts to eradicate poverty*. London: World Meteorological Organization.

Jensen, D., and Roy, M., 2013. *Food: An atlas*. [online] Available from www.kickstarter.com [Accessed 25 Mar 2022]

Jensen, P.D., and Orfila, C., 2021. Mapping the production-consumption gap of an urban food system: An empirical case study of food security and resilience. *Food Security*, 13, 551.

Kitchin, R., and Dodge, M., 2007. Rethinking maps. *Progress in Human Geography*, 31 (3), 331–344.

Lovell, S.T., 2010. Multifunctional urban agriculture for sustainable land use planning in the United States. *Sustainability*, 2 (8), 2501.

Millstone, E., and Lang, T., 2008. *The Atlas of food: Who eats what, where and why?* Berkeley, CA: University of California Press.

Morgan, K., 2014. The new urban foodscape: Planning, politics, and power. *In*: A. Viljoen and K. Bohn, eds. *Second Nature Urban Agriculture: Designing productive cities*. London: Routledge, 18.

Orwell, G., 2021. *The road to Wigan pier*. Oxford: Oxford University Press, 62.

Paxton, A., 1994. *The food miles report: The dangers of long distance food transport*. Austin, TX: SAFE Alliance.

Perez-Vazquez, A., 2002. *The role of allotments in food production as a component of urban agriculture in England*. London: Imperial College Wye, University of London.

Rockström, J., Edenhofer, O., Gaertner, J., and DeClerck, F., 2020. Planet-proofing the global food system. *Nature Food*, 1, 3–5. https://doi.org/10.1038/s43016-019-0010-4.

Simms, A., 2022. Nine meals from anarchy. [online] *New Economics Foundation*. Available from https://neweconomics.org/2008/11/nine-meals-anarchy [Accessed 25 Mar 2022].

Smit, J., et al., 1996. *Urban agriculture: Food, jobs and sustainable cities*. New York: UNDP, 11.

Smith, J., Tyszczuk, R., and Clark, N., 2012. A map they could all understand. *In*: R. Tyszczuk, J. Smith, N. Clark and M. Butcher, eds. *ATLAS: Geography, architecture and change in an interdependent world*. London: Blackdog, 5.

Solnit, R., Pease, B., and Siegel, S., 2010. *Infinite city: A San Francisco atlas*. Berkeley, CA, London: University of California Press, 2.

Sridhar, A., Balakrishnan, A., Jacob, M.M., Sillanpää, M., and Dayanandan, N., 2022. Global impact of COVID-19 on agriculture: Role of sustainable agriculture and digital farming. *Environmental Science and Pollution Research*, 1–17.

Till, J., 2013. *Architecture depends*. Cambridge, MA; London: The MIT Press.

Tomkins, M., Yousef, S., Adam-Bradford, A., Perkins, C., Grosrenaud, E., Mctough, M., and Viljoen, A., 2019. Cultivating refuge: The role of urban agriculture amongst refugees and forced migrants in the Kurdistan Region of Iraq. *International Journal of Design & Nature and Ecodynamics*, 14 (2), 103–118.

Varanka, D., 2006. Interpreting map art with a perspective learned from J.M. Blaut. *Cartographic Perspectives*, 53, 16.

Viljoen, A. (ed.), 2005. *Continuous Productive Urban Landscape: Designing urban agriculture for sustainable cities*. London: Architectural Press.

Wood, D., 2006. Catalogue of map artists. *Cartographic Perspectives*, 53, 61–68.

FOOD GROWING SITES:
Reimagining land use

Chapters in this section show that **maps and mapping underpin much of the reimagining of how city regions can re-establish connections** between their land and more resilient, equitable and sustainable urban food systems. Central to these concerns is the identification of spaces that can be re-natured and (re)connected to accommodate food growing and a diverse range of food activities and cultures. Authors speak about uniting, mediating and collaborating through mapping practices, moving beyond the dichotomy of urban/rural or human/nature.

Orthographic plans and sections merge and blend with cartography. Beyond these familiar mapping techniques, photography, narrative, collaging and painting all contribute to extending the content and meaning embodied in and attributed to mapping land use. **Urban food mapping**, as it is evolving as a method within food systems design, activities and research **has the capacity to highlight (sometimes unspoken) conflicts and potential**, aid scenario building and provide evidence for negotiating a reimagined urban habitat.

DOI: 10.4324/9781003352280-2

Dominic Walker and Tim Rodber map out an Edible London as it appears now, combining geography, cartography, photography, sketching, storytelling and anthropology to **document existing food system moments and spaces in the city**. By creating a portrait of urban agricultural endeavour, the authors establish the right and opportunity of those many moments to become the anchors for an edible city.

Ivonne Weichold explores alternative urban scenarios that are inclusive of productive agricultural land. Composite mapping is used to apply a landscape suitability analysis methodology. Developed from that, Luxembourg has been remapped for its ecological soil quality to **uncover potential agri-urban landscapes**. This mapping generates an agri-urban design reference catalogue for future use.

Jacques Abelman and Matthew Potteiger's chapter, situated in Brazil and the USA, describes the use of urban food mapping and a research-by-design methodology to re-conceptualise infrastructure as a hybrid human-ecological system. This mapping process includes observation of everyday food systems

activities and informs and articulates a **re-negotiating of the boundaries between infrastructure and landscape, generating potential for new typologies of productive urban spaces**.

André Viljoen works with abstracted and applied mappings to explore the methods used for making maps that are propositional and generative in relation to urban design in Nerima City, Tokyo, Japan. Fieldwork provides the raw material for a set of collages using **photography and drawing to communicate new readings of functional agricultural land use** and develop replicable strategies for reintegrating fragmented farmland into the city's urban fabric.

Viviana Ferrario and Fabrizio D'Angelo present an experimental series of agro-urban landscape maps about the City of Padua in Italy. The city has been conceptualised since the 2010s as part of an "agropolitan" region. The maps gather food spaces, activities as well as the voices of various stakeholders and act as **a mediation tool between citizens and the local administration, to aid the co-creation of an agro-urban park** at metropolitan scale.

Food growing sites

	Purpose WHY?	Citizen WHO?
	recording *counting* *comparing* *uncovering* *responding* *proposing*	*urban farmers* *food system activists* *food initiatives* *consumers* *local communities* *public institutions*
Walker et al. Edible London: A greater London Agriculture	recording food places proposing change 	local communities / food initiat 
Weichold Agroecologics: Reimagining an agri-urban design for Luxembourg	recording land use proposing change 	(urban) farmers 
Abelman et al. Re-negotiating the boundaries between infrastructure and landscape: Mapping infrastructural ecologies	uncovering food spaces recording produce  	urban farmers / local communi
Viljoen Mapping urban agriculture potentials in Nerima City, Tokyo	recording land use proposing change 	urban farmers food system stakeholders  
Ferrario et al.. Mapping multifunctional agro-urban landscape to manage edible cities in North-Eastern Italy	responding to change recording land use  	(urban) farmers / food system act 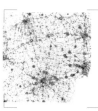 

Place WHERE?	**Time** WHEN?	**Methods** HOW?
the peri-urban city borough neighbourhood building open space	*historical begin UA movement recent past present near future future*	*Mapping methods, practices and products*
city / building	recent past / present	**Drawing Narrating**
the peri-urban / city	present / future	**Drawing Collaging**
neighbourhood / borough	recent past / present	**Photographing Collaging**
city	present / near future	**Drawing Collaging**
the peri-urban	recent past / present / near future	**Drawing Interviewing**

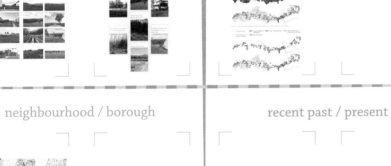

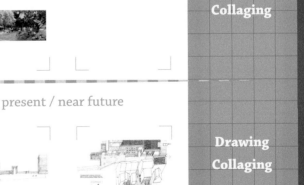
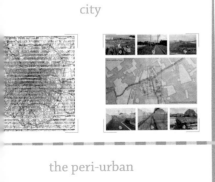
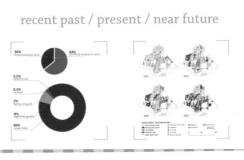

Edible London: A greater London agriculture

Dominic Walker and
Tim Rodber

Fig. 1: Mapping the existing edible city

This chapter depicts a personal journey that set out to explore portraits of an edible city in London. As authors, our interest in this subject stemmed from our success in an architectural competition to rethink the post-pandemic city.[1] Through our proposal we discovered two salient points. First, there are a number of arguments that suggest that food, farming and biodiversity play an integral role in the creation of a resilient, sustainable and healthy ecosystem. Second, in London (and elsewhere) there is already a huge range of existing initiatives and passionate

DOI: 10.4324/9781003352280-3

Production

Consumption ─── Waste

Ecology

Education ─── Economy

Existing Green Spaces

- Parks
- Woodland
- Marshland
- Brownfield sites
- Sites of natural interest

Existing Amenities

- ✛ Hospitals
- ✝ Cemeteries
- ◯ Schools
- △ Ports and docks
- ⋯ City boundary

Existing Green Hubs

- ◇ Urban growing spaces
- ☐ Food markets
- ⩔ Community or charity
- ⩔ Education and research
- ⩔ Businesses and start-ups

Proposed Networks

- ⋯↙ Biodiverse corridors
- ─ Ecological trails
- ⊕ Green innovation district
- ⌇ Marine-based agriculture
- ✾ Green energy sites

groups, from the intimate to the institutional, that are questioning the way we feed ourselves in the modern city. Figure 1 details our initial desktop survey of such spaces and groups in London. We overlaid this patchwork of existing spaces with a layer of our own proposals, aiming to stitch and weave the mapped fabric of existing spaces together into a diverse network. It was by no means exhaustive, but a useful vehicle through which to graphically express the potential London has to become a great contemporary sustainable food city.

In this chapter, we take our academic desktop pursuit and connect it to real world case studies that we have visited in London – a small and subjective selection of portraits that document the edible city (highlighted in red in fig. 1). We present an illustrated selection of four of our case studies based on themes that we believe are integral to establishing our vision of a sustainable food city.[2] We hope that our personal and analytical observations of these case studies can be read in conjunction with the academic texts elsewhere in this book. We end by compiling our case study research into a speculative drawing of an imagined edible neighbourhood in East London.

Portrait 1: Integrated urban farming – Calthorpe Community Gardens

Calthorpe Gardens was our first encounter with an intensely planted urban growing space, and it has remained in our minds since our visit on a sunny September afternoon in the middle of the Covid-19 pandemic. The gardens sit on a once contested site, sandwiched between a row of four-storey Georgian terraces to the north and the late 1920s Eastman Dental Hospital to the south. The site is decidedly urban, with the busy Gray's Inn Road demarcating its western boundary. Yet upon passing through a collection of modest timber-framed buildings you are presented with a calm but densely programmed community garden.

There are sports pitches for local communities, fluid and concaved play facilities that reminded us of the modernist sculptor Noguchi,[3] an earthen pizza oven and a mosaic-faced formal garden not dissimilar to Nek Chand's rock garden in Chandigarh.[4] Sandwiched between these nodal points of human activity is an intensive off-grid growing system, composed of richly planted raised beds, wormeries and translucent poly-tunnels that enclose hydroponic growing systems (fig. 2). The timber-framed buildings by architect Walter Segal[5] are home to a community café and educational facilities. This, in our minds, is one of the great successes

of Calthorpe: its ambition to not only generate sustainable produce, but to do so with an inherently social bias.

Many of the raised planters are tended to by various groups in the local community. For example, one area of the garden has become popular with Bengali women, and on certain days groups of elderly people meet to cook the food that they have grown as a collective. There are horticultural and environmental classes for all ages and classes for those with learning disabilities. The social mission of Calthorpe is as crucial as its sustainable one; in fact, they are intimately connected. The gardens help to combat isolation and overcrowding; they have brought disparate groups together to grow, cook, and eat healthy and sustainable food in the heart of the city.

Calthorpe operates as much as possible in a closed-loop off-grid system, and thus waste is as important as produce. After seasonal vegetables are cooked and consumed in the café, any food waste is fed into an anaerobic digester which generates renewable biogas and liquid fertilizer. This energy in turn is fed back into the system to heat the poly-tunnels and fertilise new crops.[6] A closed-loop system like this embodies the idea that we ought to view our products of waste as a resource, especially in times of scarcity and flux.

The gardens at Calthorpe present us with an intensive agricultural model in an urban environment, operating in an organic and autonomous manner. They also demonstrate to us the clear potential for urban growing spaces to enrich the social life of a community. Calthorpe is more than just a growing space; it is a site of environmental education, and a sustainable and decentralised social enterprise. Places like this remind us of Aldo van Eyck's playgrounds[7]: they are truly democratic spaces in the heart of the city, both for play and for learning. There is also a profoundly warming mentality of a 'making do and getting by'[8] at Calthorpe, where one can see that

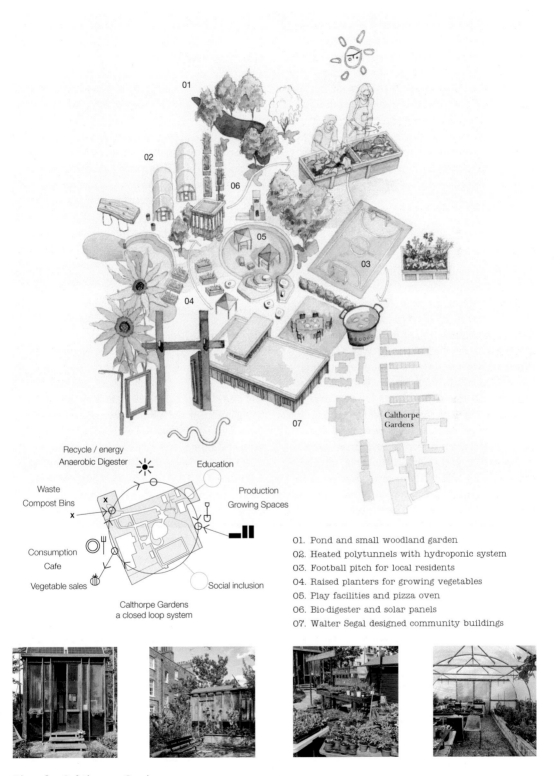

Recycle / energy
Anaerobic Digester

Waste
Compost Bins

Education

Production
Growing Spaces

Consumption
Cafe

Vegetable sales

Social inclusion

Calthorpe Gardens
a closed loop system

01. Pond and small woodland garden
02. Heated polytunnels with hydroponic system
03. Football pitch for local residents
04. Raised planters for growing vegetables
05. Play facilities and pizza oven
06. Bio-digester and solar panels
07. Walter Segal designed community buildings

Fig. 2: Calthorpe Gardens

the buildings have been repaired informally, and furniture has been constructed from logs and leftover sections of timber. In times of relative scarcity, we might look to community gardens like this as sources of inspiration, not just for ways to grow vegetables sustainably, but as an ideological approach that respects not just the value of concrete things, such as materials and buildings, but also the intangible; the social institutions of our cities.

Portrait 2: Peri-urban farming – Forty Hall Farm, Enfield

Forty Hall Farm is situated within the grounds of the Forty Hall Estate in Enfield, North London. The estate is now largely public access parkland and woods, with a Jacobean Manor House and associated courtyards and beautiful walled gardens. The entrance to the farm is integrated within the complex of buildings that form the manor house, on one of the main pathways through the park (fig. 3). This prominence of location allows for a natural flow of people past the farm, which hopefully encourages an interest in growing food and eating healthily. It is also an important factor in the economic stability of the farm, which sells its produce directly to the end user. There is a small shop by the entrance gate, a monthly farmers' market, and 200 vegetable boxes are sold to the local area each week on average.

Rare breeds of sheep are reared at the farm, and these surprisingly cater to the needs of the local end user. The sheep are of a smaller size and thus the cuts of meat are more suited to the size of families in the local area. Sales to the end user are made at a higher price than wholesale, and thus the farm can be less intensive but still economically stable. At the same time, the local community can enjoy the satisfaction of knowing where their food comes from.

The farm is intimately connected to its community through a network of volunteers and educational outreach with local schools. Angelika, Forty Hall's manager, described to us

the excitement of schoolchildren watching a cow urinate or a pig eating, perhaps for the first time. The farm allows children to experience a tangible and visceral connection to the food that they eat (even if they do want to clean off their trainers with wet wipes afterwards).[9]

During our visit, we enjoyed seeing the wilder parts of the site that had been left for nature, yet these still felt quite integrated within the productive fields of the farm. There were a number of timber structures around the site made by volunteers and farm staff. We also ran into two beekeepers who house their bees on a small plot of the farm in exchange for honey. In our minds, these elements establish a sense of openness and care towards both people and nature – an oasis closely connected to the lively bustle of Enfield and Edmonton.

Portrait 3: Latent spaces – wild hedgerows and nature occupying the city

The city should have, and in fact already does have, latent or dormant spaces that possess the capacity to be populated with wildlife and wild flora and fauna. In a city like London, many of these spaces do exist in both highly densified sections of the city and in its industrial areas and outer suburbs. Using the Thames and its tributaries as a reference point, we studied and mapped as many of these found conditions as we could in order to establish the potential for leftover urban sites to be planted – both for urban agriculture and to increase biodiversity in the city (fig. 4). We found that nature demonstrated an incredible resilience in the city, with wildflowers flourishing in gravelly underpasses and rusting post-industrial sites.

There was a rich diversity in both the types of wildlife and the varied site conditions where planting had taken over. We discovered an informal garden planted in an alleyway in Deptford, and wild lilies growing in a small disused dry dock in Wapping, East London (fig. 5). There are, in addition, many sites that, we feel, have an incredible potential for wild planting,

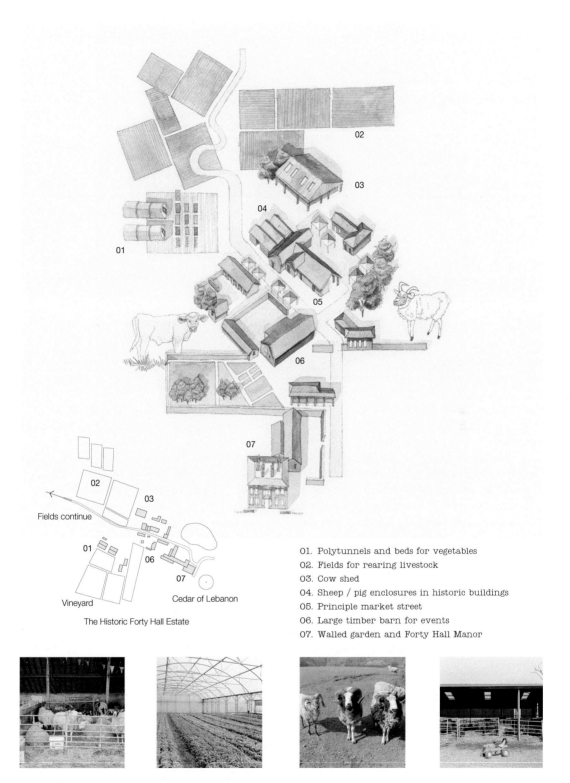

Fields continue

02

03

01

06

07

Vineyard

Cedar of Lebanon

The Historic Forty Hall Estate

01. Polytunnels and beds for vegetables
02. Fields for rearing livestock
03. Cow shed
04. Sheep / pig enclosures in historic buildings
05. Principle market street
06. Large timber barn for events
07. Walled garden and Forty Hall Manor

Fig. 3: Forty Hall Farm

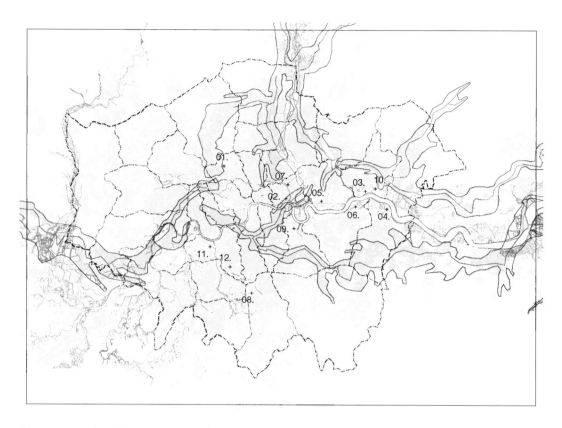

Fig. 4: Mapping latent spaces for nature

such as the numerous abandoned dry docks along the East End of the Thames. These sites simply require the catalyst to begin growth and to develop their own local ecosystems.

We believe it is important, however, to recognise the difference between these informal 'hedgerow' sites and more formally planted gardens and nature reserves. They often constitute a more piecemeal addition of wildlife to the city, as opposed to dedicated sites with hard borders, and this unconsciously integrated aspect of the hedgerow site is very important. It enables wildlife and planting to become more embedded in daily urban life, and for our cities to develop a richer ecology and biodiversity that is intimately threaded throughout our streets. We saw, for example, locals foraging for wild berries besides Haggerston Park, and a small plot of vegetables and sunflowers growing

in raised planters in Herne Hill. Where these sites have spawned out of a 'guerrilla' community planting approach, we feel they also provide an essential social benefit, in that they promote the importance of biodiversity and healthy eating throughout a community. They also provide communities with a much-needed sense of ownership and a comforting sense that the public streets outside their homes are spaces they can inhabit.

We should design the public spaces and buildings in our cities so that they have areas which are 'baggy': they have room to breathe and room for more organic programmes to develop over time, just like the spaces skateboarders have appropriated at the Southbank Centre in Central London.[10] Where the Southbank had a democratic sense of openness in terms of social programming, we can take this approach

01. Skip herb gardens in
Kentish Town

02. Lilies in an abandoned
dry dock in Limehouse

03. The latent potential of
abandoned jetties

04. Wildflowers growing by a
Dagenham cement plant

05. Marshlands in the East
India Basin

06. Overgrown industry in
Woolwich

07. An informal allotment on
in Poplar

08. Greening of the Former
Beddington Sewage works

09. A wild garden in the
Deptford Creek

10. Wildflowers by the
Beckton Sewage Plant

11. Backyard allotments by
the river in Wandsworth

12. A guerrilla community
garden in Mitcham

Fig. 5: Latent spaces survey

ecologically as well. Rather than specifying planting, we can instead facilitate the means or framework for a natural and local ecosystem to flourish on its own. As urban centres grow, we should endeavour to make more space for wild planting and for animal life to embed itself within the ebb and flow of our cities.

Portrait 4: Food education – Grow! Totteridge Academy

We visited Grow! on a damp October Saturday in 2021. Despite these conditions, there were a number of families and young children enjoying their day selecting bouquets of sunflowers and dahlias, which were nestled between pumpkins and courgettes. The farm is sited on a 6-acre plot of land on the edge of the green belt in North London. Unlike Calthorpe, its surrounding context is far less urban, but there is a large school – Totteridge Academy – directly adjacent, which the farm is partnered with. Seasonal vegetables, fruits, herbs and flowers are the principal crops of the farm, mostly grown outdoors and with agroecological principles.

When we visited, the plot of active farmland was not as intensively cultivated as Calthorpe Gardens, but we learned that the roots of connections of the charity organisation spread much further than its physical presence above ground. Firstly, Grow! provides vegetables and other ingredients for the chefs in the school canteen. This enables a very close connection between production and consumption and thus the children at the school are explicitly aware of where their food comes from.[11]

The farm's social and ethical mission stretches much further through its 'rhizomatic' network than the neighbouring school. Grow! runs after school clubs and holiday programmes where children learn about a local forest and the farm. Much of the farm's activities are focused on children, which we found particularly inspirational and important. Their 'Learning from the Land' course, a 20-hour outdoor forest school, encourages the children to rehabilitate

and continue to tend to a 'learning site' within the school that the children attend. We believe this engenders within the children a sense of ownership over their space; it is safe and permanent and constructed both physically and symbolically by themselves, much in the fashion of how Herman Hertzberger imagined his classroom spaces within his school designs.[12] It also teaches the children vital lessons of land stewardship, care and maintenance over their site, in order to keep it flourishing long after the course has finished. Again, a sense of the value, time and care for ecology is implied to the students, hopefully establishing the true value of food and its impact on land and resources (fig. 6).

Like the farm's agroecological approach to farming, there is a long-term agenda that stretches far beyond the 20-hour 'Learning from the Land' course. Grow! believes that the farm and its outdoor learning sites, as well as other places, like forest schools, can be exciting resources for all tuition subjects in a school. It is about learning lessons from ecological processes as much as learning about them. We were greatly inspired during our visit and our impassioned conversation with Lucy Gray, head of fundraising at Grow!, and a few passing visitors, each with a keen desire to transform the education system.[13]

Portrait 5: The Lower River Lea – a speculative edible neighbourhood

We end with a portrait of a speculative edible neighbourhood. Taking the Lower Lea as a case study, beginning at its confluence with the Thames, we draw upon the other portraits in this chapter to envision a part of the city integrated with sustainable food production.

The Lower Lea acts as a membrane between the boundaries of a number of urban districts; from Poplar and Bow, via the industrial sites that can be found throughout, to the more residential neighbourhoods eastwards in Newham and Barking. This conceptual drawing imagines a

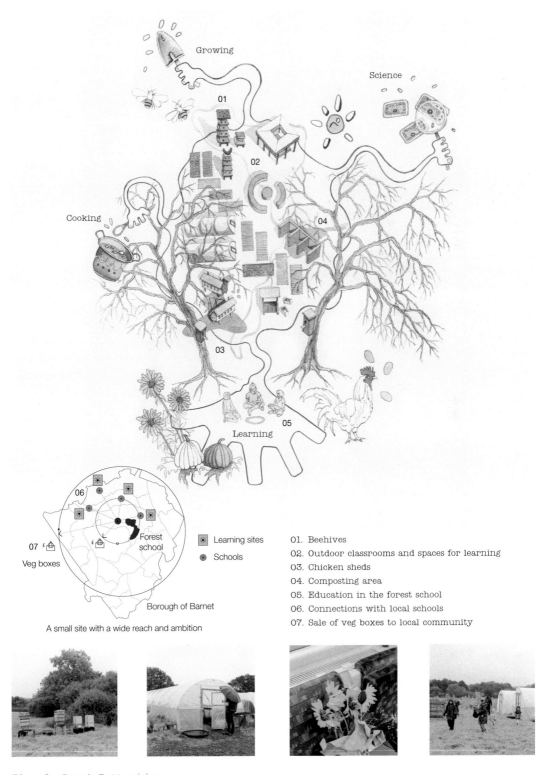

Growing

Science

Cooking

01

02

04

Cooking

03

05

Learning

06

Forest school

07 Veg boxes

A small site with a wide reach and ambition

* Learning sites

⊕ Schools

Borough of Barnet

01. Beehives
02. Outdoor classrooms and spaces for learning
03. Chicken sheds
04. Composting area
05. Education in the forest school
06. Connections with local schools
07. Sale of veg boxes to local community

Fig. 6: Grow! Totteridge

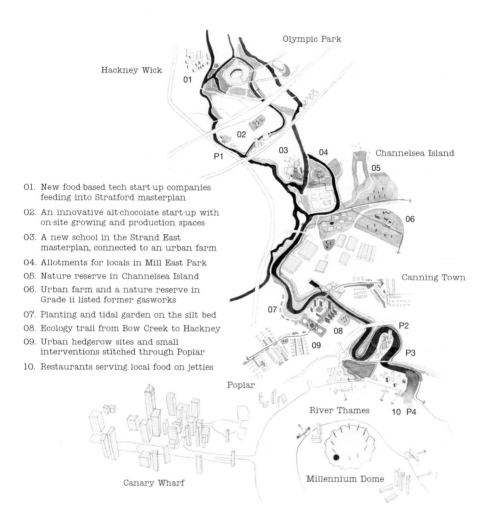

Hackney Wick

Olympic Park

01

02

03   04

P1

Channelsea Island

05

06

Canning Town

07

08   P2

09   P3

Poplar

River Thames   10 P4

Canary Wharf

Millennium Dome

01. New food-based tech start-up companies feeding into Stratford masterplan

02. An innovative alt-chocolate start-up with on-site growing and production spaces

03. A new school in the Strand East masterplan, connected to an urban farm

04. Allotments for locals in Mill East Park

05. Nature reserve in Channelsea Island

06. Urban farm and a nature reserve in Grade ii listed former gasworks

07. Planting and tidal garden on the silt bed

08. Ecology trail from Bow Creek to Hackney

09. Urban hedgerow sites and small interventions stitched through Poplar

10. Restaurants serving local food on jetties

The Lower Lea as a green and porous membrane between a number of urban districts, parks, nature reserves, and industrial sites

10. Local food on a concrete jetty

03. A new school in Strand East

P1. Cement plant

P2. Canning Town

P3. Bow Creek

P4. Jetties

Fig. 7: The Lower Lea - an edible neighbourhood

stretch of green spaces and urban buildings that weave themselves through current and post-industrial sites, through new large-scale developments and post-war council housing, stretching up from the Thames and feeding into the *Olympic Park Legacy Masterplan* (fig. 7).

Where the Lea meets the Thames, we imagine pop-up restaurants and theatres and growing spaces housed on the disused jetties that jut out from the embankments, with great views of the city to the West. Tidal silt beds and marshlands are planted with a range of both edible produce and products that can be utilised in sustainable manufacturing. As the river narrows towards Poplar, we imagine a new mixed-use development, stitched into the neighbouring community of Poplar with a series of urban growing sites. At Bow Creek, several disused industrial sites provide the perfect location for a new urban farm, with a school set within its boundaries. Here, we imagine a farm that is part ecology park, part educational facility and part recreational space; an ecologically and socially diverse space that brings its community much closer to the food it consumes. An existing trail along the river joins these sites together, leading up to the existing green spaces of the Olympic Park, its design now fully integrated into the rest of the edible city.

Notes

1 Post-pandemic in the sense of post-Covid-19. The RIBA competition was titled 'Rethink: 2025 – Design for life after Covid-19'.
2 Our selection of case studies has grown organically. It began with responses to our competition entry, which allowed for the roots of connections to develop between different groups, both inside and outside of academia and the architectural profession.
3 Isama Noguchi was a Japanese sculptor known for his abstract pieces in stone. 'The Noguchi Museum', *The Noguchi Museum*, accessed 27 February 2022, www.noguchi.org/.
4 The Rock Garden in Chandigarh was constructed by local resident Nek Chand out of construction rubble that he collected.
5 Walter Segal was a German born architect who was a proponent of self-build timber buildings. Alongside Calthorpe Gardens, another well-known example is the 'Walter's Way' self-build housing scheme in Lewisham. Alice Grahame and John McKean, *Walter Segal, Self-Built Architect* (London: Lund Humphries, 2021).
6 M. Chang, From a conversation with Marina Chang at Calthorpe Gardens, September 2021.
7 Aldo van Eyck was a Dutch architect who designed a series of playgrounds in bombed-out spaces in post-war Amsterdam. Robert McCarter and Herman Hertzberger, *Aldo van Eyck* (New Haven; London: Yale University Press, 2015).
8 In reference to the artist Richard Wentworth.
9 From a conversation with Angelika Hauses on the farm in March 2022.
10 The Southbank Centre is an arts centre facing the River Thames. A number of the external spaces were designed without a specific programme and were subsequently appropriated by groups including local skateboarders. Iain Borden, *Skateboarding, Space and the City: Architecture and the Body* (Oxford; New York: Berg, 2001).
11 Carolyn Steel states that there is no such thing as 'fast food'; there is always something along the process that pays the true price for fast or cheap food, which is not often visible at the point of consumption. Carolyn Steel, *Sitopia: How Food Can Save the World* (2021).
12 Herman Hertzberger is a Dutch architect with a strong interest in the human occupation and sense of ownership over spaces in his buildings. His *Lessons for Students of Architecture* (1991) described, amongst other ideas, ways that schools could be designed and managed to enable young children to feel comfortable and have a sense of belonging to their classroom spaces. Herman Hertzberger, *Lessons for Students in Architecture*, 4. Aufl (Rotterdam: 010 Publishers, 2001).
13 From a conversation with Lucy Gray, Grow! Totteridge Academy, October 2021, and also 'GROW', GROW, accessed 3 March 2022, http://wearegrow.org/.

Agroecologics: Reimagining an agri-urban design for Luxembourg

Ivonne Weichold

The interconnected issues and associated challenges of current urbanisation processes – regarding the existing food system, weather and climate, the ecological debate, and governance[1] – frame the overarching need to explore an alternative planning paradigm. One key to meeting this challenge is the use of multiple mapping methods to explore alternative urban densification strategies without giving up productive agricultural land.

Within this context, this chapter seeks a new balance between the built and unbuilt environments by introducing the notion of "Agroecologics". The term refers to the spatial logics of an agroecological urbanism presented in the form of an agri-urban design (see Weichold, 2021). The definition of Agroecologics, however, tries not to give a blueprint solution. Instead, it defines a new planning strategy that incorporates and accommodates agriculture and soil as a tool for urban planning, by approaching it from different mapping techniques. Agroecologics were explored through a mix of different mapping tools from field observation, sketching and retracing the exiting situations towards developing a soil suitability index. By applying such different mapping methods, it proposes a planning reference – an agri-urban design – that provides a way of thinking about agro-ecology and its spatial implications. Thus, an agri-urban design proposes a new re-imagination of land that alters agriculture within the existing planning paradigm and processes, by valuing multiple perspectives such as agroecological principles.

The case of Luxembourg provides a useful starting point for rethinking agriculture in terms of spatial and socio-economic implications within planning. Despite the enormous pressure on land and real estate in Luxembourg, the country has a noticeable amount of buildable but vacant land (L'Observatoire de l'Habitat, 2019a, 2019b; Paccoud, 2020) (see fig. 1).

However, a highly uneven distribution of land ownership, a symbolic ground tax and a non-exercised right of pre-emption by the municipalities make it challenging to stimulate new developments (see, amongst others, Hertweck, 2020; Becker et al., 2019; Chilla and Schulz, 2011). The increase in agricultural land prices, a conversion of subsidised agricultural plots to non-agricultural purposes and cross-border renting of Luxembourgish agricultural holdings are consequences of such land planning practices (Weichold, 2021). Moreover, the inclusion of agriculture in urban design and planning is at present mostly absent in Luxembourg. Another crucial issue is the exclusion of agriculture and soil assessment, at all planning levels, despite the land use analysis demonstrating that an alternative method of evaluating land for development by considering the quality of soil is an essential factor within the urbanisation process (Ibid.).

A reflection divided into three parts will address those issues. Part one situates this chapter within the study and sets out the reason for formulating a prospective agroecological agenda using design suggestions and

DOI: 10.4324/9781003352280-4

Fig. 1: Luxembourg's built and unbuilt landscape

mapping techniques. Part two illustrates the Agroecologics, i.e., implications based on a series of alterations applied to the example of Luxembourg case studies. Part three concludes with a summary of how to make use of such mapping techniques for defining an agroecological design reference catalogue in the future.

Agroecologics: Mapping the spatial logics of an agri-urban design

Mapping Agroecologics should be seen as a first attempt to formulate an agri-urban design for Luxembourg's territory. The concept of Agroecologics draws on the distinction made by Michel De Certeau (2002) between the "strategy" as the product of the formal structures of practice, and "tactics", as a seizing of opportunities and manipulation of events to alter the course set out by the dominant forces of production. Those

strategies and tactics are applied to a series of alterations distributed within the territory of Luxembourg. In other words, through the use of iterative processes, a series of conflicts and paradoxes will be reformulated with alternative strategies and tactics in order to define potential Agroecologics, i.e. spatial logic for an agri-urban design for Luxembourg. Just as Christopher Alexander (Alexander *et al.*, 1977)[2] created a new language perceived as a building code, Agroecologics attempts to create a similar code, i.e. "pattern", for an agri-urban design. Just as there is a reference book like the Neufert[3] for the built space, the un-built space needs to be further defined, particularly for an agroecological urbanism (Tornaghi and Dehaene, 2021) through agroecological mapping techniques and a design references catalogue. Therefore, the spatial logic for an agri-urban design builds upon different mapping strategies which require different scales and planning instruments by involving several disciplines such as architecture, urbanism, agriculture, landscape planning and geography. Certain strategies need to be mapped and implemented on the scale of the territory, or on the scale of the municipality, some on the scale of a neighbourhood, others on the scale of a building, and still others on the scale of a field or parcel. In order to achieve such an interdisciplinary level, the method applied explored a multiple dimensional process of mapping: through defining existing agriculture fabric, potential agri-urban landscape, existing public spaces, the impermeabilisation gradient (from 0 to 45) and the level of soil suitability of an area.

Seven suggestions for an agri-urban design

Overall, seven basic suggestions for an agri-urban design have been formulated that include different gradients of scales and strategies for Luxembourg, as seen in figure 2:

The first suggestion proposes **agri-urban developments,** characterised as a "new" zone, for production, protection and housing, called the agri-urban zone. This will be implemented by a minimum quota of agricultural production within new developments.

The second suggestion proposes to **guarantee agricultural landscape by reserving the most fertile land** for sustainable farming practices, furthermore guaranteeing land access through collective management, leases and ownerships.

The third one proposes to implement **multifunctional agriculture and land use by** fostering the diversification of farmers' incomes by integrating many aspects – like initiatives for community-supported agriculture, for example – in the discussion of agricultural preservation and production.

The fourth one proposes a **regulatory framework – adaptable urbanism** – to foster a

normative framework that is flexible and adaptable for a long-term planning and implementation period, and which allows for new zoning as well as adapting existing planning instruments.

The fifth one suggests **regenerate and (re) activate land by** "economising the extensive gaps"[4] through activating potential land, either unused, left-over, or used as public parks or forests.

The sixth suggests implementing **diversifications in the management of the landscape** through a crop rotation plan which fosters different farming methods from small-scale farming (0.5–2 ha), medium-scale farming (2–30 ha) and intensive farming (above 30 ha).

The seventh and final suggestion proposes **land development according to soil quality,** by respecting the agricultural soil fertility while planning and developing land. This will be achieved by avoiding developments on valuable agricultural land and by densifying land within the existing building perimeter by following a sustainable, compact development.

By mapping an agri-urban design, I propose an alternative planning paradigm which is flexible, adaptable, which will conciliate, densify, de-densify, hybridise, regenerate, retrofit and restructure. This list is by no means exhaustive. Instead, it attempts to offer a starting point for further discussion and experimentation around the spatialisation of an agroecological urbanism in the form of an agri-urban design. In doing so, it distinguishes between various strategies that need to be thought of in a new way and, above all, in relation to each other as well as to the built environment. Above all, mapping the Agroecologics shows various potentials for dealing with urban expansion while integrating

Fig. 2: A transformative agenda towards an agroecological urbanism: Seven suggestions for an agri-urban design

1
AGRI-URBAN
DEVELOPMENTS

2
GUARANTEEING
AGRICULTURAL
LANDSCAPE

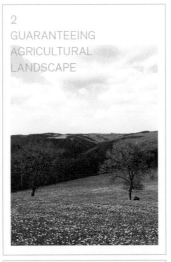

3
MULTIFUNCTIONAL
AGRICULTURE AND LAND USE

5
REGENERATE AND
(RE)ACTIVATE LAND

4
REGULATORY FRAMEWORK –
ADAPTABLE URBANISM

6
DIVERSIFICATIONS IN THE
MANAGEMENT OF THE
LANDSCAPE

7
LAND DEVELOPMENT
ACCORDING TO
SOIL QUALITY

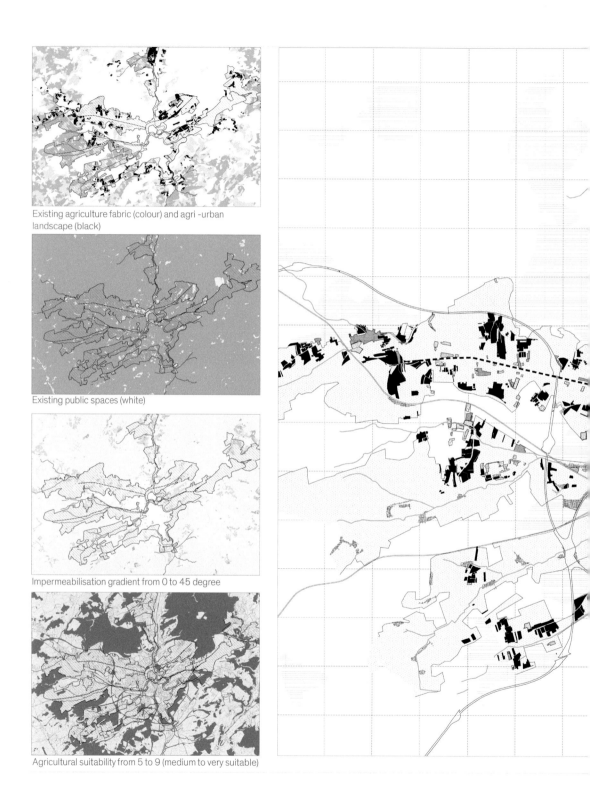

Existing agriculture fabric (colour) and agri -urban landscape (black)

Existing public spaces (white)

Impermeabilisation gradient from 0 to 45 degree

Agricultural suitability from 5 to 9 (medium to very suitable)

Fig. 3: An agroecological corridor as an essential infrastructure within the agglomeration zone of Luxembourg. The left side shows the list of layers used to define the corridors. The right side shows the projected situation for the agglomeration Luxembourg City

Agroecological corridors - Projected situation for the agglomeration Luxembourg city.

0   1 km

productive land, i.e., respecting agriculture and its soil fertility. In the next section, two different Agroecologics mappings of an agri-urban design are first described and then visualised by proposing alterations applied in Luxembourg.

Mapping strategies and alterations of an agri-urban design for Luxembourg

The strategy *From Greenbelts towards Agroecological Corridors* proposes to guide urban growth in Luxembourg's agglomeration zone by implementing agroecological corridors. While the concepts of a green belt and green radial (see amongst others Eberstadt *et al.*, 1910) at the end of the nineteenth century tried to rehabilitate the 18th- and 19th-century industrial city towards the outside of the city, the agroecological corridor offers a hybrid form of using open land by interlinking the urban and the peri-urban fringes.

The agroecological corridor limits urban expansion on fertile land by reserving a territorially demarcated area for agroecological food production and recreational space. The agroecological corridor is not simply a corridor, it instead comprises multiple functions such as: a corridor for providing access to land and supporting small-scale farming practices; a corridor along an existing water artery to steward the watershed through agroecological practices; a corridor for leisure, recreational space – public parks and squares; a corridor for education; a corridor for the rising demand for allotment gardens; a corridor for securing food production through open (public) spaces; a corridor for "air" for cooling the urban heat islands by guaranteeing enough air circulation within the urban area; a corridor for agri-urban developments; and a corridor for supporting "agro-forestry."

In addition to the implementation of an agroecological corridor, the centre also continues to develop further through farming the unused space and regenerating conflicting land uses. Instead of intensive farming, small-scale farming with an educational and recreational potential will be implemented in those green corridors.

The agroecological corridors orientate towards ideas which have been proposed through the "City Country Fingers" (see Alexander *et al.*, 1977) or the *CPULs* concept (Viljoen, 2005) to secure a place in cities for food production through open (public) and green corridors. The agroecological corridors can be applied to all the agglomeration zones in Luxembourg's South and North zones. Figures 3–5 show an alteration for the agglomeration zone of Luxembourg city.

The strategy of *Towards the Development of Agri-Urban Estates* defines areas between the three agglomeration zones (Agglo Nordstadt, Agglo Luxembourg and Agglo South) along the Alzette river and major infrastructural networks in Luxembourg. Those areas are growing fast and have reasonable accessibility through public transport which display optimal conditions of densification potential within the existing building perimeter. In order to guide an agri-urban development in those areas, this strategy is adopting the maxim that the German Landscape Architect L. Migge once formulated as "*No house construction without land cultivation.*" (Haney, 2001). In other words, all new developments have to include an agricultural quota – either per building or per land plot – for new urban developments. Eventually, those areas can be defined as the so-called agri-urban zones within spatial planning. Furthermore, this strategy adopts the Almere Oosterwold project's approach (see Structuurvisie in Gemeenteraad van Zeewolde and Almere, 2013) by differentiating between four agri-urban plots: the agriculture plot, the landscape plot, the standard plot and the urban plot. In principle, a standard plot can be realised anywhere in the urban planning area, apart from the existing forests, the protected areas and the current and future infrastructure. An urban plot allows for the development of proportionally more dense housing, for example, within the pressure and agglomeration zone. An agricultural plot can be realised anywhere, except for the existing forests and the present and future infrastructure and allows for the development of proportionately more agriculture, for example, in the quiet zone (rural areas). A landscape

Fig. 4: Agricultural corridor from Route d'Arlon to the Plateau de Kirchberg

Undefined Spaces

Large Superficies Of
Parking Lots

Public Spaces And Parcs

Existing Argriculture To
Reinvent Along The Road

Existing Argriculture To
Reinvent In Phase 2

Agri-Urban Zones

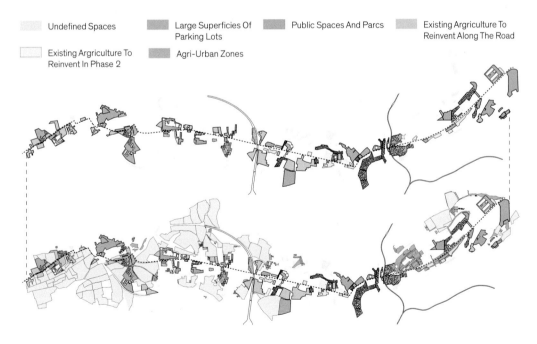

Fig. 5: The implementation of those corridors in two phases. Phase 1: implement an agricultural corridor along roads and watercourses and use all the empty spaces for agricultural production; activate public spaces as a new place for agriculture.
Phase 2: gradually grow towards the outside by connecting the corridors with intensive farming fields and transform existing monocultural fields into a more responsible, diverse agriculture which follows agroecological principles

Fig. 6: Towards the development of agri-urban estates. Projected situation in Steinsel. The implementation of those agri-urban estates could take place in different phases

plot will be linked to existing forests to support the agro-forestry and ecological structures in that zone. This plot will have a more significant proportion of greenery, which is particularly fitted to the protected zone, defined through the Natura 2000. Overall, every land area needs to fulfil a minimum quota of cultivation carried out either by the residents themselves or outsourced to a collective or a farmer, who takes care of the available productive greenery. In general, small-scale farming is defined within the agri-urban zone, while intensive farming is foreseen outside the agri-urban zone. The implementation of those plots follows a gradual growth, i.e. an "organic growth instead of uniformity" over time, towards a "self-managed agro-neighbourhood." Ultimately, this is just the first proposal. Figures 6 and 7 show an alteration of such a potential zone demonstrated in the City of Steinsel.

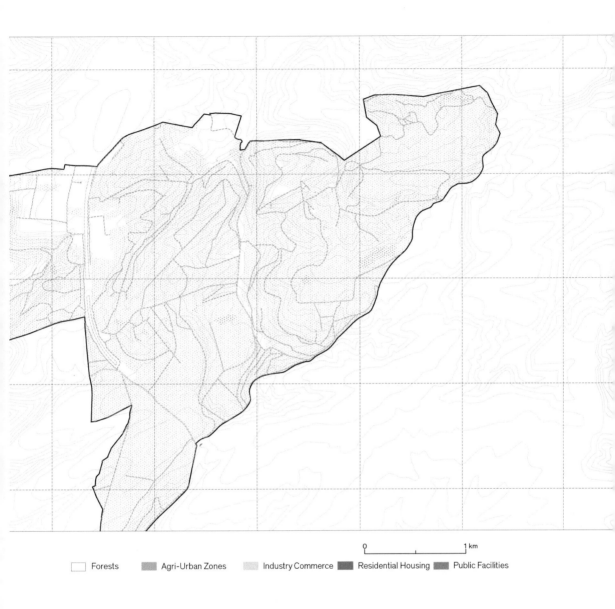

0 _____ 1 km

☐ Forests   ▨ Agri-Urban Zones   ▨ Industry Commerce   ■ Residential Housing   ▨ Public Facilities

Towards an agri-urban design

In this chapter, several mapping techniques from field observation, sketching, retracing the exiting situations towards developing soil suitability indexation have been used to define Agroecologics. Such agroecological mapping methods were thereby essential tools to start developing a new re-imaginary of the land towards an agri-urban design. Instead of

formulating a scenario, this chapter provides a direction for an agri-urban design applied to the territory of Luxembourg. It formulated an alternative planning paradigm that can guide land development according to the qualities of its soil, i.e. agroecological qualities.

The agroecological design proposals have shown a transformative agenda towards an agri-urban design, reflecting thereby on its

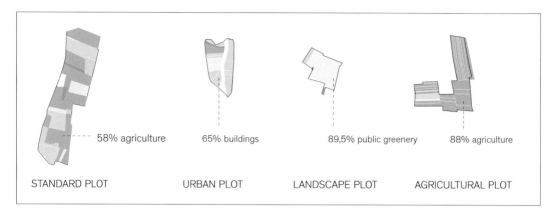

58% agriculture   65% buildings   89,5% public greenery   88% agriculture

STANDARD PLOT   URBAN PLOT   LANDSCAPE PLOT   AGRICULTURAL PLOT

Fig. 7: Proposing four different agri-urban plots for the agri-urban zone

land and soil, space and governance. The list of agroecological design proposals is by no means exhaustive. Those strategies set out earlier are in no way intended to be prescriptive, but merely suggest ways of approaching a renewed relationship between the urban and the agri-cultural through an agroecological lens. They demonstrate a multifarious answer – applied on different scales within Luxembourg – to harness the potential ecological, social and spatial bene-fits associated with agroecological practices. In this light, agri-urban design can be considered a flexible strategy to guide the development of sustainable cities and regions in the future.

While the agri-urban design started from the ground, from the soil fertility and how this could be better protected and integrated in the planning process, it requires further differ-ent experts and practitioners to define such a set of "new" rules, including the additional aspects of economy and labour, for instance. After all, each of those Agroecologics should be developed further through design research on a more detailed urban and architectural scale to explore the implications of these strategies as a design approach. A different study with a different methodological approach would be required in order to do so. Lastly and crucially, remains the question of the feasibility of such a planning concept and whether Luxembourg's existing planning system is even made for such a change. Ultimately, this chapter does

not seek to directly answer the questions of refunctionalisation and transferability of an agri-urban design by citing specific cases. Each city, after all, has its own complex set of underlying dynamics that allow for the incorporation of trends, and its own capacity to reject or counteract them. Instead, this chapter investigates the potential and limits of integrating an agri-urban design for sustain-able urban development by discussing the case of Luxembourg.

Notes

1 See the vision for EU Green Deal strategies and the No land net take strategy by 2050.
2 Christopher Alexander formulated 253 patterns in his publication "A Pattern Language." In his work Alexander addressed several scales from human settlements to the design of towns and buildings, to the arrangement of households.
3 The Neufert book was first published in 1936 by Ernst Neufert. It is an architects' reference book for spatial requirements in building design and site planning.
4 See L. Migge, *Deutsche Binnenkolonisation* (Berlin: Deutscher Kommunal Verlag G.M.B.H., 1926).

References

Alexander, C., Ishikawa, S., and Silverstein, M., 1977. *A pattern language: Towns, buildings, construction*. New York: Oxford University Press.
Becker, T., Hesse, M., and Schulz, C., 2019. Qualitatives Wachstum in Stadt und Land? Elefant im Raum und zugleich leerer Signifikant. *In*: C. Reckinger and

R. Urbé, eds. *Sozialalmanach 2019*. Luxembourg: Caritas Luxembourg, 273–288.

Certeau, M., 2002. *The practice of everyday life (1980)*. Berkeley, Los Angeles, London: University of California Press.

Chilla, T., and Schulz, C., 2011. *Raumordnung in Luxemburg/ Aménagement du Territoire au Luxembourg*. Luxembourg: Éditions Guy Binsfeld.

Eberstadt, R., Moehring, B., and Petersen, R., 1910. *Groß-Berlin. Ein Programm für die Planung der neuzeitlichen Großstadt*. Berlin: Wasmuth.

Haney, D., 2001. "No house building without garden building!" ("Kein Hausbau ohne Landbau!"): The modern landscapes of Leberecht Migge. *Journal of Architectural Education*, 54 (3), 149–157.

Hertweck, F., 2020. *Architecture on common ground. The question of land: Positions and models*. Zurich: Lars Müller Publishers and University of Luxembourg.

L'Observatoire de l'Habitat, 2019a. *Le degré de concentration de la détention du potentiel foncier destiné à l'habitat en 2016*. Luxembourg: La Note de l'Observatoire de l'Habitat, N° 23.

L'Observatoire de l'Habitat, 2019b. *Le potentiel foncier destiné à l'habitat au Luxembourg en 2016*. Luxembourg: La Note de l'Observatoire de l'Habitat, N° 22.

Migge, L., 1926. *Deutsche Binnenkolonisation*. Berlin: Deutscher Kommunal Verlag G.M.B.H.

Paccoud, A., 2020. The top tail of the property wealth distribution and the production of the residential environment. *International Journal of Housing Policy*, 20 (1), 100–119.

Tornaghi, C., and Dehaene, M., 2021. *Resourcing an agroecological urbanism: Political, transformational and territorial dimensions*. New York and Abingdon: Routledge.

van Zeewolde, G., and Almere, 2013. *Intergemeentelijke Structuurvisie Oosterwold*. Available from www.almere. nl/fileadmin/files/almere/bestuur/beleidsstukken/10.7_ Intergemeentelijke_structuurvisie_Oosterwold__2013_. pdf [Accessed 15 Oct 2020].

Viljoen, A., 2005. *Continuous productive urban landscapes*. London and New York: Routledge.

Weichold, I., 2021. *Agroecologics. Towards a territorial, integrative agri-urban design. Luxembourg as a case study*. Thesis (PhD). Luxembourg: University of Luxembourg, Department of Geography and Spatial Planning.

Re-negotiating the boundaries between infrastructure and landscape: Mapping infrastructural ecologies

Jacques Abelman and Matthew Potteiger

May, 2016, Callowhill area of Philadelphia:

In early spring of 2016, in order to get onto the Reading Viaduct, an abandoned elevated rail line near center city Philadelphia, you had to crawl through a cutout in the chain link fence (see fig. 1). There, set apart and above the city, new systems are emerging – vegetation and "wildlife" find niches, build soil, create habitat and a food web – including plants that people might forage and consume.

What is observable here is a process Bélanger (2016) refers to as an "infrastructural inversion" when the large-scale, mechanical, engineered infrastructures open to multiple trajectories and indeterminate forms. This essay sets out to explore a re-conceptualisation of infrastructure as a hybrid system of human and ecological systems, where, both design intention and aleatory processes intersect and overlap to re-negotiate the boundaries between infrastructure and landscape and between formal and informal practices. Such re-conceptualising is also a re-mapping project that reveals hidden or marginalised practices and processes.

"Infrastructural inversion" provides an alternative model for the redesign of infrastructure as complex socio-ecological systems, as *infrastructural ecologies* -- interlinked, synergistic systems operating as ecological fabric at a landscape scale. We see the potential of these *infrastructural ecologies* for providing a new framework for multi-functional landscapes for urban agriculture, edible ecologies, and food system infrastructure.

As in the initial story of the Reading Viaduct, a locus of change and nascent model for infrastructural ecologies can be found in the *left over* spaces between properties, or vacant lots, abandoned right-of-ways, under freeways, and other marginalised land uses that are *left open* to emergent processes (see fig. 2). In these spaces, "spontaneous vegetation" pre-adapted to compacted soils, less water and other challenges, creates novel ecological assemblages. These overlooked spaces are also openings for informal social practices, activities such as foraging, user-created skate parks, community gardens, or other activities that operate outside of municipal codes and therefore do not appear on officially sanctioned land use maps (Mukhija and Loukaitou-Sideris, 2014). Increasingly, designers recognise the importance of understanding such hybrid ecologies (Del Tredici, 2014) and engaging their informal practices as a means not only for making new forms of public space but also to acknowledge the agency of different social groups to expand the rights to the city (Hou, 2012; Mitchell, 2000).

This chapter explores the potential for designing infrastructural ecologies in two parts. It begins by following one informal cultural practice, foraging for edible plants and fungi, as it reveals the nascent forms and relationships of infrastructural ecologies. While finding food is the ostensible purpose of foraging, foragers are also at the vanguard of creating infrastructural ecologies. Foraging is described as a form of counter mapping that explores and claims new un-mapped territories from the ground up.

DOI: 10.4324/9781003352280-5

Fig. 1: Reading Viaduct, Philadelphia, before it was transformed into the Rail Park (Matthew Potteiger)

wild lands · parks · streets · campuses & institutions · cemeteries · community gardens · parking lots · cracks & interstitial spaces · fences & boundaries · vacant lots · yards

public   semi-public   ambiguous   private

Fig. 2: Gradient of typology of foraging spaces in Syracuse, NY (Matthew Potteiger)

Foraging, like other informal practices, also offers potential for new design strategies for engaging the emergent nature of urban ecologies. The second part of this work therefore highlights how design can work with these strategies to create flexible frameworks for promoting infrastructural ecologies. This is explored through a series of speculative design scenarios in Porto Alegre, Brazil. The scenarios emerge from a process of mapping potential spaces within the urban fabric for the purpose of creating various typologies of agroforestry food production and options for community activation of these spaces, based on a diversity of social practices. The approach throughout this collaborative work is iterative rather than linear. The structure alternates between and seeks to integrate spatial narratives and informal practices with design strategies for creating spatial/social/ecological infrastructures.

Foraging as informal social practice engaging emergent ecologies

Compared to the vast and complex infrastructures of global commodity chains that feed contemporary cities, foraging can seem inconsequential and a marginal practice. However, it represents a fundamental "infrastructural inversion". Instead of dependence on distant ecologies, foraging reveals ecologies that already exist albeit in novel form and context. Foraging can be seen as part of the larger effort of AFN (Alternative Food Networks)

to internalise and localise flows of nutrients, water, labour, knowledge, and all the dynamics of food systems and these productive uses into urban spaces (Lawson, 2005). Like foraging, many of the actions of AFN's, such as community gardens, pop-up markets, and buying clubs, began as informal social practices often unsanctioned by municipal codes. At the same time, if recorded, foraging can provide alternative mappings of local vegetation. An excerpt from a set of field notes taken during a project to document the production metrics of community gardens in Syracuse illustrates fundamental, yet latent potentials of foraging urban ecologies that already exist:

Met with the three Bhutanese gardeners at 7:00 pm. One of them was harvesting "Betu" and other "weeds" from a vacant lot. She came back into the garden through a gap in the chain link fence. The gardeners showed us the different "weeds" they harvest:
Betu – lamb's quarters
Palungi – pig weed, they compare it to Swiss chard
Kali Sag – looks like a nightshade (Kali=black)
Kangi Sag – purslane
Jaringo – looks like pokeweed

We realised that this group of gardeners was finding more fresh produce in the vacant lots, rights-of-way, cemeteries, and many other spaces in the city, than was being produced in the compost-filled raised beds that had been built by the coordinated effort of several non-profit organisations. This revelation was also a provocation to follow the very elusive, often hidden, yet extensive practices of foraging, not only by "New American" refugee groups but also by many other urban foragers representing a diverse range of ethnic, income, and other social groups.

The implications of this multi-year study foraging in Syracuse and other North American cities for mapping and designing productive infrastructural ecologies are summarised next as a series of inter-related social, spatial, and ecological discourses that are already re-making the city.

1. The social discourse: Informal and emergent practices

What is foraged, who forages, and for what purposes all have implications for mapping these landscapes. Foraged foods include wild plants and fungi, "feral" plants (cultivars that spread without human intervention), parts of plants originally intended for ornamental uses (flowers, stems, seeds, etc.), as well as "invasive" "weeds" (McLain et al., 2014). As a social practice outside conventional, domesticated food production, the knowledge necessary for identification, use, and location of foraged foods tends to be produced and shared within specific cultural groups – traditional, place-based, or increasingly on social media. One common finding from recent foraging research around the globe is that foraging is a vital prac-tice across all income levels and various ethnic groups. It is engaged in by people of all ages, recent migrants as well as long-term residents, by people in the developed world and develop-ing world (Shackleton et al., 2017). The reasons for foraging are equally diverse, ranging from finding free food for those with limited income (or not), health motivations and medicinal uses, market and non-market exchange, main-taining cultural memory and identity, culinary values, and ceremonial purposes (McLain et al., 2014). These foraging practices are dependent on and vital to the creation of social groups through sharing critical knowledge of edible species, sourcing locations, seasonal timing, and different ways of eating and cooking.

Yet, despite the values of foraging, it is often marginalised as a pre-agricultural phase of civilisation, offering limited amounts of food, or a passing hipster trend. Since the social practice of foraging occurs outside conven-tional domesticated agriculture, there is little economic incentive for research, leaving this landscape seriously understudied and unmapped.

2. The spatial discourse: Remapping the landscape

If maps represent power and knowledge, the value of mapping the act of foraging is in it being a counter-mapping project that reveals alternative forms of knowledge and experience, questioning and exploring alternatives to dominant land use categories. This begins from the ground up rather than the totalising view of conventional cartography (de Certeau, 1988). Through interviews, foraging, cooking, and other forms of engagement, this mapping follows the changing and contingent nature of foraging in emergent infrastructural ecologies.

Since foraging involves seeking edibles any-where a plant or mushroom will grow, it traverses a diversity of urban spaces, crossing social/spatial boundaries in the process. The diversity of foraging spaces (see fig. 2) includes vacant lots, public spaces (parks), rights-of-way (including sidewalks), institutional grounds (schools, campuses, hospitals), cemeteries, natural forms/elements (creeks, steep slopes), and interstitial spaces (cracks, medians, boundaries).

The level of engagement or intervention in these spaces and systems also falls along a gradient. At one end of the gradient is *gathering* from spaces or systems where the foraging has not had any role in managing. However, forag-ers may distribute seeds, clear plants around favoured species, or in other ways tend to the places. The other end of the gradient moves toward *cultivating* as people actively manage the conditions that support harvesting such as berry borders of backyards or the *Philadelphia Orchard Project* that plants fruit trees on vacant lots that are managed for public harvest.

Foraging in-between: Interstitial spaces

The interstitial spaces, the spaces between socio-political boundaries of property and land uses, as well as the edges between ecological zones, provide important niches for spontaneous vegetation and foraging. It is the very ambiguity of these spaces between authorities that creates openings for plants and behaviour that is considered transgressive in most other contexts (Galt *et al.*, 2014). At the margins of the community garden or New American Refugee farm, maintenance regimes (mowing, ploughing, weed whacking) end, and weeds find space to flourish. At these margins, New Americans find stinging nettle, black nightshade (*Solanum nigrum L.*), and more lamb's quarters. Around the vast acreage of Syracuse's Inner Harbor area, an extensive brownfield once known locally as "oil city", a chain-link fence supports a spontaneous linear vineyard of wild grapes. Along fences, backsides of buildings, and property lines where maintenance fades, plants find spaces to colonise. These lines grow as interstitial spaces so that while they appear to separate, as a network they also create textures of connectivity (Wehi *et al.*, 2009). For foragers, interstitial spaces allow them to gain access to plants growing there, yet they can quickly retreat to a safe public or private space. The interstices also operate across scales ranging from the cracks in the sidewalk to the borders between land uses and the successive and complex edges of urban development.

3. The ecological discourse: Emergent and novel ecologies

The diverse purposes of foraging mean that people are actively searching, selecting, and in other ways changing the interpretative value of the maps of vegetation, land uses, and infrastructure systems. Whether a stated intention or not, urban foragers find edibles in the cracks of sidewalks and median strips, as well as creek corridors, park woodlands, institutional lawns, and vacant lots. Through these actions they develop relationships and knowledge of unique and often novel urban ecologies. Instead of seeing these urban spaces as degraded natural systems, new paradigms of ecological systems focus on the dynamic processes of disturbance, adjustment, and change in which humans have played a significant role (Ellis, 2014). Human interaction with ecologic systems – altering species distribution, hydrologic patterns, soil compaction, and micro as well as global climates – produces ecologies characterised by their heterogeneity and multifunctionality (Ellis, 2014).

Foraging and novel ecologies are necessarily adaptive and resilient in response to the dynamics of urban processes. The urban landscape is constantly being made and remade – a perpetual state of disturbance. Spontaneous urban vegetation, weeds, and novel ecologies are disturbance adapted (Seiter, 2016) and respond to the constantly shifting situations. As a result, urban ecologies are dynamic mosaics.

Foraging generates new foundational relationships for productive infrastructural ecologies. Foraging across a diverse typology of spaces offers an expanded conception of the productive city. While urban agriculture has played an important role by reinserting productive functions into urban space, breaking down the dichotomy of rural vs. urban, it still separates out production as a discrete space assigned to vacant lots, rooftops, or raised planting beds. Foraging practices work across boundaries. Going beyond the well-coordinated efforts to garner resources and materials to construct raised beds and secure land tenure for the community gardens created for their benefit, New Americans use their own knowledge of plants and observations of their new surroundings to forage across multiple sites throughout the city. They apply their traditional knowledge to discovering a new urban ecology and thus re-code the city as a much more diverse system of productive spaces.

The research into foraging begins to identify the existing, but largely unrecognised landscape of these practices. Most importantly, it identifies the ecological discourse and spatial typologies that open new conceptions of urban spaces and systems. These discourses then provide understandings and incentives for design to work with the cultural practices of foraging as well as other informal social practices to explore the potential of emerging infrastructural ecologies.

Fig. 3: Guerrilla gardening in Praça Bernardo Drehr, Porto Alegre (Jacques Abelman)

Design strategies for engaging the informal and emergent infrastructural ecologies

April 2015, Ipanema Suburb of Porto Alegre, Brazil
The Praça Bernardo Drehr is a quiet pocket park in the suburb of Ipanema, near downtown Porto Alegre. I am being given a tour of the park by Oscar. Now retired, Oscar is an avid gardener. He is showing me the latest results of his guerrilla gardening campaign: a goaiba (Acca sellowiana) seedling inserted into the park's thick lawn, protected by a ring of sawn-off broom handles (see fig. 3). He raised this seedling from seed, and when it was big enough, transplanted it out into the park. The municipal workers who come to mow the park lawns steer clear of the protected seedlings and young trees. Once the trees are established they seem to be absorbed into the design of the park. A dozen new fruit trees planted here over the years have transformed the sterile landscape of decorative trees and lawn into a productive landscape. Other residents have joined in this practice over the years, adding their favourite food species. A seed of pitanga (Eugenia uniflora) or araça (Psidium cattleianum), for example, will quickly grow into a shrub, then a tree in the favourable sub-tropical conditions and produce bushels of fruit each year. Varieties such as araça (strawberry guava) are not often commercially available as they are very delicate and must be consumed immediately. The food in this neighbourhood park is free for all who care to pick it. These small acts of guerrilla gardening have become a shared neighbourhood practice, bringing residents out to meet each other. The network of social relationships and exchanges, based on the cultivation and exchange of food, has begun to give the park a new form. This spatial negotiation remains open to future evolutions.

The network of relationships and interactions established around this informal urban agroforestry project is an example of practices inscribed across public and private spaces forming an emergent social and spatial ecology. In contrast to the design of the initial park, issued as a blueprint planting plan by a city planner, the materialised food space of the park is an emergent property of a series of negotiations and mediated actions. This is an inversion of the standard design process – spaces and forms are articulated by community interactions over time. Rather than public space designed with the hopes of supporting or containing civic life, social interaction, needs, and desires drive the creation of new spaces.

Design for/with informal and emergent systems is almost paradoxical and requires a paradigm shift in design thinking. The transgressive and opportunistic strategies of foraging that respond to the dynamics of changing urban ecologies pose challenges for

47

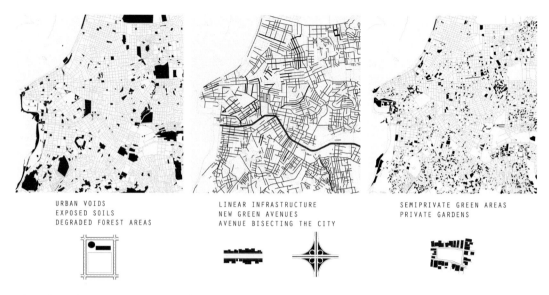

URBAN VOIDS
EXPOSED SOILS
DEGRADED FOREST AREAS

LINEAR INFRASTRUCTURE
NEW GREEN AVENUES
AVENUE BISECTING THE CITY

SEMIPRIVATE GREEN AREAS
PRIVATE GARDENS

Fig. 4: Urban LACE as a multi-scale synthesis of infrastructural ecological approaches (Jacques Abelman)

conventional approaches to design, planning, and policy development (Poe *et al.*, 2013). For instance, regulating land-based resources is a fundamental practice of urban planning; however, foraging is more knowledge-based and adaptive to changing land-based conditions, emphasising rights of use rather than property ownership. However, contemporary landscape design theory that embraces systems thinking and engages the novel ecologies of urban sites offers new strategies for meeting the challenges and potentials posed by urban foraging (Marris, 2011; Waldheim, 2006).

In addition to foraging, many spatial practices relate to establishing infrastructural ecologies. Exploring the full potential of this perspective requires a structured approach necessitating the establishment of multi-layered design strategies. Urban LACE (Local Agroforestry Collective Engagement), a two-year study project on the potential of infrastructural ecologies in Brazil, sets out such an approach. This prospective design project begins with urban mapping and reconnaissance of spatial practices in the city through sets of informal interviews with gardeners, street vendors, horticulturalists,

specialists, and inhabitants. The project is framed by a landscape architectural approach leading to projective design of novel productive spaces. The resulting designs are meant to serve as catalysts showing the potential of these practices as spatial narratives, provoking further action.

Urban LACE envisions networks of diverse typologies of productive infrastructural ecologies in the southern Brazilian capital of Porto Alegre. In the first phase of the project, fieldwork reveals a wealth of available spaces throughout the urban fabric (see fig. 4). These spaces, apt for productive landscape insertions, include the space around infrastructure such as roads and highways, heavily hardscaped sterile public spaces, and abandoned lots and degraded "wild" local ecosystems that are peri-urban in nature. These areas are catalogued according to soil type, elevation, and ecosystem type. The combination of specific characteristics in each site reveals what typologies of productive landscape could be established there – permutations of agroforestry ranging from orchards to perennial permaculture food forests. Agroforestry variations are selected for the project because of their relative ease of maintenance alongside intensive capacity for food production compared to high-intensity annual vegetable production. Once established, agroforestry systems are perennial, increasing in productive and ecological value over time. The fruiting species are selected from the hundreds of food bearing and medicinal tree, shrub, and plant varieties present in southern Brazil's Atlantic Forest ecosystem.

Taken as a whole, the network of spaces colonised by calorie-producing plants snakes its way through the city in a multitude of shapes, sizes, and intervention types, creating a lace-like landscape layer. The initial phase of the project seeks the spatial and ecological potential of the system, setting out matrices of spatial analyses cross-linked with species references and ecological parameters. In the second phase, a closer look is taken at the social context of specific sites and the actors involved in their creation and maintenance. Each site is specific because it relates to a community; demographic realities are brought to bear to potential patterns of socio-spatial occupation. Does it relate to leisure for citizens or is it purely a productive space like a production orchard? Is it near a favela or a wealthy area? Would the city maintain it? Do people need jobs? Is there a local market for food produced there? Would the food go to local schools, foodbanks, or upscale juice bars? Each site is a unique narrative of daily life, potentials, and problems, people, and opportunities. These different scenarios do not connect through aesthetic or programmatic uniformity, but rather like multi-textured, variable, and contingent pieces of a lace-like composition. Each narrative generated by the LACE strategy explores a potential constellation of people, space, and production. Taken together as a multitude of recombinant spatial relationships, they embody the concept of infrastructural ecologies.

The practice of landscape architecture in this context moves from fieldwork and analysis to normative illustration of spatial change, tracing a path from analysis of existing spaces to their

ecological and social transformation, engaging the infrastructural inversion referenced in the beginning of this chapter. Large-scale urban and landscape mapping creates a framework for establishing the structure and linkages of the network. The network relies on and reacts to the ecological as well as human capacity found within it, allowing "associations and synergies to become infrastructural" (Bélanger, 2016). The project coordinates potentials of spatial configuration, social structure, and ecological capacity. Foraging is one key practice associated with specific spatial typologies of productive landscape. Foraging is a dispersed spatial typology; orchard production is a concentrated productive typology. Food forest plantings, inspired by the classic Permaculture section of a multi-layered forest with seven productive levels, is in between. To engage the full potential of the infrastructural ecological idea, the "re-design of infrastructure as complex ecology", we must begin to assemble, catalogue, map, represent, and design these spaces, creating pathways towards actual creation of these new hybrid social-ecological-urban territories (see fig. 5).

Prospective pathways for engagement

Taken together, emergent ecologies and informal practices constitute the hybrid social and ecological spaces we offer as a definition of infrastructural ecologies. The first part of this chapter dealt with the importance for designers to recognise the nature and dynamics of these complex, hybrid phenomena, and how to engage them through mapping that begins from the ground up. It is a form of embodied mapping tracing the discursive paths of foragers themselves and integrating this to change the valence parcel maps and land use and mapping categories. If those steps can be successfully engaged, what prospective pathways emerge? Initially, we are faced with a paradox. Design as instrument of government or private interests to control programs, processes, and aesthetics seems antithetical to the very nature of the systems we are seeking to map that are indeterminate, fragile,

Fig. 5: Projective design of productive plantings for Praça Bernardo Drehr (Jacques Abelman)

aleatory, evolutionary, and chaotic. However, we believe that engaging with these processes opens up the field of design to new critical potentials: an evolution of landscape architectural practice, a new framework for productive landscapes in the city, and finally the emergence of a new form of urban commons.

The emergence of infrastructural ecologies first depends on their capacity to be seen, mapped, and then framed as emergent processes within which new negotiations transpire. The idea of design as negotiation, and designer as mediator, challenges traditional roles. In this context, the role of landscape architect is more as collaborator or mediator of spatial as well as social processes that lead to spatial transformations over time. This is new territory to be explored by an investigation into these spatial negotiations and how the landscape architect's ability to think through scale, systems, and time can beneficially frame such convergences of novel forces and stakeholders.

We see the potential of infrastructural ecologies as critical for providing a new framework for productive landscapes, urban agriculture, and food system infrastructure in the urban context. Infrastructural inversion alludes to grassroots efforts and informal practices whose potentials need to be mapped in order to reveal the spatial potential of these otherwise overlooked practices in design. Once the spatial and productive potentials of informal practices

are understood, they could potentially be augmented by newly informed design practices which create optimal or bettered conditions in which activities like foraging could take place. These new frameworks are based on intersections of ecological, social, and spatial practices and thus multiply productive potentials, site by site, in dense urban environments.

Finally, the spaces of infrastructural ecologies are co-emergent with collective social relationships involving design negotiation within shared systems and spaces. These spaces are hybrid in nature. Formed by shared actions and mutual agreement, they operate as an intermediary social space between the authorities of private property and government ownership. Because of these qualities, these spaces contain a kernel of a potential new form of urban commons. Also, since their spatiality is rooted in the extent and configuration of the resources it is based on, there is great variety of spatial typologies and scales for design engagement. For instance, the infrastructure of foraging spaces for New American refugees includes the space of the weeds growing between row crops as well as the stream corridor that links multiple spaces throughout the city. As illustrated in the LACE proposal, the intersection and overlap of interests and communities produce novel social and ecological spaces to create a dispersed network operating at multiple scales. This can be extended to conceiving of systems design of common resource spaces as infrastructural ecologies at the regional scale.

Urban agriculture and other informal practices as illustrated here by foraging are critically important for creating new productive spaces and ecologies. Infrastructure, as it is intended to facilitate and enable collective purposes is a commons project. As these potentials of the interstitial and informal become elucidated and mediated by design negotiations, they open new pathways for participation and productive urban landscapes. The proposition of infra-structural ecologies makes a new realm of urban potentials explicit by rendering previously unseen social and spatial practices visible.

References

Bélanger, P., 2016. Is landscape . . .. *In*: G. Doherty and C. Waldheim, eds. *What is landscape: Essays on the identity of landscape*. New York: Routledge.

de Certeau, M., 1988. Walking in the city. *In: Practice of everyday life*. Berkeley, CA: University of California Press, 91–110.

Del Tredici, P., 2014. The flora of the future. *In*: N. Lister and C. Reed, eds. *Projective ecologies*. New York: Actar Publishers, 338–257.

Eizenberg, E., 2011. Actually existing commons: Three moments of space of community gardens in New York City. *Antipode*, 44 (3), 764–782.

Ellis, E., 2014. Anthropogenic taxonomies: A taxonomy of the human biosphere. *In*: N. Lister and C. Reed, eds. *Projective ecologies*. New York: Actar Publishers, 338–257.

Galt, R.E., Gray, L.C., and Hurley, P., 2014. Subversive and interstitial food spaces: Transforming selves, societies, and society–Environment relations through urban agriculture and foraging, local environment. *The International Journal of Justice and Sustainability*, 19 (2), 133–146. https://doi.org/10.1080/13549839.2013.832554

Gibson-Graham, J.K., 2008. Diverse economies: Performative practices for "other worlds". *Progress in Human Geography*, 32 (5), 613–632.

Hou, J., 2012. Beyond Zuccotti Park: Making the public. *Places Journal*, September. Available from https://placesjournal.org/article/beyond-zuccotti-park-making-the-public/ [Accessed 20 Sept 2013].

Lawson, L.S., 2005. *City bountiful: A century of community gardening in America*. Berkeley, CA and Los Angeles, CA: University of California Press.

Linn, K., 2007. *Building commons and community*. Oakland: New Village Press.

Marris, E., 2011. *Rambunctious garden: Saving nature in a post-wild world*. New York: Bloomsbury.

McLain, D.J., Hurley, P.T., Emery, M.R., and Poe, M.R., 2014. Gathering "wild" food in the city: Rethinking the role of foraging in urban ecosystem planning and management. *Local Environment: The International Journal of Justice and Sustainability*, 19 (2), 220–240. https://doi.org/10.1080/13549839.2013.841659.

Mitchell, D., 2000. *Cultural geography: A critical introduction*. Oxford: Blackwell Publishers.

Mukhija, V., and Loukaitou-Sideris, A. (eds.), 2014. *The informal American city: Beyond taco trucks and day labor*. Cambridge: MIT Press.

Nasseaur, J.I., 1995. Messy ecosystems, orderly frames. *Landscape Journal*, 14 (2), 161–170.

Poe, M.R., McLain, R.J., Emery, M.R., and Hurley, P.T., 2013. Urban forest justice and the rights to wild foods, medicines, and materials in the city. *Human Ecology*, 40, 6. https://doi.org/10.1007/s10745-013-9572-1

Seiter, D. with Future Green Studio., 2016. *Spontaneous urban plants: Weeds in NYC*. New York: Archer.

Shackleton, C.M., Hurley, P.T., Dahlberg, A.C., Emery, M.R., Nagendra, H., 2017. Urban foraging: A ubiquitous human practice overlooked by urban planners, policy, and research. *Sustainability*. https://doi.org/10.3390/su9101884

Syracuse Community Geography., 2014. Putting down roots: Refugee agricultural practices in Syracuse, NY. *GIS Story Map*. Available from http://bit.ly/1wLWiwh [Accessed 3 Mar 2016].

Waldheim, C. (ed.), 2006. *The landscape urbanism reader*. New York: Princeton Architectural Press.

Wehi, P.M., and Wehi, W.L., 2009. Traditional plant harvesting in contemporary fragmented and urban landscapes. *Conservation Biology*, 24, 594–604.

Mapping urban agriculture potentials in Nerima City, Tokyo

André Viljoen

Thematically, this chapter focuses on urban food growing sites and their potential to catalyse spatial and place-making innovations. An inductive approach is applied to original primary place-based mappings made by the author to explore and describe mapping as a design research method and technique. The research questions that led to this mapping exercise in Tokyo, namely how could disparate fields be better integrated into a neighbourhood by developing a *Continuous Productive Urban Landscape (CPUL)* strategy, were posed by a local farmer and the municipality. The *CPUL* design strategy advocates the coherent introduction of a networked landscape that includes urban agriculture (Viljoen, 2005).

The type of mapping described is place-based, in a neighbourhood of Nerima City, Tokyo, at the scale of a ten-minute neighbourhood walk then focussing in on one specific urban agriculture site. The mapping is propositional and generative, set in a near future scenario that values green infrastructure, nature-based solutions and walkable neighbourhoods. This study adds to Bohn&Viljoen's ongoing research project *Laboratories for Urban Agriculture* (Viljoen and Bohn, 2014, pp. 122–154).

Digital media are used as tools for representation, e.g. images provided by *Google Earth* and graphic programmes, but the mapping techniques are essentially analogue, utilising walking, conversation, photography, drafting, collage and montage as primary working methods.

In considering mapping as a design research tool, the method described here can be used to quantify crop yields based on food growing areas and conditions for cultivation, but in this instance that was not required as the sites mapped were already being used commercially as farms.

Collage and mapping

Collage is fundamental to the mapping methods described here; it usually consists of cutting or tearing images on paper or fabric and sticking them on to a larger background sheet or panel. Butler-Kisber and Poldma (2010) describe the use of collage in experimental research, indicating its emergence, for use in this way, around the turn of the 21st century, focussing on its ability to reveal tacit understandings and uncover relationships otherwise difficult to articulate verbally.

Collage represents ideas by creating links between fragments that represent emergent feelings first and then ideas. These fragments are reconstructed to represent feelings that when viewed can suggest new meanings, or a whole new take on a phenomenon because of the artful way the pieces are put together and portrayed. (Butler-Kisber and Poldma, 2010, p. 13)

They refer to the ambiguity inherent in collage that offers alternative insights, one of the characteristics that make it valuable in generating new knowledge.

DOI: 10.4324/9781003352280-6

Fig. 1: Exploded London (Bohn&Viljoen Architects, 1998)

In Europe, collage is best known as an arts practice that was used about a century ago by early modernist painters, such as George Braque and Pablo Picasso, to explore abstracted representations of people or objects, aiming to simultaneously present several views of the same situation, simulating the way we perceive them. At the same time, the process also created unexpected juxtapositions of objects and fragments of objects, with this aspect being taken forward by practitioners such as Kurt Schwitters (Elderfield, 1985) as a more purely abstracted form of composition, where meaning and relation to the material world became less direct. Schwitters associated his early work with the *Dada* movement, a loose but impactful movement that reacted against the social norms seen to have led to the first world war. The collages of Schwitters with their ambiguity invite visual engagement and a pleasure in

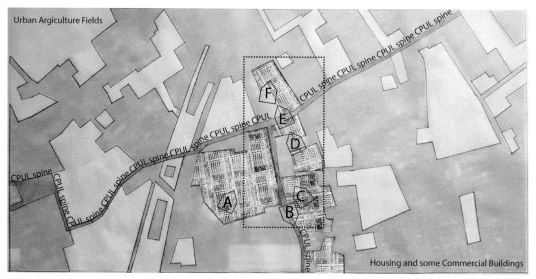

Fig. 2: Neighbourhood urban agriculture mapping in Nerima City (Bohn&Viljoen Architects, 2022)

looking at surfaces. Several of his collages have an inherent landscape and spatial quality, due to fields of colour, sometimes edged with an accentuated boarder, e.g. *Bild mit heller Mitte*, 1919, or *Oorlog*, 1930. But it is the totality of his collage work that generates an impression of spatial territories, fields and curiously engaging juxtapositions. This duality of collage as a specific artefact and something inviting interpretation led to my use of it in 1998 as a research method for food mapping to produce the collage *Exploded London* (see fig. 1).

Exploded London is a visual thought experiment; it is the openness and ambiguity in the interpretation of colleges that led to its choice as a method. The image provided a visual means of mapping how much space would be needed to supply all of London's 1998 population of about 7 million people with fruit and vegetables based

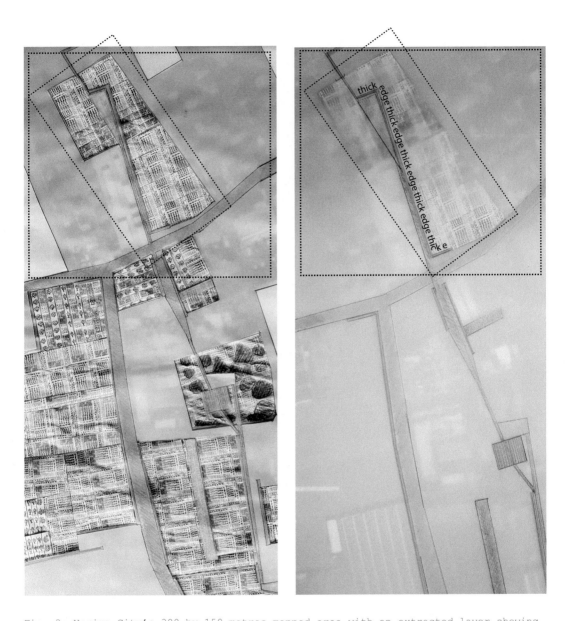

Fig. 3: Nerima City's 300 by 150 metres mapped area with an extracted layer showing proposed design interventions (Bohn&Viljoen Architects, 2022)

on needing 100m^2 of growing area per person. The collage was made using a scale "A-Z map" of London, cut up into horizontal strips between which the required food growing area of 70,000 hectares was inserted. The resulting image was both accurate and a fantasy. With regards to accuracy the viewer could make a judgment about how feasible it would be to include this additional space for urban agriculture in cities.

At the same time, they could imagine what strips of agricultural land would be like if the new exploded map of London was imagined as a reality. In our own design research, this image gave us confidence that the agricultural areas required for self-sufficiency in fruit and vegetables looked plausible if cities were to retain spaces with the density necessary for a vibrant urbanity.

Fig. 4: Ogawa Farm, Tokyo, experience
mapping (Bohn&Viljoen Architects, 2022)

Fig. 5: Raymond Farm, Tokyo experience mapping
(Bohn&Viljoen Architects, 2022)

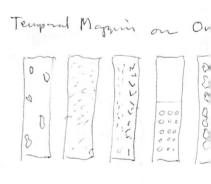

Day 28ᵗʰ November 2018

50 m =

5000 cm

$\frac{5000}{60}$ 83

plastic

peg.

$\oplus$

$\updownarrow$

egs 8 Plastic.

Montage and mapping as a visualisation method

The rest of this chapter refers to food mapping as a visualisation tool within design research. The methods for visualisation utilise scale maps and site plans as underlays for revealing urban spatial structure to which collage and drafting are applied as generative tools for specific design interventions. The techniques used here are more accurately described as a hybrid between collage and montage. Whereas collage celebrates the chance and unexpected associations that arise from the juxtaposition of materials not usually considered having an association with each other, montage in image making, uses a deliberate arrangement of images, usually including recognisable objects to articulate a specific narrative or proposition. Sudhalter (2017), in discussing the use of photographs and drawing in perspective images by the architect Mies van de Rohe, describes the method as being "developmental and demonstrative" and the same can be said for the food mapping methods that follow.

In addition to the hybrid collage and montage methods that will be described here, photographs edited and composed in spatial sequences are also used as a means of mapping the experience and perception of urban agriculture sites.

Food mapping in Nerima, Tokyo

Figure 2 shows a mapping study of a neighbourhood in Nerima City, which retains significant areas of active privately owned urban agriculture fields, resulting in a patchy landscape. The author has documented the complex planning and policy context for urban agriculture in Nerima City elsewhere (Viljoen and Bohn, 2020, pp. 82–92). The city authority's decision to support urban agriculture and farmers' desires to work with the city to find long-term solutions to retaining farmland resulted in Bohn&Viljoen being asked to develop propositions for a Continuous Productive Urban Landscape on land belonging to a particular farmer. Figure 2 maps an area including the farmers' land of about one kilometre by half a kilometre, equating to approximately ten- and five-minute walking distances. This scale of mapping is used to foreground urban agriculture fields, shown in white or by using line drawings of crops. The differentiation of fill distinguishes between sites physically visited by the mapper and ones identified using a Google Earth image. A visual assessment of fields, roads and paths leads to a proposition for a primary connective *CPUL* spine that can accommodate multiple modes of transport off which secondary routes prioritising walking and cycling are established. The mapping image is made using an underlay image from Google Earth, overlaid with two layers of tracing paper; the lower layer has fields collaged onto it, and the upper layer outlines field edges and the *CPUL* spine. The fields visited by the mapper are cut away in the upper layer to give the black and white line drawings of crops more visual prominence. For the mapper, the physical act of cutting and drawing on to paper strengthens their appreciation of the sites being considered, and in my experience as a mapper, I developed a tacit connection with the process and experience of the fields and the act of cultivation. Photographs taken while walking in the neighbourhood record actual site conditions and aid viewers of the mapping to reconcile the abstraction of the collage with the actual locality.

Figure 3 zooms into the area mapped in figure 2 to show an area approximately 300 metres by 150 metres, corresponding to an area walked by the mapper, the farmer and a representative from the city authority, and was chosen because it covers the land between field A (fig. 2) and fields E and F (fig. 2) belonging to the farmer we were working with.

All of the sites in this area were visited on three different occasions to gain an understanding of the landscape, its uses and characteristics. With this level of knowledge, it is possible to identify key points for design interventions, which are indicated on the mappings using colour coding, blue for "thick edges" and yellow for "micro squares", these interventions will be described later in this text. The process for making this mapping is the same as for figure 2, but figure 3 shows the value of being able to isolate particular layers of a mapping; in this case, on the right-hand side the layer showing design interventions is extracted, accentuating the elements that will give coherence to the *CPUL* network.

Experiential mapping

The writing and research of Lickwar and Thoren (2020) is re-evaluating eighteenth- and nine-teenth-century concepts, such as the *Ferme ornée [Ornamental Farm]* and the picturesque, which advocated landscape design strategies to include an aesthetic appreciation of farmed landscapes, then typically reserved for a landowning elite. These strategies indicate a longstanding recognition that agricultural landscapes have an aesthetic potential, but they tended to hide the exploitative labour practices that enabled them. A central argument for introducing *CPULs* into neighbourhoods is that they add value to places by enhancing the access of non-farming residents to the experience of agricultural landscapes as a second nature, and much of this will be by seeing, smelling and hearing urban agriculture sites. The concept of *Second Nature*, as a product of culture, environment and human agency is one that resonates with the processes of collage and montage, comparable to Swyngedouw and Heynen's (2003) reflection that the notion of *Second Nature* "paves the way to understanding the complex mix of political, economic and social processes that shape, reshape and reshape again urban landscapes". In rethinking the role of urban agriculture, we have developed the idea of a shared visual experience, whereby the every-day elements of agriculture are appreciated as part of an organic urban ornamentation. This approach draws in part on optics, when the eye of an observer in motion is considered in relation to a field, and on an appreciation of surface

and spatial aesthetic, found in some of the materials commonly used for crop protection. Figures 4 and 5 show mappings of crop protection structures, variously known as hoop houses or polytunnels found in the vicinity of Nerima City. Mappings like this aim to tell the story of a walk alongside or through an urban agriculture field and make visible the rich material and ambiguous spatial qualities of functional landscapes. The aesthetic draws on the same values explored by collagists like Schwitters or later multimedia artists, such as Robert Rauschenberg, Jasper Johns or the British artist Tom Phillips with whom the author undertook field trips to Cuba to study these phenomena.

Primary paths and desire lines

The order in which mapping takes place does not have to follow a particular sequence, for example from the scale of a city to municipality, to neighbourhood, to a single site. But when working at a particular scale often different mapping steps are done in parallel, as is the case in figures 6, 7 and 8.

Figure 6 examines selected urban agriculture fields in detail at the request of the farmer who owned them. The mapping methods described here are generative, made using conventional architectural orthogonal plans overlaid in sequence with a hierarchy of interventions. The primary driver for this mapping is to define a desirable pedestrian and cycle friendly path for use by residents and to provide spaces to linger and engage with adjacent urban agriculture fields. Figure 6 shows how desire lines, routes that provide easy paths from one destination to another, can generate a *CPUL* path (see A), in this case encouraging walking from a residential area towards an environmental centre and local commercial district (see B). Desire lines encourage walking, and, in this instance, their geometry encourages the creation of a small gathering space, or micro square (see C), where the two desire lines intersect. By thickening the *CPUL* path, the passage of people can slow down when another *CPUL* typology, the thick

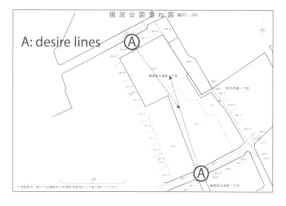
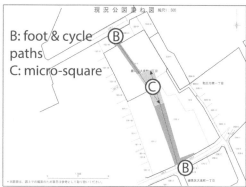
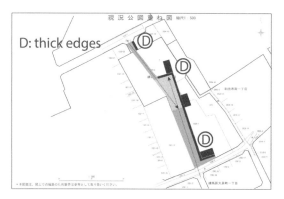

Fig. 6: Generative mapping applied to selected urban agriculture fields (Bohn&Viljoen Architects, 2019)

edge (see D), is introduced. Thick edges provide an occupiable interface between fields (see E) and neighbourhood residents, without interfering with farming activities. Since these mappings were made Iida *et al.* (2023) have demonstrated, by analysing responses from 3135 adults who participated in an online survey, how the subjective well-being and physical activity of residents in Tokyo, living in walkable neighbourhoods with urban agriculture, increased compared to residents who did not actively participate in urban food growing. Of particular significance for the *CPUL* concept was their observation that the greatest increase in physical activity was associated with the use of greenways, in other words, the types of paths advocated in the *CPUL* concept.

Figures 7 and 8 translate the two-dimensional mappings into three-dimensional images that should enable visualisation by a wide range of stakeholders. Utilising the same graphic methods as used in figures 2 and 3, the relationships between the *CPUL* strategy at a neighbourhood level and its experience by an individual is encouraged. Figure 7 isolates the *CPUL* thick edge, showing how a boundary wall between public and private space can become a device for occupation by people, including benches, outdoor kitchens, gathering spaces, storage for community items, e.g. chairs and tables, and a farm stall for the direct sale of farm goods.

Figure 9 transforms these specific *Nerima Mappings* into a speculative study that was used to communicate how the *CPUL* concept could be transferred to a city like London. This transformative possibility is in part due to the semi-abstract nature of the mapping methods developed as part of our *CPUL* design research.

60

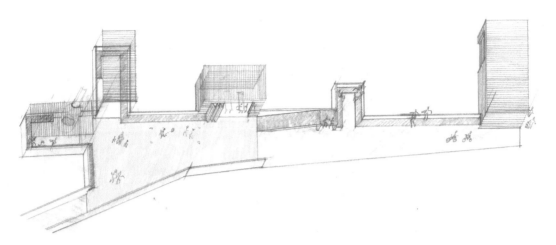

Fig. 7: Translation of a two-dimensional mapping into a three-dimensional image, showing a CPUL thick edge (Bohn&Viljoen Architects, 2019)

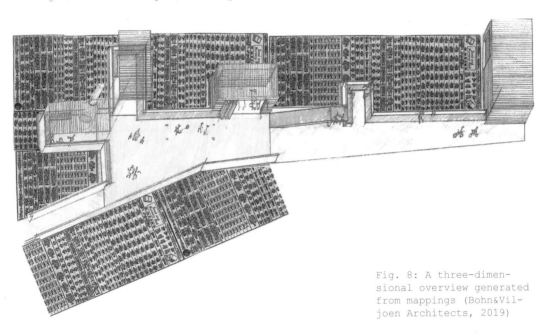

Fig. 8: A three-dimensional overview generated from mappings (Bohn&Viljoen Architects, 2019)

This description of food mapping concentrates on the application of the method, and the qualitative experiences made available to residents in a walkable neighbourhood. The mappings presented here have been used to communicate the *CPUL* concept to multiple stakeholders in Nerima City. While they have not yet been implemented, feedback from Nerima City's urban agriculture department indicate that the mappings have been successful in communicating the design intentions. In addition to these, the mappings described can be used to generate metrics to assess the increased potential for residents' interaction with urban agriculture sites. For example, by measuring the length of paths and thick edges, an indication of increased opportunities for interactions between resident, food spaces and outdoor activity may be judged.

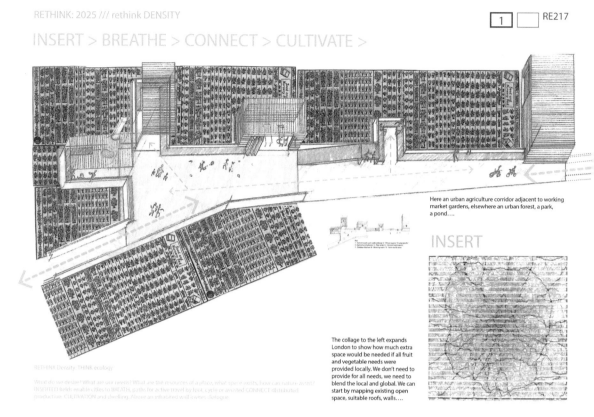

RETHINK: 2025 /// rethink DENSITY

1   RE217

INSERT > BREATHE > CONNECT > CULTIVATE >

Here an urban agriculture corridor adjacent to working market gardens, elsewhere an urban forest, a park, a pond....

INSERT

The collage to the left expands London to show how much extra space would be needed if all fruit and vegetable needs were provided locally. We don't need to provide for all needs, we need to blend the local and global. We can start by mapping existing open space, suitable roofs, walls....

Fig. 9: Rethink 2025: A post-Covid architectural competition entry drawing reworking transferable ideas from the Tokyo mappings to an imagined neighbourhood in the UK (Bohn&Viljoen Architects, 2020)

Hybrid mapping

Hybrid mapping methods, utilising mixed media, collage and montage, have the potential to address many of the questions that arise during a design process. Initial mappings utilising collage's ability to suggest new meanings and reveal opportunities can be further employed in a more instrumental way using a hybrid collage and montage method as design and visualisation tools. Concepts like the *CPUL* strategy, that have been validated, in part, by developing the mapping methods described here are now beginning to be validated by independent research. Iida *et al.* (2023) provide a good example of this validation by assessing the perceived improvement in well-being and increased physical activity associated with the kinds of food-related spaces these mapping methods have helped design and describe.

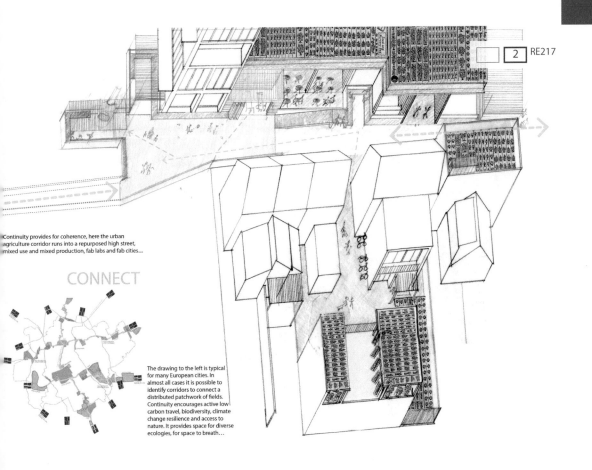

2 RE217

Continuity provides for coherence, here the urban agriculture corridor runs into a repurposed high street, mixed use and mixed production, fab labs and fab cities....

CONNECT

The drawing to the left is typical for many European cities. In almost all cases it is possible to identify corridors to connect a distributed patchwork of fields. Continuity encourages active low carbon travel, biodiversity, climate change resilience and access to nature. It provides space for diverse ecologies, for space to breath…

References

Butler-Kisber, L., and Poldma, T., 2010. The power of visual approaches in qualitative inquiry: The use of collage making and concept mapping in experiential research. *Journal of Research Practice*, 6 (2), Article M18. Available from http://jrp.icaap.org/index.php/jrp/article/view/197/196

Elderfield, J., 1985. *Kurt Schwitters*. London: Thames and Hudson.

Iida, A., et al., 2023. Urban agriculture in walkable neighborhoods bore fruit for health and food system resilience during the COVID-19 pandemic. *NPJ Urban Sustainability*, 3 (1). https://doi.org/10.1038/s42949-023-00083-3.

Lickwar, P., and Thoren, R., 2020. *Farmscape: The design of productive landscapes*. London: Routledge Taylor & Francis Group.

Sudhalter, A., 2017. Friedrichstrasse: The contexts of an image, 1922–1924. *In*: A. Beitin, W. Eiermann and B. Franzen, eds. *Mies van der Rohe Montage Collage*. London: Koenig Books, 68–85.

Swyngedouw, E., and Heynen, N.C., 2003. Urban political ecology, justice and the politics of scale. *Antipode Special Issue*, 35 (5), 898–918.

Viljoen, A. (ed.), 2005. *Continuous Productive Urban Landscape: Designing urban agriculture for sustainable cities*. Oxford: The Architectural Press.

Viljoen, A., and Bohn, K., 2014. *Second Nature Urban Agriculture: Designing productive cities*. London: Routledge.

Viljoen, A., and Bohn, K., 2020. Building continuous productive (peri-)urban landscapes. *In*: J.S.C. Wiskerke, ed. *Achieving sustainable urban agriculture*. Cambridge: Burleigh Dodds Science Publishing, 61–100.

Mapping multifunctional agro-urban landscape to manage edible cities in North-Eastern Italy

Viviana Ferrario and Fabrizio D'Angelo

The North-Eastern Italian region of Veneto is renowned worldwide for the historic city of Venice built upon the water of its lagoon. Perhaps not everyone knows that its historical fortune is mainly due to the relationships the city has established over time with the mainland, a fertile alluvial agricultural plain with some medium-sized cities. From the 1970s onwards, a very intense and dispersed urbanisation process overtook this region, where now highly fragmented cultivated and functionally mixed urbanised areas are amazingly interwoven (fig. 1).

The central part of this territory lies between the cities of Venice, Padua, Treviso and Bassano. This area is an urban-rural continuum (or, better, an agro-urban continuum) where 50% of its 2.500.000 dwellers live in municipalities with less than 15.000 inhabitants. Considerable public and private wealth, good accessibility (two international airports, three highways, the Pan-European corridor V) and a dense network of public and private services give it an urban character. Despite this, far from being marginal, agriculture is still vital, both in terms of production and income and in the number of cultivated areas that occupy more than 65% of the land. Residences, small and medium-size industries, tertiary activities and agriculture live together side by side.

Agro-urban landscapes in the Veneto region

For a long time, this area has been studied in the light of concepts such as urban growth, urban sprawl, land consumption and farmland misuse. At the regional level, agricultural policies and spatial planning proceeded separately. This is due to the absence of any specific agricultural policy for farming in such an urbanised area, as well as of an adequate spatial policy for such an intertwined agro-urban continuum able of managing territorial transformation. This problem cannot simply be explained with a lack of political will alone. Perhaps, at the core, local authorities have difficulties in envisioning the future of a territory of this kind.

This agro-urban landscape can carry mutual benefits for farming and housing, but also reciprocal disturbances. Nearby quality food production is probably the most important benefit of the Venice agro-urban continuum: wheat, fruits, vegetables (like the famous "red lettuce" of Treviso) and well-known wines (like "Prosecco") are produced within the metropolitan area. Farmland provides renewable energy sources and improves flood safety. Green infrastructure within the farming land contributes to biodiversity, connecting the mountainous ecological network and the coastal wet areas. Finally, urban dwellers use farming spaces as a huge park, walking on gravel roads and along the field borders. However, it must also be said that all these benefits are more potential than real. For example, agricultural production may not always be ecologically and productively diverse, may fail to make an urban connection and, overall, may not be as sustainable as it could be. Additionally, the more urbanisation spreads and agriculture intensifies, the more conflicts emerge regarding land use, pesticide pollution, tensions for mobility,

DOI: 10.4324/9781003352280-7

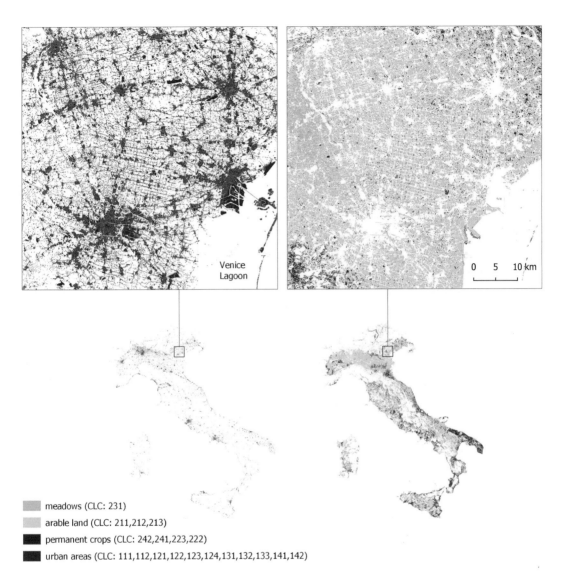

Venice
Lagoon

0 5 10 km

■ meadows (CLC: 231)

□ arable land (CLC: 211,212,213)

■ permanent crops (CLC: 242,241,223,222)

■ urban areas (CLC: 111,112,121,122,123,124,131,132,133,141,142)

Fig. 1: Components of the agro-urban continuum in the central Venice plain, in an area of 60 × 60 km (V. Ferrario; source: CLC – Corine Land Cover, 2018, at 1:100.000; Regional land cover database, 2018, at 1:10.000)

etc. This intertwined situation needs a reciprocal adaptation between farmers and inhabitants with common objectives, shared rules and integrated policies. Within the agro-urban continuum, agriculture must be different, while at the same time, inhabiting and governing an agro-urban continuum needs new geographic interpretations and unconventional urban planning (Ferrario, 2016).

In recent years, concepts such as "agro-urban" (Yokohari *et al.*, 2008; Poli, 2017; Ávila Sánchez, 2018) and "agropolitan" (Friedman, 1979; Abramson, 2020) have aroused new interest in the academic community around the world. At the same time, urban agriculture and food policies began to enter the urban planning and spatial policies agenda. Agriculture is a multifunctional activity, providing food, feed and energy sources, but it can also be a guarantee for environmental values, as well as supporting leisure and other social services. It is possible to talk about farming space as a multifunctional landscape (Brandt and Vejre, 2004). Spatial and functional proximity between agricultural and urban space can shorten the supply chains between production and consumption (in food, energy, etc.) and gives the possibility to close urban cycles in a smaller area (Dewaelheyns and Gulinck, 2008; Cartiaux *et al.*, 2018), introducing a certain level of self-sufficiency that can make the metabolism of the city more resilient (UA Magazine, 2009; Torre, 2013). Moreover, concepts such as *Continuous Productive Urban Landscape (CPUL)* and the edible city perspective assign to farming within metropolitan areas a vital role in the ecological transition towards sustainable development (Viljoen *et al.*, 2005; Azunre *et al.*, 2019).

In the last 15 years, three factors were of great importance for this increasing understanding of agro-urban landscapes: a larger availability of spatial data from the early 2000s, the global food crisis in 2008 and, more recently, the Covid pandemic in 2020. Satellite images and high-resolution land use maps allowed us to capture from above the strong interwoven pattern between cultivated and developed land which is hardly visible at the ground. Around the same time, the global food crisis raised the attention towards the importance of "feeding the planet" (to use the slogan of the 2015 Expo in Milan), and the Covid pandemic increased the awareness for the need of green open space nearby to practice outdoor sports and spend free time. This chapter focuses on the first of these three factors, particularly on GIS land-use data, whose reliability and precision has greatly improved in the last few years.

The importance of mapping for agro-urban landscape management

Several research works in the last decade have highlighted that quantifying the agricultural dynamics in urban and peri-urban spaces is

significant in bringing the food system discourse into geography and urban planning. This goes beyond the dichotomies of city/rural areas and human being/nature (Morgan, 2015), by adding an important focus on food security as well as ecological and sustainable development within urban and peri-urban areas (Ollison *et al.*, 2016) at the local scale (Feagan, 2007). While the use of GIS is particularly useful in urban and peri-urban contexts, its use in investigating urban cultivation is limited by the hybrid characteristic of such spaces and the general multifunctionality of agri-food systems (Pérez Campaña and Valenzuela Montes, 2014; Xia *et al.*, 2021).

There are also some significant challenges in GIS data collection: most of the spatial food system data are not available, and mapping the domestic or informal food system seems to be particularly complicated, due to hybrid configuration of spaces, undefined borders and different configurations for various urban patterns (Ghosh, 2021). Finally, there are limits on the use of conventional land use data, such as CORINE land cover (CLC) to study local urban dynamics and represent dispersed urbanisation (Díaz-Pacheco and Gutiérrez, 2013). A reliable land-cover map based on the CLC classification system (using maximum level 5 of the nomenclature) for the entire Veneto region at a scale of 1:10.000 was published in 2011. Its spatial detail (minimum mapping unit of 0,25 ha) can be sufficient for analysing dispersed urbanisation at the regional scale, but not for a fundamental understanding of agro-urban landscape at a closer level. This is because several agricultural fields are included within the same polygon (small areas of cultivation typical of agro-urban areas do not exceed 0,25 ha) and the presence of buildings and of other artificial surfaces dispersed throughout the fields are generally ignored (Geronta and Ferrario, 2018). In 2018, the regional authority responsible for agricultural payments from the *Common Agricultural Policy* (AVEPA) made available a new set of spatial data annually updated from 2015 onwards. These new data can be used to communicate in a novel way the specific agro-urban characters of the Venice central plain, contributing to a better geographic understanding of ongoing processes and establishing new planning practices. The opportunity to test these data showed up during the preparation of the *Plan for Urban Green Areas* of the city of Padua which started in January 2021. The research group of the Università Iuav di Venezia has been charged with preliminary research on urban and peri-urban agriculture (UPA) at the municipality level. The *Plan* recognises that multifunctional UPA, though practised in private areas, can provide several public services to the city and its citizens.

The maps shown in this chapter have been made within this framework, to better represent and communicate the multifunctional agro-urban fabric around the city of Padova. Land use data do not exhaust the complexity of the multi-functional agro-urban landscape; so they have been completed with other datasets, taken in part by other public sources and in part mapped *ex novo* by the research group, following previous experiences (Ferrario, 2016) (fig. 2). Some of these new maps were included in the *Plan for the Urban Green Areas* of the city of Padua and became the basis for new strategies for urban and peri-urban open land. Such an approach could be a way to provide a new understanding of the agro-urban character of the Venice region, and eventually of other agropolitan areas and urban-rural continuums around the world.

Data sources and methods

Our maps are based on a database partly provided by public institutes (the regional administration and the regional Authority for *Common Agricultural Policy payments* AVEPA) and partially realised by the research group. AVEPA provided two different land-use databases. The first open-source database, updated in 2020, represents the eligibility of agricultural areas for EU Community aid schemes, returning particularly detailed data that categorise the areas under

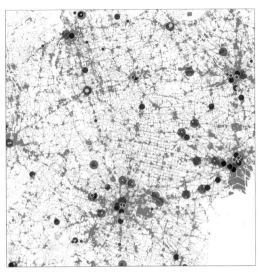

social vegetable gardens
Kmzero restaurants
raw milkmachines (coldiretti + milkymaps)
direct milk sell (coldiretti)
ethical purchasing groups (reteGAS)
farmers' markets

Fig. 2: Kmzero initiatives (short distance food transportation) in the agro-urban continuum: farmers' markets, Kmzero restaurants, Ethical Purchasing Groups, direct milk sell, social vegetable gardens (V. Ferrario; source: fieldwork; official and unofficial lists)

actual cultivation and include other landscape elements. A second database collects data taken from the collection of farm plans (Piano Colturale Grafico), based on farmers' annual declarations. This geo-spatialised survey campaign of requests for European Union subsidies in 2021, based on cadastral parcels, returns a more detailed use of agricultural land, albeit referable only to the cultivated spaces subject to declaration. The two databases made it possible to not only represent the extension and distribution of the cultivated areas, but also to roughly distinguish the main supply chains (food, feed, energy crops, ornamental, woods, livestock) and to identify other farming landscape elements, such as those that form the edge-of-field complex system (hedges, ditches, grassy strips) so crucial for agrobiodiversity.

The research group directly collected some data missing in the existing databases, in particular vegetable gardens and home vineyards. These datasets were created by photo-interpreting Google satellite WMS (2018 frames) and comparing it with other web map services (ESRI satellite; Bing Maps; Google Street View) within the municipal area of the city of Padua. Desk study results were then verified on-site through sample inspections. This work has produced unpublished data of particular importance, revealing what has never been mapped so far because it is too minute, outside the logic of the market and outside the agricultural payments system. The datasets are composed of polygonal vectors, categorised as family or professional production. The following map production drew on both the international food-mapping literature (Sweeney *et al.*, 2016) and local experiences (Ferrario, 2010, 2016; Ferrario *et al.*, 2018; De Marchi, 2020).

Mapping agro-urban landscape around the city of Padova

Food, feed, non-food

Figure 3 shows how the farmland in and around the city of Padua is used, distinguishing between food, non-food and indirect food production (feed for breeding). Within the food-dedicated farming spaces, we find horticultural crops, orchards, vineyards, the cultivation of medicinal plants, and food cereal crops (e.g. different varieties of wheat for the production of flour). Feed production includes fodder and arable crops to produce feed (e.g., corn, sorghum). Non-food farming spaces include energy crops (e.g., short-forestry, waxy maise, rapeseed), industrial crops such as sugar beet or tobacco, and nurseries to produce ornamental plants or fruit trees. The representation shows how approximately only one-third of the farming space is dedicated to direct food production (fig. 4). However, its reliability is limited because information on the final destination of the production is not always available. Interestingly, fresh food production in Padua covers a respectable surface.

Sell, share, self

Figure 5, limited to the municipal area of Padua, represents spaces for fresh food production (vegetables and fruit), distinguishing between production for sale, shared/community production and production for self-consumption. The first category includes all the spaces relating to commercial vegetable gardens, vineyards, orchards and specialised horticultural productions. The second includes urban vegetable gardens and community gardens as well as ethical purchasing groups for food. The third category describes farming spaces for self-consumption and maps home gardens, family vineyards and family orchards.

Multifunctional agro-urban spaces

These four maps (fig. 6) describe the multifunctionality of farming space in the municipality of Padua. The first relates to the agro-ecosystem and highlights the dense presence of green infrastructures in the agro-urban continuum, such as hedges, groves, rows, isolated trees, streams, canals, etc. The second map refers to agro energy and represents hypothetical energy crops, selecting land use categories such as soybean, waxy maise, sunflower and beet, generally used in biomass production for biogas plants, and short forestry wooded areas to produce woody biomass for biomass thermal power plants. The map also locates renewable energy plants such as ground photovoltaic and biogas. The third theme represents three functions particularly connected to cultivated spaces: health, education and free time. In densely populated contexts, agricultural spaces are used for education (educational farms), sociality (urban and collective gardens) and leisure (green areas, sports areas and cycle-pedestrian paths). The fourth map represents some clues of short supply chains, mapping self-production (vineyards and domestic gardens, collective and urban gardens), the points of sale of the short supply chain, such as the city markets (where local producers and solidarity buying groups also confer) and food distributors (raw milk).

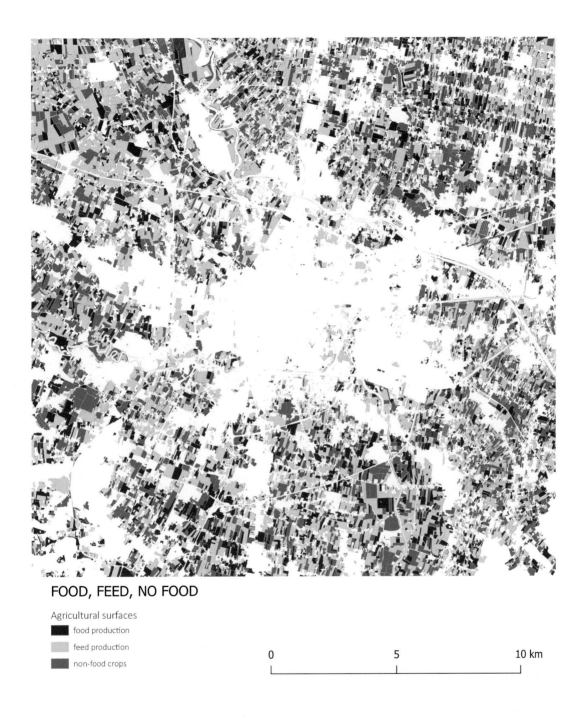

FOOD, FEED, NO FOOD

Agricultural surfaces

- food production
- feed production
- non-food crops

0   5   10 km

Fig. 3: Food, feed, non-food. Farming land around the city of Padua produces food, feed and other non-food products (V. Ferrario; source: AVEPA, land use database 2020, and collection of farm plans (Piano Colturale Grafico) 2021)

SELL, SHARE, SELF

COMMERCIAL PRODUCTION
■ commercial vegetable
gardens, vineyard,
orchard, greenhouse

DOMESTIC PRODUCTION
■ domesticvegetable
gardens, vineyard,
orchard, greenhouse

SHARED PRODUCTION
urban vegetable garden
fairtrade purchasing group

cultivated area

0   2 km

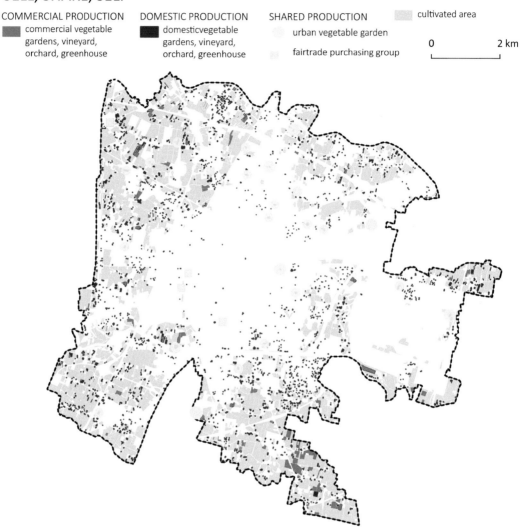

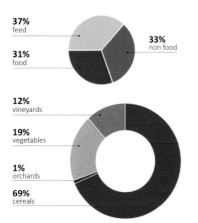

37%
feed

31%
food

33%
non food

12%
vineyards

19%
vegetables

1%
orchards

69%
cereals

Fig. 5: Sell, share, self. Food is produced
not only in the farming space but also inside
the city (F. D'Angelo; sources: AVEPA, land
use database 2020; AVEPA, collection of farm
plans 2021; Regione del Veneto, Regional land
cover database 2018 and Ethical Purchasing
Groups; Comune di Padova, Orti urbani. Domestic
productions: photo-interpretation and fieldwork)

Fig. 4: Share of farming land in Padova,
according to production. The data are
approximate and refer only to the cultivated
areas subject to EU Community contributions
(V. Ferrario; sources: AVEPA, Collection of
farm plans, 2021)

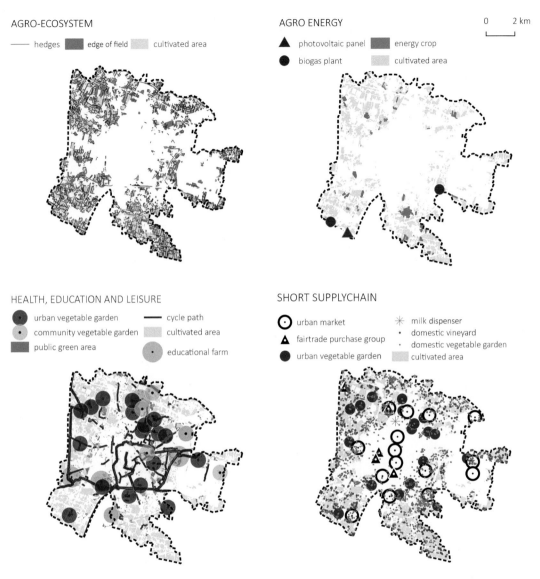

Fig. 6: Multifunctionality in the agro-urban continuum around the city of Padua (F. D'Angelo; sources: Regione del Veneto, Regional land cover database 2018, AVEPA, land use database 2020; AVEPA, collection of farm plans, 2021; GSE – Gestore Sistemi Energetici, bioenergy and solar plants; Comune di Padova, parks and green areas; Regione del Veneto, educational farms; Comune di Padova, local markets; Regione del Veneto, cycle paths)

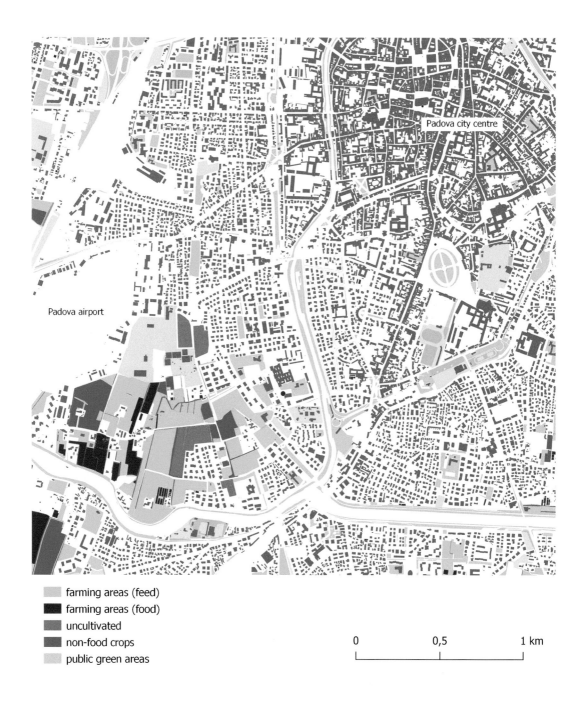

Padova city centre

Padova airport

farming areas (feed)
farming areas (food)
uncultivated
non-food crops
public green areas

0   0,5   1 km

Fig. 7: Farming spaces in the Basso Isonzo area in Padua, less than 500 metres from the ancient city walls, where citizens ask the municipality to stop urban development and establish an agro-urban park (V. Ferrario; sources: Regione del Veneto, Regional land cover database 2018; AVEPA, land use database 2020; AVEPA; AVEPA, Collection of farm plans, 2021)

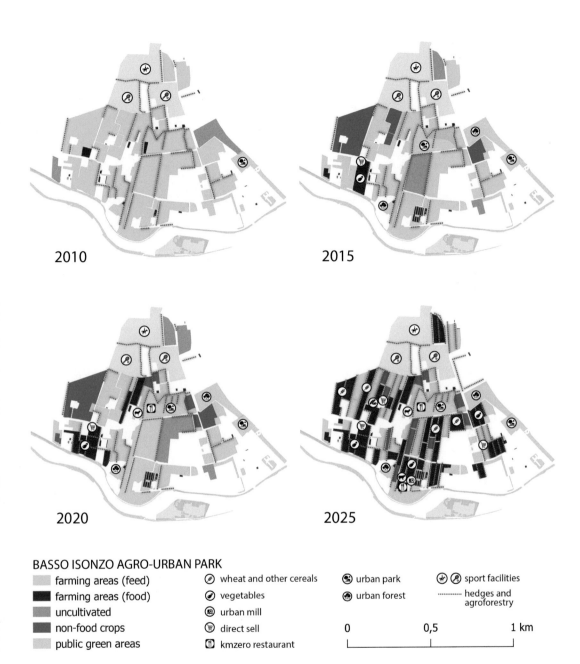

2010

2015

2020

2025

BASSO ISONZO AGRO-URBAN PARK

farming areas (feed)	⊘ wheat and other cereals	🏙 urban park
farming areas (food)	⊘ vegetables	🌳 urban forest
uncultivated	🏭 urban mill	
non-food crops	🛒 direct sell	
public green areas	🍴 kmzero restaurant	

✈ ⊘ sport facilities

.... hedges and agroforestry

0   0,5   1 km

Fig. 8: Land use change in the Basso Isonzo area from 2010 to 2020 and 2025 scenario for agricultural transition to an agro-urban park. In 2025, more land is expected to produce food, and the number of animals increases. Agroforestry contributes to agroecology and provides space for leisure under the trees and at field borders (V. Ferrario)

Mapping for the new agro-urban park in Padova

A new trend can be observed in the last few years: several cultivated areas are changing from conventional feed-oriented crops to food production, direct transformation and direct sale. The southwestern sector of the city is particularly interested in this new trend, in an area that is continuously cultivated despite it being enveloped into the urban fabric and situated at less than 500 metres from the ancient city walls (fig. 7). In 2010, the municipality bought 12 hectares of farming land to create a new urban park. Some years later, a new organic farm was established nearby, producing and selling fresh vegetables, followed by another organic farm, producing wheat. A group of citizens gathered around the two new farms, asking the municipality to stop urban development and create not an urban park but an agricultural park to develop sustainable agriculture at the city's service.

Figure 8 shows this trend from 2015 to 2020 and provides a land-use scenario for the new agro-urban park, where direct food production is preferred, according to the idea expressed by the citizens (Feagan, 2007). The main principles are new areas for growing fresh vegetables, a new supply chain wheat-flour-bread with the establishment of a new collective oven and a new community mill, financed by the municipality. Also, a community farm, offering services to the citizens and the local farms and silvoarable agroforestry as an answer to climate change and the need for leisure space and ecosystem services.

Mapping agricultural transition

Visualising the amazing agro-urban interwoven in the Venice region is full of potential to increase the awareness of citizens and policymakers. Despite the new databases provided in the last few years by some institutions (such as AVEPA), mapping farming land and its use is still difficult, mainly due to the lack of public data about the food supply chain. Methodologically speaking, it is crucial to observe and document these trends at different scales.

Mapping farming land in the Veneto region highlights an extraordinary self-sufficiency potential due to the great amount of agricultural land and its proximity to urbanised land. At the same time, it also shows a paradoxical situation, in which a great part of the farming land is used to produce feed, alimenting the long chain of meat, produced primarily for export. However, the agricultural transition of the next few years will probably change this situation. European agricultural policies are changing their objectives of sustainability, and this will lead to profound transformations in farming land and agricultural landscapes: support for the reconstruction of agro-ecosystem networks, organic farming and quality certification are strong drivers who also rely on food spaces. Representing these changes is fundamental to predict the transformations and imagine scenarios for a right and sustainable future, enhancing the local food potential.

The Padua case study highlights the fact that good practices exist and must be documented. Citizens ask for healthy, fresh, local food and for proximity to green spaces: these two needs can be met within an alliance with farmers, who in turn need citizens for their business. The success of these experiences suggests that a new sustainable agriculture in closer proximity to citizenship is possible. Apparently "empty" spaces within the city have a great potential for urban farming, both for professionals and self-production. As shown in the case of the bottom-up proposal of the agro-urban park of Basso Isonzo in Padua, there is a need for tools able to manage the tensions between farming and urban areas, thus offering new insights for spatial planning and geography.

Note

Authors discussed the topic together. Viviana Ferrario wrote the introduction and the paragraphs 1, 2, part of 4, 5, 6. Fabrizio D'Angelo wrote paragraph 3 and part of 4.

References

Abramson, D.B., 2020. Ancient and current resilience in the Chengdu plain: Agropolitan development re-'revisited'. *Urban Studies*, 57 (7), 1372–1397. https://doi.org/10.1177/0042098019843020

Ávila Sánchez, H., 2018. Agricultura urbana y periurbana. Reconfiguraciones territoriales y potencialidades en torno a los sistemas alimentarios urbanos. *Investigaciones Geográficas*, 98. https://doi.org/10.14350/rig.59785.

Azunre, G.A., Amponsah, O., Peprah, C., Takyi, S.A., and Braimah, I., 2019. A review of the role of urban agriculture in the sustainable city discourse. *Cities*, 93, 104–119. https://doi.org/10.1016/j.cities.2019.04.006

Brandt, J., and Vejre, H., 2004. Multifunctional landscapes. Motives, concepts and perceptions. *In*: J. Brandt and H. Vejre, eds. *Multifunctional landscapes, I, Theory, values and history*. Southampton: WitPress.

Cartiaux, N., Mazzocchi, G., Marino, D., and Jijakli, H., 2018. Improving urban metabolism through agriculture: An approach to ecosystem services qualitative assessment in Rome. *Vertigo*, 31. https://doi.org/10.4000/vertigo.21655De Marchi, M., 2020. Lo spazio del cibo nella città diffusa. Il sistema agroalimentare del Veneto tra urbano e rurale. *In*: K.Z. De Marchi, eds. *Territori post rurali. Genealogie e prospettive*. Roma: Officina.

Dewaelheyns, V., and Gulinck, H., 2008. Rurality near the city. *In*: *Proceedings of the international seminar*. Leuven: Department of Earth and Environmental Sciences.

Díaz-Pacheco, J., and Gutiérrez, J., 2013. Exploring the limitations of CORINE land cover for monitoring urban land-use dynamics in metropolitan areas. *Journal of Land Use Science*, 9 (3), 243–259.

Feagan, R., 2007. The place of food: Mapping out the 'local' in local food systems. *Progress in Human Geography*, 31 (1), 23–42. https://doi.org/10.1177/0309132507073527

Ferrario, V., 2010. About agricultural space in the città diffusa and its importance for the future. *In*: P. Viganò and L. Fabian, eds. *Extreme city. Climate change and the transformation of the waterscape*. Padova: Il Poligrafo.

Ferrario, V., 2016. Contemporary city and food areas. The basso isonzo in padua: Campagne urbaine or urban farming? [Città contemporanea e spazi del cibo. Il Basso Isonzo a Padova: campagne urbaine o urban farming?] *Territorio*, 79, 74–78. https://doi.org/10.3280/TR2016–079013.

Ferrario, V., Geronta, C., and D'Angelo, F., 2018. La costruzione di un quadro conoscitivo per l'implementazione del PaAM, Parco agropaesaggistico metropolitano di Padova. L'esperienza del progetto Urban Green Belts. *In*: M.C. Tosi, a cura. *Veneto. Temi di ricerca e azione*. Milano: Mimesis, 116–137.

Friedmann, J., 1979. Basic needs, agropolitan development, and planning from below. *World Development*, 7 (6), 607–613.

Geronta, C., and Ferrario, V., 2018. Creation of a preliminary database for monitoring and evaluating the transformations of the peri-urban landscape of Padua (Italy). *GI_Forum*, 6 (1), 117–125. https://doi.org/10.1553/giscience2018_01_s117

Ghosh, S., 2021. Urban agriculture potential of home gardens in residential land uses: A case study of regional City of Dubbo, Australia. *Land Use Policies*, 109, https://doi.org/10.1016/j.landusepol.2021.105686

Morgan, K., 2015. Nourishing the city: The rise of the urban food question in the Global North. *Urban Studies*, 52 (8).

Ollison, A., Kerselaers, E., Søderkvist Kristensen, L., Primdahl, J., Rogge, E., and Wästfelt, A., 2016. Peri-urban food production and its relation to urban resilience. *Sustainability*, 8 (12).

Pérez Campaña, R., and Valenzuela Montes, L.M., 2014. Agro-urban open space as a component of agricultural multifunctionality. *Journal of Land Use Science*, 9 (1), 82–104. https://doi.org/10.1080/1747423X.2012.751561

Poli, D., 2017. Food revolution and agro-urban public space in the European bioregional city. *Agroecology and Sustainable Food Systems*, 41 (8), 965–987. https://doi.org/10.1080/21683565.2017.1331178

Sweeney, G., Hand, M., Kaiser, M., Clark, J.K., Rogers, C., and Spees, C., 2016. The state of food mapping: Academic literature since 2008 and review of online GIS-based food mapping resources. *Journal of Planning Literature*, 31 (2), 123–219.

Torre, A., 2013. Introduction. In *Natures urbaines: l'agriculture au coeur des Métropoles?* París: Demeter.

Urban Agriculture, 2009. Building resilient cities. *UA Magazine*, 22.

Viljoen, A., Bohn, K., and Howe, J., 2005. *Continuous productive urban landscapes: Designing urban agriculture for sustainable cities*. London: Elsevier.

Xia, H., Ge, S., Zhang, X., Kim, G., Lei, Y., and Liu, Y., 2021. Spatiotemporal dynamics of green infrastructure in an agricultural peri-urban area: A case study of Baisha district in Zhengzhou, China. *Land*, 10, 801.

Yokohari, M., Takeuchi, K., Watanabe, T., and Yokota, S., 2008. Beyond greenbelts and zoning: A new planning concept for the environment of Asian mega-cities. *Urban Ecology: An International Perspective on the Interaction between Humans and Nature*, 783–796. https://doi.org/10.1007/978-0-387-73412-5_50.

FOOD SYSTEM ACTIVITIES: Recording economies, patterns and crises

This section includes **maps and mappings that make evident our actions on and with food** thereby providing a permanent record of these transient activities. Food – where it comes from; how it is produced, transported, traded, prepared, consumed and its waste recycled; and what this signifies to individuals, social groups, societies and the environment – provides an essential focus from which to understand themes that include identity, the senses, economy and place-making.

Often, it is **the altering of everyday food environments** that **makes visible their underlying structures and constraints**. The Covid-19 pandemic, for example, affected us all, probably most through changes that happened at the individual scale. At the other end of that scale, there is the global food landscape, equally hard to detect, which explores how food travels from field to fork almost invisibly. Urban food maps can capture such patterns using a wide range of mappings methods, from quantifiable to qualitative, including drawing, redrawing, photographing, counting, calculating, journaling, walking and eating.

DOI: 10.4324/9781003352280-8

Amélie André uses mapping across a diverse range of practices, including drawing, redrawing, photographing and labelling, to **explore twentieth-century Letchworth Garden City, UK, as a model to support a local sustainable food economy**. Food mapping as a groundwork method, combined with an ethnographical approach, emphasises the importance of characterising food spaces, key local stakeholders and activities to envision the integration of more reliable and resilient urban food systems.

Howard Lee and Will Hughes argue that pressures to feed people will lead inevitably towards recognising the importance of productive urban space. Employing digital mapping techniques and quantitative methods, they propose Integrated Development Areas to **examine (map) the value certain social groups place on heterogenous micro-urban spaces**, such as entrepreneurial market gardens and community gardens, that will necessarily become part of future urban agriculture activities.

Patrick S. Ford and Nina Yiu Lai Lei encourage us to dive deep into urban food landscapes through consumption practices. Setting out on foot each day during the same week, Monday to Friday, the authors **discover the spatial occurrence and social popularity of different types of local cuisine**. Through these informal food walks, they develop abstract and alternative maps to complement food narratives highlighting the multi-cultural nature of residing in an edible urban framework.

Natacha Quintero González and Anke Hagemann widen the geography of food supply activities by mapping the global journeys of food, from fields to plates. By working across scales and line drawing techniques, they focus on socio-political issues through food mapping. **A clearer understanding emerges of current consumption patterns** implying opportunities for better use of hitherto inconspicuous or unknown food sites.

Gesine Tuitjer et al. explore the disruption of urban food retail by the Covid-19 pandemic. Their photographic, drawn and verbal recordings **map the effects that public health strategies had on the spatial designs and usage of food consumption sites** in Hannover, Germany. This practice of collecting, sharing and discussing images in pandemic times, they argue, helped them to reconnect with the estranged urban terrain.

Food system activities

	Purpose WHY?	Citizen WHO?
	recording *counting* *comparing* *uncovering* *responding* *proposing*	*urban farmers* *food system activists* *food initiatives* *consumers* *local communities* *public institutions*

André
Using visual methods
to map
green infrastructure
for a sustainable
food economy in
Letchworth Garden City

counting food spaces
recording land use

local communities
food system activists

Lee et al.
A participatory digital
mapping practice:
Proposing Integrated
Development Areas
for food secure
systems in cities

comparing food production
proposing change

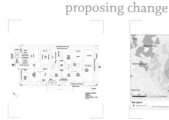
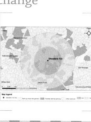

urban farmers / local communit

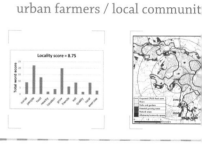

Ford et al.
Walking out for dinner:
Discovering and
mapping food choices
in Saigon

uncovering stakeholders
recording food consumption

food initiatives / consumers

**Quintero González
et al.**
Follow the food...
and the spaces it shapes

recording food system activities
uncovering produce

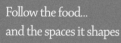

food system stakeholders
public institutions

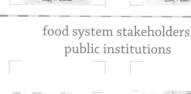

Tuitjer et al.
Rupturing the mundane
in times of crisis:
New geographies of food
in Hannover, Germany

responding to food crises
recording change

food initiatives / consumers

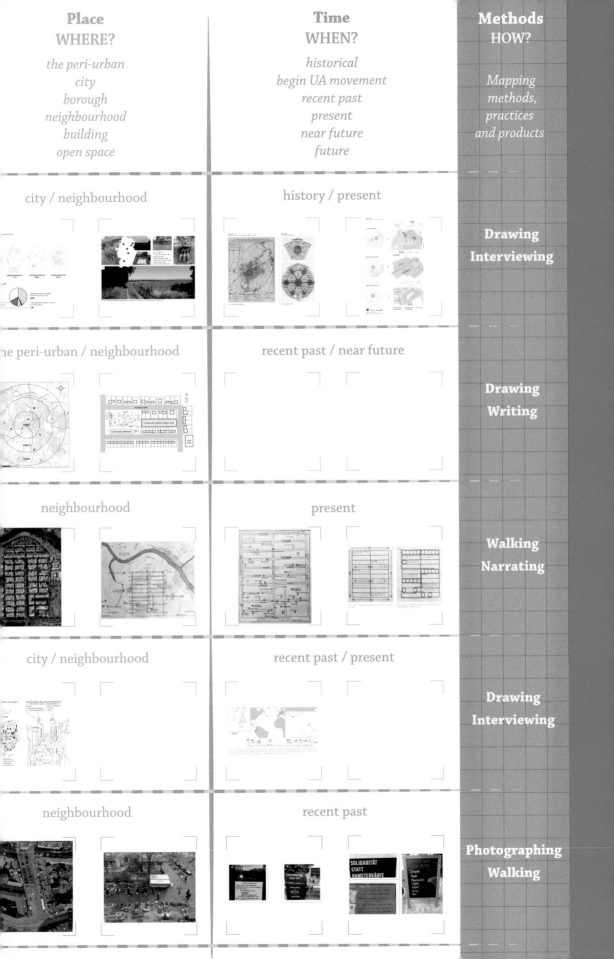

Using visual methods to map green infrastructure for a sustainable food economy in Letchworth Garden City

Amélie André

Today, relationships between food systems and cities are of growing interest to practitioners, policymakers, and academics from different backgrounds, whether in urban planning (Duany and Duany Plater-Zyberk, 2011; Morgan, 2009), food policies (Lang *et al.*, 2009), urban food movements (Cockrall-King, 2012) urban design (Parham, 2015a), edible landscapes (Parham, 2015b; Viljoen *et al.*, 2005) or planning history (Imbert, 2017; Steel, 2008; Vitiello and Brinkley, 2014). While the garden city is a landmark in the urban planning development, the food integrated into its three core features (physical, social, and politico-economic) has not been fully explored. Hence, as compelling works have suggested (Pothukuchi and Kaufman, 2000; Viljoen and Wiskerke, 2012; Wiskerke and Verhoeven, 2018), the garden city principles demonstrate relevant interplays between food and the fields of urban planning, design and policies. This chapter gives a glimpse of a research project that investigated how the garden city principles, as a spatial and political blueprint, could provide alternative models for a healthy and sustainable food economy accessible to the local community (Andre, 2020). Reporting on the mapping-based methodology that explored the overall food set-up of Letchworth Garden City, the focus of this chapter are the green infrastructure and edible landscape opportunities in the town.

Theoretician of the garden city movement, Sir Ebenezer Howard shared in his books (Howard, 1898) a vision for new cities of 32,000 inhabitants where land use and food were intended as strategic economic resources: available for the local community yet open to competition and world-wide food trade (Howard, 1898, p. 24, p. 75). In 1903, architects Barry Parker and Raymond Unwin proposed the physical translation of the world's first garden city with the masterplan of Letchworth (see fig. 1), to this day the closest version of Howard's idea of layout and administrative organisation. The nineteenth-century garden city model influenced urban planning theory and practice through its fascinating graphic sets (see fig. 2), with which Howard communicated and convinced a spectrum of enthusiastic investors regardless of their political streams (Buder, 1990). Driven by this illustrative tradition, the research project applied food mapping and visual methods to examine the garden city theory and layout that include a holistic approach to food in cities.

Mapping food in a garden city

The research project's methodology combined techniques from different fields, including geography, urban design, and ethnography. The first step was to map out every food-related location in Letchworth with geographic information system (GIS) software. The GIS dataset provided then details that in a second stage enabled close-ups of different areas of the town to examine different urban morphologies (Kropf, 2017) and the relationships between green infrastructure and the built environment. Throughout the research process, archives and documents from the early Letchworth helped understand the town's layout evolution.

DOI: 10.4324/9781003352280-9

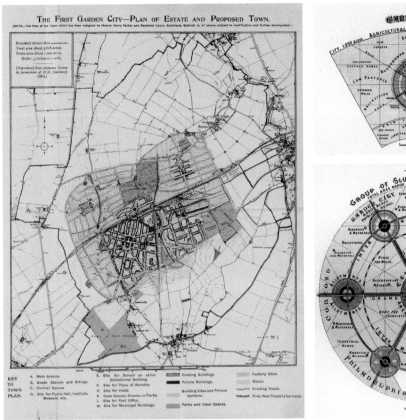

Fig. 1: Letchworth Development Plan, circa 1908 by Parker and Unwin (© Garden City Collection, Letchworth Garden City Heritage Foundation)

Fig. 2: The Garden City diagrams (Howard, 1898)

The desk-based food mapping was cross-examined on site. A part of the data collection entailed documenting bike rides and recording each exploration retrospectively on a map. This process was inspired by the Situationists' *Derive*, a form of urban exploration questioning the psychogeographical effects of a specific environment (Debord, 1958). Another aspect of the field trips involved an ethnographic approach with observation and participation in the town's food life. From 2018 to early 2020, volunteering regularly in local groups for food waste rescue and community food gardens created connections with key stakeholders. Specific observation sessions included joining public discussions that local groups or institutions organised, taking part in the daily life of the town throughout the week and attending food-related events (food festival, farmers' markets).

Inspired by how Shove *et al.* (2012) defined product or service as effective once embedded in daily life (Dagevos and Veen, 2020, p. 101), healthy and sustainable food practices in this study encompassed notions such as closeness, convenience, knowledge and affordability. In this view, interacting with local stakeholders unravelled distinct food 'realities' that food mapping snapshots did not capture (Duncan, 2006): an additional dataset consisted of hearing their voices to understand how food was embedded in daily routines (Castelo *et al.*, 2021).

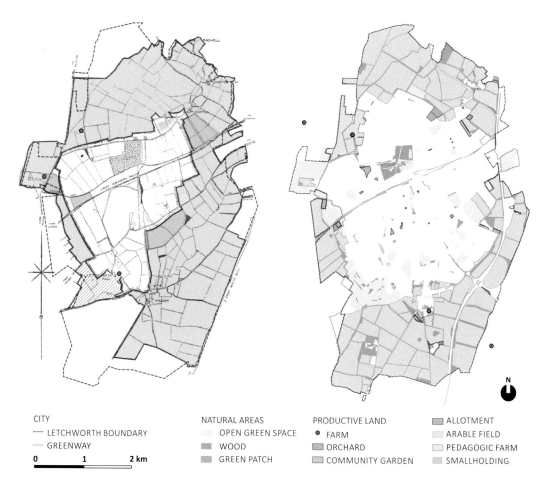

CITY
--- LETCHWORTH BOUNDARY
---- GREENWAY

0   1   2 km

NATURAL AREAS
OPEN GREEN SPACE
WOOD
GREEN PATCH

PRODUCTIVE LAND
• FARM
ORCHARD
COMMUNITY GARDEN

ALLOTMENT
ARABLE FIELD
PEDAGOGIC FARM
SMALLHOLDING

N

Fig. 3: Rural and town estates, 1917 and 2020

Out of 51 participants, six were experts in their fields (food strategy, urban planning, garden city), 16 were representatives of local authorities, six were home-grown food initiative champions, five were working in the private sector, and three were involved in farming activities. In addition, 15 residents responded to the call for participation in the study. Non-residents were chosen for their field of expertise and invited via their public contact details. No specific criteria were required for the residents, recruited through online advertisement and word of mouth, but their interest in the study may suggest a form of awareness regarding food and the environment. Albeit specific to

each category in terms of focus and jargon, the different question sets covered the common topics of food access in town, perception of what a garden city is, the governance model in place and partnership, and their expectations in terms of food.

Inputs from residents were crucial to express how food spaces and green infrastructure played out in their daily life. During semi-structured interviews (SSIs), participants could elaborate on their food environment by reflecting on their food practices. Some of them also commented on pictures they shared beforehand (Harper, 2002; Lapenta, 2011).

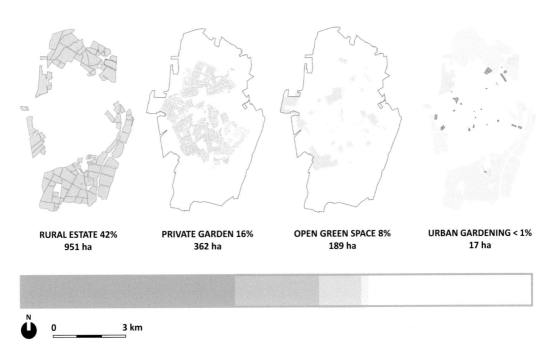

RURAL ESTATE 42%   PRIVATE GARDEN 16%   OPEN GREEN SPACE 8%   URBAN GARDENING < 1%
951 ha   362 ha   189 ha   17 ha

N
0   3 km

Fig. 4: Main green infrastructure proportion in Letchworth Garden City, 2020

Once most SSIs were conducted, a group discussion with four residents outlined the different outlooks on the local food economy, personal definition of healthy and sustainable food, and perceptions of the town for food experience. The group was invited to discuss photographs from the *Garden City Collection* (GCC, 2022) representing food-related activities in early-day Letchworth. These photographs opened a debate about the imaginary of the garden city model these archives conveyed compared to participants' food experience in Letchworth today (Margolis and Pauwels, 2011).

Food mapping of a theorised layout

The work strategically started with a GIS mapping project. This stage had two objectives: firstly, establishing a comprehensive list of food-related spaces and venues in Letchworth's area to identify a physical food setting and secondly, comparing the graphic outcomes with the garden city's illustrations and early

masterplan. The first noticeable element visible in the food mapping is the partition of the garden city that respects Howard's text and diagrams: the rural and the town estates (see fig. 3). Not intended as a food self-sufficient city per say (Howard, 1898, p. 75), the garden city was however a productive town that offered economic opportunities to its residents (p. 17) with various shapes and forms of available land (Adams, 1905), including large fields, fruit farms, smallholdings and allotments. Today, smallholdings have disappeared, merged into the fringe of the arable land and town estate, or transformed in smaller allotment sites, but the rural estate corresponds to around 42% of the total area of the city and is still dedicated to food production for 90% of it, while the remaining 10% belongs to a pedagogic farm (see fig. 4).

Letchworth's original masterplan resulted in a sound green infrastructure (Freestone, 2002). The size and shape of each green space type could be appropriate for different food-related activities: open green spaces (public wide green space), 'semi-common' (green areas in the public realm yet close to housing), nature strips (continuous patches of green buffering pedestrian and car-related infrastructure, term borrowed from Couchman, 2005), wooden patches, productive land (including allotments, orchards, large arable fields), shared common (green patches hidden behind several houses) and private gardens. A photographic survey in southeast neighbourhood displaying an iconic 'Radburn layout' (Schaffer, 1982) showed a prevalence of 'semi-common' resulting from its layout, seemingly serving an unspecified purpose (see fig. 5).

The inventory of these green areas as actual or potential edible landscape suggested many variations of the natural network within the built environment and showed the different infrastructure opportunities for food as described in Howard's book (1898, p. 18, p. 24). To this end, food mapping provided a dataset for three-dimensional models that characterised the prevalence of each green typology in three neighbourhoods' layouts (see fig. 6). Each model indicated that urban morphology influences the green infrastructure, while fieldwork informed on the land use status for a potential food retrofit.

Food mapping linked with socio-spatial practices

The cartographic outcomes suggested how the garden city model, embodied in Letchworth's layout, offered a remarkable physical backbone for food and edible landscape. These preliminary morphological outputs required nevertheless cross-examinations with local stakeholders to understand the decision-making process and food practices in town. For some residents, the town's genesis carries a sense of place, creating a social backdrop for a local, alternative, and sustainable food economy. When reflecting

on pictures of the early Letchworth during the group discussion (see fig. 7), participants acknowledged the town's legacy for productive spaces but challenged the direct benefits of the local food production for the community. Similarly, during interviews, green spaces were not always associated with food but systematically recognised as a well-being feature for Letchworth (see fig. 9). Nonetheless, on-site investigations and some pictures shared by the residents reflected the diversity of the food experiences (see fig. 8) and the use of green spaces in their daily food procurement.

The garden city model embraced a distinctive and independent administrative framework, holding a strategic power over the land that could initiate a local food strategy while regulating land cover and land use for an edible green infrastructure using land stewardship (Howard, 1898). Today, a charitable institution, the Letchworth Garden City Heritage Foundation, owns and manages land and properties across Letchworth Garden City and reinvests assets to create wealth for municipal purposes on behalf of the residents (LGCHF, 2022). While both, representatives of the local institution and residents described Letchworth's rural estate as a 'missed opportunity' for the local food economy, interviews with farmers mentioned the general disconnection between food policies and local authorities, usually not involved in these matters (see fig. 9). This suggested that the decision-making structure could represent an additional lever to underpin sustainable food practices and bolster food in green areas for the benefit of the community.

Exploring food realities, the role of urban food mapping and visual methods

A fine-grained exploration of Letchworth's green infrastructure using different visual methods revealed the legacy of the garden city spatial theory. As the early advocates of the movement described over a century ago,

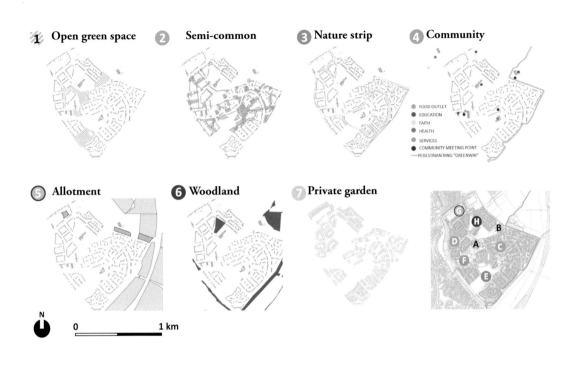

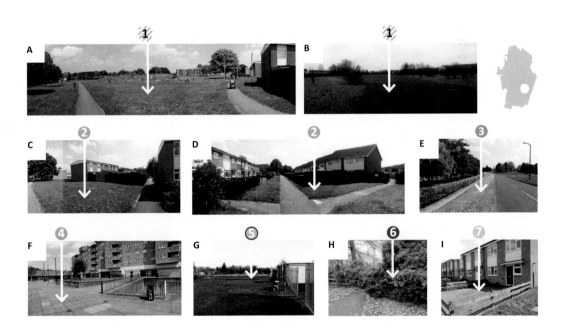

Fig. 5: Green typologies in the southeast neighbourhood and photographic survey

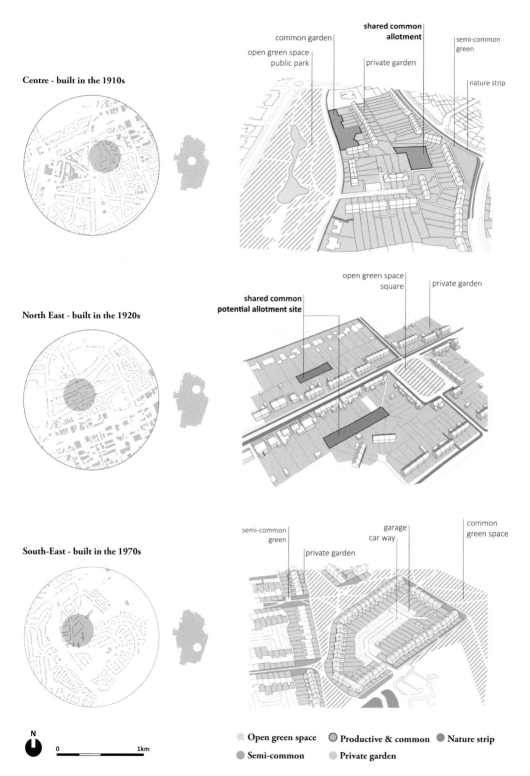

Centre - built in the 1910s

common garden

shared common
allotment

semi-common
green

open green space
public park

private garden

nature strip

North East - built in the 1920s

open green space
square

private garden

shared common
potential allotment site

South-East - built in the 1970s

semi-common
green

garage
car way

common
green space

private garden

N

0   1km

▨ **Open green space**   ◯ **Productive & common**   ● **Nature strip**

● **Semi-common**   ● **Private garden**

Fig. 6: Close-ups on three neighbourhoods of Letchworth

Gentleman digging his garden, Birds Hill - date unknown

Haven Social Club picking apples - circa 1940

Farm land of vegetables - circa 1940s or 1950s

Co-operative Society Ltd. Fish Department- date unknown

Fig. 7: Some of the archives discussed during the group discussion (© Garden City Collection, Letchworth Garden City Heritage Foundation)

today green areas represent a large proportion of Letchworth Garden City with various sizes and characteristics suitable to different appropriations for food. In addition, an independent local administration, establishing long-term strategic plans and place-based decisions in partnership with local stakeholders, could address possible gaps left by centralised food policies (Lang *et al*., 2009, p. 82). Of course, the garden city principles implemented in Letchworth today could not address all the issues related to today's agri-food systems, but the use of visual methods in this research suggested valuable insights for place-making and edible landscape retrofitting.

Food mapping underpinned by visual methods in this research provides a food-location overview as a support for connecting the town layout, socio-spatial experiences, and garden city guidelines. The techniques to rediscover these food principles can contribute to resilient urban-rural interplays, offsetting the apparent separation of the productive rural land on one hand, and the consuming urban realm, on the other. Learning from the garden city model, the study's outcomes add to the urban food research field, looking at place-based approaches to food systems, and Letchworth gives us food for thought about the holistic approach of multi-functional green infrastructures and nature-based solutions to create resilient edible cities.

1
3
5
6
2

1: Greta's allotment
2: Letchworth rural estate: cattle grazing in the shade
3: Adrian: blackberry bushes
4: Adrian: community garden
5: Grace's front garden
6: Judith's apple tree and jui

Fig. 8: Food in green areas, including material sent by residents (collected by the author 2020-21) - names are pseudonyms

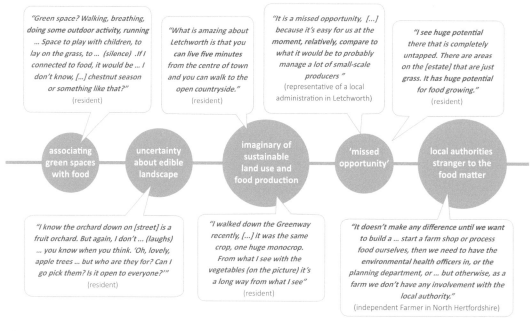

"Green space? Walking, breathing, doing some outdoor activity, running ... Space to play with children, to lay on the grass, to ... (silence) .If I connected to food, it would be ... I don't know, [...] chestnut season or something like that?"
(resident)

"What is amazing about Letchworth is that you can live five minutes from the centre of town and you can walk to the open countryside."
(resident)

"It is a missed opportunity, [...] because it's easy for us at the moment, relatively, compare to what it would be to probably manage a lot of small-scale producers"
(representative of a local administration in Letchworth)

"I see huge potential there that is completely untapped. There are areas on the [estate] that are just grass. It has huge potential for food growing."
(resident)

associating green spaces with food

uncertainty about edible landscape

imaginary of sustainable land use and food production

'missed opportunity'

local authorities stranger to the food matter

"I know the orchard down on [street] is a fruit orchard. But again, I don't ... (laughs) ... you know when you think. 'Oh, lovely, apple trees ... but who are they for? Can I go pick them? Is it open to everyone?'"
(resident)

"I walked down the Greenway recently, [...] it was the same crop, one huge monocrop. From what I see with the vegetables (on the picture) it's a long way from what I see"
(resident)

"It doesn't make any difference until we want to build a ... start a farm shop or process food ourselves, then we need to have the environmental health officers in, or the planning department, or ... but otherwise, as a farm we don't have any involvement with the local authority."
(independent Farmer in North Hertfordshire)

Fig. 9: Food and green areas: Participants' interview extracts (conducted by the author, 2020-21)

References

Adams, T., 1905. *Garden city and agriculture, how to solve the problem of rural depopulation*. London: Unknown Binding.

Andre, A., 2020. *Food economy and Garden City legacy: Letchworth Garden City in our present day – Part 2, International Garden City Institute*. Available from www.gardencitiesinstitute.com/think-piece/food-economy-and-garden-city-legacy-letchworth-garden-city-in-our-present-day-0 [Accessed 25 Jan 2021].

Buder, S., 1990. *Visionaries and planners, The Garden City movement and the modern community*. New York: Oxford University Press.

Castelo, A.F.M., Schäfer, M., and Silva, M.E., 2021. Food practices as part of daily routines: A conceptual framework for analysing networks of practices. *Appetite*, 157, 1–10.

Cockrall-King, J., 2012. *Food and the city, urban agriculture and the new food revolution*. New York: Prometheus Books.

Couchman, S., 2005. Nature strips: A forgotten feature of urban history. *The Garden History Society*, 33 (1), 127–134.

Dagevos, M.J., and Veen, E.J., 2020. Sharing a meal: A diversity of performances engendered by a social innovation. *Journal of Urbanism*, 13 (1), 97–113.

Debord, G., 1958. Theory of the derive. *International Situationniste #2*. Available from www.cddc.vt.edu/sionline/si/theory.html.

Duany, A., and Plater-Zyberk, D., 2011. *Garden-cities: Theory and practice of agricultural urbanism*. London: The Prince's Foundation for the Built Environment.

Duncan, S., 2006. Mapping whose reality? Geographic information systems (GIS) and "wild science". *Public Understanding of Science*, 15 (4), 411–434.

Freestone, R., 2002. Greenbelts in city and regional planning. *In*: K.C. Parsons and D. Schuyler, eds. *From Garden City to Green City*. Baltimore: The Johns Hopkins University Press, 67–98.

GCC, 2022. *Home page, Garden City Collection website*. Available from http://www.gardencitycollection.com/themes [Accessed 23 Jul 2022].

Harper, D., 2002. Talking about pictures: A case for photo elicitation. *Visual Studies*, 17 (1), 13–27.

Howard, E., 1898. *To-morrow: A peaceful path to the real reform*. London: Swan Sonnenschein & Co Ltd.

Kropf, K., 2017. *The handbook of urban morphology: Aspects of urban form*. Chichester: John Wiley & Sons.

Lang, T., Barling, D., and Caraher, M., 2009. *Food policy: Integrating health, environment and society*. Oxford: Oxford University Press.

Lapenta, F., 2011. Some theoretical and methodological views on photo-elicitation. *In*: E.M. Margolis and L. Pauwels, eds. *The SAGE handbook of visual research methods*. SAGE Publications, 201–213. Available from https://ebookcentral.proquest.com/lib/herts/reader.action?docID=786862.

LGCHF, 2022. *How we are funded, Letchworth Garden City Heritage Foundation website*. Available from https://www.letchworth.com/what-we-do/how-were-funded [Accessed: 22 Jun 2022].

Lim, C., 2014. *Food city*. 1st ed. New York: Routledge.

Margolis, E.M., and Pauwels, L., 2011. *The SAGE handbook of visual research methods*. SAGE Publications. Available from https://ebookcentral.proquest.com/lib/herts/detail.action?docID=786862.

Morgan, K., 2009. Feeding the city: The challenge of urban food planning. *International Planning Studies*, 14 (4), 341–348.

Parham, S., 2015a. *Food and urbanism: The convivial city and a sustainable future*. London: Bloomsbury Publishing.

Parham, S., 2015b. The productive periphery: Foodspace and urbanism on the edge. *In: Localizing urban food strategies. Farming cities and performing rurality. 7th International Aesop sustainable food planning conference proceedings*.

Pothukuchi, K., and Kaufman, J.L., 2000. The food system: A stranger to the planning field. *Journal of the American Planning Association*, 66 (2), 113–124.

Schaffer, D., 1982. *Garden cities for America: The Radburn experience*. Philadelphia: Temple University Press.

Shove, E., Pantzar, M. and Watson, M., 2012. *The dynamics of social practice: Everyday life and how it changes*. Los Angeles: SAGE Publications.

Steel, C., 2008. *Hungry City: How food shapes our lives*. London: Vintage.

Viljoen, A., Bohn, K., and Howe, J., 2005. *Continuous productive urban landscapes: Designing urban agriculture for sustainable cities*. Edited by A. Viljoen, K. Bohn and J. Howe. Oxford: Elsevier.

Viljoen, A., and Wiskerke, J.S.C., 2012. *Sustainable food planning: Evolving theory and practice*. Edited by A. Viljoen and J.S.C. Wiskerke. Wageningen: Wageningen Academic.

Vitiello, D., and Brinkley, C., 2014. The hidden history of food system planning. *Journal of Planning History*, 13 (2), 91–112.

Wiskerke, J.S.C., and Verhoeven, S., 2018. *Flourishing foodscapes, Designing city-region food systems*. Edited by J.S.C. Wirskerke and S. Verhoeven. Amsterdam: Valiz & the Academy of Architecture Amsterdam.

A participatory digital mapping practice: Proposing Integrated Development Areas for food secure systems in cities

Howard Lee and Will Hughes

Growing urban food has been reviewed by Martellozzo *et al.* (2014) with a focus on food security, who has suggested that, spatially, urban agriculture would require a commitment of roughly one-third of urban land to meet the vegetable demands of urban dwellers. Tacoli (2017) also considers urbanisation and poverty, linking it to living space and access to food. This spatial focus has its earliest review in Bohn and Viljoen (2005) who estimated that about a third of the fruit and vegetable needs of a (European) city could be met from within, but also Müller *et al.* (2020) who modelled food security across global to household scales and Vonthron *et al.* (2020) for spatial approaches to 'urban foodscapes' (food within landscapes). Some towns and cities have been specifically studied in terms of spatial food distribution. For good examples, see London in Ontario, Canada (Larsen and Gilliland, 2008); Melbourne, Australia (Lyons *et al.*, 2013), and Haifa, Israel (Toger *et al.*, 2016).

Urban food space

The authors of this chapter have a background in agronomy and geography. Our working hypothesis is that a mapping focus is vital for urban food production in the context of local food security, i.e. that the sustainable management of food growing in towns and cities can only be achieved through a mapping lens. Three mapping projects for growing food are presented to explore this hypothesis: a community allotment in Hadlow, Kent, UK; a student teaching exercise focussed

on a mapped urban foodshed (as defined by Zasada *et al.*, 2019) for Shooters Hill, London; and a project to map a potential CPULs (first defined by Viljoen *et al.*, 2005) food zone across Maidstone, Kent, UK. These mapping examples are then developed towards the concept of a new proposed term: *Integrated Development Areas (IDAs)*. An IDA is thought as a mapped, urban agroecological management zone in which up to 500 neighbouring citizens can work together as a community and *via* entrepreneurism, to maximise local food security.

Mapping example 1: Digital mapping for a community food allotment, Hadlow, Kent, UK

In 2006, one of the authors (Lee) started a twelve-year collaboration with a low-carbon community group from Hadlow village, who were invited to develop an allotment on Hadlow College land. The original site of 50m × 25m was allocated by the author for this essay. Figure 1 shows a plan of the site as of 2009. This working map was facilitated by members of the group utilising skills in gardening, graphic design and IT. The group then started in the west of the site (on the left of the map), installing a shed and developing the vegetable beds over the next three years. The mapping process was thus a vital precursor to the project and a result of full participation within the group. Using the map, the group decided what and where to grow fruit and vegetable species, and their mapping and growing expertise were

DOI: 10.4324/9781003352280-10

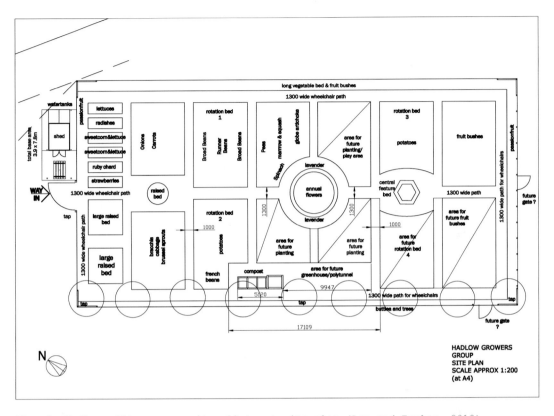

Fig. 1: Hadlow village community allotment site plan (Lee and Taylor, 2010)

impressive. Although college horticulture staff and students were 'offered' in support, the village community allotment group were almost entirely independent.

The use of digital mapping technologies by communities is discussed in a relatively old report by Craig and Elwood: "*Strong neighbourhoods make healthy cities. . . . People who have access to GIS have come to feel they might have a resource that could help neighbourhoods by providing maps and geographic information*" (Craig and Elwood, 1998. p. 1). In this example, training of community members in the use of GIS is recommended: "*Seeing the potential of these grassroots community groups to use GIS also may prompt . . . education to these groups about the full and appropriate uses of geographic information and analysis*" (Craig and Elwood, 1998, p. 14).

Mapping example 2: Urban foodshed exercise at Shooters Hill, London

As part of curriculum delivery to BSc Hons Agriculture students at Hadlow College, an exercise was undertaken to define the urban foodshed for a 1-km-diameter zone around Shooters Hill in London. Students were tasked with using *ArcGIS* to map this zone in terms of land potentially available for growing food, possible yields of vegetables and fruit crops and how many citizens this could support (the estimated foodshed). One mapping example is shown in figure 2. Mapping is the key focus in this chapter, so detailed metrics are not shown, but it was determined that land available for growing food within the 1-km-diameter zone could potentially feed most or all of the fruit and vegetable needs of the 13,433 citizens living in that area. Of course, a clear answer depends upon the growing systems used, the crops grown, access to nutrients, pest-, weed- and disease management and post-harvest storage and processing (for a review see Lee (2012)).

Mapping example 3: A food security assessment of Maidstone, Kent, UK

A case study for Maidstone, Kent, was under-taken remotely. A series of *ArcGIS* maps was developed to clarify land suitable for community food production. The GIS software package *ArcMap* (10.6.1) was used with *OS Mastermap* data downloaded to extract pre-digitised layers for green spaces, allotment sites and community growing areas.

Figure 3 shows the existing food growing sites (all are allotments) in Maidstone. These are relatively small, and the intention still is to explore the potential of suitable additional land for growing food. The urban settings of sites were then studied in relationship to Zones 1, 2 and 3, as described by *Growing Communities* (Growing Communities, 2021).

Local communities in Maidstone were to be consulted next, but this was delayed due to the Covid-19 pandemic. Instead, the process was undertaken remotely as a preliminary measure (see fig. 4). Here, additional layers were added for parks, gardens and natural areas. Then, potential food production zones were drawn as 'Continuous Productive Urban Landscapes' (Viljoen and Bohn, 2014). They represent the areas across Maidstone where a greater focus on additional community food growing would be recommended, based on proximity to existing allotments, available open spaces and potential access by citizens. *CPUL* areas are also intended to create continuous corridors for movement of wildlife and so aid biodiversity.

As of mid-2021, Maidstone's population was 176,700 citizens (Kent Analytics, 2023), and we wanted to establish if the mapped *CPUL* area was sufficient to provide fruit and vegetables

for all these people. Such calculations will again not be elaborated here but have been considered in the literature (Fairlie, 2007) and by one author of this chapter (Lee, 2012). Potential yields are affected by interacting factors: the blend of open site *versus* protected (polythene or equivalent and glass) production, species grown, management expertise and weather variability. Early metrics suggest that at least half of the citizens of Maidstone could be provided with sufficient fruit and vegetables from the *CPUL* zone in figure 4. Most importantly of all, it is posited that effective mapping of edible zones as clarified by Tomkins (2012) will be key in the development of optimal urban food production efficiency, and this is likely to be based on community cooperation for use of smaller sites (approximately < 0.1 ha) and entrepreneurial development of larger areas (Lee, 2017).

Urban space attachment and the IDA

Tobler (2004) has stated that the science of geography involves the relation between events and spaces of social interaction. More specifically, urban studies of space have focussed on food production (Lyons *et al.*, 2013), connectivity (Toger *et al.*, 2016), socio-economic factors (Pinho and Oliveira, 2009), environmental impact (Adolphe, 2001) and wellbeing (Newton, 2022). Urban space is considered vital for human residents, and the potential disappearance of urban open spaces is seen as concerning for urban planners (Toger *et al.*, 2016). This includes planned open spaces (public parks, lawns and gardens, sport and recreation facilities) and unplanned open spaces (unbuilt, vacant and abandoned lots, wastelands, fallow and abandoned agricultural lands, creeks and ravines, flood plains and riverbeds, coastlines, wetlands, roadside vegetation, backyards and other unbuilt patches of land) (Toger *et al.*, 2016).

Feagan (2007) critiques the local food system (LFS) movement, predicated upon "*spatially referenced concepts*" (Feagan, 2007). Most importantly, Feagan states that: "*LFS objectives . . . all*

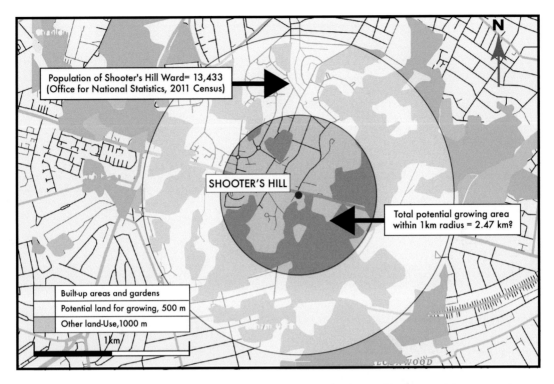

Population of Shooter's Hill Ward= 13,433
(Office for National Statistics, 2011 Census)

SHOOTER'S HILL

Total potential growing area
within 1km radius = 2.47 km?

Built-up areas and gardens
Potential land for growing, 500 m
Other land-Use,1000 m
1km

Fig. 2: ArcGIS image of Shooters Hill, London. Part of a college teaching exercise
to consider potential land available for growing food within a 1-km radius

converge around particular places" (Feagan, 2007, p. 28). For local groups, this has been termed place attachment (Lewicka, 2010) and has been established as a powerful and emotive factor for community gardens (Hajba, 2018).

At Hadlow College, the community allotment referred to in figure 1 comprised 12 families from Hadlow village, who independently managed this site. In 2013, one of the authors undertook semi-structured interviews with 11 adult members of the group. A Likert scale (Joshi *et al.*, 2015) was utilised based upon the importance of locality to the community allotment (sense of place), here termed the 'Locality score.' The question was phrased: "How important to you is the actual location of your allotment at Hadlow?" (1 = low, 9 = high), and the average result obtained was 8.75. Further comments from members were also assessed via *Thematic Analysis* (Maguire and Delahunt, 2017), and all these results can be seen in figure 5.

Specific comments relevant to location were:

- "*It's a pleasant spot – we can walk or cycle there.*"
- "*The location is only a 5-minute walk away – a bit of exercise. Walkable access to the site is very important.*"
- "*The plot is near to where we live – this is very important – it gives a great sense of community.*"

Members emphasised to one author (Lee) the profound effects of their participation in this allotment group. Many had found it to be a turning point in their lives – giving new meaning, enabling new friendships to be formed and contributing hugely to personal wellbeing. Some even talked about a sense of peace when on the allotment site and how they valued any time there.

We thus have realised that place attachment is a potentially powerful 'glue' for food growing

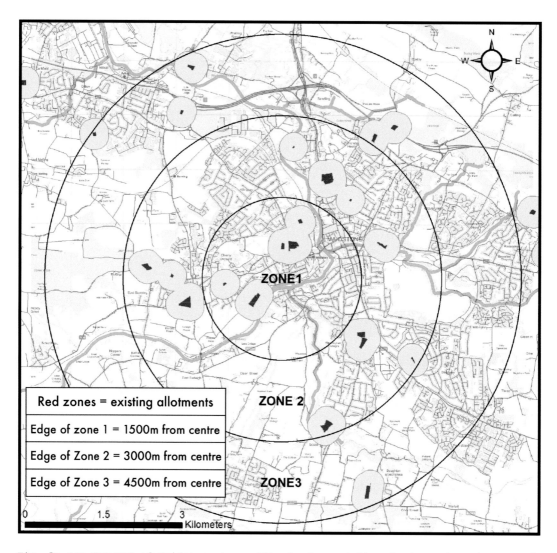

Fig. 3: Arc GIS map of Maidstone town, UK, showing existing food growing sites; each one has a buffered surround (data source: see end of the chapter)

communities who can identify very positively with a specific site. As an urban agroecological management zone of about 500 neighbours, an IDA can represent that site, with tangible borders which enclose a food production area and a community of growers. So, Tomkins' (2012) concept of edible mapping could be extended within an IDA context and the Hadlow allotment described earlier in Mapping example 1 could be considered part of an IDA.

However, place attachment theory has limitations too, especially when quantifiable data are needed to advance urban development as is the case for questions around food security. Brown *et al*. (2015) suggest the following actions: "*Whereas place attachment appears to be a rather blunt instrument to assess the potential for place-protective and place enhancement behaviour, mapped landscape values* [IDAs as suggested here] *provide more specific information about the potential motivations for place-based behaviour*

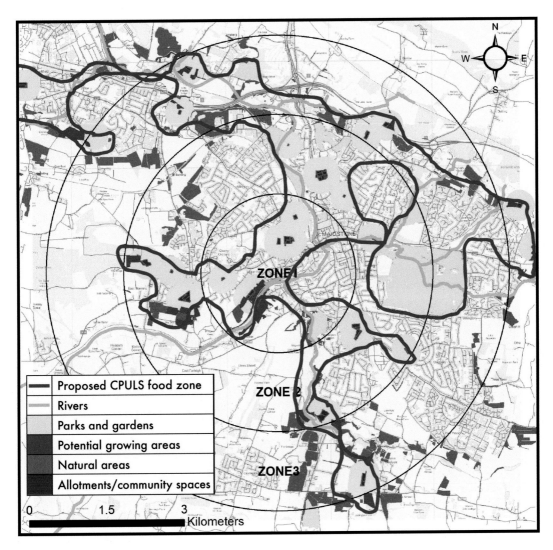

Fig. 4: ArcGIS map of Maidstone town, UK, showing 'Continuous Productive Urban Landscape' (CPUL) food zones (data source: see end of the chapter)

over a larger geographic area" (Brown et al., 2015, p. 52). They have concluding recommendations for future mapping of place attachment areas:

1. Assess the intensity and structure of place attachment;
2. Offer greater mapping precision;
3. Link/associate place attachment to mapped landscape values;
4. Link place attachment mapping to place-inspired behaviour.

Integrated Development Areas (IDAs)

How can digital food mapping be developed for urban food production?

IDAs need to function agroecologically (holistically) with boundaries which integrate inputs (soil organic matter, nutrients, water and energy) and with an awareness of human needs (physical, mental, cultural) and the wider environment (such as wildlife biodiversity). But the ultimate driving priority must be food security and the efficiency of that space for food production depends upon mapping, to allow land to be allocated for open or protected (polythene, glass, etc.) production by community groups or entrepreneurial enterprises. IDAs are thus seen as dependent upon mapping, allowing relatively efficient food production *via* accurate land allocation. In class teaching, we have explored with students the challenges of choosing appropriate urban land for growing food, ranging across micro sites including domestic gardens, larger spaces (< 0.1 ha) where small groups (30 people?) might work together (as for the Mapping example 1 earlier) and spaces > 0.1 ha where the expertise of specialist horticulture entrepreneurs might rationalise maximum yields and provide some local employment.

How large might an IDA be? How might it function? In terms of size, the number of participants is important. Lewicka (2010) states that: "*studies found a linear negative relationship between size of community and level of place attachment*" (p. 210). Dunbar and Sosis (2018) studied the size of community groups for effective function and longevity: "*Community sizes of 50, 150 and 500 are disproportionately more common than other sizes; they also have greater longevity*" Dunbar and Sosis (2018, p. 106). Thus, in an urban setting of relatively high density across Zones 1 and 2 and probably 3 (see fig. 3), it is probably worth considering IDAs containing upper limits of 500 citizens, though of course many will

not necessarily be active in growing food (the young, elderly, otherwise employed, etc.).

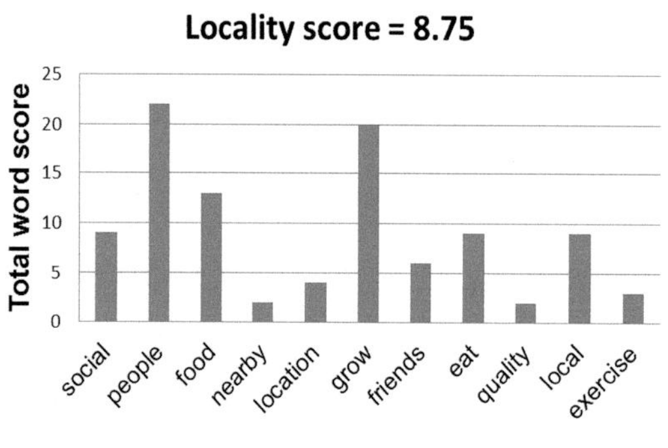

A schematic of a proposed portion of an ideal urban IDA is presented in figure 6. Land for growing food can be seen to cover a complex mosaic of gardens and an open space as a community allotment. A nearby, larger space (not shown) might also be suitable for a specialist horticulture enterprise.

The challenge is to consider a town like Maidstone and allocate IDAs that each encompass a maximum of 500 residents for optimal urban food production. The intention is that each IDA would contain the houses where these people live and some adjoining land where they might singly or jointly grow food. A horticulture enterprise could also fit within or, if larger, adjacent to IDAs. The success of this potentially complex scenario is seen as dependent upon effective planning. The concept of 'counter mapping' might be employed (De Master and Daniels, 2019) and blended with other multimedia techniques, and perhaps linked to a Situationist International theory and psychogeographic approaches. In other words, the participation of local people in determining the borders and function of the IDA in which they become sited must be fully participative and flexible, conceptual, and artistic, even spiritual. An institutional imposition of any form could be seen as a complete anathema.

Thus, the mapping of IDAs will depend upon a survey, which:

Locality score = 8.75

Fig. 5: Thematic analysis of comments made by 11 members of the Hadlow community allotment group

- Combines disparate data sources such as remote sensing and ground based economic, sociological and environmental metrics (for an example of a fusion of remote and economic ground data to facilitate urban mapping see Rosier *et al.*, (2022));
- Monitors on a site-by-site basis what land is available – a la Tomkins's edible mapping (Tomkins, 2012) to cover all possible urban spaces as listed by Rosier *et al.*, (2022);
- Urban land access for development. Russell *et al.*, (2022) review the challenges for

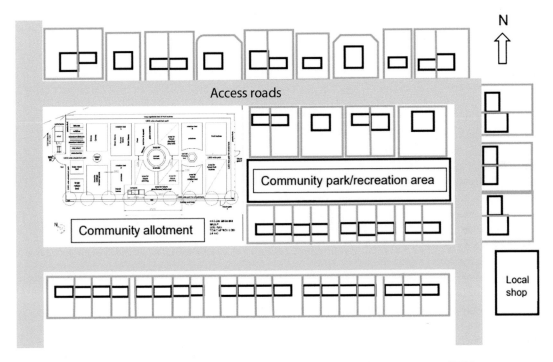

Fig. 6: Schematic of portion of possible Integrated Development Area (IDA).
This IDA portion is estimated to contain 100-150 citizens, so an ideal IDA would be
three to four times larger. A community allotment site is shown, taken from figure 1
with houses outlined in black and the garden perimeter in green

urban land access and propose Public-Common Partnerships (PCPs) *"for a new democratic common sense to emerge around urban development."* Thus, consultation with citizens is seen as a vital aspect of the development of IDAs;

- Urban food production as a contributor to national food security. The current international problems in Europe (Behnassi and El Haiba, 2022) are leading towards a greater focus on national food security. Spatial approaches to 'urban foodscapes' (Vonthron *et al.*, 2020) to enhance urban food production, as already reviewed here, will be based upon effective mapping.

Mapping IDAs: Developing the concept further

It is proposed that some 'pilot' towns/cities be sought that can take part in this approach. Any such urban centre would be consulted for the views of its citizens and their participation sought. Participative mapping would then take place – informally/formally – to consider potential IDA borders. If agreed, the IDAs would be declared and place-inspired behaviour encouraged, all as listed earlier by Brown *et al.* (2015). This would involve:

- Local food production and post-harvest processing – individually or in groups on available land, with advice/mentoring as needed;
- Water access;
- Nutrient access – recycling of municipal wastes;
- Marketing – bartering or sales;
- Biodiversity, wildlife encouragement;
- Collaboration between IDAs – on all of the aforementioned aspects.

If successful, a town or city would then become defined by its IDAs, which would contribute to the nutrition and wellbeing of its residents. The food production of all IDAs in a pilot planning study would need careful assessment, to help determine the proportion of fruit and vegetable needs that can be satisfied – *i.e.*, the level of self-sufficiency.

The success (or failure) of IDAs will ultimately depend upon their ability to feed people. It is forecast that local food production will become increasingly important for urban citizens. Many people who have no experience of mapping land and growing food need to be encouraged to do so. Formal training courses need to be offered by institutions such as Hadlow College, but there also needs to be informal sharing of mapping and growing expertise, *via* social media and other modes of linkage. The timeline for such developments is seen as less than ten years – *i.e.*, by the end of this decade (2030). External pressures are already affecting national food security, and a national policy is urgently needed. In many nations, at least half of its citizens live in or near towns and cities. Thus, mapping and planning for enhanced urban food production is a priority that cannot be ignored.

References

Adolphe, L., 2001. A simplified model of urban morphology: Application to an analysis of the environmental performance of cities. *Environment and Planning B: Planning and Design*, 28, 183–200.

Behnassi, M., and El Haiba, M., 2022. Implications of the Russia–Ukraine war for global food security. *Nature Human Behaviour*, 6, 754–755.

Bohn, K., and Viljoen, A., 2005. Urban Agriculture on the map: Growth and challenges since 2005. *In*: A. Viljoen and K. Bohn, eds. *Second Nature Urban Agriculture. Designing productive cities*: Routledge, 312.

Brown, G., Raymond, C.M., and Corcoran, J., 2015. Mapping and measuring place attachment. *Applied Geography*, 57, 42–53.

Craig, W.J., and Elwood, S.A., 1998. *How and why community groups use maps and geographic information*. Report (NPCR 1109). MN: University of Minnesota, 24.

De Master, K.T., and Daniels, J., 2019. Desert wonderings: Reimagining food access mapping. *Agriculture and Human Values*, 36, 241–256.

Dunbar, R.I.M., and Sosis, R., 2018. Optimising human community sizes. *Evolution & Human Behaviour*, 39, 106–111.

Fairlie, S., 2007. Can Britain feed itself? *The Land*, 4, 18–26.

Feagan, R., 2007. The place of food: Mapping out the 'local' in local food systems. *Progress in Human Geography*, 31 (1), 23–42.

Growing Communities, 2021. *The food zones. [Web site]*. https://growingcommunities.org/food-zones [Accessed 20 Feb 2023]

Hajba, G., 2018. Struggling with temporality. A case study of place attachment and displacement of an urban agriculture community in Hungary. *Socio.hu, Special Issue*, 94.

Joshi, A., Kale, S., Chandel, S., and Pal, D.K., 2015. Likert scale: Explored and explained. *British Journal of Applied Science & Technology*, 7 (4), 396–403.

Kent Analytics, Kent County Council, 2023. *2021 Mid-year population estimates: Total population in Kent*. Kent: Kent County Council, 13.

Larsen, K., and Gilliland, J., 2008. Mapping the evolution of 'food deserts' in a Canadian city: Supermarket accessibility in London, Ontario, 1961–2005. *International Journal of Health Geographics* 7, 1–16.

Lee, H.C., 2012. Chapter 36. How food secure can British cities become? *In*: A. Viljoen and J.S.C. Wiskerke, eds. *Sustainable food planning: Evolving theory and practice*. Wageningen: Wageningen Academic Publishers, 453–466.

Lee, H.C., 2017. Chapter 27. Antifragile urban entrepreneurialism as a contributor to food security in Europe. *In*: R. Roggema, ed. *Agriculture in an urbanizing society*, Vol. 2. Cambridge: Cambridge University Press, 705–730.

Lee, H.C., and Taylor, J., 2010. The HadLOW carbon community: Behavioural evolution in the face of climate change. *In*: M. Peters, S. Fudge and T. Jackson, eds. *Low carbon communities: Imaginative approaches to combating climate change*. London: Edward Elgar Publishing, 237–251.

Lewicka, M., 2010. Place attachment: How far have we come in the last 40 years? *Journal of Environmental Psychology*, 31, 207–230.

Lyons, K., Richards, C., Desfours, L., and Amati, M., 2013. Food in the city: Urban food movements and the (re)- imagining of urban spaces. *Australian Planner*, 50 (2), 157–163.

Maguire, M., and Delahunt, B., 2017. Doing a thematic analysis: A practical, step-by-step. Guide for learning and teaching scholars. *All Ireland Journal of Teaching and Learning in Higher Education (AISHE-J)*, 9 (3), 3351–3354.

Martellozzo, F., Landry, J-S., Plouffe, D., Seufert, V., Rowhani, P., and Ramankutty, N., 2014. Urban agriculture: A global analysis of the space constraint to meet urban vegetable demand. *Environmental Research Letters*, 9 (6), 064025.

Müller, B., Hoffmann, F., Heckelei, T., Müller, C., Hertel, T.W., Polhill, J.G., van Wijk, M., Achterbosch, T., Alexander, P., Brown, C., Kreuer, D., Ewert, F., Ge, J., Millington, J.D.A., Seppelt, R., Verburg, P.H., and Webber, H., 2020. Modelling food security: Bridging the gap between the micro and the macro scale. *Global Environmental Change*, 63, 102085. https://doi.org/10.1016/j.gloenvcha.2020.10208

Newton, D.W., 2022. Identifying correlations between depression and urban morphology through generative deep learning. *International Journal of Architectural Computing*, 1–22.

Pinho, P., and Oliveira, V., 2009. Cartographic analysis in urban morphology. *Environment and Planning B: Planning and Design*, 36, 107–127.

Rosier, J.F., Taubenbock, H., Verburg, P.H., and van Vliet, J., 2022. Fusing earth observation and socioeconomic data to increase the transferability of large-scale urban land use classification. *Remote Sensing of Environment*, 278, 113076.

Russell, B., Milburn, K., and Heron, K., 2022. Strategies for a new municipalism: Public–common partnerships against the new enclosures. *Urban Studies*, 1–25.

Tacoli, C., 2017. Food (In)Security in rapidly urbanising, low-income contexts. *International Journal of Environmental Research Public Health*, 14, 1–8.

Tobler, W., 2004. On the first law of geography: A reply. *Annals of the Association of American Geographers*, 94 (2), 304–310.

Toger, M., Malkinson, D., Benensen, I., and Czamanski, D., 2016. The connectivity of Haifa urban open space network. *Environment and Planning B: Planning and Design*, 43 (5), 848–870.

Tomkins, M., 2012. You are hungry: *Flâneuring*, edible mapping and feeding imaginations. *Architecture Culture and the Question of Knowledge: Doctoral Research Today*, 15–36.

Viljoen, A., and Bohn, K., 2014. *Second Nature Urban Agriculture. Designing productive cities*. London: Routledge, 312.

Viljoen, A., Bohn, K., and Howe, J. (eds.), 2005. *Continuous Productive Urban Landscapes: Designing urban agriculture for sustainable cities*. London: Architectural Press, 272.

Vonthron, S., Perrin, C., and Soulard, C.-T., 2020. Food-scape: A scoping review and a research agenda for food security-related studies. *PLoS One*, 15 (5), e0233218. https://doi.org/10.1371/journal.pone.0233218

Zasada, I., Schmutz, U., Wascher, D., Kneafsey, M., Corsid, S., Mazzocchi, C., Monaco, F., Boyce, P., Doernberg, A., Sali, G., and Piorr, A., 2019. Food beyond the city – Analysing foodsheds and self-sufficiency for different food system scenarios in European metropolitan regions. *City, Culture and Society*, 16, 25–35.

Data source acknowledgements for figures 3 and 4

OS MasterMap 1:25,000 scale Raster

1:25 000 Scale Colour Raster [Shape geospatial data], Scale 1:25,000, Tile(s): TQ 75ne,TQ75nw,TQ 75se,TQ75sw, Updated: December 2019, Ordnance Survey, Using: EDINA Digimap Ordnance Survey Service, *https://digimap.edina. ac.uk/webhelp/os/data_information/os_products/25k_colour_ raster.htm*, Downloaded: July 2020

OS Greenspace

OS MasterMap Topography Layer [Shape geospatial data], Scale 1:25,000, Tile(s): TQ 7050, TQ 7055, TQ 7550, TQ 7555, Updated: November 2020, Ordnance Survey, Using: EDINA Digimap Ordnance Survey Service, *https://digimap. edina.ac.uk/webhelp/os/data_information/os_products/ os_open_greenspace.htm*, Downloaded: July 2020

OS Open Rivers

OS Open Rivers [Shape geospatial data], Scale 1:25,000, Tile(s): TQ 75ne,TQ75nw,TQ 75se,TQ75sw, Updated: April 2020, Ordnance Survey, Using: EDINA Digimap Ordnance Survey Service, *https://digimap.edina.ac.uk/web-help/os/data_information/os_products/os_open_rivers.htm*, Downloaded: July 2020

OS Open Roads

OS Open Roads [Shape geospatial data], Scale 1:25,000, Tile(s): TQ 75ne,TQ75nw,TQ 75se,TQ75sw, Updated: April 2020, Ordnance Survey, Using: EDINA Digimap Ordnance Survey Service, *https://digimap.edina.ac.uk/web-help/os/data_information/os_products/os_open_roads.htm*, Downloaded: July 2020

Walking out for dinner: Discovering and mapping food choices in Saigon

Patrick S. Ford and Nina Yiu Lai Lei

Since the 1960s, the field of creative walking has exploded with individuals and groups utilising psycheography and the concept of the dérive to study and/or examine everything from urban planning, public and private space, ecological status, and more. The scope of this chapter concerns a rectangular grid of roads within *'Phu My Hung'*, a local area within District 7 of Ho Chi Minh City, Vietnam (see fig. 1).

District 7 is a new area in the city, developed to cater for the growing population of the city, constructed on a previously empty landscape. The nature of the neighbourhood's rectilinear structure meant the authors' recorded directions could be easily tracked (see fig. 2). This district is comprised predominantly of Vietnamese with the addition of a large percentage of Koreans along with Taiwanese, Indian and Western expatriates.

This perambulatory approach to data-gathering has been described by several authors and published as field-guides that could be catalysts for subsequent walks (Overall, 2021; Qualmann and Hind, 2015). The area had also previously been the subject of study by the authors in 2018 (Ford, 2018).

As so much of the social life of the city seems to revolve around eating, the current plan was to set out on foot each day during the same week, Monday to Friday, aiming to discover the different types of food available to cater for the multi-cultural nature of the residents and customers in the area (see fig. 3).

The project sought to investigate the types of food establishments available within the area under study by adopting a peripatetic approach borrowed from psychogeographical research. The perambulatory aspect of the project would also discover more about how the various types of eateries are located in relation to one another within the study area.

To do this it was necessary to create a map of where each restaurant was for future reference. Over five days a particular type of food was selected each day and the authors would walk from the same starting point each time to locate five examples (see fig. 4). The routes the authors took were recorded as maps, one each day, and at the end of the week the five routes were combined into an abstracted, conceptual map of the food types available. Each food type was graphically differentiated using colours within the maps, enabling the location and incidence of each food type to be examined: green for Vietnamese food, blue for Korean food, yellow for Indian food, orange for Chinese food and finally red for Western Style food (including Italian, French, American, British, etc.).

Monday

On the first day of the project the food choice was simple as it seemed logical to eat Vietnamese food and so the authors set out south along Dương Phạm Văn Nghị for one block before turning east along Khu phố Hưng Gia 2. This road led to Bùi Bằng Đoàn after which it continued as Khu phố Hưng Gia 1. Almost

DOI: 10.4324/9781003352280-11

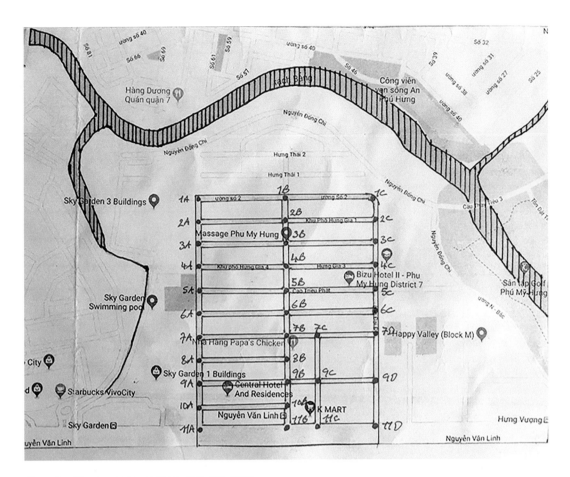

Fig. 1: Study area within Phu My Hung

at the junction with Đặng Đại Độ, the authors found *Dê Trương Định*, the first stop. After a few delicious starters, the authors were becoming a little thirsty and, rather than opting for the offered can of **Tiger** beer, it was thought preferable to move on to another local establishment for a street-side drink.

Exiting southward along Đặng Đại Độ, it is only a short walk before turning west again along Đ. Phan Khiêm Ích. After a few minutes the authors found *Hà Nội Corner*. Ignoring the wonderful North-Vietnamese dishes, it was decided to sample some cool **Hà Nội Bia**.

Leaving *Hà Nội Corner*, the walk backtracked along Đ. Phan Khiêm Ích and turned south once

again on Đặng Đại Độ. Passing three side-streets, on the right is *Bún bò Vỹ Dạ Xưa*. This restaurant specialises in **Bún bò**, a beef noodle soup, especially **Bún bò Huế**, named after the central Vietnamese former capital. A bowl of **Bún bò Huế** is surprisingly light with a spicy soup and added lemongrass, a perfect addition to Monday's walk.

Reluctantly leaving *Bún bò Vỹ Dạ Xưa* by the exit on Lê Văn Thiêm, the authors walked west until they reached Bùi Bằng Đoàn, where they found *Phở Việt Nam* – part of a local food chain. Despite **Phở** being the most famous Vietnamese dish, the authors decided that eating another soup-based dish at a chain restaurant would not be the best way to follow the wonderful **Bún bò Huế** and so the walk continued across Bùi Bằng Đoàn to

Fig. 2: Overview of study area

Hoàng Triều Garden for the final sample of the walk. This restaurant had a good selection of set menus, but they all seemed too much to finish on whereas the coconut ice cream **Kem** seemed the perfect way to round-off the walk (see fig. 5).

Tuesday

For the second walk this week, the choice was, once again, not difficult. Being in District 7, we could not miss out on sampling the plentiful Korean food on offer.

The authors walked due south down Dương Phạm Văn Nghị, but this time walking one street farther, turning east into Đ. Phan Khiêm Ích the authors discovered the *Jeon Joo Oak* restaurant. Here they enjoyed a plate of delicious **spicy squid** and a bowl of **fried vegetables**, a Korean version of **tempura**.

Returning to Dương Phạm Văn Nghị, the authors continued south one more street and turned east into Khu phố Hưng Gia 4. After a short walk, *Seoul Restaurant* came into view. This restaurant offered a wide variety of **soups** with an emphasis on **beef**: **Oxtail**, **ox-bone**, etc. but the favoured dish was the **Sizzling**

Stone Pot Bibimbap, which included **beef**, **vegetables**, and **bean sprouts** with an **egg** broken on top – a good choice.

Backtracking to Dương Phạm Văn Nghị, the authors continued south, to the junction with Khu Phố Hưng Phước 2 where the *Korean BBQ Restaurant Lee Cho* occupies the corner plot. On the outdoor terrace, a lovely **hot-pot** dish was served, along with a side-dish of **kimchee**.

Continuing along Khu Phố Hưng Phước 2, turning north up Bùi Bằng Đoàn and then east along Cao Triều Phát the authors discovered the *Makchang Dodook*. The authors decided to share a couple of small dishes of **squid** and **vegetables**, cooking them themselves at their table.

Following this tasty dish and backtracking along Cao Triều Phát they turned south down Bùi Bằng Đoàn, strolling leisurely until the turn west along Khu Phố Hưng Phước 3, where the final eatery was located, the *Hansol Restaurant*.

The combination of these dishes, each of them substantial, eventually proved enough and so the evening was rounded off with a nice glass of **Soju**, the traditional Korean beverage (see fig. 6).

Wednesday

The first Indian restaurant was within sight of the daily start-point, and this observation determined the choice of food for Wednesday's walk.

A two-minute walk south down Dương Phạm Văn Nghị is *Dahi Handi*, a newcomer to the locale. The authors ordered the flavourful **prawn curry**, along with an **Aloo Paratha**, which was a superb way to begin the walk.

Leaving Dahi Handi and continuing south down Dương Phạm Văn Nghị before turning east along Khu Phố Hưng Phước 2, the authors found *Swagat Restaurant*, located about halfway along the street. Unfortunately, this eatery had closed.

Continuing along Khu Phố Hưng Phước 2, turning south down Bùi Bằng Đoàn and then turning west once more, along Khu Phố Hưng Phước 3, reveals *Roti Mojo*. This eatery offers an interesting menu with several dishes being a Chinese Indian blend of flavours. To avoid repetition, the authors avoided the **tiger prawn**, and instead opted for a shared dish of **Haryali Chicken Tikka** washed down with a glass of **coconut juice**.

The menu offered desserts such as **Kheer** and **Gulab Jamun**, but it was decided to leave that choice for later.

A short stroll farther west along Khu Phố Hưng Phước 3 lies *Ganges Restaurant*. Here the authors enjoyed a plate of **vegetarian samosas** served with a combination of **dips** and **sauces**. The selection proved to be a successful complement to the previous **chicken** dish.

Continuing west along Khu Phố Hưng Phước 3, turning south down Dương Phạm Văn Nghị and west along Đường số 6 brought the authors to their final stop of the walk, *Ganesh Restaurant*. This restaurant offered yet another wonderful array of choices, but the authors opted for a delicious tub of **Kulfi** and a **mango lassi** to finish off Wednesday's walk (see fig. 7).

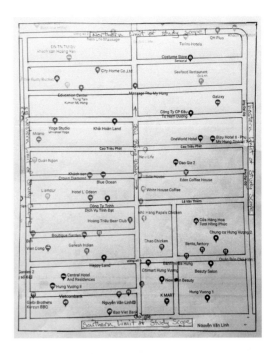

Fig. 3: Detail of study area

Thursday

Thursday evening's choice continued the Asian theme and began by walking south down Dương Phạm Văn Nghị for one block before turning east along Khu phố Hưng Gia 2. After crossing Bùi Bằng Đoàn, *Mỳ Dimsum* can be found. This brightly lit restaurant features a covered terrace with large tables. It was pleasant to find that the **steamed and fried dishes** were definitely worth the visit. A good start to today's walk.

Continuing south down Bùi Bằng Đoàn for two blocks and a turn west along Khu Phố Hưng Phước 2 brought the authors to *Chuen Heung Choy Guen*. In this small restaurant, the authors enjoyed a bowl of **flat noodles**, **stir-fried beef** with **chopped spring onion** and **green peppers**. So far so good!

Backtracking a little farther down the street, lies *Phúc Mãn Lầu*. The frontage of this restaurant had been decorated with a large collection

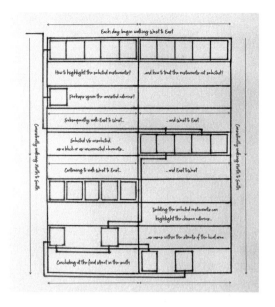

Fig. 4: Proposed general walking directions and method for indicating restaurant locations

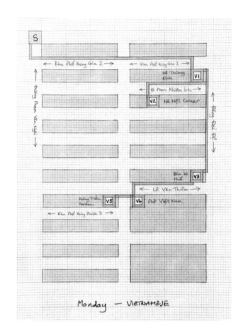

Fig. 5: Monday's walking map

of paper lanterns. A bowl of **Kung Po Chicken** proved just the job, delighting the palette without filling the stomach thereby allowing us to continue our culinary walk.

Turning back along Phố Hưng Phước 2, crossing Bùi Bằng Đoàn once more and progressing farther west along Nội khu Hưng Phước 1, the authors found *Il Pum Gag*, a Korean owned Chinese Restaurant, targeted at the local Korean community. Considering this was to be our fourth eatery of the walk, we decided to try an **egg fried rice** dish, with a small bottle of **soju** to complete the experience.

Returning once more to Bùi Bằng Đoàn and following it south until the junction with Nguyễn Văn Linh, the authors broke with the project format again by not completing a full list of eateries. Situated on the corner of Bùi Bằng Đoàn and Nguyễn Văn Linh stands the large *Nathalie's Thai Restaurant*. The fact that the geographical limit of the project's scope had been reached, the authors decided to end the day's walk here, with a selection of **Grass Jelly**

with Lychee, **diced fruit** and a small bowl of **Thai Black Sticky Rice**. Another successful day (see fig. 8).

Friday

On the final day it was decided to try an assortment of Western themed restaurants as a way of completing the project. The authors walked due east along Đường số 2, then turned south down Bùi Bằng Đoàn to *The Tavern*, essentially a bar that also serves food. The order was an **aperitif** and a few simple **bar snacks** whetting the appetite for the coming walk.

Leaving *The Tavern* on Bùi Bằng Đoàn and turning east along Hưng Gia 3, *Red and Round* is located on the south side of the street. The menu boasted a large selection, **appetizers**, **pizzas**, **pasta dishes**, **risotto** and even **gnocchi**. The eventual choice was one of the restaurant's best sellers, **Carpaccio**. Made with **Australian beef** and served with **rocket**, **parmiggiano** and a **lemon dressing**, this was a great choice.

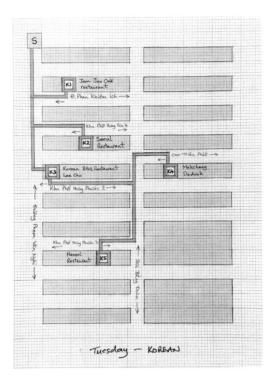

Fig. 6: Tuesday's walking map

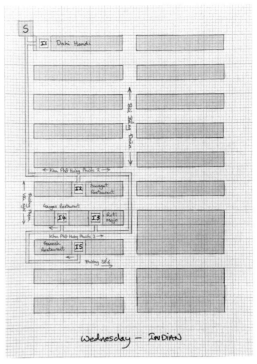

Fig. 7: Wednesday's walking map

The walk then retraced the street back to Bùi Bằng Đoàn before turning south for one block and a turn west along Cao Triều Phát. Almost at the end of the street is *Moo Beef Steak*. The interior featured subdued lighting, a vast and impressive wine list, polite and eager staff and a very detailed breakdown of the **beef** available, including **Black Angus** from Australia and **Wagyu** from Japan. It was a treat to eat such a **steak**, washed down with a glass of **Argentinian Malbec**.

Retracing the walk along Cao Triều Phát and then south down Bùi Bằng Đoàn, *La Forchetta* can be found. Appearing nightly on the terrace of the BlueSky Global building, this restaurant presents dishes well above what you would expect from a pop-up type eatery. The **arancini siciliani** were wonderful.

The final stop was found by turning east along the next street that turns off from Bùi Bằng

Đoàn. *Speakeasy* is situated not far along Lê Văn Thiêm and was the final stop of the week. As it is another bar that serves simple snacks; the day's walk was rounded off with a **negroni** (see fig. 9).

Five days of interactive mapping

After five days of walking and eating, the authors combined the five walking maps and reflected upon the week's observations (see fig. 10).

Despite the restaurants being the targets each day, the authors soon realised that it was the street itself that was the true 'heart' of the city. The lack of an efficient bus service and the stalled development of the city's mass transit rail system meant that most people used mopeds and motorcycles to navigate the city. In many cities around the world, the streets have become 'non-places' as Marc Auge would describe them (2008), somewhere that only

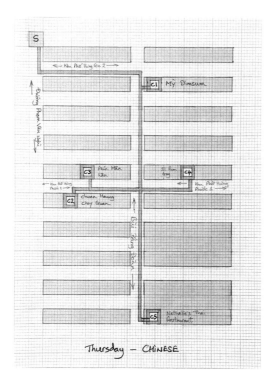

Fig. 8: Thursday's walking map

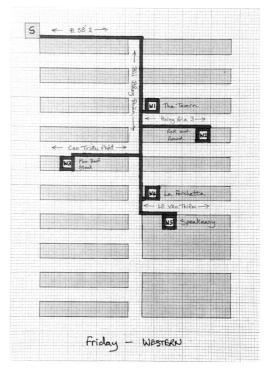

Fig. 9: Friday's walking map

exists to link one desirable location to another. Here in Ho Chi Minh City, the life is lived mostly out on the street. Everyone rides around the streets, deliveries are made (also mostly using motorcycles), food is cooked and sold on the streets, repairs are made to motorcycles on street corners, temporary cafes appear from nowhere on pavements and just as quickly disappear, hawkers slowly cruise the streets (also on motorcycles) advertising their wares or services such as knife-sharpening, fresh snacks, gas bottle deliveries. Walking the streets exposes us to the sounds and the smells of the city, and we are also more aware of the weather. The streets of HCMC have not yet lost their sense of place and become a 'non-place' as they have in many cities around the world.

Another observation made by the team was which of the restaurant types had been transformed by the proliferation of international customers in the area. Most of the restaurants seemed to offer a 'core' of national dishes,

supplemented by a selection of other dishes that could be palatable to customers from other countries and continents. The 'fusion' approach seemed to have been adopted with great success and all the busiest restaurants offered a mixed menu of international fare.

The open-ended nature of the project means that to keep up to date with the status and nature of the eateries within the area it would be necessary to conduct this type of study at regular intervals, perhaps at least once or twice per year.

References

Auge, M., 2008. *Non-places*. London and New York: Verso.
Ford, P.S., 2018. Walking as cartography: Collecting colours in Saigon. *Living Maps Review* [online], 5. Available from http://livingmaps.review/journal/index.php/LMR/article/view/131 [Accessed 30 Jan 2022].
Overall, S., 2021. *Walk write (Repeat)*. London: Triarchy Press.
Qualmann, C., and Hind, C., 2015. *Ways to wander*. London: Triarchy Press.

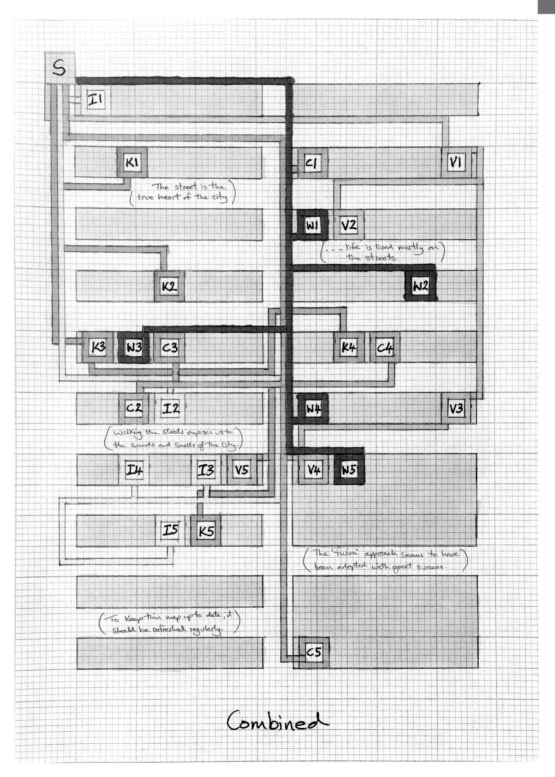

Fig. 10: The combined map of the week's walks

Follow the food . . . and the spaces it shapes

Natacha Quintero González and Anke Hagemann

Food is all around us and can evoke multiple senses including a sense of place and identity. Yet, food not only affects the individual or the collective through the senses, imagination or metabolism, but its materiality and associated requirements shape the various spaces in which it circulates: from the dense urban centres where it is consumed and disposed of to the rural, industrial and infrastructural spaces where it is extracted, grown and processed.

Food supply has traditionally linked cities and their close hinterlands, and although this link has not been entirely broken, it has, on the other hand, reached planetary dimensions. The radical reconfigurations of urbanisation processes that we have witnessed since the 1980s have blurred categorical distinctions such as 'urban/rural' and de-territorialised the former 'hinterland', creating global urban networks and new scales of urbanisation over time (Brenner and Schmid, 2011). Instead of consuming food that is produced with local resources, know-how and agricultures in the surrounding region, expanding metropolises benefit from large-scale agribusinesses that conform national or supra-national networks and produce exactly what the modern citizen demands: low-priced and predictable food that is in constant supply (Steel, 2009, p. 59). A useful pedagogical exercise to analyse the myriad socio-material relations embedded in these translocal food networks is to "*trac[e] back all the items used in the production of [a regular] meal*" (Harvey, 1990, p. 422). Doing so reveals the various dependencies that tie together

diverse labour conditions, diverse geographies of production and consumption, and what Marx called the "*fetishism of commodities*", i.e. the concealment of information as well as social and geographical relations by markets (Harvey, 1990, p. 422). Such exercise also provides an opportunity to engage with 'food pedagogies', 'critical food literacy' (Sumner, 2008) and 'food geographies' (Jensen et al., 2013).

In this chapter, we explore links between food, urbanisation and architecture. We present a mapping methodology developed for graduate-level teaching that aimed at exploring the status quo of food supply chains as well as their urban and architectural implications. The chapter draws on the outputs of a master's seminar entitled "*Feeding the City*", held during the COVID-19 pandemic for students of architecture and urban planning (Hagemann and Quintero González, 2021) who, confined to their homes, began interacting with food and space in new ways. Using this situation as an opportunity, the seminar focused on products found in the students' kitchens and explored them through spatial mappings. The resulting maps aimed at unveiling the origins, transformation and journeys of conventional food products in order to understand the impact of multi-local and multi-actor processes on the built environment at different spatial scales. The approach required students to use digital tools to examine and visualise multi-scalar processes and the physical infrastructures involved in translocal commodity chains. They were asked to draw on relational perspectives, such as systemic

DOI: 10.4324/9781003352280-12

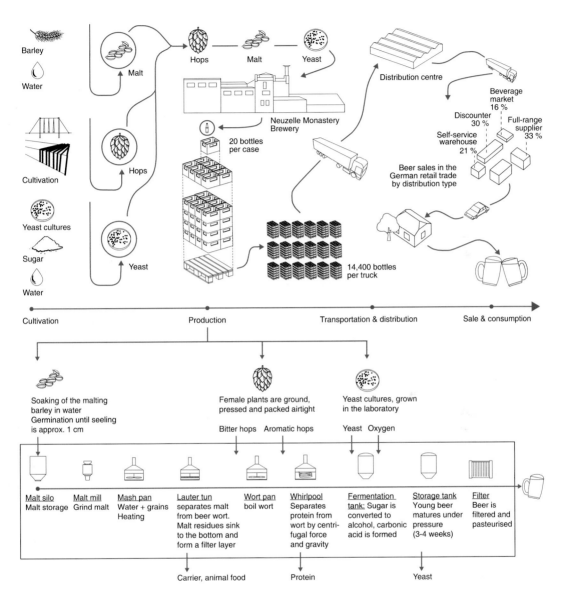

Fig. 1: Elaboration of beer from its main components: Water, hops, malt and yeast to its liquid state. The drawing shows the transformation of the individual ingredients into beer during the brewing cycle, including the machines and logistics, as well as packaging and the journey of beer to the home for consumption (Tim Heinzmann, Lars Matthias, Lara von Thienen and Hanna Zeißig)

thinking and actor-network theory, and to explore different graphic design methods for the mappings. Thus, students participated in an interdisciplinary and iterative activity in which they could explore the intersections between geography, urbanism, architecture, graphic and

communication design, critical urban studies, ecology, political economy and cartography.

In favouring *maps* as methods for spatial analysis (Baur *et al.*, 2014, p. 8), we did not conceive mapping as the mere reproduction of reality but as a practice that can recompose, accentuate and interpret its underlying narratives. Accordingly, our methodology focuses on the capacity of mapping to reveal hidden links and *"uncove[r] realities previously unseen or unimagined"* (Corner, 2011, p. 89), a powerful capacity when it comes to processes within the food system we are usually unaware of (Kiyooka *et al.*, 2013).

Following and mapping food supply chains

Tracing consumer goods through increasingly complex and spatially fragmented supply networks to the places of their extraction and production has become a didactically effective means of gaining a better understanding of globalisation and the workings of the world economy. Since the early 1990s, several research approaches linking actors and places involved in commodity production and consumption have emerged from various fields of study. While many scholars have focused on global commodity chains, global value chains or global production networks (Gereffi and Korzeniewicz, 1994; Henderson *et al.*, 2002; Bair, 2005), and others have described commodity circuits (Hughes and Reimer, 2004), some have been simply 'following things' through the most diverse spatial and cultural contexts (Cook, 2004; Knowles, 2014; Hulme, 2015). Within those *follow-the-thing* approaches, generally coming from anthropology and cultural geography, food has been a prominent commodity to trace (Cook, 2004; Cook *et al.*, 2006; Tsing, 2015). Following edibles has proven to be a formidable strategy for linking systems of global reach to both our everyday consumption patterns as well as to the social micro level, including our own metabolic systems (Bennett, 2010; Strüver, 2020). However, in linking geographies interconnected through various social and market systems, most commodity tracing approaches – although partly applied in spatial sciences – have hardly included physical urban structures and their architectural manifestations in the analysis.

More recent efforts coming from urban and architectural scholarship have begun to chart spatial patterns and physical infrastructures of logistical systems, material flows and global connectivity, providing valuable models for our mapping practice (Beyer *et al.*, 2020; Lyster, 2016; LeCavalier, 2016; Hein, 2018; Topalovic *et al.*, 2013).

The methods presented in this chapter expand on research contributions that aim to stimulate transdisciplinary synergies by linking urban and architectural research with the study of commodity chains, thereby focusing on the interplay between the relational space of networks and the built environment (Krätke *et al.*, 2012; Hagemann, 2015; Hagemann and Beyer, 2020). By linking commodity studies with spatial analysis, the focus on food allows for an integrated study of the gigantic efforts involved in food supply chains as well as a closer look into how these efforts ultimately give shape to urban or rural environments and buildings (Steel, 2009). The multiscalar approach and style of the maps were based on the methodology of the research seminar titled *"Architectures of Circulation"* and the cartographic practice from the research project *"Transnational Production Spaces"* (2016–2019), which includes the analysis of global commodity networks, urban situations of the commodity trail as well as architectural structures (Hagemann and Beyer, 2020).

What follows is a critical and methodological reflection on how five mappings with five different foci can depict conventional food supply chains, exploring how they shape and are shaped by the spaces through which they travel. We present an analysis of exemplary and very basic food items typically found in large numbers and at low prices in supermarkets, namely, beer, bananas, Darjeeling tea, eggs and sugar. The order of the sections in the chapter follows the analytical structure and the steps that the students took with their respective products during the seminar.

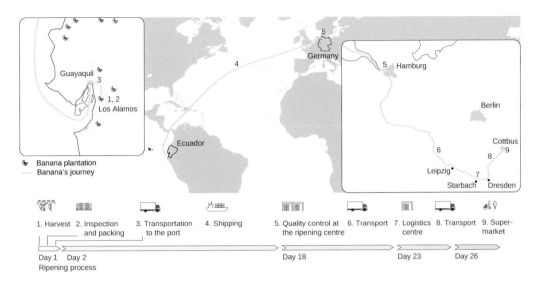

Fig. 2: Exemplary journey of bananas from the plantation in Ecuador to the supermarket in Cottbus. The mapping shows the various stations and means of transportation linked to the temporalities involved in banana trade (Jana Assef, Wenjie He, Birgit Jeschke and Anna Tombroff)

Students adhered to a strict framework of five mappings (including annotations): the first mapping characterised the *product* and its composition; the second traced an exemplary *supply chain* from its place of origin (usually the farm/plantation) to the supermarket; in a third mapping students explored the complexity of food production systemically with the aid of a *network* diagram; the fourth mapping illustrated one characteristic *architecture* along the route; and the fifth and final map investigated the spatial significance of the selected product in the *city* of Cottbus, either historically or presently. The maps were developed using CAD software, vector-based illustration and layout designing software and were collectively discussed on a weekly basis. Research on the food products was gathered from journal and online newspaper articles, websites of the relevant actors, aerial satellite imagery, interviews, visits to supermarkets and a few production sites and social media posts. We argue that this approach, i.e. linking the spatial mapping of the geographies and physical environments of commodity flows

with the mapping of relational networks, allows for a better understanding of the translocality of food supply chains and their built manifestations.

Understanding food products

When thinking about the ways we interact with food on a daily basis, we might think of the obvious: cooking and eating. Yet we also consume food visually, and with the rise of online food communities, various forms of food imagery have come forth (Turner, 2016). Among these forms are illustrations, a type of visualisation capable of evoking sensory experiences of food (Turner, 2016).

Aware of the power of visual communication tools such as illustrations and infographics to convey knowledge in an easily digestible format (Smiciklas, 2012; Ainsworth and Scheiter, 2021), students were encouraged to start their food journey by characterising products and trying to visually tell what is not usually told in recipes or food advertising. The first map is the result of a process of synthesising information, becoming familiar with the products through drawing and understanding food as more than its *finished* or marketed form.

The team working on beer created a narrative by drawing a flow chart of the successive transformation of seeds, hop cones and fungi into beer's carbonated liquid form – a process that has historical and cultural significance in

Germany (Heinzmann *et al.,* 2021). They relied mainly on online resources by major national stakeholders of beer brewing as well as on personal conversations with experts in the field.

This first map (fig. 1) serves as a stand-alone infographic on the selected products and their constituents. It does not address in detail political, ethical and social issues related to food production and trade, but facilitates the

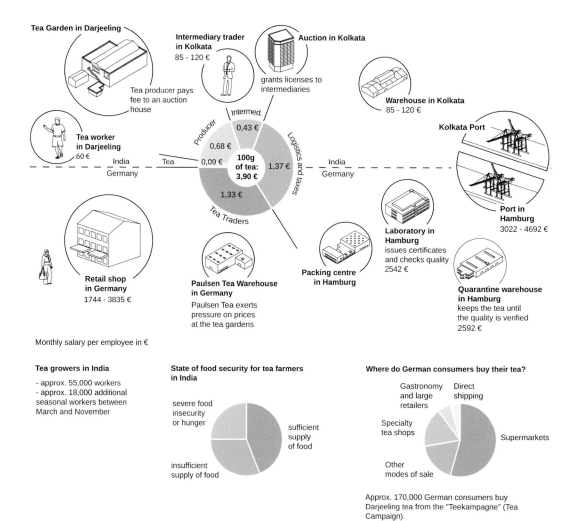

Fig. 3: Network of actors and processes behind the retail price of 100g of Darjeeling tea. The map highlights human actors, their roles and incomes as well as the role of buildings in tea production and trade (Julia Fritsche, Laurin Roman Henklein, Julia Theite Piro and Leonard Zappe)

analysis of what is embodied in food products. Visual representations are a form of communication that allows large amounts of research to be summarised and reduced to manageable scales. In doing so, creators coherently define and arrange the most important aspects of the information so that the viewer can grasp the whole picture (Schraw *et al.*, 2013). This exercise of synthesis and translation through drawing can lead to the discovery of various themes for further analysis.

Charting global commodity chains

Grasping the spatial reach of food supply chains, be it regional, supra-regional or global, means being confronted with highly debated issues, such as the origins of food, the transparency and ethics of supply chains and how those can distinctly influence consumer's decisions (Ermann, 2015). To investigate these issues, students were asked to trace the selected food (quite literally) back to its roots and map its journey to the supermarket. This mapping had to consider relevant stations, means of transportation, required infrastructures and the temporal dimension of the supply chain.

This exercise required students to make assumptions and often troubling decisions, as many aspects of supply chains were untraceable or remained in the dark. Yet, discussing and *"attempting to understand the unfollowable bits of the commodity trail"* (Hulme, 2015, p. 157) contributed to a better understanding of how capitalist food supply systems operate. Field research showed to be especially challenging under restrictions posed during the COVID-19 pandemic. Methodologically, most students relied on desktop research (Bereskin and Quintero González, 2022), except for the few who focused on regional products and were able to visit livestock farms or see processing plants at least from the outside.

The group following bananas focused on the fruit's journey from Ecuador's large monocultures to Germany, where they can be bought in

any supermarket for less than 2 Euros per kilo. The mapping shows the bananas' path from the plantations to the country's port, from where they are shipped to Hamburg. From there, they continue by truck to a ripening centre and the trader's logistics centre before reaching the supermarkets in Cottbus. Figure 2 not only shows the global scale of the banana supply chain, but also highlights the critical aspect of time in banana trade as its ripening process requires precise logistical operations (Assef *et al.*, 2021). For this map, students used online information provided by the respective global banana trade company, Ecuadorian tourism marketing, local administration, fair trade organisations, critical journalistic sources and conversations with supermarket employees. By defining an exemplary journey and specifying the various stations in the map, the generic banana on the supermarket shelf is given a more individual connotation. However, the map raises further questions about the respective local production and working conditions as well as the character of these places and their infrastructures.

Tracing actor-networks in food systems

In writing about the *"epistemology of the shopping cart"*, Raj Patel (2019, p. 20) argues that *"[t]o know things through their supply chains is to know everything and nothing"*. He explains that, while we can nowadays trace food back to its origins and clearly know *what* we eat, the question of *why* we eat what we eat is much more important if we are to understand the historical, social, political and market forces behind the logic of our food consumption (Patel, 2019).

To address some of these 'why' questions, we sought to capture this bigger picture and explore the different forces that interact along the food trajectory by relying on a relational perspective. This relational approach views food systems as socio-material entanglements that operate inside and outside our bodies and which acutely embody various forms of injustice (Bennett, 2010, Strüver, 2020); and planning – including theory, practice and knowledge – as intricately linked to networks made up of material, social, cultural, historical, political and legal contexts (Kurath and Bürgin, 2019).

Based on the relational approaches of systems thinking and actor-network theory, students were encouraged to pay attention to privileged, excluded, essential or subordinate (human and non-human) actors and to depict their power relations, cyclical processes or newly discovered patterns graphically. The maps included network diagrams, flow charts or organisational charts using pictograms, geometric shapes, lines and arrows to differentiate and link actors, places and processes or to express hierarchies. In the case presented here, students focus on the retail price of 100g of tea as a starting point to unfold the complexities and embodied inequalities in the tea industry. The analysis shows various actants involved in tea production and trade along with their roles as they unequally assemble to make up the price of tea. The most striking features shown in figure 3 are the minimal share of profit that goes to the tea-pickers, the substantial price increase that occurs once market forces and taxes come into play and how buildings operate as key agents in tea production and trade. Another illustrative 'move' that underlines the unjust balance is the 'North-South' divide in the middle of the graph (Fritsche *et al.*, 2021).

The architectures of food production

The integration of architectural analysis into our food-following journey was distinctly illustrated in the fourth mapping. Students focused on the physical articulation of food production in specific buildings or facilities and consequently explored a selected station of their respective commodity trail, such as the farm, the plantation or the food processing plant.

Most of the analysed stations are located in rural or peri-urban settings, and yet their large dimensions and mass production character

underlines their centrality in translocal production networks. Standing in stark contrast to a traditional imagination of the countryside, they have become part of an extended urbanisation that increasingly incorporates all types of spaces on the planet's surface (Brenner and Schmid, 2015). This is illustrated by a conventional laying hen farm in southern Brandenburg (fig. 4). This huge farm houses around 1 million hens and, being completely surrounded by forest, is protected from prying eyes. There are 40 multi-storey hen houses clustered in several clearings, connected by access roads. The mandatory floor husbandry is achieved by intermediate levels, which allow 18 hens per square metre of barn surface area (Chen *et al.*, 2021). The interior of the buildings is so efficiently organised that the interaction of hens and technical equipment creates an egg production machine that requires little human intervention. Students working on the origin of eggs struggled with the strategies of 'dissociation' (Ibert *et al.*, 2019) and the lack of transparency of the notorious large-scale egg industry. To bring to light the 'black box' of the laying hen farm – which was not only hidden by trees – they had to reconstruct information from the most diverse sources, such as satellite images, tabloid newspaper articles and press photographs, or technical norms and standards communicated through business associations and public authorities. While the site plan highlights the large size, rational layout and isolated location of the stables, the anonymous industrial architectures are characterised by reduced isometric drawings highlighting their efficient internal production machinery.

Zooming in on specific stations of the food supply chain can reveal the most inconspicuous or hidden places that have not yet been considered in urban research (Choplin and Pliez, 2015; Beyer *et al.*, 2020). Furthermore, mapping the architectures of food production renders visible those functional buildings which, despite their enormous size and significance, are often overlooked.

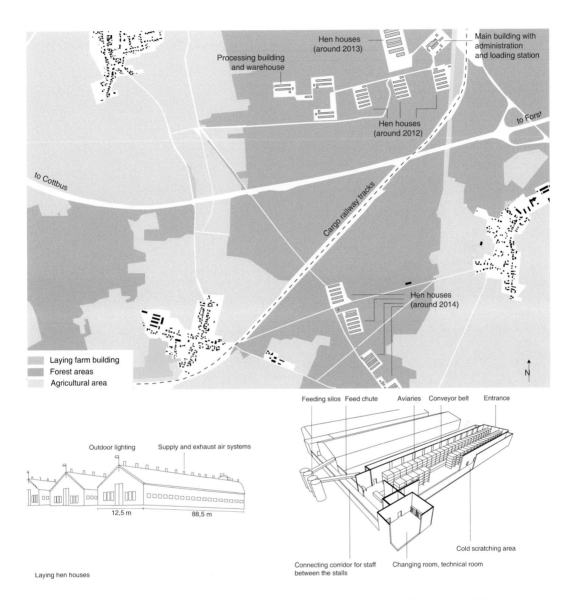

Fig. 4: Spatial layout and typical buildings of a laying hen farm in southern Brandenburg. Left, the laying hen house with its access points and internal organisation. Right, location of hen houses and administrative buildings surrounded by forest (Mingyun Chen, Vivienne Heiden, Noelle Kliesch and Jonas Müller)

Shaping the city through food

The fifth and final mapping exercise of our food tracing journey sought to demonstrate the enormous physical presence of food in the city of Cottbus as well as its influence on urban space.

Students were asked to reflect on the role of the selected food products in shaping the built environment (Steel, 2009), be it as spaces of production, trade or consumption. Several groups highlighted the availability and omnipresence of certain products by mapping where they were

Places of sugar consumption: inner city area

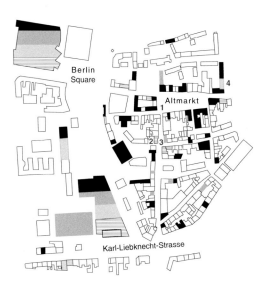

Consumption of sugar in public space: example Spremberger Street

	Gastronomy	1	Eiscafé Da Capo
	Shopping	2	Bakery Heimat & Herz
	Local supply	3	Confiserie arko
	Bakery/Confectionery	4	Asian market

Points of sale and consumption

Stand sale:

Outdoor gastronomic areas:

1   Markets (weekly and festivals)   3   Cafés and confectioneries
2   Ice cream and convenience shop   4   Restaurants
5   Bakeries

Sugar consumption of the city of Cottbus as a bulk cone (2018)

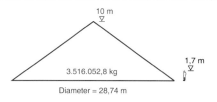

10 m

1,7 m

3.516.052,8 kg

Diameter = 28,74 m

Shelf in the "Cotti" Späti at the Karl-Marx-Strasse 14
Quantities and grey bars: sugar content per 100 g

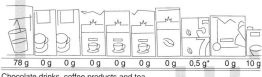

| 78 g | 0 g | 0 g | 0 g | 0 g | 0 g | 0 g | 0,5 g* | 0 g | 10 g |

Chocolate drinks, coffee products and tea

| 8,5 g | 3,2 g | 4,9 g | 5 g | 3 g | 0 g | 100 g | 100 g | 100 g | 0 g |

Milk, sugar and baking ingredients

Südzucker products

| 13 g | 41 g | 12,9 g | 15 g | 14,6 g | 75 g | 70 g | 55 g* | 56,3 g |

Jams, honey and nut nougat cream

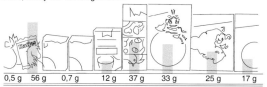

| 0,5 g | 56 g | 0,7 g | 12 g | 37 g | 33 g | 25 g | 17 g |

Breakfast cereals and sweets

Fig. 5: The omnipresence of sugar in the city centre of Cottbus. Left, a mapping of sales points including products with sugar, the map in the middle highlights the spatial significance of sugar consumption in Cottbus' major shopping street. Right, an analysis of the amounts of sugar in common food products (Daniel Cardué, Theres Marthaler, Natalie Schubert and Lukas Teschner)

sold. The group working on sugar focused on the old town of Cottbus and mapped all types of retail outlets that offered sugar in any form: supermarkets, cafés, bakeries, etc. (Cardué *et al.*, 2021). By means of perspective drawing based on photography and observation, they highlighted the spatial importance and visibility of sugar consumption in a major shopping promenade. They also visualised the amount of sugar in a wide range of everyday products based on a photographed shelf in a corner shop (fig. 5).

Rethinking the synergies between food mapping and architectural and urban analysis

This chapter presented a synergy of methods for following food, possibly the most basic requirement for urban life and urban growth. As argued in the first sections, the practice of *following things* is certainly not new. However, a focus on the representation and visualisation of different spatial scales, the operational role of architecture in the food industry, the different translocal processes embodied in products and the myriad of interconnected actors and networks involved in food supply chains can offer new opportunities to explore the performative power of maps in urban food mapping.

In their most basic form and through their selective nature, maps can shed light on hidden or unnoticed spaces and their importance for urban food supply (henhouses, for example). In conventional methodology, they support urban and architectural analysis by isolating certain dimensions or layers of the built environment (Bentlin, 2021). But maps can also reformulate spatial realities and make visible diverse and, at times, contrasting conditions beyond the physical attributes of a site (Corner, 2011). This is an important capacity as it allows us to consider the various hidden forces at work in, within and across a given space (Corner, 2011). Accordingly, mapping embodies two important operations: "*[the] digging, finding and exposing on the one hand, and relating, connecting and structuring on the other*" (Corner, 2011, p. 93). From a pedagogical point of view,

these operations – researching, representing, linking and structuring – can be reinforced by an iterative process of continuous discussion and revision of the maps (Bereskin and Quintero González, 2022). During the seminar, these discussions helped students improve their graphic and verbal skills to convey interdisciplinary research and gave us (the instructors) multiple opportunities to emphasise the importance of practices of "*thinking through drawing*", even in an increasingly digitalised field (Brown, 2006, p. 62). In the subsequent process of editing the maps for a collective digital publication, the students also grappled with finding a coherent graphic language, general legibility, data transparency and correct referencing.

With the teaching methodology and examples presented in this chapter, we would like to contribute to a 'pedagogy of food mapping' in architectural and urban planning education. This pedagogy is centred on teaching and learning about food issues, while establishing links between a multiplicity of processes taking place at global and local scales (Sumner, 2008) and underlining the importance of visualising such relations. As agents for learning and communication, maps (and the act of mapping) open new avenues for food studies, urban research and pedagogy to come together.

References

Ainsworth, S.E., and Scheiter, K., 2021. Learning by drawing visual representations: Potential, purposes, and practical implications. *Current Directions in Psychological Science*, 30 (1), 61–67. https://doi.org/10.1177/0963721420979582.
Assef, J., He, W., Jeschke, B., and Tombroff, A., 2021. Bananen. *In*: A. Hagemann and N. Quintero González, eds. *Feeding the city: Food cycles and the production of urban space*. Senftenberg: BTU Cottbus, 27–33. https://doi.org/10.26127/BTUOPEN-5505.
Bair, J., 2005. Global capitalism and commodity chains: Looking back, going forward. *Competition & Change*, 9 (2), 153–80. https://doi.org/10.1179/102452905X45382.
Baur, N., Hering, L., Raschke, A., and Thierbach, C., 2014. Theory and methods in spatial analysis. Towards integrating qualitative, quantitative and cartographic approaches in the social sciences and humanities. *Historical Social

Research/Historische Sozialforschung, 39 (2), 7–50. https://doi.org/10.12759/hsr.39.2014.2.7-50.

Bennett, J., 2010. Edible matter. *In: Vibrant matter: A political ecology of things*. Durham: Duke University Press, 133–145. https://doi.org/10.1215/9780822391623.

Bentlin, F., 2021. Städtebauliche schichtenanalyse. *In*: A.J. Heinrich, S. Marguin, A. Million and J. Stollmann, eds. *Handbuch qualitative und visuelle Methoden der Raumforschung*. Bielefeld: Transcript Verlag, 309–326.

Bereskin, E., and Quintero González, N.Q., 2022. Going to places and staying at home: Reflections on critical cartography and desktop documentation in online education. *In: Understanding site in design pedagogy*. London: Routledge, 29–50.

Beyer, E., Hagemann, A., and Misselwitz, P., 2020. Commodity flows and urban spaces. An introduction. *Articulo – Journal of Urban Research*, 21. https://doi.org/10.4000/articulo.4522.

Brenner, N., and Schmid, C., 2011. Planetary urbanisation. *In*: M. Gandy, ed. *Urban constellations*. Berlin: Jovis-Verl, 10–13.

Brenner, N., and Schmid, C., 2015. Towards a new epistemology of the urban? *City*, 19 (2–3), 151–182. https://doi.org/10.1080/13604813.2015.1014712.

Brown, M., 2006. For_getting drawing: Toward an architectural pedagogy for digital media. *In: Changing trends in architectural design education*. Rabat and Morocco: CSAAR, 59–79.

Cardué, D., Marthaler, T., Schubert, N., and Teschner, L., 2021. Zucker. *In*: A. Hagemann and N. Quintero González, eds. *Feeding the city: Food cycles and the production of urban space*. Senftenberg: BTU Cottbus, 34–40. https://doi.org/10.26127/BTUOPEN-5505.

Chen, M., Heiden, V., Kliesch, N., and Müller, J., 2021. Eier. *In*: A. Hagemann and N. Quintero González, eds. *Feeding the city: Food cycles and the production of urban space*. Senftenberg: BTU Cottbus, 41–47. https://doi.org/10.26127/BTUOPEN-5505.

Choplin, A., and Pliez, O., 2015. The inconspicuous spaces of globalization. *Articulo – Journal of Urban Research*, 12. https://journals.openedition.org/articulo/2905.

Cook, I., 2004. Follow the thing: Papaya. *Antipode*, 36 (4), 642–64. https://doi.org/10.1111/j.1467-8330.2004.00441.x.

Cook, I., et al., 2006. Geographies of food: Following. *Progress in Human Geography*, 30 (5), 655–666. https://doi.org/10.1177/0309132506070183.

Corner, J., 2011. The agency of mapping: Speculation, critique and invention. *In*: M. Dodge, R. Kitchin and C. Perkins, eds. *The map reader*. Chichester: John Wiley & Sons, Ltd, 89–101. https://doi.org/10.1002/9780470979587.ch12.

Ermann, U., 2015. '"Wissen, wo's herkommt"– Geographien des guten Essens, der Transparenz und der Moral der Herkunft von Lebensmitteln'. *In*: A. Strüver, ed. *Geographien der Ernährung – Zwischen Nachhaltigkeit, Unsicherheit und Verantwortung* (Hamburger Symposium Geographie 7). Hamburg: Institut für Geographie der Universität Hamburg, 77–94.

Fritsche, J., Henklein, L.R., Piro, J.T., and Zappe, L., 2021. Tee. *In*: A. Hagemann and N.Q. González, eds. *Feeding the city: Food cycles and the production of urban space*. Senftenberg: BTU Cottbus, 62–68. https://doi.org/10.26127/BTUOPEN-5505.

Gereffi, G., and Korzeniewicz, M. (eds.), 1994. *Commodity chains and global capitalism* (1. publ. Contributions in Economics and Economic History). Westport, CT: Praeger.

Hagemann, A., 2015. 'From flagship store to factory: Tracing the spaces of transnational clothing production in Istanbul'. *Articulo – Journal of Urban Research*, 12. https://doi.org/10.4000/articulo.2889.

Hagemann, A., and Beyer, E., 2020. Globalizing urban research, grounding global production networks. Transnational clothing production and the built environment. *Articulo – Journal of Urban Research*, 21. https://doi.org/10.4000/articulo.4622.

Hagemann, A., and González, N.Q. (eds.), 2021. *Feeding the City. Lebensmittelkreisläufe Und Die Produktion Städtischer Räume*. Cottbus: Brandenburgische Technische Universität Cottbus-Senftenberg, IKMZ – Universitätsbibliothek.

Harvey, D., 1990. Between space and time: Reflections on the geographical imagination. *Annals of the Association of American Geographers*, 80 (3), 418–34. https://doi.org/10.1111/j.1467-8306.1990.tb00305.x.

Hein, C., 2018. 'Oil spaces: The global petroleumscape in the Rotterdam/The Hague Area'. *Journal of Urban History*, 44 (5), 887–929. https://doi.org/10.1177/0096144217752460.

Heinzmann, T., Matthias, L., von Thienen, L., and Zeißig, H., 2021. 'Bier'. *In*: A. Hagemann and N.Q. González, eds. *Feeding the city: food cycles and the production of urban space*. Senftenberg: BTU Cottbus, 55–61. https://doi.org/10.26127/BTUOPEN-5505.

Henderson, J., Dicken, P., Hess, M., Coe, N., and Wai-Chung Yeung, H., 2002. Global production networks and the analysis of economic development. *Review of International Political Economy*, 9 (3), 436–64. https://doi.org/10.1080/09692290210150842.

Hughes, A., and Reimer, S., 2004. *Geographies of commodity chains*. London: Routledge.

Hulme, A., 2015. *On the commodity trail. The journey of a Bargain Store product from east to west*. Bloomsbury Publishing. Available from www.bloomsbury.com/uk/on-the-commodity-trail-9781472572868/.

Ibert, O., Hess, M., Kleibert, J., Müller, F., and Dominic Power., 2019. Geographies of dissociation: value creation, "dark" places, and "missing" links. *Dialogues in Human Geography*, 9 (1), 43–63. https://doi.org/10.1177/2043820619831114.

Jensen, D., Roy, M., and Jaffe, K., 2013. *Food: An atlas*. Oakland: Guerrilla Cartograph.

Kiyooka, S., Smith, F.C., and Slobodian, Q. (eds.), 2013. Mapping food matters. A resource on place based food system mapping. *GroundWorks, LifeCycles, Common Ground, and Oxfam Canada*. Available from https://foodsecurecanada.org/sites/foodsecurecanada.org/files/Mapping_food_matters.pdf.

Knowles, C., 2014. *Flip-flop: A journey through globalisation's backroads*. London: Pluto Press.

Krätke, S., Wildner, K., and Lanz, S., 2012. The transnationality of cities: Concepts, dimensions and research fields. An introduction. *In: Transnationalism and urbanism*. New York: Routledge, 1–30.

Kurath, M., and Bürgin, R., 2019. Einleitung: Planung relational denken. *In: Planung ist unsichtbar*. Transcript Verlag. Available from www.degruyter.com/document/doi/10.14361/9783839448533-001/html.

LeCavalier, J., 2016. *The rule of logistics: Walmart and the architecture of fulfillment*. University of Minnesota Press. https://muse.jhu.edu/book/47864.

Lyster, C., 2016. *Learning from logistics: How networks change our cities*. Basel: Birkhäuser.

Patel, R., 2019. The epistemology of the shopping cart. *In*: A. Cezar and D. Burrows, eds. *Politics of food*. London: Delfina Foundation, Sternberg Press, 16–26.

Schraw, G., McCrudden, M.T., and Robinson, D., 2013. *Learning through visual displays*. London: IAP.

Smiciklas, M., 2012. *The power of infographics: Using pictures to communicate and connect with your audience*. Indianapolis, IN: Que Pub.

Steel, C., 2009. *Hungry City: How food shapes our lives*. London: Vintage.

Strüver, A., 2020. Urbane Metabolismen: Verkörperte Politische Ökologien des e/Essens. *sub\urban. zeitschrift für kritische stadtforschung*, 8 (1/2), 99–116. https://doi.org/10.36900/suburban.v8i1/2.497.

Sumner, J., 2008. Eating as a pedagogical act: Food as a catalyst for adult education for sustainable development. *In: Thinking beyond borders: Global ideas, global values. proceedings of the Canadian Association for the Study of Adult Education (CASAE)*. Vancouver: CASAE, 352–356.

Topalovic, M., Knüsel, M., and Jäggi, M., 2013. *Architecture of territory – Hinterland: Singapore, Johor, Ria Institut Für Geschichte Und Theorie Der Architektur (Zürich)*. Zürich: ETH Zürich DArch. http://topalovic.arch.ethz.ch/materials/hinterland/.

Tsing, A.L., 2015. *The mushroom at the end of the world: On the possibility of life in capitalist ruins*. Princeton, NJ: Princeton University Press.

Turner, J., 2016. Food illustration: A morsel on the medium. *Cuizine: The Journal of Canadian Food Cultures/Cuizine: Revue Des Cultures Culinaires Au Canada*, 7 (2). https://doi.org/10.7202/1038481ar.

Rupturing the mundane in times of crisis: New geographies of food in Hannover, Germany

Gesine Tuitjer, Leonie Tuitjer and Anna-Lisa Müller

Grocery shopping is a mundane yet essential task, whereas eating out and take-away are pleasures many people enjoy within the city. Food connects us to each other, to distant places and to the local neighbourhood (Edwards and Mercer, 2010). Emotions and affects, as well as politics, shape the socio-spatial and material flows of urban food provisioning (Edwards and Davies, 2018). Both the mundane necessity and the pleasures attributed to food practices came to a sharp halt in 2020. The worldwide spread of the Sars-CoV-2 virus caused rampant suffering and loss: through June 2022, more than 6 million lives were mourned worldwide. Lockdowns, stay at home orders and the closure of many social and cultural institutions warranted a social, cultural, political and geographical reckoning with complex consequences (Ho and Maddrell, 2020; Sparke and Anguelov, 2020).

Everyday food shopping under Covid measures

We explore how this crisis produced severe changes in the spatial order and related practices of perhaps the most mundane everyday activity: buying and consuming food. For 12 months, we observed two inner-city neighbourhoods in northern Germany by collecting photographs and drawing maps of their food provisioning. These images record the changed relations between consumers, food and the city during the pandemic. They become tools to our aim of making visible and archiving pandemic ruptures which would otherwise be quickly forgotten as the changes they induced stabilise

into new "normal" routines and practices. Our chapter contributes to literature on urban (food) mapping within times of crisis and on the Covid-19 pandemic especially (Cattivelli and Rusciano, 2020; Gundersen et al., 2017; Donaldson et al., 2020).

Mapping inner-city food procurement in times of crisis

Our two research sites – Linden-Mitte and Nordstadt – are located in Hanover, the capital city of Lower Saxony in northern Germany which has approximately 500,000 inhabitants. They are densely populated neighbourhoods with a majority of four-storey brick buildings from the 1880s, erected to lodge workers and executives of the then industrialising city. Today, the two neighbourhoods show clear signs of gentrification. They are "ordinary" and typical of northern Germany's urban features, as well as being understudied places (Robinson, 2006). We argue that our mapping of food access and consumption during the pandemic can be indicative of changes experienced in similar-structured neighbourhoods across the country.

This chapter is inspired by the collaborative auto-ethnography approach (CAE) proposed by Roy and Uekusa (2020) in the context of doing research in pandemic times. CAE is a particularly suitable research method when social distancing and "stay at home" measures limit social interactions as this method enabled us to "[study] society through *ourselves*" (Roy and

DOI: 10.4324/9781003352280-13

Fig. 1a+b: Changes to the way space is being used happened indoors and outdoors as seen in a supermarket and outside of it

Uekusa, 2020, p. 384, original emphasis). CAE entails a meshwork of data, comprising of short notes, vignettes, photographs and maps. In our case, photographs were taken during routine walks through the two neighbourhoods, mostly while food shopping ourselves (fig. 1). Cohen (2012) pointed out that crisis situations bear the opportunity to reflect anew upon one's relationship with familiar environments. Mapping changes by taking pictures was our initial pre-reflexive and non-verbal way to document the changes that we saw. We then used the photographs to share observations within the group for collaborative interpretation (Parkin *et al.*, 2021). Later on, we drew maps of the photographed changes to *"visualise the relationship between ethnographic observations (of activities, events, work) and underlying (social, economic, environmental and institutional) processes"* (Parkin *et al.*, 2021, p. 560). For example, the position of people who adhere to social distancing becomes visible in the pictures, standing at least 1 metre apart from each other (see figs. 3 and 7). This new use of space is orchestrated by

multiple signs, such as tape on the floor, which, however, is mostly invisible in the pictures. In this manner, the many small activities and signs we caught in photographs were subsequently interpreted and condensed into a drawn map, bringing together in one visualisation the most substantive structural changes as observed from our perspective.

Accessing food procurement in times of crisis

Diverse literature on consumer behaviour, retail and business management tells us that behaviour in times of crisis differs from routine practices (Boost and Meier, 2017; Saridakis, 2012; Sarasa *et al.*, 2020). For much of western society, food consumption involves dispersed sites and increasingly sensitive timings of production, storage and distribution and thus connects people and products across vast time-spaces in dispersed food networks (Crang, 1996). These food networks (or supply chains) can become subject to disruptions in times of crisis (Hall *et al.*, 2020). In contrast, for many

Fig. 2: Regulation signage

Fig. 3: Floor signage

people on the planet, food provision is always in crisis. In Linden-Mitte and Nordstadt, we focused on changing regulations, structures and spaces in two types of food outlets: supermarkets and farmers' markets.

Shops in the first national lockdown (March 2020)

While German supermarkets stayed open during lockdowns throughout the pandemic, how food was bought in supermarkets changed. In the first lockdown, people had to use supermarket-provided baskets or trolleys to do their shopping. This strategy helped supermarket staff to regulate the number of people within the market. People were advised to keep their distance from each other, and supermarkets erected barriers between customers and clerks to maintain social distancing rules. In supermarkets all over the city, new markings appeared, telling people where to queue in front of shops and the required distance to keep apart (see figs. 2 and 3).

The ordinary task of buying bread or vegetables required re-learning how to navigate the city

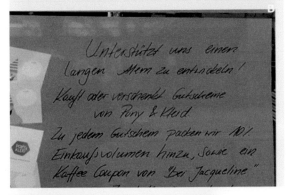

Fig. 4: Signs of solidarity and thank you

and the modifying of one's mental maps of the city (Lynch, 1960). Figures 1–3 contribute to a relational understanding of the space within the supermarket where bodies and objects were spatially re-ordered to conform to distancing rules. Social distancing re-evaluated how (close) we could move and how to (re)position our bodies when obtaining food. The images show how the pandemic challenged geographic categories like proximity, distance and inside/ outside. The entrance of the supermarket for example became an unsurpassable border for those who forgot to bring their mask, and new practices such as putting on a face mask marked the transition between "inside" and "outside". The conversion of the supermarket from a once "ordinary" into a now potentially dangerous space resulted in a significant increase in online grocery shopping (Dannenberg *et al.*, 2020). Furthermore, supermarket staff were honoured

Fig. 5: Location of Linden-Mitte Market within the neighbourhood (source: Google, 2022)

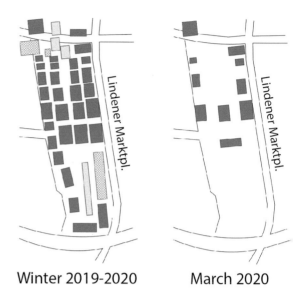

Winter 2019-2020 **March 2020**

Fig. 6: Changes to the spatial set-up of stalls on the market in accordance to changing public health regulations

as essential brave workers, as expressed by German news outlets. The pandemic thus not only altered spatial practice but also changed the symbolic meaning of everyday shopping.

The pandemic also changed the relationship between consumers and businesses and the way how shopping from small shops works. In the course of the pandemic and the subsequent lockdown, especially small-shop owners had to adjust to this difficult situation. They did so by calling onto the solidarity of their local customers (Tuitjer *et al.*, 2023) and by inventing new modes of shopping. In contrast to supermarkets, where the new regulation of the flow of people, their position in space and the health-related requirements for customers made it possible to maintain shopping on site, small shops were temporarily forced to close. However, a new mode of shopping established quickly, with the small shops offering different sorts of "remote" shopping. The following photos bear witness to the creativity of these

makeshift alternatives to large online stores. Thus, window-shopping was proposed by the small stores, orders could be placed via phone or mail and purchased items had to be picked up during announced "pick-up" times (fig. 4).

The farmers' market (June 2020)

In many countries, particular features of market spaces, such as store density, open boundaries and public character, were considered a risk during the Covid-19 pandemic, because of their linkage to previous outbreaks of zoonotic diseases (Munster *et al.*, 2018; van Eck *et al.*, 2020). Despite the prevalence of supermarkets for food retail in Western countries like Germany, farmers' markets still play a considerable role in urban food provisions across the world (Gonzaléz, 2019).

The Linden-Mitte farmers' market researched here provides organic and small food manufacturers' products as well as take-away food and

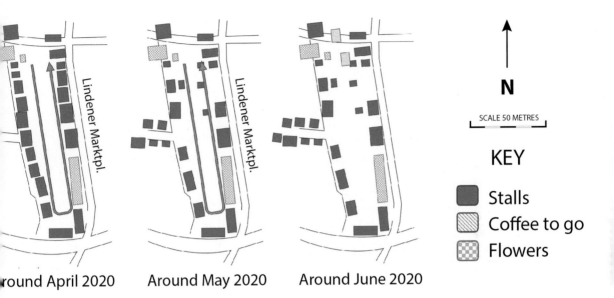

N

SCALE 50 METRES

KEY

■ Stalls
▨ Coffee to go
▦ Flowers

Around April 2020   Around May 2020   Around June 2020

beverages, some of them catered from the cafés surrounding the market space, which altogether makes it a very popular place in the neighbourhood and even beyond (fig. 5). Before the Covid-19 pandemic, the Linden-Mitte farmers' market had about 40 stalls and more than 200 visitors during its peak hours on Saturday mornings in summer. This popularity changed profoundly during the pandemic. From the beginning of the pandemic in March 2020 until about June, the order of the market stalls changed almost monthly due to revised public safety measures. First, flower and take-away stalls and other "non-essential" stalls were banned from the marketplace. This way, the remaining food stalls could spread out over the entire marketplace, providing more space for people to maintain distance. By summer 2020, a one-way path was introduced to the market where people were asked not to move against the flow. This way, grocery shopping took much longer. By no longer allowing the on-site consumption of food and coffee the market lost its function as a place to mingle. Because sampling the food from the stalls was forbidden, too, the lively and

atmospheric relationship between people, food and the senses changed. The contained chaos of the market was replaced by orderly rows and a uni-directional path (Black, 2012) (fig. 6).

This new ordering resembled the historical evolution of western supermarkets with their highly organised aisles of different product types and increased distancing between customers and staff, making food shopping more efficient (Humphery, 2012). Indeed, the subsequent loss of conviviality at the farmers' market was decried as a temporary "death" of public space by Dutch researchers who noticed similar interventions (van Eck, van Melik and Schapendonk, 2020, p. 374). While there was a decline of conviviality at the Linden-Mitte market, our map shows that the absolute physical space of the market actually expanded to include the adjacent street to accommodate the original number of stalls to allow for social distancing. Hence, the map does not capture the lost opportunities for socialising and the market's altered atmosphere, reminding us that maps are selective in what they can or cannot make visible (Carolan, 2021).

Fig. 7: Customers queuing in an expanded line at Linden-Mitte farmers' market

Disrupting local symbolics

The current pandemic has altered the way we relate to food in the city. Public health measures challenged routines and practices, and shared understandings of space, belonging and home. Eating in the city acquired a new dimension of uncertainty as routines were de-stabilised and rules and regulations regarding grocery shopping were in flux. These disruptions to urban food practices are by no means trivial, revealing profound changes in everyday procurement and consumption. Such a *"temporary death . . . is likely to impact people's sense of reflexive awareness and common experience of community and belonging"* (van Eck *et al.*, 2020, p. 376). Our photographs and maps make visible how disruption of procurement practices stemming from a global crisis can profoundly impact local symbolic and social dimensions within neighbourhoods (fig. 7).

References

Black, R.E., 2012. *Porta Palazzo. The anthropology of an Italian market*. Philadelphia, PA: University of Pennsylvania Press.

Boost, M., and Meier, L., 2017. Resilient practices of consumption in times of crisis – Biographical interviews with members of vulnerable households in Germany. *International Journal of Consumption Studies*, 41 (3), 71–378. https://doi.org/10.1111/ijcs.12346

Carolan, M., 2021. Putting food access in its topological place: Thinking in terms of relational becomings when mapping space. *Agriculture and Human Values*, 38, 243–256. https://doi.org/10.1007/s10460–020–10149-y

Cattivelli, V., and Rusciano, V., 2020. Social innovation and food provisioning during COVID-19: The case of urban-rural initiatives in the Province of Naples. *Sustainability*, 12, 4444. https://doi.org/10.3390/su12114444

Cohen, E., 2012. Flooded: An auto-ethnography of the 2011 Bangkok flood. *Aktuelle Südostasienforschung/Current Research on South East Asia*, 5 (2), 316–334. https://doi.org/10.4232/10.ASEAS-5.2–8

Crang, P., 1996. Displacement, consumption, and identity. *Environment and Planning A, Economy and Space*, 28 (1), 47–67. https://doi.org/10.1068/a280047

Dannenberg, P., Fuchs, M., Riedler, T., and Wiedemann, C., 2020. Digital transition by COVID-19 pandemic? The German food online retail. *Tijdschrift voor Economische en Sociale Geographie*, 111 (3), 543–560. https://doi.org/10.1111/tesg.12453

Donaldson, A., Brice, J., and Midgley, J., 2020. Navigating futures: Anticipation and food supply chain mapping. *The Transactions of the Institute of British Geographer*, 45, 606–618. https://doi.org/10.1111/tran.12363

Edwards, F., and Davies, A.R., 2018. Connective consumptions: Mapping Melbourne's food sharing ecosystem. *Urban Policy and Research*, 36 (4), 476–495. https://doi.org/10.1080/08111146.2018.1476231

Edwards, F., and Mercer, D., 2010. Meals in metropolis: Mapping the urban foodscape in Melbourne, Australia. *Local Environment*, 15 (2), 153–168. https://doi.org/10.1080/13549830903527662

Gundersen, C., Dewey, A., Hake, M., Engelhard, E., and Crumbaugh, A., 2017. Food insecurity across the rural-urban divide: Are counties in need being reached by charitable food assistance? *AAPSS*, 672, 217–237. https://doi.org/10.1177/0002716217710172

Gonzaléz, S., 2019. Contested marketplaces: Retail spaces at the global urban margins. *Progress in Human Geography*, 44 (5), 877–897. https://doi.org/10.1177/03091 32519 859444

Hall, M.C., Prayag, G., Fieger, P., and Dyason, D., 2020. Beyond panic buying: Consumption displacement and COVID 19. *Journal of Service Management*, 32 (1), 113–128. https://doi.org/10.1108/JOSM-05–2020–0151

Ho, E.L.E., and Maddrell, A., 2020. Intolerable intersectional burdens: A COVID-19 research agenda for social and cultural geographies. *Social & Cultural Geography*, 22 (1), 1–10. https://doi.org/10.1080/14649365.2020.1837215

Humphery, K., 2012. *Shelf life: Supermarkets and the changing cultures of consumption*. Cambridge: Cambridge University Press.

Lynch, K., 1960. *The image of the city*. Illustrated ed. Cambridge, MA: MIT Press.

Munster, V.J., et al., 2018. Outbreaks in a rapidly changing Central Africa – Lessons from Ebola. *New England Journal of Medicine*, 379, 343–358. https://doi.org/10.1056/NEJMp1807691

Parkin, S., Locock, L., Montgomery, C., and Chisholm, A., 2021. Team ethnography visual maps': Methods for identifying the ethnographic object in multiple sites of fieldwork. *Ethnography*, 22, 556–577.

Robinson, J., 2006. *Ordinary cities: Between modernity and development. Questioning cities*. London and New York: Routledge.

Roy, R., and Uekusa, S., 2020. Collaborative autoethnography: "Self-reflection" as a timely alternative research approach during the global pandemic. *Qualitative Research Journal*, 20 (4), 383–92. https://doi.org/10.1108/QRJ-06–2020–0054.

Sarasa, M.A., de Castro Pericacho, C., and Paz Martín, M.P., 2020. Consumption as a social integration strategy in times of crisis: The case of vulnerable households. *International Journal of Consumption Studies*, 44, 111–121. https://doi.org/10.1111/ijcs.12550

Saridakis, G., 2012. Introduction to the special issue on enterprise activity, performance and policy during times of crisis. *International Small Business Journal*, 30 (7), 733–735. https://doi.org/10.1177/0266242612457404

Sparke, M., and Anguelov, D., 2020. Contextualising coronavirus geographically. *Transactions of the Institute of British Geographers*, 1–11. https://doi.org/10.1111/tran.12389

Tuitjer, A.L., Tuitjer, G., and Müller, A.L., 2023. Buycotting to save the neighbourhood? Exploring the altered meaning of social infrastructures of consumption during the Covid-19 crisis in Linden, Hannover, Germany. *Social & Cultural Geography* 24 (3–4), 640–660. https://doi.org/10.1080/14649365.2022.2115537

van Eck, E., van Melik, R., and Schapendonk, J., 2020. Marketplaces as public spaces in times of the Covid-19 coronavirus outbreak: First reflections. *Tijdschrift voor Economische en Sociale Geographie*, 11 (3), 373–386. https://doi.org/10.1111/tesg.12431

FOOD STAKEHOLDERS: Proposing change for communities

This section acknowledges a new wave of emerging urban food maps that disrupt traditional mapping approaches. The most radical of these are often called 'counter or guerrilla mapping' where **critical cartography democratises the practice of mapping** to make counterclaims, to express competing interests around food, to make practical plans for social change or to imagine utopian worlds.

The chapters show how through participation with maps, locals can be invited to insert detailed knowledge about food practices and spaces within their cities. Such **urban food mappings can help advocate for the actions and desires of residents to make something happen**, such as aiding informal food security or urban agriculture. Often, counter-maps are used to lay claim to land with clear political and ecological goals. Counter cartography can highlight diversity within the urban food system whilst harnessing opportunities for socio-ecological change through revealing new connections between people, place and what we eat. Map makers apply the entire breadth of mapping methods and techniques, from oral interview via drawing and performance to digital and satellite imagery.

DOI: 10.4324/9781003352280-14

Janie Bickersteth et al.'s chapter describes how the Incredible Edible Lambeth initiative in London, UK, used two **mapping projects to catalyse change within municipal decisionmakers**, where urban food growing can contribute to improved health and wellbeing. Working with engineering firm Arup, they combine new digital mapping technologies, citizen science and participatory methods to highlight yet unknown potential food growing spaces.

Adrian Paulsen and Bradley Rink dissect the artificial divide between formal and informal food networks, both spatially and socio-economically. Their mappings consist of drawn, photographed and narrated visualisations, rich in context and detail, **challenging what it means for citizens to be food (in)secure** in Delft, South Africa. These inform local food security strategies, responding to the complexities of wider survival options.

Mikey Tomkins explores the potential Edible Urban Landscape through drawn maps, walking tours, performance and growing. His essay documents over ten years of participatory mapping projects, focusing on one project in Newcastle, UK. Here, initial **map walks were transformed into a year of community wheat growing, harvesting and baking**. The project ends with a performance, where a new costumed entity walks into the city to protect the urban harvest.

Paula Restrepo echoes Lefebvre's 'right to the city' and calls for inhabitants to challenge and transform an economic system that supports unfair, unequal and dangerous cities, asking: Could urban farmers contribute positively to social and environmental change? As an activist-researcher, she uses **mapping to strengthen the networks of urban agriculture practitioners and practices** in Medellín, Colombia.

Katrin Bohn explores the relationships between 'mapping food' and 'mapping food opportunities' in spatial planning and urban design focussing on **urban food maps as communication tools in participatory and co-design processes**. Comparing urban food mapping projects in two cities, she demonstrates how spatial and network visualisations that emanate from existing local food system activities can support strategies for resilient urban food futures.

Food stake-holders

	Purpose WHY?	Citizen WHO?
	recording *counting* *comparing* *uncovering* *responding* *proposing*	*urban farmers* *food system activists* *food initiatives* *consumers* *local communities* *public institutions*
Bickersteth et al. Lambeth plots: Highlighting existing and potential inner-city spaces for food growing	counting food activities recording land use 	local communities / public institu 
Paulsen et al. The practice of sharing: Mapping food networks in Delft, South Africa	recording food culture comparing food activities 	food initiatives / consumers 
Tomkins Six feet high and rising: Mapping the Edible City as a theatre of food	uncovering food spaces proposing change 	food system activists public institutions 
Restrepo Mapping seeds of freedom with Red de Huerteros Medellín	uncovering stakeholders counting spaces 	local communities / public institu 
Bohn Food in urban design and planning: The CPUL Opportunity Mapping Method	recording stakeholders counting spaces 	urban farmers / food initiative 

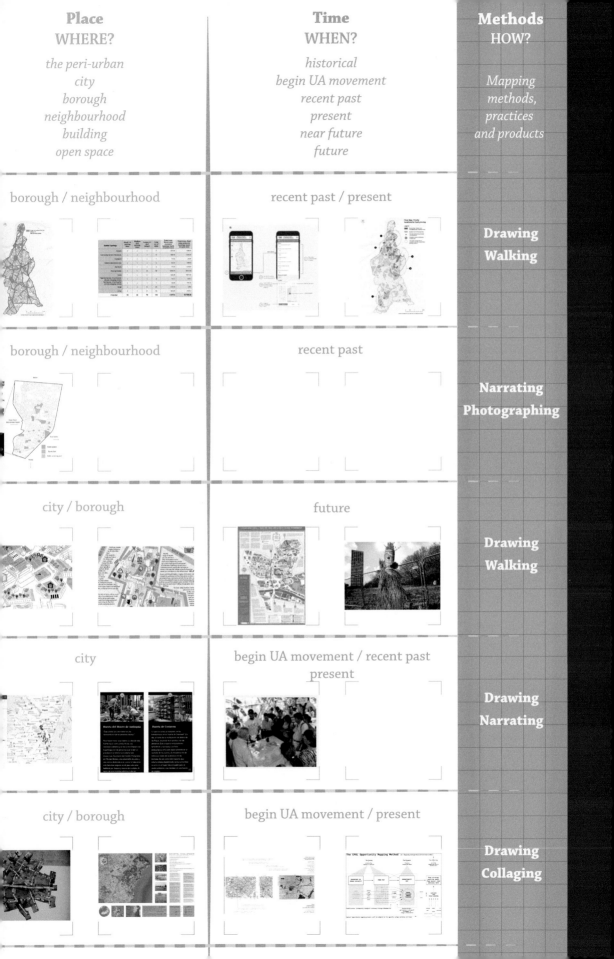

Lambeth plots: Two mapping projects highlighting existing and potential city spaces for food growing

Janie Bickersteth, Joana Ferro, Marjorie Landels and Stephanie Robson

The links between inequity, access to food and land are important to recognise, even in wealthy nations such as the UK. In many cities, a significant proportion of households are classed as food-insecure and in London this figure is 20% (Greater London Authority, 2019). The poorest urban communities often also have the least access to quality green space and are at higher risk of mental and physical wellbeing issues (Groundwork UK, 2021).

The London borough of Lambeth, population 325,000, is ranked the 44th most deprived local authority in England (from 326), with 31% of the population living in areas of high deprivation (Lambeth Council, 2017). The North of the borough is densely populated with housing estates and neighbourhoods that have poor access to fresh food. Most estates are managed by Lambeth Council and have some land surrounding them, historically managed for minimum effort (with short mowing and pruning cycles) (see fig. 1), leaving these spaces as unattractive areas where there is little chance for biodiversity to flourish and nothing to make them places you would want to linger. The challenge is how to engage and encourage many more residents to help transform these (currently) barren spaces into areas for recreation, food growing and biodiversity, with a happy 'bi-product' being the knitting of communities and an improvement to social wellbeing (Veen et al., 2015). This is the remit of the *Incredible Edible* movement.

Incredible Edible Lambeth (IEL) is one of 150 *Incredible Edibles* across the world with the inclusive motto of '*If you eat, you're in*'. It is working

to support the re-localisation of food. IEL, with its 120 community and 562 individual members (mostly food growers), is uniquely placed to work in the more deprived areas of the borough, as many members live on housing estates. IEL recognises the multiple advantages of growing food as mentioned earlier, especially in a community garden context, with additional gains including enhanced nutritional content of meals, mental health benefits, being outside in nature, putting your hands in the soil (which boosts your immune system), socialising, sharing food and reducing one's carbon footprint.

Acknowledging that it is the deprived communities who would most benefit from more local food, IEL has been focusing on the land surrounding the 150 council-owned housing estates and is starting to support local communities to transform these spaces into community gardens for food (see fig. 2). Food growing is anything but mainstream in our cities, perceived as an older generation's 'hobby', not as a 'must have'. It is evident that in just one generation, the knowledge around growing food has been lost. IEL is trying to understand the triggers that shift people back to the land, helping them to engage more with their immediate outdoor space, bringing with it the many benefits already outlined.

We have found that how these spaces are occupied is deeply affected by social economics. Through recent work funded by the Mayor of London's *Grow Back Greener* initiative, IEL has witnessed land ownership issues, suspicion of residents, a reticence to volunteer and work with neighbours,

DOI: 10.4324/9781003352280-15

Fig. 1: A Lambeth estate

Fig. 2: Valcie in ALTHTRA Community Garden

a lacking sense of solidarity, no clear steer from the housing officers or the main contractors working on estates in Lambeth and, most of all, a lack of agency for these communities. Of the six estates IEL has been working with, the two estates that have flourished have been where a group of people have freely given up their time to create new vibrant growing spaces. Their enthusiasm has been infectious and has given others the courage to get involved. One thriving green space is on an estate that is under constant threat from demolition, so that residents already had a fierce sense of solidarity about their immediate environment. Another successful green space has seen people come together to transform the land directly in front of their homes. They have witnessed immediate benefit to their households' outlooks and neighbours have begun to communicate with each other in a very positive way, sharing the care of flower and vegetable beds.

Whilst these are positive examples, IEL has also understood that multiple factors prevent engagement with green space in our cities. To overcome this, IEL is engaging in two mapping projects. IEL's ambition for all Lambeth residents to live no more than 100 metres from a food growing space has driven this work. Residents need to know where the growing spaces are and maps show the gaps, reveal current activities and highlight the possibilities. Mapping is the first stage for gathering information and an initial land audit.

Walking trails

It is a prolonged process bringing people back to nature, but by highlighting what is already happening in green spaces in the many communities that make up Lambeth, IEL wanted to help residents discover their neighbourhoods for themselves. Producing local, user-friendly pocket walking trails seemed to provide a great starting point for engagement; a bridge to connect people and places.

Despite the gloomy statistics about Lambeth's barren housing estates, the borough (like many urban landscapes) has scores of hidden food production niches. Over the past seven years, IEL has been developing walking trails of different neighbourhoods. Focusing on the green spaces (including parks and playgrounds), the primary aim of each map is to shine a light on the many food growing spaces in the borough (IEL [n.d.] a). The maps signpost people off the main thoroughfares and facilitate the discovery of local green spaces. The trails are proving to be a valuable form of social prescription and are distributed to all pharmacies, health centres, libraries, housing officers and schools along the route. The maps are easy to read, beautifully illustrated and are provided in hard copy as an A6 double-sided cross-fold that easily fits into a pocket, or as a downloadable pdf. Each map contains two trails of different lengths, with toilets and benches marked (two barriers to people

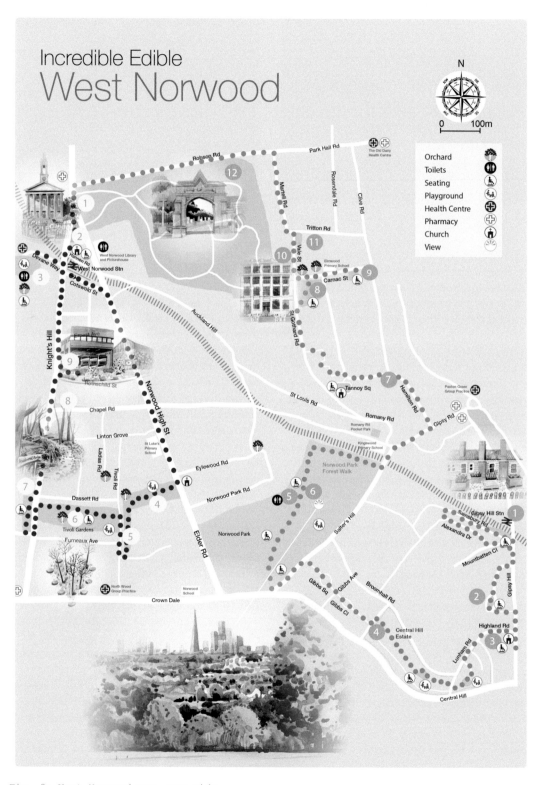

Fig. 3: West Norwood map, map side

These two trails take you on a voyage of discovery around the many green spaces and secret outdoor spots in West Norwood and Gipsy Hill. On the map we have highlighted places for children to play and enjoy Nature, places to grow food, places to eat and places to sit. We hope it enables you to connect with your local community and get growing!

Incredible Edible Lambeth is a network of food growers, food entrepreneurs and food activists all working to improve our communities.

Our motto is 'If you eat, you're in' ... it's that simple, everyone can get involved with us - join our network today by signing up to become a member at www.incredibleediblelambeth.org/join.

Membership is free and you will immediately be linked in with hundreds of other growers, green spaces, allotments, gardens, parks and more throughout the borough.

Get in touch:
www.incredibleediblelambeth.org
☐ questions@incredibleediblelambeth.org
☐ ediblelambeth
☐ incredibleediblelambeth
☐ EdibleLambeth

Incredible Edible
West Norwood
illustrations by Lis Watkins

Two trails exploring hidden green spaces and food growing in West Norwood and Gipsy Hill

Incredible Edible West Norwood
Please refer to the map for the location of the projects listed

West Norwood route

1 West Norwood Cemetery
2 St Luke's Church *
3 West Norwood Health and Leisure Centre
(Orchard and Playground)
4 Wood Vale Community Garden
5 Wood Vale Orchard and Wildflower Garden
6 Tivoli Park Orchard and Wildflower Garden
7 Knight's Hill Wood
8 West Norwood Gateway Garden
9 West Norwood Bzz Garage

4,531 steps / 3.157km

* (FEAST every 1st Sunday of the month 10am - 4pm
https://westnorwoodfeast.com/)

Gipsy Hill route

1 Gipsy Hill Station Garden
2 Becondale Road Garden
3 Christ Church Memorial Garden
4 Central Hill Community Garden
5 Norwood Park Community Allotments
6 Norwood Park Orchard
7 Gipsy Hill Brewing Company
8 Resistance Memorial
9 Carnac Street Community Garden
10 Parkhall Business Centre
11 Tritton Vale Pocket Garden
12 West Norwood Cemetery

7,421 steps / 5.171km

Fig. 4: West Norwood map, back and front cover (when folded)

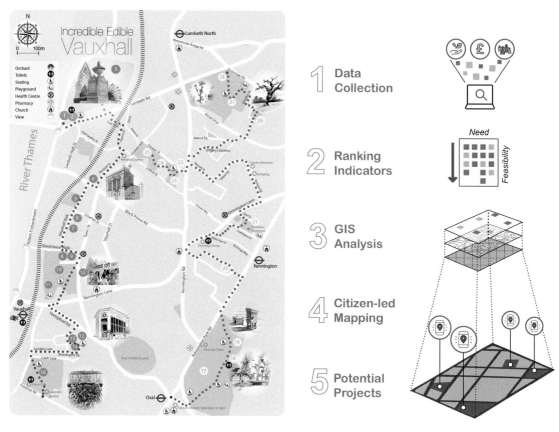

Fig. 5: Vauxhall map   Fig. 6: Mapping analysis process (Arup, 2021)

taking a walk are the lack of both). Parks, local cafes, playgrounds, health centres, schools and community gardens are marked along the trails and in later maps, IEL has provided distance and steps, for those wanting to use the trails as part of a fitness programme. In 2018 IEL's Brixton map was used by 50 schools for a *Clean Air Week*, revealing to young people (and their families) how to navigate their neighbourhood away from the more polluted main roads. The maps highlight community gardens to encourage more people to get involved with food growing.

IEL's newest trails (West Norwood [see figs. 3 and 4] and Stockwell) contain a QR code that

directs people to the IEL website for further information. Eventually, IEL plans to map the whole borough, funding allowing.

The Vauxhall map (see fig. 5) has been taken up by a local pharmacy and several NHS link workers as a social prescribing tool, offered to clients who would benefit from a more active lifestyle.

Increasingly, these trails will be used for guided tours, which IEL hopes will enable funders and the Council to see at first hand the multiple benefits of transforming what would otherwise be barren land into fruitful community spaces.

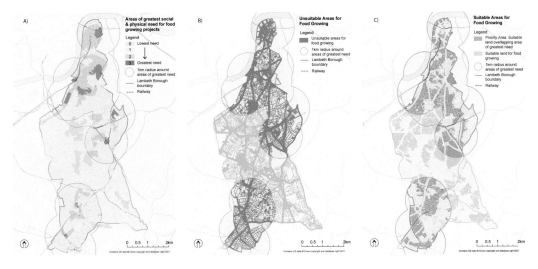

Fig. 7: Need and feasibility maps (Arup, 2021)

Lambeth plots: Mapping land for food

In 2020, IEL partnered with Arup's GIS and landscape architecture consultants to explore opportunities for a sustainable food future in the London borough of Lambeth. The partnership began during the first nationwide Covid-19 lockdown when a member of the Arup team attended *Lambeth Food Stories* hosted by IEL (IEL [n.d.] b). The *Lambeth plots* project developed a comprehensive urban food growing map for Lambeth that identified existing and potential food growing spaces in the borough. The project used a combination of geographic information system (GIS) software using collated open source datasets and conducted citizen-led mapping for the analysis (see fig. 6 for the process) (IEL [n.d.] c). This research revealed opportunity areas for potential urban food growing across different spatial typologies, to systematically increase urban food production by bringing together bottom-up food growing with strategic city priorities using a scalable and replicable methodology. The intention is for this methodology to be easily applied in different boroughs across London or in urban areas further afield to inform future local development and investment, particularly in neighbourhoods with poor access to open space and/or healthy food options. This work aligns

with London's Food Strategy and supports Lambeth Council's goals to '*increase access to publicly owned land for community food growing*' (Lambeth Council, 2021), as well as helping to identify the potential to fulfil community aspirations around ownership and agency within their environment.

The series of maps were developed using GIS and open source spatial data to analyse and identify areas in '*need*' of healthy food options and access to green open space, while assessing the feasibility of creating new spaces for urban food growing in the borough. The input datasets selected for the analysis of '*need*' reflected the social and physical environment related to food and access to green open space; these included data such as income and health deprivation, public open spaces and biodiversity, for example. We focused on indicator data that could be categorised into three groups: social, economic and environmental. These three indicator categories were selected in recognition that urban food production initiatives need to respond to the principles of sustainability, as well as consider the numerous interdependencies between all three pillars, or it could limit the wider benefits and opportunities that urban food growing presents. For the feasibility analysis, spatial data informed the potential opportunities for new

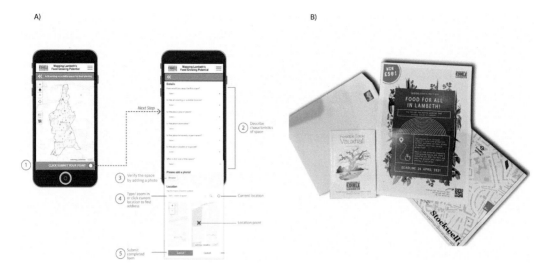

Fig. 8: Citizen-led mapping (Arup, 2021)

food growing spaces. Information about land ownership, air quality and level of land contamination for example was useful data to include in the analysis. In total, nine indicator datasets were spread across the '*need*' and used in the GIS mapping analysis to develop a series of insightful maps (see fig. 7). The indicators were ranked and categorised through consultations with key local stakeholders, including Lambeth Council and key Arup experts, to inform appropriate weightings for calculating the results use and visualisations.

Three GIS spatial analytical maps were produced for the study (see fig. 7). The first map shows areas of greatest social and physical need for food growing projects which combine socio-economic indicators into a single spatial layer producing a heatmap. The areas of greatest vulnerability are illustrated in red. The second map highlights unfeasible land for food growing which included factors such as land ownership, land-use constraints (industrial zones, roads and rail reserves, etc.), land contamination and air quality considerations. The third map is a combination of figs. 7a and 7b, creating a single map using a 'union' computation which summed the indicator scores to reveal the most suitable areas for urban food growing. Creating a distinction between

indicators of need and indicators of feasibility allowed us to consider them separately which was useful in identifying areas that have a high need but low feasibility, for example.

The Covid-19 pandemic caused a rapid shift to online engagement and many projects had to pivot in response to social distancing restrictions. This shift created barriers to face-to-face engagement with the community. A digital mapping tool was developed to overcome this limitation, with residents mapping locations in real-time using mobile devices (see fig. 8a). Information such as food growing typology, approximate plot size, public accessibility, surface type and photographs of the site could be included. Several online feedback sessions were held with the mappers to test and improve the usability of the app. To address issues around digital exclusion, an 'analogue' alternative was created which included a printed map, colour-coded stickers representing food typologies, an instruction leaflet and a pre-paid envelope (see fig. 8b). For recipients of the analogue mapping tool living close to IEL's published *Walking Trails*, they also received the appropriate trail, to encourage exploration of their local area and participation in the project. We partnered with a local

Food Growing Typologies	Small 1-2 parking bays	Medium (2-3 parking bays)	Large (+4 and larger)	Total no. of sites	Total Area: Worst case scenario/ typology (sqm) (smallest size)	Total Area: Best case scenario/ typology (sqm) (largest size)
Carpark	2	2	3	7	207.36	668.16
Community Garden/Allotments	x	2	7	9	368.64	1359.36
Courtyard	1	x	x	1	11.52	23.04
Derelict/ abandoned sites	x	x	2	2	92.16	368.64
Flat Roofs	1	1	3	5	172.8	610.56
Housing Estates	5	11	30	46	1693.44	6024.96
Parks	1	x	9	11	426.24	1681.92
Vegetated surfaces: Church yards/ schools/ shopping centres	x	1	2	3	115.2	403.2
Hard surfaces: Church yards/ schools/ shopping centres	x	x	1	1	46.08	184.32
Road verges	3	6	11	20	679.68	2304
Others	3	1	11	15	564.48	2131.2
Total Potential Area	16	24	79	120	4 332.6	15 759.36

Fig. 9: Results of citizen-led mapping (Arup, 2021)

cooked meals food charity to distribute the packs to their beneficiaries.

Between the period of March to May 2021, participants plotted 120 spaces across 11 different typologies of good growing space (see fig. 9). We used a qualitative approximation based on the dimensions of a vehicle parking bay as a universal standard of measure that could be understood by urban dwellers. On the conservative side, just under 5,000 m² of available land with the potential for food growing was mapped and, as best-case scenario, over 15,000 m² were identified.

The result of the final map was produced by combining the three GIS maps with the citizen-led mapping (see fig. 10a+b). The findings revealed significant potential identified by citizens in both the areas of need and feasibility. However, many of the identified potential food growing spaces did not overlap with the areas of greatest need, suggesting that our audience may have been from a specific, perhaps privileged

demographic background. These insights tell us that areas in 'red' and 'orange' zones that did not receive any points will need future engagement to explore urban food growing opportunities which could meaningfully impact the lives of those frequently experiencing hunger. This is not to suggest that increasing food growing in other parts of the borough would not have benefits, but underserved areas, lacking access to green space and/or access to fresh, healthy food options are the priority for this project.

This was an accelerated study to test, explore and develop new methods of mapping and community engagement. The study revealed insights into the current state of urban food growing in Lambeth, highlighting the spatial barriers as well as the possibilities. Whilst we acknowledge the limitations of this rapid study due, in part, to the challenges presented by the pandemic, we also celebrate the opportunity to have developed a bottom-up community-driven methodology. City authorities are increasingly recognising the importance of food and making it a focus in city strategies so we hope that this work will bridge top-down strategies and bottom-up community initiatives in the future.

Through these projects, we have designed two different ways to highlight the importance of green and productive space in the urban environment and engage the local community. We have found that the *Walking Trails* are more accessible, with fewer barriers to use – but they only focus on what already exists. Engaging people with the online mapping option was more challenging but offered data-driven insight into the possible and a future of food-growing in our local areas. We learned that we need to think more critically about how we engage with disadvantaged communities to ensure that the value of increasing biodiverse green space and food growing will benefit those in most need. Mapping is the first step; this work now needs to be evaluated and will hopefully provide valuable information for Lambeth Council and other landowners in the borough.

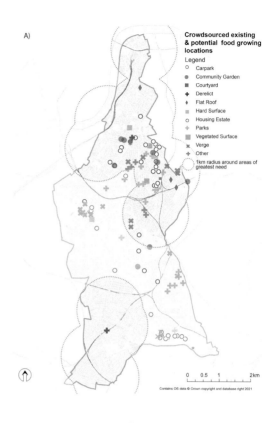

References

Greater London Authority, 2019. Survey of Londoners headline findings. Available from https://data.london.gov.uk/dataset/survey-of-londoners-headline-findings

Groundwork UK, 2021. Out of bounds: Equity in access to urban nature. Available from www.groundwork.org.uk/wp-content/uploads/2021/05/Out-of-Bounds-equity-in-access-to-urban-nature.pdf

IEL., n.d.-a. Incredible Edible Lambeth Walks. Available from www.incredibleediblelambeth.org/walks/ [Accessed 16 Mar 2023]

IEL., n.d.-b. Incredible Edible Lambeth Food Stories. Available from www.incredibleediblelambeth.org/lambeth-food-stories/) [Accessed 16 Mar 2023]

IEL., n.d.-c. Lambeth plots. Available from www.incredibleediblelambeth.org/lambeth-plots/ [Accessed 16 Mar 2023]

Lambeth Council, 2017. Demography factsheet. Available from www.lambeth.gov.uk/sites/default/files/ssh-demography-factsheet-2017.pdf

Lambeth Council, 2021. Lambeth food poverty and insecurity action plan 2021–2024 final draft. Available from https://beta.lambeth.gov.uk/sites/default/files/2021-01/Lambeth%20Food%20Poverty%20and%20Insecuity%20action%20plan%20final%20draft.pdf

Veen et al., 2015. Community gardening and social cohesion: Different designs, different motivations. *Local Environment*, 21 (10), 1271–1287. Available from www.tandfonline.com/doi/abs/10.1080/13549839.2015.1101433

Fig. 10a+b: Combined mapping analysis results (Arup, 2021)

B)

Final Map: Priority locations for food growing

Legend

Priority Area: Suitable land overlapping area of greatest need

Suitable land for food growing

Potential food growing location *(crowdsourced)*

Potential location overlapping suitable land

1km radius around area of greatest need with potential food growing locations

0 0.5 1 2km

Contains OS data © Crown copyright and database right 2021

The practice of sharing: Mapping food networks in Delft, South Africa

Adrian Paulsen and Bradley Rink

The aim of this chapter is to challenge essentialist notions of food security while disrupting the artificial divide between formal and informal food networks. We attempt to accomplish both goals through an exploration of the practices of food sharing in the community of Delft in Cape Town, South Africa. The practices of sharing that we explore are amongst a variety of strategies that individuals and communities employ toward fulfilment of the complex social phenomenon that is food security. Much of the existing literature on food security focuses on using research tools that locate food security either as a temporal or spatial phenomenon. While this may be an adequate way of discussing the lived realities of those individuals and communities deemed to be food insecure, such an approach frames food insecurity within limited temporal and spatial constraints. Our focus on food sharing recognises the lived experiences of food security and highlights the social aspects of food – and other elements of everyday life – that are not lived in isolation but as part of a community of individuals and families faced with similar challenges.

Existing tools such as the *Household Food Insecurity Access Scale (HFIAS)* help us to understand the temporality of food access and its impact on diet, but it only does so within the temporal limits imposed by the survey itself. Such limitations may lead to a false sense of food insecurity and strategies to deal with it. Another approach to food insecurity is the mapping of food systems, visualising the flows of food into and out of geographical locations from the small scale of a suburb to larger scales nationally and globally. The advantage of this approach over the *HFIAS* is that we can map food systems at larger scales, looking at a broader range of methodological tools to uncover food-related phenomena outside of the limited scale of the *HFIAS*. These scalar approaches also have their own problems since they overlook how individuals interact with and share food on a daily basis. In our effort to map food networks in Delft, we offer food mapping as a tool to visually represent sharing. Beyond classifying degrees of food security, it is our aim to understand the nuances of food security and the strategies that those who are food insecure employ. Our approach to understanding food security uses neighbourhood-scale mapping to visualise and to take into account the lived realities of the Delft community. The findings that we present in visual and narrative form illustrate strategies for ensuring food security for Delft residents.

Situating Delft

Delft is a suburb within the city of Cape Town, South Africa. It lies on the fringes of two of Cape Town's primary urban nodes: to the east of Cape Town's central business district (CBD) and to the south of the suburb of Bellville's CBD (see fig. 1). It is situated on the Cape Flats, an area on the geographic and economic periphery of the city, known for its poverty and crime and designated by the apartheid government to house coloured[1] and black people. Delft has experienced a rapid expansion over the past decade, leading to an influx of residents. According to data from the 2011

DOI: 10.4324/9781003352280-16

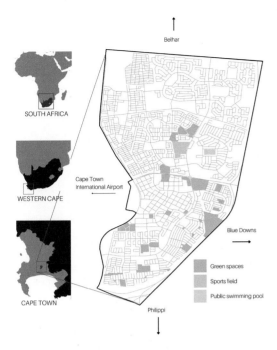

Belhar

Cape Town
International Airport

Blue Downs

Green spaces

Sports field

Public swimming pool

Philippi

Fig. 1: Map of Delft

Census (Statistics South Africa, 2012; Frith, n.d.), Delft has a population of approximately 152,030 and covers an area of 11.08 square km giving it a population density of 13,721 people per square km. It has approximately 39,575 households with an average of 3.8 people per household. There is nearly an equal share of coloured and black residents (51.44% vs 46.22% respectively) and an equal distribution of male and female residents. The racial profile of Delft sets it apart from typical residential areas in South Africa that have clear racial majorities as a legacy of apartheid segregation. Delft is a relatively built up area that has few public green spaces for recreation. The suburb has one formal sports field and one public swimming pool. The green spaces that do exist are mostly empty fields used as de facto dumping sites or as improvised sports fields. In spite of the existence of such public green spaces, none are used to grow food on a large scale.

Locating the practice of sharing

The field of food security interrogates relationships between people and food. Our exploration of the practice of sharing is framed by an understanding of food security through the related concepts of food deserts and food networks. We visualise these concepts through food mapping. According to the Food and Agriculture Organization of the United Nations (FAO) a state of food security is one where individuals and groups have "both physical and economic access to the basic food that they need" (FAO, 2006, p 1). Food security is further defined by a range of factors (FAO, 2006), including:

- *Food availability* measured by sufficient quantities of food of appropriate quality, supplied through domestic production or imports (including food aid);
- *Food access* to adequate resources (entitlements) for acquiring appropriate foods for a nutritious diet;
- *Utilisation of food* through adequate diet, clean water, sanitation and health care to reach a state of nutritional well-being, highlighting the importance of non-food inputs in food security; and
- *Stability* through access to adequate food at all times, without risk of losing access to food as a consequence of sudden shocks (e.g. economic or climatic) or cyclical events (e.g. seasonal food insecurity).

In Africa, hunger affects 21% of the population. Within South Africa, figures from 2017 demonstrate that out of 16.2 million households, more than 20% reported that their food access was inadequate or severely inadequate (Statistics South Africa, 2019). Black and coloured South Africans reported the highest levels of inadequate and severely inadequate food access levels in the country.

Many of those South Africans who suffer from inadequate food access live within what are deemed "food deserts". These areas are defined by the absence of modern retail outlets and poor access to healthy and affordable food (Battersby and Crush, 2014). Whether induced by demographic change imposed by apartheid spatial policies (Kroll, 2016) or the closure of stores (Walker, Keane and Burke, 2010), a variety of causes may lead to the development of food deserts. However they may form, Battersby and Crush (2014) assert that supermarket access as a food desert metric in the South African context is somewhat inappropriate. They argue that Eurocentric models tend to focus on proximity to supermarkets as a proxy for food security, whereas the informal food retail environment in African cities is marked by great fluidity. Food desert mapping often fails to capture the everyday mobility of residents whose lives are not restricted by the neighbourhoods in which they live.

In order to spatially represent such food-related issues, food mapping visualises indicators such as access, security and poverty. Food mapping makes use of a range of variables and takes place at various spatial resolutions – from community to global levels. By using remote sensing, first-hand knowledge and GIS software, food maps can represent complex phenomena (Hubley, 2011; Hallet and McDermott, 2011) yet small – and especially informal – food retailers are frequently overlooked, leading to an understatement of food availability and the exaggeration of the size and frequency of food deserts. This also questions the supremacy of the formal retail sector that is only one component of food networks. We approached food mapping in Delft from a bottom-up perspective, doing in-field mapping of all food sources and conducting interviews with Delft residents to develop a deeper understanding of the food networks in Delft.

Food networks refer to the institutions within a community to which each person and household has access containing formal, informal and, as underscored in our findings, alternative food networks. The formal food network is well-studied and understood, comprising food retailers regulated and taxed by the government (Essop and Yu, 2008) and including most prominently retailers within shopping malls. In contrast, the informal food network operates outside systems of regulation and taxation. In South Africa, much of the informal trade in food takes place through what are known

as spaza shops (or tuck shops) that are small convenience shops often operated from the home (Skinner and Haysom, 2016). Goods sold within this sector are nonetheless sourced from the formal sector, evidenced by the fact that more than half of sales by formal retailers in South Africa are to the informal retailers for resale (Skinner and Haysom, 2016). This demonstrates the coexistence and reliance of formal and informal food networks on each other (Battersby et al., 2016; Crush and Frayne, 2011; Ligthelm, 2003). The formal sector provides foods that are cheaper and more regulated in comparison to the informal sector, whereas the informal sector provides foods that are sold in smaller quantities and at price points accessible to individuals with precarious income streams that restrict bulk purchases.

An underexplored feature of the food system, alternative food networks in the form of sharing complicate the formal/informal binary. Alternative food networks encompass household and community domains where cultures around food are formed and where community bonds are established by neighbours sharing food with each other. Alternative food networks in the form of sharing constitute domains of food procurement within communities and family units that are altruistic and where there is no economic incentive. These food networks are reciprocal, meaning that any sharing of food or money is expected to be repaid at a later date. The practices of sharing that we explore are amongst a variety of strategies that individuals and communities employ toward fulfilment of the complex social phenomenon that is food security. It is this network that emerges as a powerful strategy for resilience.

Understanding the practice of sharing: Methodological approach

In our exploration of the practices of food sharing in the community of Delft, we used a combination of quantitative and qualitative methods. Data were collected over the period between December 2018 and March 2019 using a modified version of the *Household Food Insecurity Access Scale (HFIAS)* survey tool to gather quantitative measures of food in/security and associated coping mechanisms. The modifications included the use of 12 questions that focused on food networks and sharing. These questions probed practices of borrowing from/giving to neighbours; purchasing food items from food vendors, tuck shops, spaza shops or supermarkets; and use of public transport in food purchasing. Amongst the additional questions were those seeking a greater understanding of the Delft food environment including participants' understanding of food security; household state of food security; household diet; use of transportation in food purchasing; community resources; and types of foods purchased and/or avoided. Adding to the quantitative methods was the use of remotely sensed data to visualise the spatial elements of Delft and the relationships between individuals and neighbourhoods of the area. Considering our focus on the lived experiences of food security in Delft, our study also employed a qualitative method in the form of semi-structured interviews with Delft residents to substantiate and expand on the data analysis from the *HFIAS* survey.

Sharing food: Beyond the formal/informal divide

The qualitative results of the HFIAS survey reveal that businesses in Delft's informal sector overshadow those in the formal sector in both number and scale. Nine out of ten survey participants reported using a tuck shop during the past four weeks at the time of the survey being conducted and 8.5 out of every ten participants reported using a mall during the same period. Most residents access the mall only for bulk shopping around the time when income is received every month. In comparison, accessing a tuck shop is something that happens throughout the month and for convenience. Tuck shops and malls also serve very different niches. Tuck shops are more expensive per unit of food, but they sell foods packaged in smaller quantities (and thus price) to be accessible for those with

a limited income stream during times of the month when money is scarce.

Most residents walk to access food, enabled by the dense distribution of tuck shops and proximity to malls. The second largest proportion of residents use public transport to either access malls within the area or to access malls outside of Delft. The smallest proportion of residents use their own vehicle to access food, not surprising considering low levels of car ownership amongst Delft residents due to cost.

Sharing and lending food from family and neighbours is an important aspect of Delft's food system. Over 34% of all residents report that they had borrowed food from their neighbours but more than 65% of residents reported that neighbours had borrowed food from them. Low-income households were more likely to borrow food from neighbours since they were more likely to run out of food during the month. Figure 2 shows the disparity in sharing in the various Delft neighbourhoods.

These acts of sharing are not abstract. They are part of the lived realities of the people of Delft. Using data from the *HFIAS* survey, semi-structured interviews and observation, we have constructed representations of the people of Delft to push back against clinical representations of food insecure people as an abstract collective. In order to humanise our findings, we have aggregated our data into three personas representing the average Delft resident. Each persona represents a social class marked by the terms "poor", "middle class" and "high income" representing differences in income and livelihood strategies. These terms must be understood within the context of Delft and are relative to the predominantly low-income setting of the area. Our personas are three women representing the range of lived experiences of food security in Delft: Shamiela, Carmen and Nolu (see fig. 3).

Shamiela
Shamiela's household is a poor one. She lives in an unrenovated two-bedroom house. She

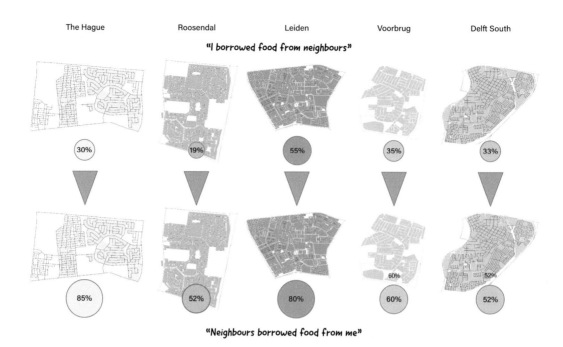

Fig. 2: Food sharing from neighbour to neighbour

has an average household size of four people with more people living in informal structures on her property, usually family members who may not pay rent but may contribute towards electricity and other utilities. The only form of household income is likely to be from social grants such as Child or Pension grants – the latter in cases where an older family member resides with them. She lives in a household where at least one family member (usually younger) has completed high school, but she herself is unlikely to have completed high school. Shamiela's household is severely food insecure, especially towards the end of the month when both money and food are running short. When this happens, she is unlikely to borrow (or admit to borrowing) any food items from neighbours, relying on family members instead. She does this for many reasons: to avoid the shame and social stigma of asking neighbours for food; because she would not be able to reciprocate; and because there is less shame and stigma in reaching out to family members for food or money to buy food.

Her household makes frequent use of local tuck shops to purchase daily necessities such as bread and milk. She walks or uses public transport to make purchases at the supermarket at least twice a month. She will sometimes travel outside of Delft to buy foods that are on sale or are cheaper. Shamiela will avoid buying certain foods all together due to cost. She considers her household to be food secure and believes that her household eats a balanced diet. When it comes to sharing food with and from neighbours, 42% of poor households reported that they lent food from their neighbours while 57% of those same households reported that their neighbours lent food from their household, of those that lent food from their households "rarely" that is to say only once or twice in the past four weeks of the survey being conducted. More than 36% of these households reported that neighbours lent food from them "sometimes" which is three to ten times in the past four weeks and 50% of these households reported that neighbours borrowed food from them often, which is more than ten times in the past four weeks.

High income household
household six of 4 people
2 working adults
highest level of education is a
diploma or degree
Makes more purchaes from
supermarkets than from tuckshops

Middle class household
1 working adult
Diverse forms of income
High school level of education
Makes frequent use of tuckshops for
small purchases
Lots of anxiety about food running
out

Fig. 3: Nolu, Carmen and Shamiela –
profiles of the Delft community

Carmen

Carmen's household is a middle class one. Her
household has access to diversified forms of
income in the form of a monthly salary or wage
as well as social grants that can include Child
and/or Pension grants depending on household
structure. Her household has at least one working adult. The fact that her household receives
social grants means that the monthly income
her household receives is within the threshold
to receive such grants or she may live with older
parents who receive a pension grant. It is very
likely that her household receives both types
of social grants because extended family such
as a parent or parents are living with her. If her
property has informal structures, they would
tend to be of higher quality than the informal
structures found on the properties of poorer
households. Her household is one where it is
likely that at least one household member has
completed high school and in rare cases where

one household member holds a diploma or
degree.

Even though her household has access to various streams of income which would serve to
protect her household from food shortages, it
still experiences anxieties over running out of
food. This is largely due to the fact that households like hers find themselves in the transi-
tional state of becoming food secure, situated
between the security of waged labour and the
precarity of social grants. When food is running
short, she is unlikely to reach out to neighbours for help or would underreport doing so.
Households like hers also report giving neighbours food at a far higher rate than they report
asking for food. Because the sharing of food
is a cultural practice depending on reciprocity,
it is likely that households like hers would
borrow from the food sharing network at the
same rate they give to it. Carmen's household
makes frequent use of the tuck shops in her
area to buy goods such as bread, milk, potatoes,
onions and small packets of sugar. Her household is sensitive to the prices of food and will
avoid buying certain foods that are perceived as
being too expensive. Our findings demonstrate
that only 30% of all middle-income households,
such as Carmen's, reported that they lent
food from neighbours, but 75% of those same
households reported that neighbours had lent
food from their households in the previous four
weeks. According to these households, neighbours lent food from them "rarely" 44% of the
time, "sometimes" 29% of the time and "often"
25% of the time.

Nolu

Nolu's is a high-income household. The only
form of income in households like hers is a
monthly salary. This is enough to push her
household above the qualifying threshold for
social grants. The average size of a household
like hers is around four people with two of them
working and earning a salary. At least one or
more members have finished high school and
in rare cases one member of the household has
completed a diploma or degree. Her property

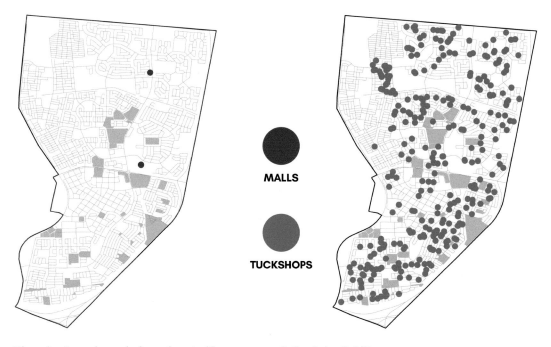

Fig. 4: Formal vs informal retail sources of food in Delft

is unlikely to contain informal structures and it is likely that her home has been renovated. Her household experiences anxieties of running out of food at a lower rate than poor and middle-class households and thus her household is highly likely to be food secure. Her household also reports giving or lending neighbours food at double the rate that they ask neighbours for food. There are two reasons for this: because households like hers have enough food to last throughout the month and thus have excess food to lend to family and neighbours; and/or because households like hers feel a certain amount of shame if they need help from family and neighbours and therefore under-report having to borrow food. Nolu's household makes more purchases from supermarkets throughout the month than from tuck shops. Households like hers will make multiple trips to the supermarket throughout the month. Our findings from Delft indicate that a mere 32% of high-income households like Nolu's reported that they borrowed food from their neighbours. Of those that did, 36% reported that they did so "rarely" or once or twice in the past four weeks, 18% reported that they did so "sometimes" or three to ten times in the past four weeks and 45% reported that they borrowed food from their neighbours "often" or more than ten times in the past four weeks.

Mapping food networks in Delft

Food networks are the systems of food procurement that arise from the interactions of multiple actors over time and space (Kroll, 2016; Skinner, 2016). These actors can include people, food retailers, food vendors, wholesalers and public transport. Food networks are complicated by various factors such as the availability, affordability, temporality, stability, utilisation and cultural appropriateness of food available to actors in the food network. Food networks can further be divided into three domains: the formal, the informal and the alternative. Our findings suggest that food security in Delft exceeds the binary of formal and informal, where the alternative food network provides a socially embedded strategy for resilience.

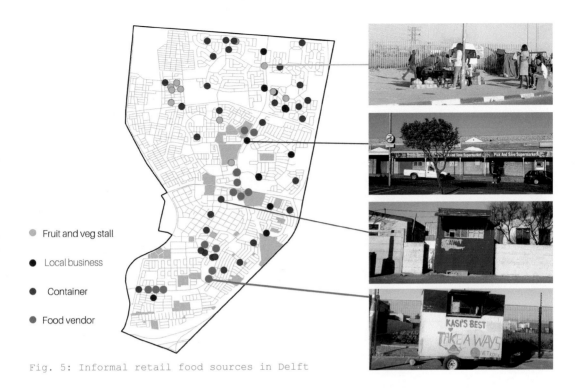

Fig. 5: Informal retail food sources in Delft

The households of our three representative personas each access the formal food network differently, both at different frequencies according to income and across various retail typologies depending on proximity and the amount and type of food sought.

The formal sector, while organised and beholden to regulation, is still complex in the way that people interact with it. Logic dictates that supermarket access would equate to access to healthier and more affordable foods, but this is not always the case. Malls that house low-cost supermarkets like those found in Delft offer affordable foods at the expense of nutritional value. Access to low-cost supermarkets in Delft is dictated by income. Those who enjoy a regular income access supermarkets more often than those who do not. Likewise, higher income means that households can expand the area in which they can shop around for food.

More than half (56%) of poor households like Shamiela's were likely to access the informal food network more than ten times in the past four weeks. Her household uses the network to predominantly buy goods such as bread and milk on a daily basis as well as items such as single use bags of coffee and sugar. On average, items such as bread and milk are cheaper at supermarkets. As a result, households like Shamiela's would save more over time if they bought these items from supermarkets, yet the reasons they do not are twofold: they do not live close enough to a supermarket; and/or they prefer the convenience of buying these items from tuck shops. In contrast, 88% of middle income households like Carmen's have access to the informal food network similar to Shamiela's. They also use the informal network to buy items such as bread and milk daily. But where Carmen's household and those like her differ from households like Shamiela's is that they buy a wider variety of items such as potatoes, rice, polony and cheese. Their mixed forms of income equip them to spend more money on items that are more expensive from tuck shops and food vendors for the trade-off of more convenience. Nolu and 91% of all households like hers – that only receive an income through a salary – access the informal food network on a frequency that ranges from semi-regular to regular. Their households also buy items such as bread, milk, onions and potatoes on a regular basis, but their income allows them to expand the range of items they can afford from tuck shops, with some households in this income bracket reporting that they buy items such as chicken and chicken necks; cheese; yoghurt and spices.

A general trend becomes apparent as income increases: patronage of the informal sector increases. This is counter to the general trend that predicts that as income increases, we should see patronage of the informal sector decrease. Delft goes against this trend since Delft is still poor overall and thus the informal sector still serves a market in the area. Another reason why residents access the informal sector more as income increases is because they value convenience over price for certain items of food and finally; the informal sector is so enmeshed within the spatiality of Delft it is likely to be accessed by all residents at least once a day.

Mapping the sharing of food: Resilience through alternative food networks

Through the process of drawn and written food mapping we have visualised the complexity of food networks in Delft and community members' reliance on formal, informal and alternative channels in the fulfilment of food security. As told through the narratives of Shamiela, Carmen and Nolu, our mappings demonstrate the need for a more nuanced approach to food security. Their stories take into account the lived realities of the so-called food insecure and shed light on the fact that food security is more complicated than previous studies would suggest. The sharing of food plays a key role in the food environment of Delft, where more than a third of all residents reported that they borrowed

food from neighbours. However, almost two-thirds of all residents reported that neighbours borrowed food from them, a discrepancy in borrowing that points to interesting dynamics in the Delft food system. Poorer households were more likely to borrow food items from neighbours as they were more likely to run out of food during the course of the month.

Food networks in Delft are complicated and interlinked, with residents making use of formal, informal and alternative food networks to access food. The formal networks are few and far between, as can be observed in figure 4: only two formal low-cost supermarkets exist at the time the study was conducted, located in the upper and lower halves of Delft. The informal network consists of tuck shops (see fig. 4) and other informal businesses (see fig. 5) located throughout Delft. Tuck shops are found within neighbourhoods while other forms of informal businesses are found near to main roads and busy intersections. The alternative food network serves as a supplementary way to obtain food as a stop-gap method between salary and social grant payments or when food runs low within households. It is accessed through social capital which can then be used to access food from friends, neighbours and family. Social capital can be exhausted, however and access to food through this network can be cut off. Reciprocity is also expected to be maintained and failure to do so can cause households to be cut off from the network. Negative feelings of shame and pride serve as a regulating mechanism so that one actor is unlikely to access too much food through this network. Sharing food within alternative networks may be a last resort for some people in Delft, but it also serves as an important means of enhancing access to food and increasing resilience against food insecurity. Our study highlights the importance of sharing as a central tenet of alternative food networks. Through a range of survival strategies including practices of sharing, Delft residents that are considered food insecure are empowered to procure food and to ensure that their households have access to food.

Note

1   The legacy of South Africa's apartheid era remains
    in the form of racial classifications including "black"
    (or African), "Indian", "coloured" and "white". These
    terms remain in use despite calls for a non-racial
    society.

References

Battersby, J. and Crush, J., 2014. Africa's urban food deserts. *Urban Forum*, 25 (2), 143–151.

Battersby, J., Marshak, M. and Mngqibisa, N., 2016. Mapping the invisible: The informal food economy of Cape Town, South Africa. *African Food Security Urban Network*, 1–26.

Crush, J. and Frayne, B., 2011. Supermarket expansion and the informal food economy in Southern African cities: Implications for urban food security. *Journal of Southern African Studies*, 37 (4), 781–807.

Essop, H. and Yu, D., 2008. The South African informal sector (1997–2006). *Stellenbosch Economic Working Papers*, 58.

Frith, A., n.d. Census 2011: Main place: Delft. *Census 2011*. Available from https://census2011.adrianfrith.com/place/199023

Hallet, L.F. IV and McDermott, D., 2011. Quantifying the extent and cost of food deserts in Lawrence, Kansas, USA. *Applied Geography*, 31 (4), 1210–1215.

Hubley, T.A., 2011. Assessing the proximity of healthy food options and food deserts in a rural area in Maine. *Applied Geography*, 31 (4), 1224–1231.

Kroll, F., 2016. Deflating the fallacy of food deserts. *PLAAS Working Paper*, 1–26.

Ligthelm, A., 2003. Informal retail structures in South Africa: An exploratory study. *South African Business Review*, 7 (1), 54–63.

Skinner, C. and Haysom, G., 2016. *The informal sector's role in food security A missing link in policy debates?* Cape Town: PLAAS, UWC and Centre of Excellence on Food Security.

Statistics South Africa, 2012. *Census 2011*. Available from www.statssa.gov.za/publications/P03014/P030142011.pdf

Statistics South Africa, 2019. Towards measuring the extent of food security in South Africa: An examination of hunger and food inadequacy (No. 03-00-14). Available from www.statssa.gov.za/publications/03-00-14/03-00-142017.pdf

United Nations Food and Agriculture Organization (FAO), 2006. Food security. 2. [online] *Food and Agriculture Organization of the United Nations*. Available from www.fao.org/fileadmin/templates/faoitaly/documents/pdf/pdf_Food_Security_Cocept_Note.pdf [Accessed 22 Aug 2021].

Walker, R.E., Keane, C.R. and Burke, J.G., 2010. Disparities and access to healthy food in the United States: A review of food deserts literature. *Health and Place*, 16 (5), 876–884.

Six feet high and rising: Mapping the Edible City as a theatre of food

Mikey Tomkins

The use of 'theatre' in the title refers to the *Theatre of the Orb of the World* (Theatrum Orbis Terrarum) by Abraham Ortelius and Gerardus Mercator from 1570. Here, the cartographic theatre is both a building but also a space of performance, which means actors. In an era of remote data sensing that feeds readily available digital maps, it is easy to forget that maps originated as a combination of both land measurements and stories (often fantastical), both provided by those who travelled. Michel de Certeau comments that modern maps have increasingly become representation of data as a "totalizing stage" alone, now devoid of the itinerate actors and their stories who have subsequently been silenced and pushed backstage (De Certeau, 1984, p. 122).

My chapter reflects on the use of mapping within my urban agriculture (UA) research which aims to place the urban resident as actor back, centre stage. As we barrel headlong into climate emergency, I argue there is a need to engage with people through their imaginations and stories about the shifts that will be required to create equitable, resilient and sustainable cities. I primarily engage using fictional maps of city neighbourhoods, called the *Edible Mapping Project (EMP)*. The maps I create present a near-future vision of an Edible City where fruit, vegetables, livestock, fish, bees and other food sources could flourish and be nurtured by urban gardeners in streets, empty rooftops and underused open spaces (figs. 1–4).

The *Edible Mapping Project* draws on the concept of the everyday regarding space as, primarily, a lived experience rather than a set of physical objects alone. This is not oppositional but cocreational where both "people and their environments are continually bringing each other into being" (Ingold, 2000, p. 87). Ingold further defines this as moving from "a 'building perspective', where worlds are made before they are lived in, to a 'dwelling perspective', where the forms people build, whether in the imagination or on the ground, only arise within the current of their life activities" (Ingold, 2000, p. 154).

One issue with inhabiting urban environment is spatial blindness. As Lefebvre states, "We no longer see that reality; we resist it, turn away from it, struggle against it, prevent its birth and development. The urban (urban space, urban landscape) remains unseen" (Lefebvre, 2003, pp. 29–30). Hence it is a blankscape rather than a possible foodscape. The *EMP* is an attempt to 'make visible' the potential Edible City, as a space of the imagination within the flow of everyday life, because you cannot farm space you can see.

The Edible Mapping Project: An accidental cartographer

I have, since 2004, used mapping extensively with UA research and latterly, I have begun to think of myself as an 'accidental cartographer'; accidental because in exploring UA, I had seen mapping as one step within a linear process to address the primary question of UA. However, the concept of urban food mapping (UFM) has enabled me to position all the stages of my work, including map making, walking,

DOI: 10.4324/9781003352280-17

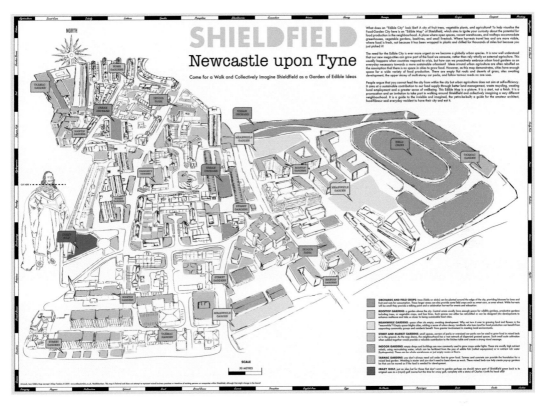

Fig. 1: The Edible Map of Shieldfield, Newcastle upon Tyne, UK. 2019. Printed on paper 420 mm × 594 mm

performance and food growing as part of an ongoing mapping practice, where maps should be "conceived as a processual . . . that maps are of-the-moment, brought into being through practices (embodied, social, technical); that mapping is a process of constant reterritorialization" (Kitchin and Dodge, 2007, p. 331).

Specifically, I created the *EMP* in 2009 and it involves creating spatially accurate neighbourhood maps, overlaid with UA data and imagined future scenarios (figs. 1–4). These maps are stand-alone images, but they are also used to support author-led public walks, exhibitions, start gardens and other creative outputs that incorporate photography, writing, performing, drawing and ceramics. While I have previously used quantitative mapping to establish some baseline for potential UA yields in cities (Tomkins, 2006, 2008, 2009), the *EMP* is a qualitative project

that aims towards provoking and empowering residents and igniting actionable outcomes.

I will discuss one project undertaken in Shieldfield, Newcastle, UK, in 2019–2020, which involved spending time in the city, getting to know residents and the community and creating a map of the neighbourhood (fig. 1). I use multiple practices to enable participation, for example, walks (fig. 6), an exhibition, creating urban wheat gardens (figs. 7 and 8), bread baking and a celebration through a harvest festival in October 2020 (fig. 11).

Shieldfield: Mapping as walking, drawing and stories

Shieldfield is a 40-hectare Tyneside neighbourhood towards the east of Newcastle upon Tyne, bounded by main roads. It is mostly residential, a mixture of tower blocks, inter-war

Fig. 2: Edible Map of Brighton, 2022. Printed on paper 420 mm × 594 mm

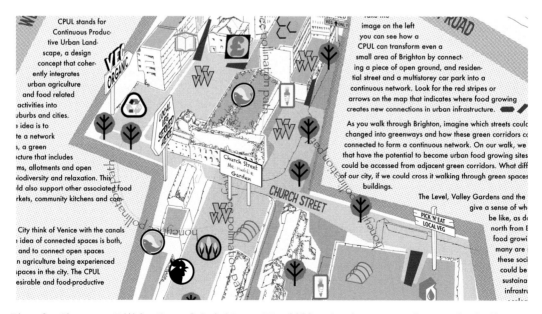

Fig. 3: Closeup, Edible Map of Brighton, UK, 2022, showing extensive UA including hydroponics, home gardens and rooftop farms

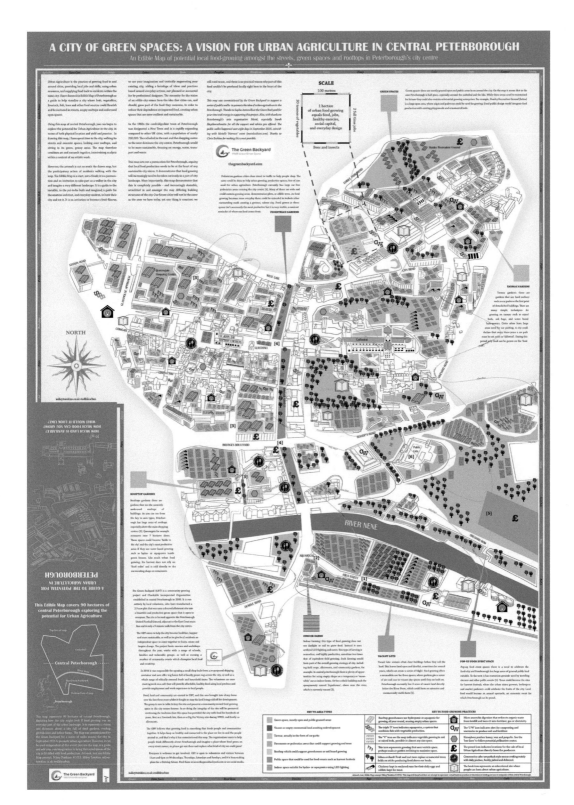

Fig. 4: Edible Map of Peterborough, UK, 2015. Printed on paper 594 mm × 841 mm

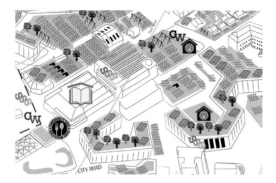

Fig. 5: Close up, Edible Map of
Peterborough, UK, 2015, showing
extensive UA including hydroponics, home
gardens and rooftop farms

semi-detached housing and newer, much more imposing student accommodation. It is also a place in transition where long-term residents mix sometimes uneasily with the newer imposing student accommodation (Whetstone, 2019).

The *Shieldfield EMP* begins with me walking around the estates and roads and imagining a near-future urban landscape full of food, gardeners, their daily rhythm and its harvests with its sounds and smells. It is a process in which I need to disrupt what I see in front of me, asking questions, a process that the landscape sometimes resists. By 'resist', I mean that the urban landscape, such as the ubiquitous grassed areas, don't typically demand attention as they don't obstruct, they often remain quiet in their typical ordinariness. Perhaps, they know they are being hunted and like any predator/prey game they use their sedentariness to repel the chase. As I stand in Shieldfield, my impression is that the ever-present grass was never meant to be used for anything, it was purely decorative, an infill between brick and tarmac. For someone wanting to conceive of food growing landscapes, the grass and its concomitant landscape offers a temptation, yet within the everyday it remains unseen. I would argue that the ubiquity of the grass means people become spatially blind to it; these spaces are not significant like parks, or areas for dog exercise, or jogging, for example, they are blankscapes.

Constructing an edible landscape in my mind is a playful, sometimes surreal exercise. It is a cut and paste practice where I insert UA into all the spaces I can see. When I begin to devise the imaginary UA map, I think of origami, as both are connected through the art of paper folding. How a single sheet can be creased, turned and folded, across its surface, to manifest different objects, in the same way that our imagination folds and turns space, to make visible differing opportunities, both latent and potential. This mutability speaks to the manifold possibilities of all urban landscapes when viewed thought the lens of UA. I am not pursuing a conflict between the existing urban plan and the UA vision; both are stories that can and should be possible. Yet as Denis Wood states, "In pointing towards the existence of other worlds – real or imagined – map artists are claiming the power of the map to achieve ends other than the social reproduction of the status quo" (Woods, 2006, p. 10).

Mapping to walking

I drew the Shieldfield map over a two-week period after which I advertised five days of walks through a local gallery, Shieldfield Art Works (SAW). SAW was a vital part of the project as they gave institutional support and connected me with the local community, individuals and institutions. Each walk was repeated three times daily and lasted one and a half hours following the same route to help meet walkers' expectations, particularly when people have limited mobility. The walks and a large version of the map formed part of a joint exhibition at SAW, from 17th May–6th July 2019 (SAW, 2019; Whetstone, 2019). The walks attracted a wide variety of people: residents, counsellors, political party members, activists, those running local food initiative members, several academics and visitors from other cities who were looking for inspiration (fig. 6).

Reflecting on walking as part of the mapping process, the map is created in my studio, alone and is under my control. However, the walks are

Fig. 6: Walking and talking on the Edible Map walk, Shieldfield, 2019

where I give up control and begin to co-create a space; the map and walk become entangled and I try to be agnostic. Walkers respond to the A2-printed maps in many ways; some might stuff maps into their pockets, while others use the map as a constant reference, following our route with fingers. Some groups remain almost silent; others chat distractedly, drifting between talking about shopping, laundry, or their day ahead. This is the everyday production of space, where we are constantly distracted by thoughts and imagination.

I see the walks as performances where participants enact space through mapping using their bodies. Here, the map is understood contextually rather than abstractly, directly experienced in relationship to people and the making of space through walking, reinserting "the biographical and bodily meaning of landscape" (Okely, 2001, p. 99). Walkers are therefore spatially and socially agile, sliding from conversations about food production to their daily schedule, or remembrances about what is no longer visible since the bulldozer and the master planners moved in the 1960s.

The walking, talking, socialising, sharing and looking demotes the primacy of the *Edible Map* as another 'master plan'; it is not here to precede construction or control the present; it stresses an enacted mapping moment, which is fluid, fleeting and itinerant, later settling into memory. With the map so intrinsically bound to the

walk, I find it disorientating to distribute maps without the walking event: it is as if I am giving out the cover of a book that will never be written by the walker-as-author (Tomkins, 2012).

Implementation

As a result of the walks, we gained funding to grow food and serendipitously chose wheat; a resident had been spreading bird seed in the neighbourhood containing wheat which had sprung to life; chance had intervened. However, in March 2020, the Covid-19 pandemic lockdown arrived, but not before we managed to plant spring wheat in disused flower beds (fig. 8), back gardens and raised beds. Before constructing them, I lay out the wood to playfully create a pattern of desire (fig. 7). The wheat grew all summer and the harvest and threshing took place in mid-August, which coincided with a break in the lockdown, allowing me to travel again.

However, lockdown returned in October 2020, excluding me from the bread making sessions with Andy Haddon at the local *Big River Bakery*. Haddon said, "This is the first time bread has been made out of wheat grown on Tyneside for hundreds of years and it is entirely appropriate that it should happen here in Shieldfield" (Goodwin, 2020). Out of our entire neighbourhood, we harvested 1.5 kg of wheat and baked 10 loaves, which were sliced and offered to residents at the SAW October harvest festival. We interviewed some residents after the bread making and overall people were thrilled with the whole process and growing urban wheat and baking bread. One resident commented on loving "seeing new growth coming up in unexpected places. People working together for a common purpose, a symbol of what might be" (SAW, 2020, p. 22.15).

Reflecting on the decision to grow wheat pivoted around two words expressed by some residents: curiosity and risk. The sense of curiosity matches how I introduce the walks: that the map is a provocation to the concept of UA. Risk, however, was a response born from

Fig. 7: Mapping the construction of wooden raised beds, Shieldfield, 2020

the deep frustration residents felt regarding the way the local council had responded to budget cuts and not maintained the open public spaces beyond grass cutting. Risk encapsulated the realisation that they had little to lose by putting the spade in the ground. The potential UA story within the map and walk advocates not a design solution but for an inquisitiveness about the boundaries between real life, imagination and action. Residents were able to imagine beyond

the visible and engage as agents of change where the *EMP* had facilitated a disruptive relation with the urban landscape: chance snuck in, for example, the bird seed mentioned earlier, which the residents were able to seize upon and make tangible.

Imagining urban rituals

As we planted the wheat in March, a conversation emerged about the spectres and old traumas of plague and harvest that still inhabit the landscape: the former redolent through the Covid-19 pandemic, the latter deferred by the limitless ability of supermarkets to fill shelves. I was plunged back in time and my thoughts turned to images of 16th century plague doctors and other costumed entities roaming the urban landscape to protect us. Over the years of the *EMP*, my thoughts had often moved beyond what the landscape might look like, to explore

Fig. 8: Harvesting wheat in public flower beds, Shieldfield, 2020

how people might inhabit it; what tasks do they perform or what new rituals might emerge? I began to imagine various costumed entities walking the city and out of this emerged the *Guardian of the Urban Wheat* costume (fig. 9), as well as other costumed entities that protect sweet corn, or an entity called the fish-spirit-catcher that celebrates the daily urban aquaponics harvest (fig. 10).

The concept behind the costumes was firstly, to address the idea that future urban agri*cultural* environments will generate a *cultural* response to food production that mirrors the way rural landscapes also have such food-related events and rituals. Secondly, I want to find a way to bring the maps to life, so to speak, to use my own body within mapping. Consequently, I created a costume of multicoloured wheat, where the mask is a map of Shieldfield, showing the location of the urban wheat fields. In this way my body,

the urban landscape and the *Edible Map* became entwined as part of a continuing 'theatrical' process, "a process of constant reterritorialization" (Kitchin and Dodge, 2007, p. 331).

The return of lockdown in October 2020 prevented me from travelling to Shieldfield and walking around in the *Guardian of the Urban Wheat* costume. However, this also created another moment of risk and chance; I constructed a green screen in my studio and 'performed' via zoom, 340 miles away at the opposite end of England, with a virtual backdrop of images from the neighbourhood (fig. 11). Some of the images were at ground level, others taken from tower blocks giving a bird's eye view. The performance was shown to residents (who were also wearing masks themselves!) as they collected their slices of urban bread from SAW and briefly celebrated the harvest. One resident, who viewed the

Fig. 9: Author wearing Guardian of the Urban Wheat costume against background of Shieldfield, Newcastle, 2020

Fig. 10: Author wearing the Fish Spirit Catcher costume against background of Shieldfield, Newcastle, 2020

Fig. 11: Still from video performance, at the Shieldfield harvest festival, October 2020. On the right is the SAW office with public, on the left is the author wearing the Guardian of the Urban Wheat costume

Zoom call commented, "is he really in Shield-field?" adding further to the surrealism implicit in the *EMP*, while another acknowledged this directly stating "that strange straw people floating through the air make it [Shieldfield] the magical, mysterious place it ought to be" (Tomkins, 2020).

Blankscapes to foodscapes

While walkers are engaged with the subject of UA as a food concept, I see that they are equally engaged with the landscape before them. However, we are a long way off from a simple equation where seeing space will equal food gardening, in the sense of turning a blankscape into a foodscape and therefore, it is important not to overclaim our work as artists or researchers. However, the multiple art practices from bread-making, to costumes, walks and paper maps demonstrate that mapping is "processual" (Kitchin and Dodge, ibid). It requires the engagement of people within the city as a theatre, a place where spatial data is already present with itinerate performance, which links back to the 'dwelling perspective' (Ingold, 2000).

The *EMP* does not present itself as a large-scale strategy for implementing food growing in cities. As we barrel headlong into climate emergency, I argue there is an urgent need to engage at all levels regarding the Edible City: as planners, artists, architects, food gardeners, residents, accident professionals, amateurs and the *EMP* is one contribution. I would also argue that change is better attended to via systemic processes while society is still reasonably stable, rather than in the predicted deep crisis. As Johnny Cash wrote in his 1959 song, *Five Feet High and Rising* (Cash, 1959):

"How high's the water, mama?
Three feet high and risin'
How high's the water, papa?
She said it's three feet high and risin'

Well, the hives are gone, I lost my bees
Chickens are sleepin' in the willow trees
Cow's in water up past her knees
Three feet high and risin'"

References

Cash, J., 1959. *Five feet high and rising*. Songs of Our Soil, Columbia Records.

De Certeau, M., 1984. *The practice of everyday life*. Berkeley, CA: University of California Press, 122.

Goodwin, N., 2020. Wheat sowed on the streets of Newcastle offers fresh hope for local baker. [online] *ChronicleLive*. Available from www.chroniclelive.co.uk/news/north-east-news/wheat-harvest-newcastle-shieldfield-loaf-19319821 [Accessed 25 Mar 2023].

Ingold, T., 2000. *Perception of the environment*. New York: Routledge.

Kitchin, R. and Dodge, M., 2007. Rethinking maps. *Progress in Human Geography*, 31 (3), 331–344.

Lefebvre, H., 2003. *The urban revolution*. Minneapolis: University of Minnesota Press.

Okely, J., 2001. Visualism and landscape: Looking and seeing in Normandy. *Ethnos*, 66 (1), 99–120.

SAW, 2019. *Shieldfield begins with your imagination: A map – Shieldfield Art Works* [online]. Available from www.saw-newcastle.org/shieldfield-begins-with-your-imagination-a-map/ [Accessed 25 Mar 2023].

SAW, 2020. Film, "Shieldfield wheat documentary. 22 mins, 15 seconds. *SAW Shieldfield Wheatfield – Shieldfield Art Works* [online]. Available from www.saw-newcastle.org/curated-by-saw/shieldfield-wheatfield/ [Accessed 25 Mar 2023].

Tomkins, M., 2006. *The edible urban landscape: An assessment method for retro-fitting urban agriculture*. Available from www.cityfarmer.org/MikeyTomkins_UA_thesis.pdf

Tomkins, M., 2008. The productive 'ugly sister' of garden history. *The London Gardener Journal*, 14.

Tomkins, M., 2009. UA magazine, 22, 9. *Building Resilient Cities*. Available from https://ruaf.org/assets/2019/11/Urban-Agriculture-Magazine-no.-22-Building-Resilient-Cities.pdf [Accessed 25 Mar 2023].

Tomkins, M., 2012. You are hungry: Flâneuring, edible mapping and feeding imaginations. *Footprint*, 15–36.

Tomkins, M., 2020. *Shieldfield Wheatfield* [online]. Available from https://mikeytomkins.co.uk/shieldfield-wheat-field. [Accessed 25 Mar 2023].

Whetstone, D., 2019. The amount of student housing in Newcastle once again in the spotlight. [online] *ChronicleLive*. Available from www.chroniclelive.co.uk/whats-on/arts-culture-news/amount-student-housing-newcastle-once-16390840 [Accessed 20 Jan 2021].

Wood, D., 2006. Map art. *Cartographic Perspectives*, 53, 5–14. Available from https://cartographicperspectives.org/index.php/journal/article/view/cp53-wood-featured-article [Accessed 16 Aug 2020].

Mapping seeds of freedom with Red de Huerteros Medellín

Paula Restrepo

While large populations need considerable amounts of food, modern cities have tended to reject local agriculture. Instead, they favour capitalist priorities that influence many other political and economic processes, accelerating both urbanisation and large-scale agriculture to an unhealthy and even dangerous level. However, potential alliances between agriculture and cities are developing which may also boost struggles that seek to resist the negative consequences of industrial-scale agriculture and reverse its damage. Urban collectives are one such alliance, fighting to transform spatial conditions by taking advantage of the transformative power of urban agriculture.

Like in many other cities (Lundberg, 2013), urban collectives and local governments in Medellín, Colombia, have started to use urban agriculture as a transformative tool. For example, local administrations might provide tools and supplies, training, as well as support to overcome difficulties in implementing urban agriculture. Many people who engage in urban food growing and urban food system activities come from economically disadvantaged neighbourhoods. Understanding this, local administrations try to demonstrate that urban agriculture can be part of a strategy to alleviate hunger and, at the same time, stop unplanned urban sprawl beyond the city's boundaries. These actions are supported by numerous research papers that regard urban agriculture as a way to address hunger and environmental issues in cities (Méndez-Lemus and Vieyra, 2017; Degenhart, 2016).

People who live in peri-urban areas often have both the initiative and space to plant crops. They may also possess agricultural knowledge from having previously lived in rural areas. Sometimes, their labour on peri-urban farms is profitable. Local governments typically intervene once such urban agriculture projects become successful, in order to demonstrate how urban agriculture works as a way of economic transformation and of improving families' diets (Corcoran and Kettle, 2015). In this way, urban agriculture becomes a tool for local governments to convey that they have achieved their goals and that communities' needs have been satisfied while investing in few resources.

Red de Huerteros Medellín

Medellín is a city with little space and whose soil and air are highly polluted. Although urban agriculture has enormous potential to transform socio-economic realities, in Medellín, that potential stems from the fact that urban farms work as social laboratories allowing citizens to become empowered political subjects that understand their role in the supply segment of the food chain and, as a result, manage to transform their subjectivities (Rivera y Calero, 2022). However, there are also other ways to view urban agriculture in Medellín which enable us to regard farms as *tools* used by families, neighbourhood groups, social organisations and institutions for ecopolitical goals and not only as "devices" for food production. We argue that it is this combination of ecology, economics and

DOI: 10.4324/9781003352280-18

Fig. 1: In 2014, members of the *Red de Huerteros Medellín* (RHM) network create Medellín's food map

food production that provides urban agriculture's most significant transforming power.

In 2013, Medellín witnessed the creation of a collective called *Red de Huerteros Medellín* (RHM). From its inception, this group has questioned the origin of agricultural products that feed cities, reflected on local practices to produce them, supported those practices that maintain biodiversity and health and created alliances with other food-focused collectives to support the establishment of vibrant cities and towns.

RHM's manifesto, *Sowing Sovereign and Solidary Worlds* (2017), supports food sovereignty, building on a concept coined by Vía Campesina that differs from food security as defined by the Food and Agriculture Organization (Medina *et al.*, 2021). While the latter only considers food availability, the former also takes into account the mode of production, the food's origin and peoples' autonomy regarding food policies. RHM's manifesto, therefore, regards urban agriculture as an eco-political practice. It acknowledges how people make decisions that contribute to maintaining or putting in question certain powers while planting, buying, cooking or waste recycling. These powers are usually encompassed within free trade

agreements, intellectual property protection rules and similar agreements among countries intended to give rise to life-based innovation and its appropriation by private hands. It is important to remember that Colombia has been a country at war for a long time, engulfed in a conflict caused by the unequal distribution of all kinds of resources: from land to education, from access to food to access to energy sources or drinking water. After the signing of the *Peace Agreement* with the FARC (Fuerzas Armadas Revolucionarias de Colombia) in 2016, citizens started to demonstrate in a more fervent way their unwillingness to accept political and police violence, inequalities and injustice. The RHM manifesto bears witness to that.

Mapping bottom-up

One of RHM's most important actions was the collective mapping of Medellín's urban farms in 2014. On a paper map made using only paper, scissors, pencils and glue, they located their farms geographically, accompanied by icons to record characteristics such as name, address, area, participants, activities and goals (fig. 1). The maps produced made visible how the network's urban farms were not isolated but were instead part of a practice that was well

01 Huerta Agroarte.
02 Huerta el Guayabo.
03 Huerta Col Mayor.
04 Huerta del Museo de Antioquia.
05 Huerta de la biblioteca Floresta.
06 Huerta Psiqué.
07 AEIOU.
08 El Oregano.
09 Mi Huerta. Huerta Comunitaria La Gabriela.
10 Huerta # 10.
11 El Huerto de la UVA.
12 Huerta de Corinven.
13 Huerta # 13.
14 La Huerta.
15 Eco Huertas Urbanas San Joaquín Bolivariana.
16 Mi Nuevo Renacer.
17 Zúñiga.
18 Entre Semillas Mi Huerta a la Vuelta.
19 Ecohuerta Castelo.
20 Huerta de la Casa de la Cultura Popular.

Fig. 2: Community-generated map showing the general distribution of urban farms across Medellín (RHM, 2020b)

established in the city. This spatial visualisation enabled RHM to identify as a group of people who contributed to a larger movement. Seen in isolation, the farms mainly functioned with production objectives; seen collectively, they became understood as a network of communicative interactions that can give rise to collective ways of inhabiting and contesting space in confrontation with neoliberal logic.

Later, RHM opened a Facebook group and were able to establish contacts with more urban farmers and ask for geo-referenced data to build new maps. Due to concerns about data privacy, RHM decided to create a map in Open Street Map (OSM) which enabled the urban farmers to participate in the map's edit using this free and open-source tool. This new platform gave RHM and its further network more autonomy and ensured that geo-referenced data would be available for everyone. The map was continually updated and reached around 70 entries.

In 2017, RHM decided to study Medellín's urban agriculture characteristics and this has greatly progressed our knowledge of the city's urban agriculture practices. On the one hand, it has allowed us to understand that seed saving is little understood or practised in urban agriculture and this has motivated us to explore further the world of biotechnological and legal details. On the other hand, it has led us to see urban agriculture in our city not as a single activity but as multiple and interconnected practices that should be evaluated one by one. Not being able to articulate the multiple different practices that constitute urban agriculture as a whole has placed us at a disadvantage. Yet, every single practice is vitally important, for example, when exploring seed-saving practices.

The data we used for our research were taken from the OSM map. Unfortunately, several farms no longer existed and some urban

Fig. 3: Screenshots of the online Story Map showing a map of farms that use cutting propagation techniques for plant reproduction and two stories about urban farms (RHM, 2020d)

farmers did not answer our written request for an interview or did not respond when we called them. Nevertheless, the previous 70 entries provided a good starting point to collect stories about urban agriculture in the city and this mapping catalysed our identity as a movement.

From those records, using the snowball technique, we interviewed a further 84 urban farmers. Each farmer answered a questionnaire that included qualitative, quantitative, relational and geo-referenced information which we then mapped. The resulting maps represent an essential feature of our research. One example is our regularly updated overview map (fig. 2), showing the general distribution of farms across Medellín. Another example is the online *Story Map* which can be found at *https://arcg.is/0nLPDK* (fig. 3). It includes location data; short geo-referenced stories about the farms' origins; pictures; classification by gender; an iconographic distinction among private, family and community farms; compost production; cultivated plants; and plant husbandry.

We highlighted the organic waste management map, which expressed how this is a strong urban agriculture practice. However, one of the most insightful maps was not a geographically based map but a relationship one (fig. 4). This relational map shows links between farms, people and organisations related to urban agriculture. It demonstrated urban agriculture as an activity constituted by diverse practices: waste management, bees and other insect preservation, seed liberation, knowledge about medicinal plants, ancestral recipe conservation, among others. These maps highlight practices of utmost importance such as seed use and safeguarding due to their global socio-political power and how they relate to other aspects of urban agriculture.

This relational map visualised a poor connection or no connection at all among urban farmers (UFs) and key organisations related to seed guardians (SGs) (fig. 4): people who protect seeds with the intention of benefiting humanity instead of them becoming private property of multinational corporations. This map supports other data outcomes: only a few Ufs actually know about the eco-political implications of the seed business and even fewer obtain their seeds from seed keepers or show any consideration for their labour. Hence the research revealed that Ufs have little knowledge about political, economic and epistemic implications related to seeds that give rise to our food, nor do they support SGs' labour.

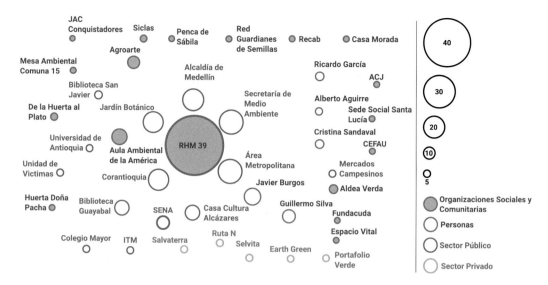

Fig. 4: This relational map shows the key links between farms, people and organisations related to urban agriculture (RHM, 2020c)

Furthermore, this map illustrates connections between UFs, organisations and stakeholders. The size of the circles shows the number of relationships with an organisation or person. RHM was the most highly related organisation: an outcome which was expected since most farmers interviewed were contacted due to their connections with this organisation through maps and geo-referenced data. Alternatively, the organisations Red de Guardianes de Semillas and Red Colombiana de Agricultura Biológica (RECAB) were two of the least related organisations, with less than five relationships among the interviewed UFs and no relation at all with individual SGs.

The most common origin of seeds were the farms themselves, who collect and store seeds from each harvest. Although most of the time this is a good practice, it is mainly carried out in response to an inability to finance buying seeds in stores. Only 29% of gardeners get their seeds from SGs and this quote illustrates motivations for using this source:

We support seed guardians because of our love of Earth and farmers. Because of our love for life, because of respect, because of the aim to preserve

and value a legacy. There is a family memoir, a preservation story of aliment and the natural rhythm of life.

(D46_LaHuertaDeGedy)

Politics versus agriculture

In 2019, a national strike declared discontent with the Colombian government and its politics. This situation was echoed in the Facebook group when administrators accepted a post that said: "*For the defense of life, I march #21N (21th November 2019)*". For some members, it was against the group's objectives, supposedly only intended to address urban farming. The aforementioned members wrote comments such as the following: "*Political posts should be eliminated. Agriculture has nothing to do with the left or right: Everyone decides who they vote for. I would ask members to respect this*".

Despite this disagreement, group administrators were not swayed. According to them, urban agriculture is meant to reflect on conflicts arising within agriculture, how cities have contributed to their worsening and how cities themselves can help to solve them. For example, in Colombia, there is an endless debate about the private property of seeds, use of soils, excessive consumption, agrotoxic usage, glyphosate usage to eradicate coca plantations and water usage in fracking (which, moreover, the government has backed all along). The pledge of many movements that work with urban agriculture worldwide was to understand food choice as a political act. Thereby, this practice becomes a way of asking for our *right to the city* (Lefebvre, 1967) to the extent that resistance is formed in response to the capitalist dynamics that have permeated the act of eating and living in the city.

The *Story Map* has allowed us to strengthen this eco-political narrative surrounding urban agriculture. For example, there is a section dedicated to the farm narratives of Medellín, where we record experiences and stories told by UFs. In the first map (see *https://arcg.is/0nLPDK*), for example, we read:

"*Agroarte was born as a form of resistance against La Escombrera, a place located in Comuna 13, where more than 300 bodies disappeared after Operación Orión (a military operation that took place on October 16 and 17, 2002)*". Other maps in the same section tell diverse stories about urban agriculture in Medellín. For example, Colectivo Tierra states: "*This is a clear example of how a space that was previously at the center of crime and the accumulation of rubbish can be the origin of a project of territorial and social transformation*". Huerta los Valores' story is also awe-inspiring, where a group of ex-guerrilla combatants originally founded this garden in 2004. Other stories are about women trying to survive and teachers teaching through gardens or collectives occupying space. Hence, our stories have to do with social struggles, regarding ecology as a political struggle and the idea that the urban agriculture can be a tool to fight for our *right to the city* from cultural, ethnic and gender diversity (Soja, 2018).

Although there are many ways of doing urban agriculture, we are focused on those that set

a scenario for important actors to transform the city into a territory of resistance to defend life. For example, some Ufs interviewed had sustainable practices and discourses related to water use in the city, urban biodiversity and urban soil regeneration, while also questioning consumption. Harvey (2012) comes to the conclusion that capitalism thrives within the city and, at the same time, transforms it into a place of inequality. Therefore, capitalism needs to invest its surplus through urbanisation, generating more surplus to be invested in the town in order for capital concentration and towns to develop at the same time and at the same rate. Both Lefebvre (1968) and Harvey (2012) maintained that a political consciousness to fight against this kind of urbanisation and production should emerge. However, they differ on who those protagonists would be. Might these protagonists also be UFs, as many people claim?

Urban agriculture is probably overrated as a tool used to seek social justice. Some local governments regard it simply as a cure for misery and a way for low-income families to guarantee food security. Projects that promote this kind of urban agriculture do not question production modes that feed cities through industrial agriculture. We at RHM assert that urban agriculture calls and works for the *right to the city* and should question capitalist methods related to food production which are mainly intended to feed urban inhabitants. Perhaps the practice that best represents this is the safeguarding of the freedom of seeds.

The politics of seeds in Colombia

RHM seeks to put seeds at the core of the urban agriculture debate in resistance to the disastrous consequences of capitalism. According to Luby and Goldman (2016), in the last 100 years, restrictions to germplasm have been increasing so much that the vision of plants as public property has eroded. Moreover, the issue of seeds has become such a sensitive topic that in many countries its administration outwith certain rules imposed by corporations such as Dupont, Syngenta and Bayer-Monsanto can be illegal. Keeping seeds is vital to guarantee production and adapt new generations of plants through artificial selection and other practices that have guaranteed agricultural and food security for centuries. Unfortunately, biotechnology and political lobbying are being used to take advantage of this and restrict their circulation, endangering ancient farming practices. As Vandana Shiva (2007) highlighted, seeds are symbols of freedom amid manipulation and monopoly. Biotechnology is used to manipulate and patents to monopolise them.

Transgenic seed companies lobby the political powers of countries to modify patent laws of living organisms such as seeds and plants so that these corporations build economic, political and juridic environments, thus, monopolising markets. Luby and Goldman argue that such actions by corporations that limit the rights of farmers to keep seeds threaten plant breeding innovation. When seeds are patented by corporations, they patent such innovations capturing humankind's heritage as "raw material". As such, seeds and the accumulated public knowledge surrounding them, being classified as private property, is ethically complex (Shiva, 2007). There is little labour directed towards seed protection in cities. Prioritising this task, however, would bring about many advantages, including empowering citizens with knowledge and the consciousness to support the defence of free, creole and native seeds, in addition to adapting seeds to urban environments.

However, RHM has not yet been able to work extensively enough in order to safeguard the freedom of seeds. One action was the construction of a seed directory where distributors of grains, cereals and nuts of native and creole seeds can be found (RHM, 2020a). We also created a study group to learn about other SGs' networks around the world, legal and educational activities that fight against seed privatisation, Colombian legislation regarding this topic and the relationship between food and seed privatisation. We are currently working

on two interventions and dialogues regarding such knowledge. One of them is called Flavors and Knowledge that brings together knowledge about creole and native seeds to make visible the link between seeds and foods that feed the city. We have also conducted gastronomic workshops to learn how to cook different ancestral seeds such as pigeon peas, chachafruto, cassava, arracacha and petaco beans. We have also used social media by making TikTok videos and developing an Instagram channel @ redhuerteros.

However, our contact with organisations related to the seeds' custody had been largely intermittent. The rights to seeds in Colombia is currently under discussion in the House of Representatives. The draft *Legislative Act number 226* of 2019 proposes to: "*prohibit the entry into the country, as well as the production, commercialization, export and release of genetically modified seeds, to protect the environment and guarantee the right of rural inhabitants and farmers to free seeds*" (2019). However, this current legislation has created some confusion. While this uncertainty has enabled some SGs to continue working with few difficulties, we are also concerned that mapping SGs may create potential repressive actions, as has emerged from historical cases of expropriation of hundreds of tons of seeds that were considered illegal by the Instituto Colombiano de Agricultura (Colombian Institute of Agriculture).

From these actions, RHM is improving relationships between Ufs and SGs, between the countryside and the city, transforming practices and knowledge about seeds by Ufs in Medellín towards a more eco-political perspective. A map is a powerful tool to further encourage consumption of these products and strengthen links between UFs and SGs. However, we have refrained from doing so for fear of facilitating retaliation against seed guardians. Although many cities and countries have forbidden GMOs in agriculture, there is yet a long way to go to build fairer agricultural standards.

Organic waste management

While seeds as a political topic were underdeveloped in Medellín's urban agriculture, waste management was received more favourably, giving rise to a Medellín-led organic waste movement. The city deployed *Paca Digestora Silva* (PDS), a device to manage organic waste by compacting leaves and kitchen waste layers. Our research showed that 83% of interviewed farmers make their own fertiliser, 67% use the compost method, 40% use PDS and 37% use vermicompost. Ufs also engage in complex discourses about soils, waste reuse and consumption decrease – aspects that relate to waste management.

This organic waste management discourse has spread throughout Colombia and other countries, where for example, Bogota has become the leader of the so-called *Movimiento Paquero*. Although the PDS produces organic fertiliser for farms and gardens, the movement also focused on reflecting on consumption practices and the collapse of landfill systems. In figure 4, we see considerably more relationships with people and organisations related to waste management than with those related to seed keeping. However, some organisations – such as Medellín's Botanical Garden – work across these issues. Although seeds and waste management seem disparate, both have had significant repercussions in the city where they represent key sites of connection between global problems and urban gardens. For example, they link the fight against an aggressive consumption system that generates enormous amounts of garbage, seeks to increase private profits and expropriates knowledge resulting from thousands of years of work. However, the countryside seems to be a more suitable place than the city to resolve these issues, especially for SG's networks that tend to address efforts by rural farmers and indigenous peoples.

According to our research, both practices and discourses, such as consumption, food sovereignty or environmental crisis, are strong in waste management. Alternatively, some UFs

keep seeds from their harvests, few are related to SGs and even fewer articulate actions related to topics such as food sovereignty or autonomy, civilisational crisis or economic model crisis. The RHM has been very interested in mapping waste management, especially in places that are using the PDS as shown in http://u.osmfr.org/m/392408/ where can be found pacas in Medellín, Colombia and the world. Bogotá has also extensively promoted community waste management using PDS, mapping their distribution by nodes (*https://linktr.ee/PacaDigestoraSilva*) (fig. 5).

Spatial struggles

Lefebvre (1968) coined the concept of the *right to the city* arguing that cities are unfair and unequal places and that cities' inhabitants were the ones called to fight against such a situation. This fight is against capitalist urbanisation and the mode of production to which it contributes. RHM recognised that the city has the power to bring people together. The city as a singular space can transform society through "spatial struggles" which can be potentialised and eased by using maps from social movements. In the 1990s, Lefebvre's concept was re-launched by the so-called *spatial spin* and gained a new force in the middle of the second decade of the 21st century (Molano, 2015). Current struggles for urban space confront the degradation of cities led by financial capitalism, such is visible in services and soil privatisation, raising inequality, erosion of urban democracy, gentrification and environmental deterioration.

Looking at the role of urban agriculture in the contemporary spatial struggles of Medellín, there are a few key imaginable scenarios: in RHM's different mappings we have learned that urban agriculture can be understood as food system activities of small collectives that aim to find ways to articulate their actions through communication networks. These scenarios are full of contradictions. They seek to fight for collective ways of inhabiting space and, at the same time, are complicit to forms of cultivation

Fig. 5: PDS registered in Bogotá Región, mapped by nodes (Red de huerteras y huerteros de Bakatá Región, n.d.)

that strengthen neoliberal logics which, in turn, can lead to the endangerment of food sovereignty and a lack of understanding in the articulation between political ecology discourses and planting practices.

When space is at the core of the debate, mapping is an urgent practice that allows us to look at the city in other ways and to appropriate it from the bottom up. These struggles are limited not only to opposing neoliberalism, but also appeal to resisting cultural, ethnic and gender injustices (Soja, 2018). Even though urban agriculture can give rise to urban communication models that enable us to inhabit space and gain our *right to the city*, it is also required to strengthen certain agricultural discourses and practices in the town that lead us to a food production closer to life. We consider that it is essential to enhance communication practices

that allow UFs to appropriate the discourses related to safeguarding seeds and caring for pollinators, responsible consumption and proper organic waste management. As Lefebvre argued regarding politicising space in the city, it is also necessary to politicise urban agriculture. As such, joint efforts must be made to understand and transform the relationship that agriculture has with global eco-politics to ensure that urban agriculture represents a site of resistance towards securing our *right to the city*.

Mapping urban agriculture as a social movement

This chapter has demonstrated how the RHM has used maps to identify as a social movement, to transform the narratives related to urban agriculture, to give visibility to the PDS and to find and connect people who are carrying out urban agriculture activities. Urban agriculture mapping has made us aware of being a collective body and, in doing so, has strengthened our work. In other words, maps have strengthened our fight for our *right to the city*. One significant difference between the work we have done around seeds and the PDS is that the latter was extensively mapped. Although its success is not limited to this act, there is no doubt that it has contributed, especially in Bogotá, to spreading this practice across the country within just a few years. The absence of a map for seeds, however, needs to be understood as a reflection of fear in the face of advancing repressive legislation, especially witnessed in the United States, the country that many Latin American governments tend to imitate. After all, maps are tools for generating and communicating knowledge – primarily related to space and social connections – and for articulating ideas and people. They have helped us change the city's speeches, stories and language. However, the question that remains is how to build and use urban food maps to reach our social goals without "handing over" this knowledge to an oppressive system that seeks to usurp us of the right to a fair and equal urban life.

References

Corcoran, M.P. and Kettle, P.C., 2015. Urban agriculture, civil interfaces and moving beyond difference: The experiences of plot holders in Dublin and Belfast. *Local Environment*, 20 (10), 1215–1230. https://doi.org/10.1080/13549 839.2015.1038228

Degenhart, B., 2016. La agricultura urbana: un fenómeno global. *Revista Nueva Sociedad*, 262, 136–146.

Harvey, D., 2012. The right to the city. *In*: J. Lin and C. Mele, eds. *The urban sociology reader*. London: Routledge, 443–446.

Lefebvre, H., 1967. Le droit à la ville. *L'Homme et la société*, 6 (1), 29–35.

Lefebvre, H., 1968. *Le droit à la ville, I, et II, espace et politique*. Paris: Anthropos.

Luby, C. and Goldman, I., 2016. Freeing crop genetics through the open source seed initiative. *PLoS Biology*, 14 (4). Available from https://journals.plos. org/plosbiology/article/file?id=10.1371/journal. pbio.1002441&type=printable

Lundberg, B., 2013. Urban agriculture and local government law: Promises, realities and solutions. *University of Pennsylvania Journal of Law and Social Change*, 16, 221–235.

Medina Rey, J.M., Ortega Carpio, M. and Martínez Cousinou, G., 2021. ¿Seguridad alimentaria, soberanía alimentaria o derecho a la alimentación? Estado de la cuestión. *Cuadernos de desarrollo rural*, 18, 1–19.

Méndez-Lemus, Y. and Vieyra, A., 2017. How social capital enables or restricts the livelihoods of poor peri-urban farmers in Mexico. *Development in Practice*, 27 (3), 301–315.

Molano, F., 2015. *El Derecho a la Ciudad en la ciudad neoliberal: una agenda estratégica para la lucha por la ciudad*. Buenos Aires: Mimeo.

Paquerxs Bogotá-Red de Huerteras y Huerteros, 2019. *Registro de pacas digestoras silva en Bogotá-Región*. Available from www.google.com/maps/d/viewer?mid=1G_KcBc_m9aH2lb95K_nYZqdfpN6vBJNL&hl=es&ll=4.5984898149 07903%2C-74.071034003303343&z=14

Proyecto de Acto Legislativo número 226 de 2019. Available from www.secretariasenado.gov.co/legibus/legibus/gacetas/2019/GC_0874_2019.pdf

Red de Huerteros Medellín, 2017. Manifiesto Red de Huerteros Medellín. *Sembrando mundos soberanos y solidarios*. Available from www.redhuerterosmedellin.org/manifiesto-red-de-huerteros-medellin/

Red de Huerteros Medellín, 2020a. Comer es un acto político. *Directorio de semillas que resisten*. Available from https://upamedellin.files.wordpress.com/2020/12/semillasqueresisten-2.pdfRed de Huerteros Medellín, 2020b. *Huertas entrevistadas Red de Huerteros Medellín*. Available from www.redhuerterosmedellin.org/wp-content/uploads/2020/07/MapaRHM.pdf

Red de Huerteros Medellín, 2020c. *Relational map between farms, people and organizations related to UA*, May 2020.

Red de Huerteros Medellín, 2020d. Story map: Aprovechamiento de los residuos orgánicos para la producción de abonos naturales. *Mayo de 2020*. Available from https://arcg.is/0nLPDK

Red de huerteras y huerteros de Bakatá Región, n.d. Paquerxs Bogotá-Red de huerteras y huerteros. *Google Maps*. Available from https://www.google.com/maps/d/viewer?mid=1G_KcBc_m9aH2lb95K_nYZqdfpN6vBJN-L&hl=es&usp=sharing

Rivera, C. and Calero, S., 2022. Soberanía alimentaria: acciones y sentidos para la construcción de nuevos sujetos. *En*: P. Restrepo, C. Rivera y S. Calero, eds. *Prácticas sociales de la agricultura urbana en Medellín*. Medellín: Fondo Editorial de la Facultad de Comunicaciones y Filología de la Universidad de Antioquia.

Shiva, V., 2007. *Las nuevas guerras de la globalizaciónsemillas, agua y formas de vida*. Madrid: Editorial Popular.

Soja, E., 2018. *Posmetrópolis, estudios críticos sobre las ciudades y las regiones*. Madrid: Traficantes de Sueños.

Food in urban design and planning: The CPUL Opportunity Mapping Method

Katrin Bohn

Food is fundamental to a sustainable and resilient urban development, yet, to the author's knowledge, most urban design and planning still does not fully provide for food system activities. As all built environment professions rely on maps, for the reasons stated elsewhere in this book, it seems imperative as well as beneficial to employ urban food mapping to advance food-focused urban design and planning processes.

One urban food mapping method, the *CPUL Opportunity Mapping Method*, has been developed by the author, with André Viljoen, as part of our ongoing and evolving design research into productive urban landscapes. This method is informed by participatory and co-design theories (Pieters and Jansen, 2017) and embedded in Bohn&Viljoen's *Continuous Productive Urban Landscape* concept (Viljoen, 2005).

Bohn&Viljoen Architects began publishing around the year 2000 on what we termed *Continuous Productive Urban Landscape (CPUL)*. A *CPUL* is an urban green infrastructure linking food-producing sites of varying scales and operating types with other (green) open spaces through and across towns or cities, connecting those parcels of land to the citizens as well as to other food system activities and, ultimately, to the rural landscape (Viljoen, 2005). It is an urban design concept proposing that urban agriculture can contribute to more sustainable and resilient food systems while also adding beneficially to the spatial and socioeconomical quality of the civic realm (Viljoen and Bohn,

2000). The planned introduction of *CPULs* into existing and emerging urban areas would create the *CPUL City*.

The Inventory of Urban Capacity

In 2012, after more than a decade of design research and practice, we brought together our observations and analyses of successful food projects and defined the *CPUL City Actions*: four recurring conditions essential for any lasting integration of urban agriculture and food system activities into cities (Bohn and Viljoen, 2012). One of those four interlinked actions we called *Inventory of Urban Capacity*.

The *Inventory of Urban Capacity* is also the first stage of the *CPUL Opportunity Mapping Method*, subject of this chapter. Using a diverse range of mapping practices including drawing, photographing, walking, writing, collaging and diagraming, it aims to create a comprehensive overview of the status quo of any given site or sites.

Through our work, we had found that "*an inventory is necessary for each location, especially of spatial, resource, stakeholder and managerial capacities in order to best respond to local opportunities*" (Bohn and Viljoen, 2014, p. 159). At that time, around 2010, emphasis (if any) was usually only given to identifying and mapping open urban space for urban agriculture (Balmer *et al.*, 2005). However, it had become clear to us in our practice and design research that engaging the local community and assessing its managerial capacities in a food growing

DOI: 10.4324/9781003352280-19

The CPUL Opportunity Mapping Method

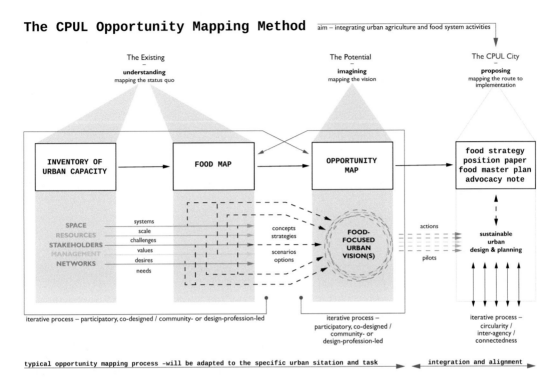

Fig. 1: The three-stage *CPUL Opportunity Mapping Method* enables the design and planning of food system opportunities for any given site (Bohn&Viljoen Architects [2012] with Ian Bailey, University of Brighton, 2021)

project were as important. Moreover, available resources also needed to be recorded and integrated into the planning and execution of any urban food projects (Bohn and Viljoen, 2014, p. 255).

The *Inventory of Urban Capacity* therefore suggests:

1) map physical sites to build a catalogue of *spatial opportunities* considering that suitability for urban agriculture includes issues such as orientation (sun), soil, air, boundaries, access, supply (e.g. water) and ownership.

2) identify existing and potential *stakeholders* as well as their goals for the project's different development stages – from start-up to establishment to long-term prominence – in order to ascertain if local capacity needs developing to maintain the project.

3) aim for no-waste systems – grow, eat, compost, grow . . . – as one aspect of maximising the ecological intensification on (open) urban space.

4) identify and map local *resource and managerial capacities* as a basis for new economic models, environmentally friendly production and fair trade for urban farmers.

A participatory design and planning tool

Based on this understanding, a productive urban landscape – regardless of its scale and typology or even as an individual urban food system activity – without supportive local population is not imaginable. The *CPUL Opportunity Mapping Method* reflects this: it is a participatory urban design and planning tool aimed at a networked integration of urban agriculture and food system activities into

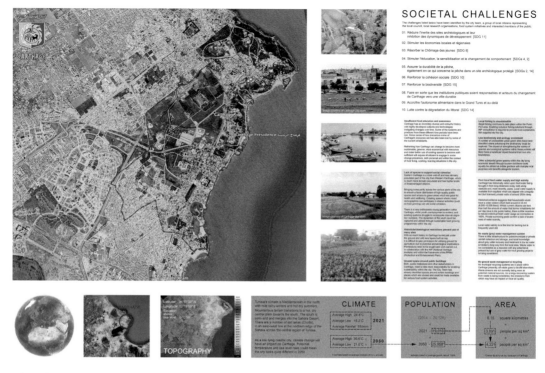

Fig. 2: Supporting the food map of Carthage is a database mapping key characteristics of the city as well as the challenges it aims to address (extract; University of Brighton (Ian Bailey, Katrin Bohn) and City Team Carthage, 2021)

cities (Viljoen and Bohn, 2014). The method equips its users with a systemic as well as systematic approach to urban food mapping processes. Outcomes of these processes are "food maps" that record/count/order and "opportunity maps" that explore/propose/ envision. Any of the urban food maps classified in the *Urban Food Mapping Matrix* (*see Introduction*) can be generated using the method (fig. 1).

It lies in the nature of the urban agriculture movement to be site-specific and stakeholder-led. Consequentially, each urban food mapping process is different. The *CPUL Opportunity Mapping Method* has been employed by the author since 2004 in various projects and for a variety of clients ranging from local authorities to local food initiatives, from arts-based to planning-based organisations. Each time, we "reinvented the method" whilst adhering to its iterative structure. Each time, everything was

new – sites, landscapes, stakeholders, climate, food system activities, aims, tasks, funding – yet, each process resulted in a number of urban food and opportunity maps and a measurable project legacy originating in this mapping-based participatory work (Bohn&Viljoen Architects, n.d.). By "making visible" through mapping, we were able to move towards edible nature-based solutions that concentrated on the locally specific to the benefit of the national and global.

Within our design practice, this approach noticeably advanced the acceptance of urban agriculture and food system activities in the cities we worked with, and it generated implementable pilots. This chapter discusses two example projects: in 2010–12, in Köln [Cologne], Germany, we facilitated the first full urban food mapping process, i.e. one that completed all stages as seen in figure 1. The author will compare this with the most recent

Fig. 3: Supporting the food map of Cologne is a database registering name, location, produce and producers of each food system activity (extract; Bohn&Viljoen Architects and DQE [2011] with Nishat Awan, Technical University Berlin, 2012)

full process, being conducted at the time of writing in Carthage, Tunisia, in order to reflect on the variability and usefulness of the method.

Opportunity mapping in Carthage and Cologne

Whilst our three-stage *CPUL Opportunity Mapping Method* usually aims for two straightforward maps – food and opportunity – the participatory mapping processes generating them are extremely diverse. This diversity mirrors the different food and stakeholder realities we encounter in specific local contexts, and it is clearly captured in the final maps, as well as in their supporting documents.

In Carthage, the project *Towards a food-focused masterplan* serves this chapter as an example of top-down, cross-disciplinary, design-profession-led, participatory urban food mapping. Triggered by environmental concerns,

members of the municipality and the local environmental research association REACT began thinking about urban agriculture as a possible land use. The food subject emerged as an opportunity for this ancient city at the outskirts of the Tunisian capital because 64% of its land is classified as an archaeological site protected by UNESCO world heritage status (Commune de Carthage, n.d.). Such distinction comes with various advantages on the one hand, for example tourism, research projects and financial support, but, on the other hand, locals consider the protection order *"stifling"* for urban development (Houman *et al.*, 2022). Neither the municipality, nor landowners, nor landusers can build on the archaeological site. This can be seen as an advantage too because it kept urban sprawl from Tunis at bay. However, coupled with high unemployment, especially amongst young people, waste management problems and biodiversity degradation, to name

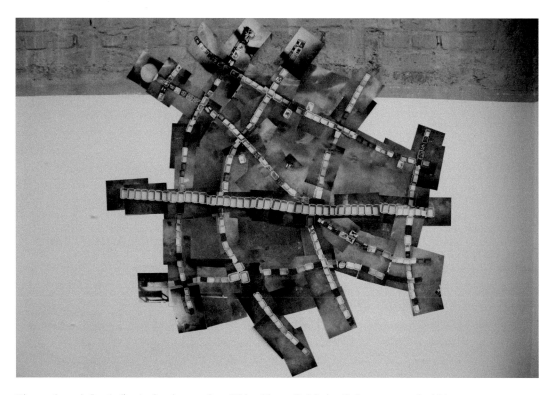

Figs. 4 and 5: A first food map for Köln-Ehrenfeld in Cologne was built as an interactive installation of the street layout to enable conversations about food in the neighbourhood (Dirk Melzer, 2010)

but a few challenges, the "loss" of territory is bitterly felt (Houman *et al.*, 2022). Within the framework of a Horizon-2020-funded project (EdiCitNet, n.d.), the author has supported the city since 2021 in envisioning sustainable urban development strategies. As part of this, the local team first conducted field research for an *Inventory of Urban Capacity* and identified the societal challenges it aimed to address through food (City Team Carthage, 2022a), of which one

image- and text-based mapping, a datasheet, is shown in figure 2.

In Cologne, Bohn&Viljoen Architects co-facilitated a complex project that serves this chapter as an example of bottom-up, cross-disciplinary, design-profession-led, participatory urban food mapping (Viljoen and Bohn, 2014, p. 216–21). Running from 2010 until 2012 and being coordinated by a team around local art historian Sabine Voggenreiter, *Urbane Agrikultur in Köln-Ehrenfeld* was, to the author's knowledge, the first project in Germany to establish food as the major tool – and major aim – in a locally driven urban regeneration process. This approach benefitted from the art-based commissioning situation of the project as part of Cologne's architecture biennale *plan10* which added its own dynamics of hands-on public discourse and engagement (Voggenreiter,

CLASSIFICATION DES
ESPACES OUVERTS

Espaces ouverts publics
de la qualité paysage

Espaces ouverts publics
éducatifs et institutionnels

Espaces ouverts archéologiques
(publics et privés)

L'agriculture urbaine
dans les zones archéologiques

Espaces ouverts privés

Espaces ouverts privés commercials

Zones côtières

Routes importantes et
ligne ferroviaire (TGM)

Limite der Carthage

Zones socio-géographiques

○ Projet existant
de la production alimentaire

♥ Projet existant
de l'élevage du bétail

CLASSIFICATION DES
ACTIVITÉS DE SYSTÈME ALIMENTAIRE

○ Production alimentaire
>>> voir les espaces de
production alimentaire ci-dessus

● Traitement des aliments
Sur le site de production
○ Entreprises de traitement
○ Boulangerie

■ Vente au détail de produits alimentaires
□ Épicerie
□ Marché local
■ Supermarché

● Consommation alimentaire
○ Restauration rapide locale
○ Restauration rapide
○ Restaurant gastronomique
○ Hôtel

◆ Recyclage des déchets alimentaires
◆ Installations de compostage

Fig. 6: Created in collaboration with local stakeholders under leadership of the municipality, Carthage's food map visualises existing urban space types and food system activities (University of Brighton (Ian Bailey, Katrin Bohn) and City Team Carthage, 2022)

2014a). Starting point was the Ehrenfeld neighbourhood, largely neglected by city officials but consisting of a healthy network of long-established, often working-class inhabitants, a transient student and immigrant population, young creative industries and small-scale businesses. Led by the *Design Quartier Ehrenfeld (DQE)* initiative, an innovative sustainable urban design approach was taken to regenerate the run-down urban quarter, so that "*small-scale and sensitive urban and socially interactive planning of the city will help it survive . . . long-term*" (Voggenreiter, 2014b, p. 222). Therefore, the first aim of the project was to bring people together and get them talking to each other – about food. To enable this, the project first generated an

Inventory of Urban Capacity to make visible the many, mostly hidden food system activities that were going on in the neighbourhood. Several interlocking mappings were trialled to support the engagement process, one of which, an interactive data base, can be seen in figure 3.

Urban food maps and food mapping

The *CPUL Opportunity Mapping Method* facilitates food maps that can either be used as stand-alone final outputs, ready to become part of local urban development projects, or as a starting point for an opportunity mapping process. In both cases, the urban food map helps to: 1) capture all relevant aspects of the existing local food system; 2) visualise the complexity of the given site in food-planning terms; and 3) enable viewers to see spatial connections between local food actors and activities that previously remained hidden.

In Cologne, the art-based participatory food maps (figs. 4 and 5), presented as a public exhibition during *plan10*, were followed by three mapping workshops spread over several months during 2010 and 2011 with locals meeting in between to advance site research. Each workshop ran for several days, allowing people to drop in and out and consisted of site visits, talks (some illustrated, some invited), joint meals and the work, often in groups, on different parts of the quarter using geographical maps. The mapping process was open-ended. Its aim was to support neighbourhood building using food as an agent for place-making and participation, also in an effort to fight off profit-led developer interests.

In Carthage, the mapping process was masterplan-oriented from its beginning in 2021, aimed at improving environmental performance of the whole city as well as achieving a proposition about the usage of the city's "dormant" open space that can be negotiated with UNESCO. In a participatory process, the local team developed its own mapping-based open urban space classification to locate the city's 10 most urgent societal challenges it had identified before. Hindered by the Covid-19 pandemic, discussions, talks and expert panels were mostly held online, using a Miro board to communicate visually, whilst fieldwork was carried out by the local team to map existing urban food system activities (fig. 6).

Food-focused opportunity maps

Food-focused opportunity maps, as Bohn&Viljoen define them, *"visualise food system activities from a spatial perspective and can serve as cross-disciplinary links and communication tools between professional designers and planners, food system actors, local authorities and lay audiences. Such*

maps are not masterplans in the traditional planning sense but act as strategic, conceptual steps ahead of them. They capture ideas, desires and possibilities and make them accessible to diverse audiences".
(Bohn, 2019)

In our practice, an opportunity map is also an urban food map. It differs from the food map in that it contains one or several propositions and therefore, usually, comes after the food map that showed the status quo. Ideally, the opportunity map is a precursor to either a food strategy or a food-focused urban masterplan or both.

In Cologne, the final opportunity map assembled all information collected, discussed and evaluated during several on-site workshops. It fulfilled two purposes: on the one hand, it made visible a large number of existing and potential food system spaces, activities and stakeholders and the spatial and organisational networks between them. On the other hand, it enabled and visualised four jointly generated productive urban landscape strategies: a) an East-to-West productive green corridor; b) a North-to-South productive green corridor; c) the redevelopment of the Helios Quarter, a former industrial hub now occupied by small creative businesses; and d) a North-West-to-South-East green corridor. The opportunity map also visualised three potential pilot projects that emerged in the workshops: 1) *Low Line Ehrenfeld*: the regeneration of a disused, ground-level railway line; 2) *Obsthain Grüner Weg*: a community orchard on an unused brownfield site; and 3) *Weinberg Güterbahnhof*: a vineyard on a south-facing slope next to a disused goods train station (figs. 7 and 8).

In Carthage, participatory workshops enabled the local team to generate and agree on visions and concepts for an *Edible Carthage*. These were not all geographically rooted, hence, a novel intermediate stage was devised and collectively developed: the opportunity mapping diagram. This diagram makes visible a complex web of three food-focused urban visions – *Edible historic urban landscape*, *Food knowledge networks* and *Sustainable coastline* – and four urban development

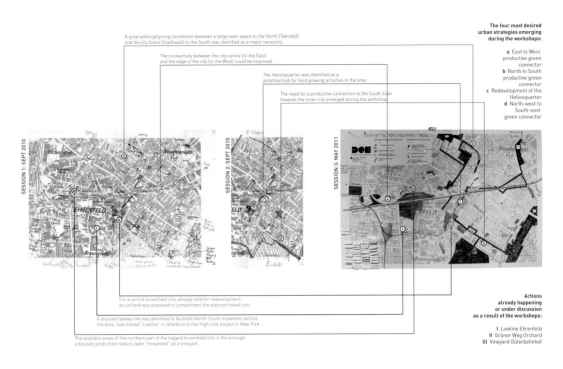

The four most desired
urban strategies emerging
during the workshops:

a East to West
productive green
connector
b North to South
productive green
connector
c Redevelopment of the
Heliosquarter
d North-west to
South-east
green connector

A good walking/cycling connection between a large open space to the North (Takufeld)
and the city forest (Stadtwald) to the South was identified as a major necessity.

The connectivity between the city centre (to the East)
and the edge of the city (to the West) could be improved.

The Heliosquarter was identified as a
potential hub for food growing activities in the area.

The need for a productive connection to the South-East
towards the inner-city emerged during the workshop.

SESSION 1: SEPT 2010

SESSION 2: SEPT 2010

SESSION 3: MAY 2011

For a central brownfield site, already sold for redevelopment,
an orchard was proposed to complement the planned mixed-use.

A disused railway line was identified to facilitate North-South movement across
the area, now named "Lowline" in reference to the High Line project in New York.

The available areas of the northern part of the biggest brownfield site in the borough,
a disused goods train station, were "reinvented" as a vineyard.

Actions
already happening
or under discussion
as a result of the workshops:

I Lowline Ehrenfeld
II Grüner Weg Orchard
III Vineyard Güterbahnhof

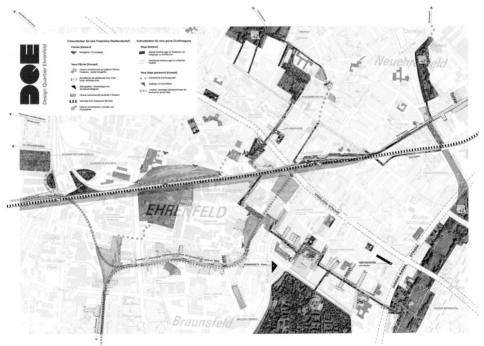

Figs. 7 and 8: The Opportunity Map for Köln-Ehrenfeld (above) emerged from a series
of food maps (far above). It visualises an urban design strategy that integrates
existing and potential food spaces as well as concrete implementation ideas
(Bohn&Viljoen Architects [2011] with Nishat Awan, Technical University Berlin, 2012)

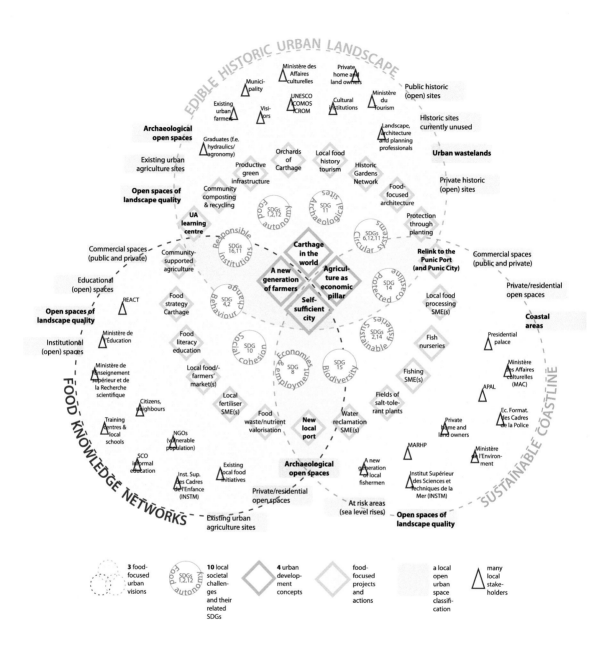

Fig. 9: Preceding the opportunity map of Carthage is this diagram which captures the richness of the locally specific edible city vision (image: University of Brighton (Katrin Bohn, Ian Bailey) and City Team Carthage [data], 2022)

concepts – *Carthage in the world*, *Agriculture as economic pillar*, *Self-sufficient city* and *A new generation of farmers*, all of which were achieved through iterative, conceptual mappings in live meetings and on the Miro board, facilitated by the author. The resulting diagram (fig. 9) shows how the visions and concepts relate to the city's societal challenges, its key stakeholders and open spaces. The diagram also names a number of potential food-focused pilot projects and actions that began emerging during the working process.

Ahead: Designing urban food transitions

Whilst each urban food mapping process starts from the existing context of its unique site and urban capacities, the two most common aims of the *CPUL Opportunity Mapping Method* are to produce credible maps and mappings aiding to develop or inform 1) a local food strategy and 2) a local food masterplan.

Neither in Carthage nor Cologne have such food-focused masterplans been adopted yet, though Cologne has had a food strategy since about five years ago. Cologne and Carthage (now) both are fully aware of the necessity to improve their urban food systems for environmental and socio-economic reasons. In both cities, (open) space plays a vital role: whilst the lacking activity on open space is threatening Carthage, the intensifying activity on open space is threatening the borough of Ehrenfeld in Cologne. In both cities, food has been identified as a tool and an aim to involve stakeholders in envisioning an alternative, sustainable urban future. Even without completed food masterplans, the two projects' experiences can confirm that urban food mapping processes will leave a legacy towards these aims and that this legacy, if pursued, will succeed in making cities more food-sustainable.

In Cologne, for the last 10 years, key ideas that carry the emerging food-focused urban design and planning in the Ehrenfeld neighbourhood were developed in the opportunity mapping process facilitated by Bohn&Viljoen with landscape architect Dirk Melzer and DQE staff. This means in spatial terms that: 1) a new housing estate includes the fruit trees of the community orchard and adopted a productive open space planning (GAG Immobilien AG, n.d.); 2) community gardening was incorporated into the redevelopment of the goods train station (Stadt Köln, n.d.) and Ehrenfeld now produces wine (Ehrenveedel, 2021); and 3) the *Low Line Linear Park* is still being discussed within the local council (veedelfunker, 2013). An associated strategic outcome is Cologne's Food Policy Council (Ernährungsrat Köln, n.d.), the first in Germany, with the local community starting its network during the opportunity mapping process.

In Carthage, it is too early to reflect on the legacy of the opportunity mapping process because it is ongoing until the end of 2023. However, what has been already achieved is the creation of a dedicated city team, a complete overview of the existing and potential food system situation and the subject anchored in civil society, city administration and politics. There are also a few pilot projects that have been formulated during the project time: two local schools are investigating the use of their school grounds for food production, the council is negotiating with the city's urban agriculture pioneer to use land on less important archaeological sites for a micro-green farm and, most importantly, the municipality is considering to develop a food strand in its ongoing urban masterplanning (Municipalité de Carthage, 2023). To kick-start the latter, the mayor has commissioned, at the beginning of 2023, a local planning practice to co-produce the final opportunity map in cooperation with the city team. It was still under discussion when writing this chapter, therefore only a draft of the map could be included here (fig. 10).

Transitioning to a food-sensitive city is a significant challenge. Whilst many cities around the globe have development plans for roads, water, air quality, housing, to name but a few subject areas, food masterplans are yet to be drawn up. Urban food practice is here, urban food research

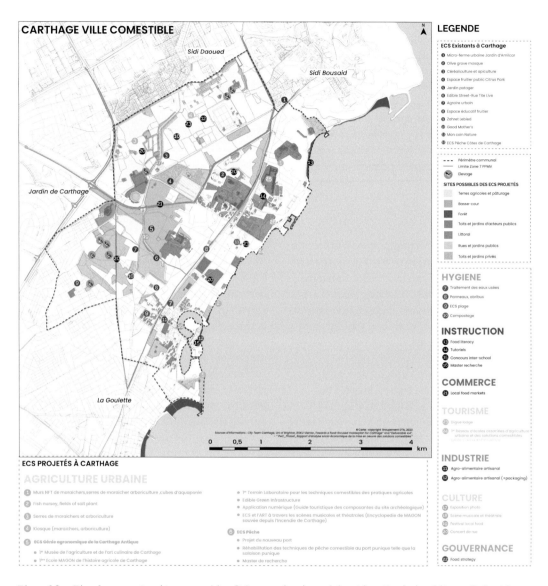

Fig. 10: Final opportunity map (draft) commissioned by the Municipality of Carthage taking forward the results of the opportunity mapping process (Groupement DTA and City Team Carthage [data], 2023)

too; what is needed are food policies and food strategies, fully integrated into municipal, regional and national planning legislation (Viljoen and Bohn, 2015). In this process, the role of urban food and opportunity maps and mapping methods cannot be emphasised enough. The local team in Carthage expressed it like this: "*[the opportunity mapping process] has enabled the city team and all its partners [. . .] to 'design' the contours of a self-sufficient, inclusive and resilient city – a city 'that we want'*" (City Team Carthage, 2022b, p. 150; Houman *et al.*, 2022).

References

Balmer, K., Gill. J., Kapliner, H., Miller, J., Peterson, M., Rhoads, A., Rosenbloom, P. and Wall, T., 2005. *The diggable* city: Making urban agriculture a planning priority. Available from https://oregonexplorer.info/content/the-digga-ble-city-making-urban-agriculture-planning-priority [Accessed 16 Nov 2022].

Bohn, K., 2019. Five facts about food mapping. EdiCitNet Andernach. Available from www.researchgate.net/publication/342132126_Five_facts_about_food_mapping [Accessed 16 Nov 2022].

Bohn, K. and Viljoen, A., 2012. The CPUL City Toolkit: Planning productive urban landscapes for European cities. In: A. Viljoen and J. Wiskerke, eds. Sustainable food planning: Evolving theory and practice. Wageningen: Wageningen Academic Press.

Bohn, K. and Viljoen, A., 2014. CPUL City Actions: An introduction. In: A. Viljoen and K. Bohn, eds. Second Nature Urban Agriculture: Designing productive cities. London: Routledge.

Bohn&Viljoen Architects, n.d. Practice. Available from http://bohnandviljoen.co.uk/practice [Accessed 16 Nov 2022].

City Team Carthage, 2022a. Les défis sociétaux. In: M. Manderscheid et al., eds. Deliverable D4.4. EdiCitNet report, 167–171.

City Team Carthage, 2022b. Processus d'élaboration du masterplan. In: M. Manderscheid et al., eds. Deliverable D4.4. EdiCitNet report, 149–151.

Commune de Carthage, n.d. La ville en chiffres. Available from www.commune-carthage.gov.tn/fr/index.php?srub=258&rub=247 [Accessed 16 Nov 2022].

EdiCitNet, n.d. Edible city solutions for a better world!. Available from www.edicitnet.com [Accessed 16 Nov 2022].

Ehrenveedel, 2021. Der erste Wein, made in Ehrenfeld' ist da. Available from https://ehrenveedel.net/imi-winery-wein-ehrenfeld [Accessed 16 Nov 2022].

Ernährungsrat Köln und Umgebung, n.d. Der Ernährungsrat. Available from www.ernaehrungsrat-koeln.de [Accessed 16 Nov 2022].

GAG Immobilien AG, n.d. Ehrenfelds Grüner Weg. Available from www.gag-koeln.de/die-gag/wohnen-mit-der-gag/unsere-objekte/wohnfuhlobjekte/gruner-weg [Accessed 16 Nov 2022].

Houman, B., Bayoudh, H., Malki, K., Bousselmi, L., Bouziri, L. and Sbei, H., 2022. Towards an Edible Carthage: Developing an inclusive, healthy, vibrant and resilient city. Municipality of Carthage. Unpublished.

Municipalité de Carthage, 2023. Groupement DTA: Présentation des données restituées. Unpublished.

Pieters, M. and Jansen, S., 2017. The 7 principles of complete co-creation. Amsterdam: BIS Publishers, 15.

Stadt Köln, n.d. Ehemaliger Güterbahnhof Ehrenfeld. Available from ww.stadt-koeln.de/politik-und-verwaltung/stadtentwicklung/gueterbahnhof-ehrenfeld [Accessed 16 Nov 2022].

veedelfunker Stadtmagazin, 2013. Ehrenfelds neue grüne Linie. Available from http://veedelfunker.de/ausgabe/ehrenfeld-pflanzt/ehrenfelds-neue-gr%C3%BCne-linie [Accessed 16 Nov 2022].

Viljoen, A. (ed.), 2005. Continuous Productive Urban Landscape: Designing urban agriculture for sustainable cities. London: Architectural Press.

Viljoen, A. and Bohn, K., 2000. Urban intensification and the integration of productive landscape. In: A. Sayigh, ed. Renewable energy: The energy for the 21st century, vol. 1. Oxford: Pergamon Press, 483–488.

Viljoen, A. and Bohn, K., 2014. Second Nature Urban Agriculture: Designing productive cities. London: Routledge.

Viljoen, A. and Bohn, K., 2015. Pathways from practice to policy for productive urban landscapes. In: G. Cinà and E. Dansero, eds. Localizing urban food strategies: Farming cities and performing rurality. Torino: Politecnico di Torino, 98–106. Available from www.aesoptorino2015.it.

Voggenreiter, S., 2014a. City, disorder, time and good life. In: K. Keitz and S. Voggenreiter, eds. Architecture in context: Developing urban living environments beyond the masterplan and façade discussion. Berlin: Jovis, 20–39.

Voggenreiter, S., 2014b. Initials. CPUL: Regenerating the urban. In: A. Viljoen and K. Bohn, eds. Second Nature Urban Agriculture: Designing productive cities. London: Routledge, 222–227.

FOOD PRODUCE AND CULTURES: Uncovering the special in the everyday

This section refers to **maps and mappings of urban collective agency, memory and food fiction, as well as of adaptation and resilience**. Through case studies, its chapters explore the role of urban food mapping especially around the everyday as they contribute to urban histories and narratives, identities and customs. They show how participatory and scientific mapping methods combined with a range of approaches, such as ethnographic observation, literature and historical analysis as well as photographic fieldwork, can make concealed connections visible. Past and present challenges can so be understood as future opportunities.

Urban food mapping understands food system activities **to be made up of everyday practices, performed by individuals and collectives** on a local level with repercussions of global reach. Spatialised across our daily work routine, domestic or social life, they often slip from our memory as each day passes. Here, authors map these small connections between individuals, social groups and the local built environment as a product of everyday life.

DOI: 10.4324/9781003352280-20

Marthe Derkzen et al. map urban food-scapes and foodscape changes in Bengaluru, India. Combining participatory mapping, interviews and photography, they show how Bengalurueans from different socio-economic, demographic and geographic back-grounds **make sense of food produce and practices not just as an edible product but also as an expression of cultural heritage**, everyday connections and imminent futures.

Diana Tung explores the preparation and consumption of aguaje (palm fruit) and its centrality to Amazonian identity. Using photography and text, she maps **how the fruit's street vendors in Iquitos, Peru, are embedded within the local tissue**, exploring their domestic and public workspaces, as well as production processes. The resulting research details the spatial distribution of aguaje and aguajina stalls in the municipality.

Mila Brill investigates how the mapping of gastronomic use preferences can help deepen public participation in inner-city development processes, especially in the context of cultural polarisation. She describes **maps of food place use and mapping processes in a very diverse district** of Bonn, Germany, highlighting the relevance of mobility and place-making for everyday practices, such as eating out.

Merel Zwarts et al. present the activities of the *Travelling Farm Museum of Forgotten Skills*. This mobile and interactive museum is centred in Leidsche Rijn near Utrecht, The Netherlands, a once agricultural area now replaced by mass housing. Using cycling, interviewing, collecting and a mobile installation, the museum **captures and maps the stories, memories and skills from local farmers and residents**.

Silvia Rosivalová Baučeková detects a rising interest in literature about food. She critically analyses the optimistic visions on London's foodscapes expressed in culinary texts by British food writers to **show how the present-day food map of London is closely intertwined not only with Britain's colonial history, but also with the city's current status** as one of the world's global capitalist metropolises.

Food produce/ culture

	Purpose WHY? recording counting comparing uncovering responding proposing	Citizen WHO? urban farmers food system activists food initiatives consumers local communities public institutions
**Derkzen et al.** Oota Kathegalu: Tracing the food stories of Bengaluru, India	recording food places comparing food cultures 	urban farmers / food initiative 
Tung Emblematic fruit: Mapping aguaje palm fruit vendors during Covid-19 in Iquitos, Peru	uncovering food stakeholders recording produce 	food system stakeholders / consu 
Zwarts et al. Reimagining the (agri)cultural city: Commoning and cultivating relationships in Utrecht, Holland	uncovering food stakeholders responding to change 	urban farmers / local communit 
Brill Participative food culture mapping in polarised urban districts	counting food places proposing change 	food system activists / consum 
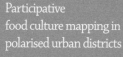**Baučeková** A fairy tale of a place: Depictions of 21st century London as a fantasy foodscape in contemporary food writing	comparing food stories recording food places 	consumers / food initatives 

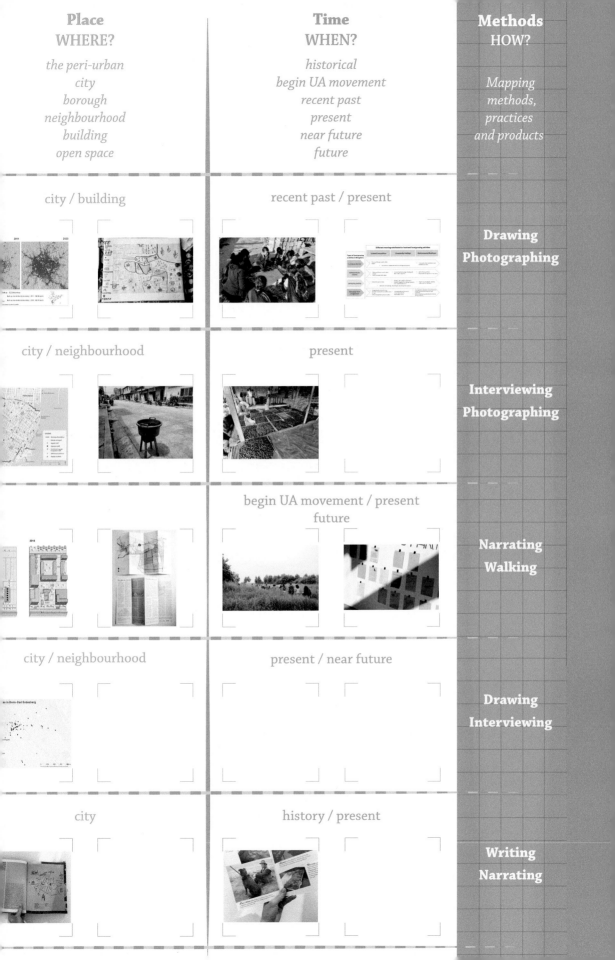

Place WHERE?	Time WHEN?	Methods HOW?
the peri-urban *city* *borough* *neighbourhood* *building* *open space*	*historical* *begin UA movement* *recent past* *present* *near future* *future*	*Mapping methods, practices and products*
city / building	recent past / present	**Drawing** **Photographing**
city / neighbourhood	present	**Interviewing** **Photographing**
	begin UA movement / present future	**Narrating** **Walking**
city / neighbourhood	present / near future	**Drawing** **Interviewing**
city	history / present	**Writing** **Narrating**

Oota Kathegalu:
Tracing the food stories of Bengaluru, India

Marthe Derkzen, Maitreyi Koduganti, Sheetal Patil and Parama Roy

Bengaluru's identity has transitioned in the past several decades: from a Garden City and Pensioners' Paradise to a hub of knowledge-driven global technology. Expanding boundary lines, changing land use and population explosion (see fig. 1) have brought significant shifts in its food system.

The city's development, evidenced first in the public sector growth and then by the information technology boom, attracted new residents from across the country. The influx of people into the city was followed by their own local cuisines which were established in pockets of newer settlements. Today, the city's many *petes* bustle with the rich culture of traditional food and its trade. These formal marketplaces were established by the founder of the city in the 16th century with *akkipete* (rice market), *balepete* (banana market), *arale pete* (cotton market) and *chika pete* (smaller market) being typical examples. At the same time, cosmopolitan food with exotic vegetables and fruits has also made its way into the supermarkets and Bengalurians' kitchens. On a parallel front, citizens are starting to get engaged in growing their own food, both individually or collectively, blurring the traditional dichotomy between the rural, peri-urban and urban, agricultural and non-agricultural spaces.

The phrase *Oota Kathegalu* used in the title means 'food stories' in the local Kannada language. This chapter will use four *oota kathegalu* to highlight a) how urban foodscape and farming are being reinvented, spatially redrawing the geography of food growing activities along the urban and peri-urban transects; and b) how different people attribute different meanings to food and food growing activities.

Mapping methods

Qualitative mapping methods were employed between 2015 and 2021 to examine and reflect on the diverse meanings of food that Bengalurians associate with. The use of maps and different forms of imagery ensured that the findings 'represented' their voice, expression and imaginations (Emmel, 2008). For instance, participatory community mapping served to understand the changes in the foodscape between 1980 and 2015 as experienced by the urban poor (Derkzen *et al.*, 2017). Two-hour mapping sessions were held with three to six residents each, across seven lake communities, with the help of A1-sized topographic maps. Using tokens that represented, for instance, livestock or a sacred tree, participants discussed what was grown on the fields, how responsibilities were being shared, and how the food landscape and farming practices evolved over time (see fig. 2).

Additionally, 214 pictogram-based household interviews were employed to incorporate attitudes, beliefs and local knowledge of community members around how they grow, use and consume their food (see fig. 3). Furthermore, audio-visual techniques like photography (Derkzen, 2015) and videography helped us contemplate personal stories and how farming found its way into the city in the form of kitchen gardens and community farms (Singh

DOI: 10.4324/9781003352280-21

Bengaluru | Karnataka　　　　**2011**　　　　　　　　　　**2020**

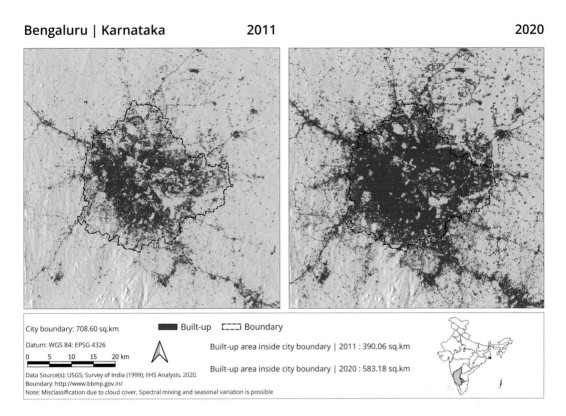

City boundary: 708.60 sq.km ■ Built-up ⌐‾‾‾¬ Boundary

Datum: WGS 84: EPSG 4326

0　5　10　15　20 km　　　Built-up area inside city boundary | 2011 : 390.06 sq.km

Data Source(s): USGS; Survey of India (1999); IIHS Analysis, 2020.　Built-up area inside city boundary | 2020 : 583.18 sq.km
Boundary: http://www.bbmp.gov.in/
Note: Misclassification due to cloud cover, Spectral mixing and seasonal variation is possible

Fig. 1: Bengaluru's expanding built-up areas between 2011 and 2020 (IIHS – Geospatial Lab, 2020)

Fig. 2: Community mapping sessions at Madivala Lake (left: Marthe Derkzen, 2015) and Puttenahalli Lake (right: Anoop Bhaskar, 2015)

et al., 2021). Finally, the UPAGrI study explored a diverse typology of urban and peri-urban agriculture through an online survey to which 379 urban farmers responded (see more details at *www.upagri.net*).

Making use of data collected through the aforementioned diverse methodologies, this chapter maps four food stories on how Bengalurueans with socio-economic, demographic and spatial diversities make sense of food and food

Fig. 3: Pictogram-based household interviews (Marthe Derkzen, 2015)

growing activities not just for cultivating edibles, but also as an expression of cultural connections, community feelings and resilience.

Oota Kathe 1: The lake landscape as a foodscape

This story captures food growing activities around Bengaluru's lakes which were the heart of many communities. A few decades earlier, people depended on the lake for water supply, fishing, cleaning and bathing. Cattle grazed in the fields around the lakes, while fuelwood was collected from the surroundings, where one could also spot mango, *sapota* and coconut trees. Fields were planted with *ragi* (finger millet), rice, beans, maize and vegetables. This is depicted on the participatory community maps (see fig. 4). Many of these subsistence and livelihood activities were driven by shared access and responsibilities over land and water (Derkzen *et al.*, 2017).

However, the lake landscape was beyond just a food-enabling environment, as it signified sacred expressions, like lake festivals

and processions, with people carrying idols, decorations and food offerings. Back in the day, all materials, like dyes, flowers, fruits and palm leaves, were locally sourced. Daily, one could find women sitting under a big shade tree combing each other's hair or weaving baskets, with men squatting in another corner to play board games. Moreover, trees were never 'just' trees, rather they provided multiple functions: food, natural material, medicinal, economic or sacred use (Gopal *et al.*, 2015).

Today, most of these subsistence and livelihood activities seemed to have disappeared from Bengaluru, for many reasons. The lakes are getting polluted and degraded, decreasing the water quality. Several lakes are encroached for constructing commercial complexes, highways or housing leading to lesser land for cultivation (Derkzen *et al.*, 2017). Despite these changes, a few communities continue to rear cattle, yet struggle to find suitable grazing lands. Also, fishing can be spotted at a few locations (see fig. 5). However, a woman from Bhatarahalli Lake lamented: "*I stopped eating fish from the lake because the water is so polluted and I don't dare to touch its fish.*"

Interestingly, however small-sized the area is that residents have in front of their home, they always keep a few plants. Most common are *Tulsi* (used in daily *pooja*), aloe vera and chillies within people's small veranda. Several others grow eggplant, tomato and pumpkin. With a little more space, people additionally keep a banana or other fruit trees. So, even though food production around the lakes is largely disrupted, many people manage to keep their cultural connections alive with edible and sacred plants.

Fig. 4: *Oota Kathe 1*: Participatory community maps of Puttenahalli Lake (above right) and Madivala Lake (below right) indicating the lake boundary in wet and dry seasons, the location of paddy fields, fruit plantations, forest, sacred trees, temples, houses and grazing land (Marthe Derkzen, 2015)

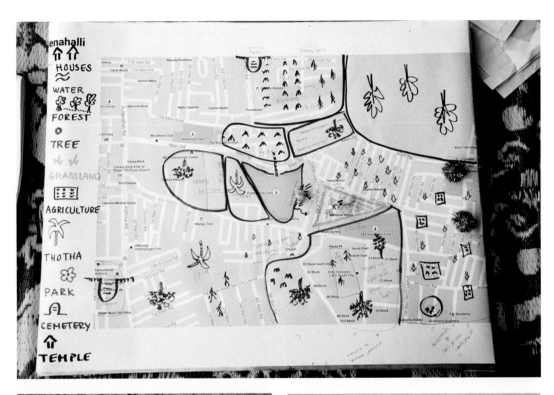

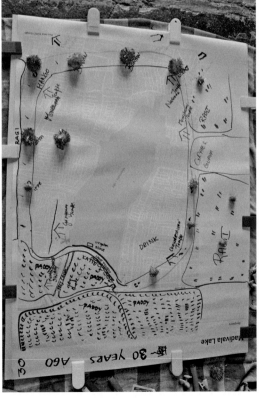

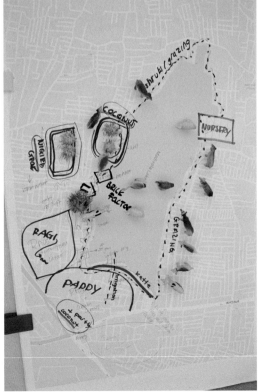

Fig. 5: *Oota Kathe 1*: At several lake communities, we found residents keeping plants and growing vegetables (Marthe Derkzen, 2015), fishing (Anoop Bhaskar, 2015) and keeping cattle (Arati Kumar Rao, 2015)

Oota Kathe 2: Beyond food: The landscape of home gardens

Home gardening is not new to Bengaluru. One can spot a few pots of basil, mint, tomatoes or chillies within many households in the city. Results from our online survey indicate that for at least 55% of respondents, growing their own food was a primary motivation to start gardening, amongst many others (see fig. 6).

Amongst the several responses, we found that two home gardeners, Nandini and Anuja, are redefining gardening activities within small urban spaces as being more than 'just a hobby.' In this *oota kathe*, we narrate their stories of their gardening practices.

Nandini is an entrepreneur by profession, and she began her journey of growing food in 2015. With the need to access vegetables, flowers

Motivations to start gardening

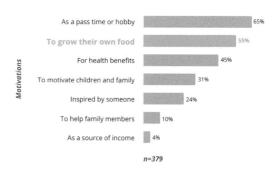

Motivation	Percentage
As a pass time or hobby	65%
To grow their own food	55%
For health benefits	45%
To motivate children and family	31%
Inspired by someone	24%
To help family members	10%
As a source of income	4%

n=379

Fig. 6: *Oota Kathe 2*: Survey responses regarding motivations to start gardening (n = 379) (*UPAGrI* project, 2020–23)

and fruits in proximity to her home, Nandini started growing them on her terrace. Sensing the hassle due to irregular garbage collection, she also started composting wet waste that added required nutrients to the plants.

Fig. 7: *Oota Kathe 2*: Produce from Nandini's terrace garden (Amruth Kiran, 2021)

Flowering plants that attract bees and other insects form the basis for pollination in her garden, owing to which her garden yields many fruits and vegetables like mango, tomatoes, strawberries, sweet potato, lemon, turmeric, beans, brinjals, okra, microgreens and a variety of gourds (see fig. 7). Flowers from her garden are also offered to the Almighty during daily prayers, indicating how growing food and praying to the divine power go hand-in-hand for her.

Fig. 8a: *Oota Kathe 2*: Edible home garden at Anuja's residence (Prathijna Poonacha, 2020)

Concerned about the quality of food available in the markets, Nandini noted that *"there is nothing that is one hundred percent organic [in the market]."* Providing quality food with minimal contamination, especially for her family, shows how she intends to create a safe and resilient food system at her own scale. Like her, the majority of our online survey respondents also perceive growing their own food to diversify their diets and improve their nutrition intake (*UPAGrI* project, 2020–23).

Anuja, an IT professional, was inspired to garden by her mother and grandmother. Gleaming with utmost delight, Anuja indicated that she grows 90% of her kitchen supplies like vegetables, herbs and fruits including guava, pomegranate, banana, strawberries and

passion fruit (see fig. 8a). She started gardening in the early 2000s with a few succulents and eventually progressed to growing herbs and fruit trees. When Anuja started to run out of space in her own terrace, she joined hands with like-minded neighbours and started to grow food gardens within a communal space (see fig. 8b). This strengthened the sense of community within her neighbourhood, since these food gardens were accessible to all other residents. To scale-up such impacts, Anuja conducts workshops which she feels help in creating awareness about the multiple benefits of sustaining edible home gardens. Believing in the concept of '*eat what you grow*,' Anuja's practices ensured self-sufficiency of quality food even in times of the Covid-19 pandemic, which had

Fig. 8b: *Oota Kathe 2*: Edible communal garden near Meenakshi's residence (Prathijna Poonacha, 2020)

disrupted food movement due to lockdowns and restrictions.

Both stories exemplify how individual efforts have the potential, not only to grow sufficient food for a healthy living, but also play a critical role in creating spaces of personal, communal, cultural and environmental importance.

Oota Kathe 3: Bengaluru's food entrepreneurs

Home gardening has paved the way for the emergence of multiple enterprises that are venturing into aquaponics, hydroponics and other tech-driven models. On the one hand, these models provide services to home garden-ers in terms of fresh produce, gardening inputs, operation and maintenance services, while on the other hand, they provide livelihoods for city dwellers, especially to the urban poor. This story is about two such innovative enter-prises, *Urban Mali Network* and *Farmizen*, which leverage the rising interest among Bengaluru's (upper) middle class to grow their own food.

Urban Mali Network, started in 2015, employs about 45 rural migrant farmers as *malis* (gar-deners) to set up and maintain home gardens. Till date, they have developed 1300 gardens for people interested in having their own gardens for varied motivations (see fig. 9). According to *Urban Mali*'s co-founder, women, includ-ing working-professionals and homemakers, who form the bulk of their client-base, want *"aesthetic spaces along with functional ones."* They wish to grow both organic vegetables and flowering plants for a healthy lifestyle, better health, for *pooja* (daily prayers) and decorative purposes. Male customers, often corporate professionals, are driven by the need to connect back to nature. They are inclined towards having gardens for growing only vegetables. Contrastingly, retired couples engage in grow-ing food simply because they find it relaxing. Despite these nuanced connections that dif-ferent age or gender groups feel with food and home gardens, value for nature and environ-mental resilience remain common. *Urban Mali*'s services strictly rest on principles of organic farming and growing native plants, thereby attracting niche customer groups, who appreci-ate connection with nature and biodiversity.

Farmizen, also started in 2015, is based on a mini-farm model that offers an improved livelihood opportunity to hundreds of tradi-tional and new young farmers on the outskirts

Fig. 9: *Oota Kathe 3*: Nursery maintained at Urban Mali premises in Bengaluru, India (Amruth Kiran, 2021)

of Bengaluru City by connecting them directly to urban consumers. Consumers pay a fixed fee to the farmer for growing an assortment of organic vegetables on a patch of land solely allocated to them. Consumers also get an option to engage in farming on a regular basis. However, *Farmizen*'s founder recalls, only few young professionals with families who want their kids "*to know where food comes from and how it's actually grown, and . . . that it does not grow in factories/shops*" get actively involved in growing food. This group enjoys their weekends working on the farms, alongside farmers, reconnecting with nature (see fig. 10). The rest of the clients are satisfied with understanding the traceability of their food, and their engagement with the farm, the farmer or farming remains minimal. They constitute a new social trend of consuming organic food but lack the time or commitment to connect with the landscape or nature.

Both these narratives signify how young entrepreneurs are enabling urbanites in

Fig. 10: *Oota Kathe 3*: A family engaging in their mini-farm (Better India, 2018)

different ways to get engaged in food growing activities.

Oota Kathe 4: Community farming for inclusivity

The awareness about unsafe and contaminated food is growing among Bengalurians. Hence, several people are growing food on their terraces and balconies, as described in *oota kathe 2*. However, several gardeners are constrained by the lack of space, labour and financial investment (Smit *et al.*, 2001). It is here that community farming is gaining popularity, contributing to social and environmental sustainability (Cabral *et al.*, 2017, Sanye-Mengual *et al.*, 2020).

This last *Oota Kathe* is about community garden initiatives that are driven by active civil society groups. One such initiative is the community garden at Jakkur lake, where urban commons are used for both productive purposes and bringing together the local community that includes fishermen, grazers, garden workers, local lake users, residents and wildlife. Native varieties of jackfruit, mango and avocado form a necessary canopy in the first of three layers. The second layer consists of native shrubs like sapota, pomegranate, guava, rose apple and mulberry. The last layer is dotted by hibiscus, lemongrass, rosella and gourds, while the root layer has tubers (see fig. 11). Using indigenous varieties preserves the local biodiversity

Fig. 11: *Oota Kathe 4*: Jakkur Community Garden set up in layered manner following permaculture practices (*ANANAS*, 2017)

and supplies nutritional food to surrounding communities.

Volunteers take turns in groups and spend four to five hours every week on removing weeds, watering, sowing new plants, applying natural inputs, composting and harvesting. Gardening collectively enhances a sense of inclusivity and togetherness within the community. Whenever volunteers work alongside other community members, they exchange new ideas for the garden and thoughts about culture and cuisine (*UPAGrI* 2020–23).

A similar cultural diversity exists among the subscribers of micro-plots at Village Story, a community farming initiative that was set up with a dual objective to connect people to their roots and consume fresh vegetables (see fig. 12). At Village Story, customers subscribe to a piece of land to grow vegetables. They also actively exchange ideas, play traditional games, cook traditional food, watch folk performances, meet local farmers and share their vegetables with friends and family.

A subscriber proudly stated that "*the time spent gardening brought back memories of childhood with my parents.*" These cases exemplify how land can elicit a sense of cultural connection amidst communities apart from providing safe, diverse, fresh and nutritious food.

Redrawing Bengaluru as an Edible City

All the four *Oota Kathegalu* (food stories) signify how Bengalurians are involved in creating localised food systems, building and enhancing cultural connections, community feelings and environmental resilience (see fig. 13).

The *Oota Kathegalu* depict a pattern of how Bengaluru has been reinventing and reimagining itself as an *Edible City* (Sartison and Artmann, 2020). The pattern starts with communities growing food around lakes for subsistence and livelihood purposes, with most of the landscape being used for food-related activities (*Oota Kathe*

Fig. 12: *Oota Kathe 4*: The premises of Village Story (Prathijna Poonacha, 2020)

1). Such community-driven natural resource management tends to embody environmental resilience, while fostering cultural connections and community feelings. Furthermore, the interconnectedness with natural areas is typical for low-income communities in cities (Duraiappah, 2004), however these spaces are severely threatened by pollution and rampant urbanisation.

As exemplified in *Oota Kathegalu 2, 3 and 4*, nature connections are being reinvented by citizens of middle and upper-income groups, who either grow or consume locally grown organic food. This points to the emergence of a social trend coupled with a sense of growing awareness for health and environment.

Our stories also signify how the relevance of urban-peri urban-rural boundaries are getting rather faint by such food transformations from a mass-produced and marketed commodity to carefully cultivated produce largely for self-consumption. Amidst rampant urban development, pollution and climate variability, these stories ranging from individual home gardens and community farming, to farming by the lakes and food-enterprises, serve as a starting point for planning transitions in urban food systems. This requires policy level attention for leveraging these non-traditional forms of agricultural practices to foster greater environmental and community resilience in cities like Bengaluru. Special attention is needed for resource-poor communities, to enable them to co-shape the changing urban foodscape.

These practices which involve stakeholders from social, cultural and economic diversities exemplify how cities can enable food production and contribute not only to food security and healthy diets but also to environmental resilience and community cohesion for a global urban population that is estimated to be over 9 billion by 2050.

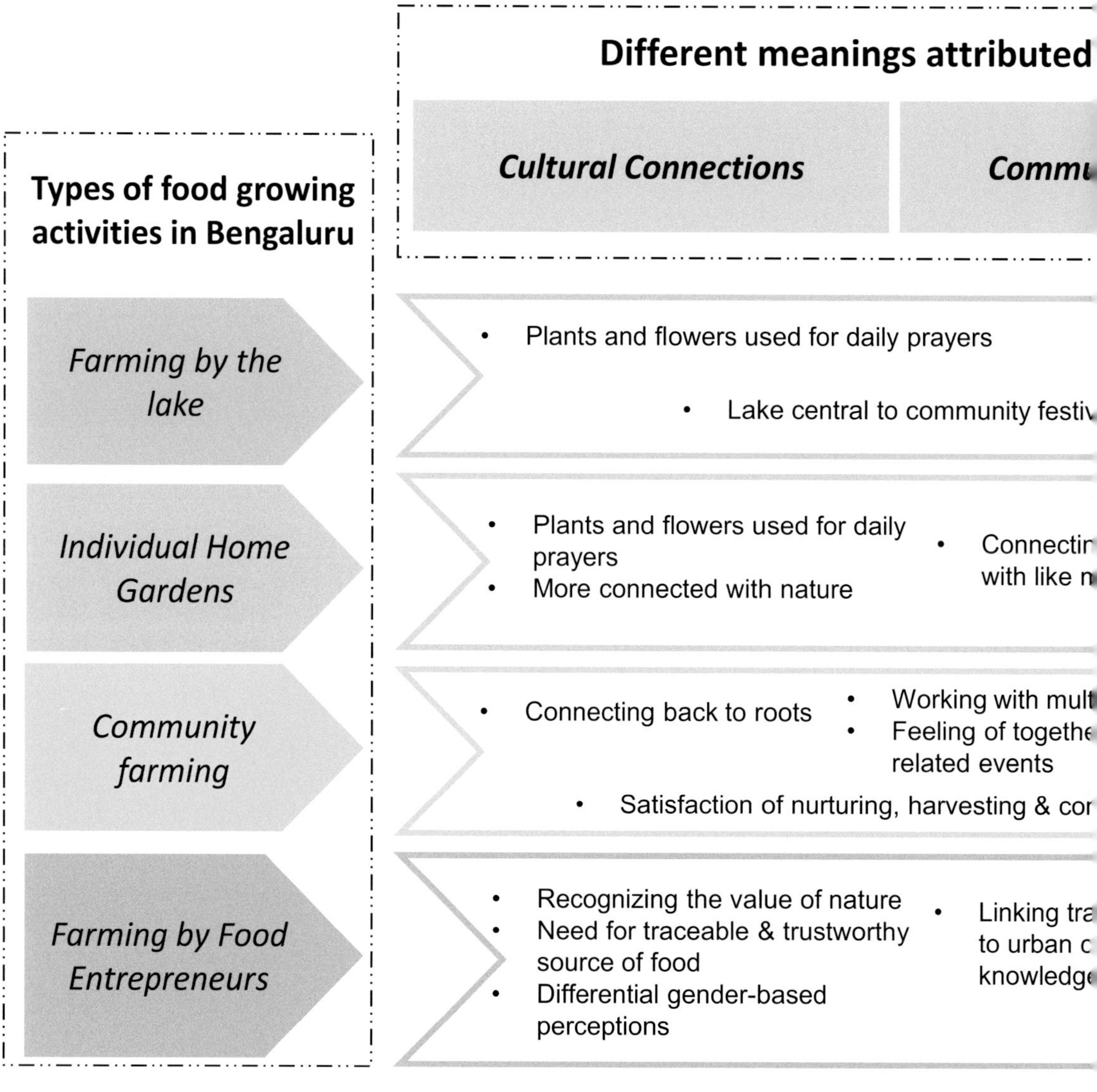

Different meanings attributed

Types of food growing activities in Bengaluru	Cultural Connections	Commu
Farming by the lake	• Plants and flowers used for daily prayers • Lake central to community festiv	
Individual Home Gardens	• Plants and flowers used for daily prayers • More connected with nature	• Connectir with like n
Community farming	• Connecting back to roots • Satisfaction of nurturing, harvesting & cor	• Working with mult • Feeling of togethe related events
Farming by Food Entrepreneurs	• Recognizing the value of nature • Need for traceable & trustworthy source of food • Differential gender-based perceptions	• Linking tra to urban c knowledge

Fig. 13: Different meanings attributed to food and food growing

References

Cabral, I., Keim, J., Engelmann, R., Kraemer, R., Siebert, J., and Bonn, A., 2017. Ecosystem services of allotment and community gardens: A Leipzig, Germany case study. *Urban Forestry and Urban Greening*, 23 (4), 44–53. http://dx.doi.org/10.1016/j.ufug.2017.02.008

Derkzen, M.L., 2015. *Photo essay: Untold stories of change, loss and hope along the margins of Bengaluru's lakes*. London: Blogpost for The Nature of Cities

Derkzen, M.L., Nagendra, H., Van Teeffelen, A.J.A., Purushotham, A., and Verburg, P.H., 2017. Shifts in ecosystem services in deprived urban areas: Understanding people's responses and consequences for well-being. *Ecology and Society*, 22 (1), 51. https://doi.org/10.5751/ES-09168-220151

Duraiappah, A.K., 2004. *Exploring the links: Human well-being, poverty & ecosystem services*. Nairobi: The United Nations Environment Programme.

Emmel, N., 2008. *Participatory mapping: An innovative sociological method*. London: Real Life Methods Toolkit #3.

Gopal, D., Nagendra, H., and Manthey, M., 2015. Vegetation in Bangalore's slums: Composition, species distribution, density, diversity, and history.

food and food growing activities

...ty Feelings	Environmental Resilience

- Community driven subsistence and livelihood activities

...and large processions.

...knowledge sharing
...ed neighbors

- Self sufficiency of food
- Responsible management of wet waste

...stakeholders
...ss via games & other food-

- Regreening, recycling & restoring urban commons like lakes

...ning fresh produce

...onal farmers
...umers &
...aring

- Growing native varieties to increase biodiversity
- Increasing awareness through training & workshops
- Enhance livelihood opportunities for traditional farmers in the city

Environmental Management, 55 (6), 1390–1401. http://dx.doi.org/10.1007/s00267-015-0467-3

Sanye-Mengual, E., Specht, K., Vávra, J., Artmann, M., Orsini, F., and Gianquinto, G., 2020. Ecosystem services of urban agriculture: Perceptions of project leaders, stakeholders and the general public. *Sustainability*, 12, 10446.

Sartison, K., and Artmann, M., 2020. Edible cities – An innovative nature-based solution for urban sustainability transformation? An explorative study of urban food production in German cities. *Urban Forestry & Urban Greening*, 49, 126604.

Singh, C., Patil, S., Poonacha, P., Koduganti, M., and Sharma, S., 2021. When the "field" moves online: Reflections on virtual data collection during COVID-19. *Ecology, Economy and Society–the INSEE Journal*, 4 (2), 149–157.

Smit, J., Nasr, J., and Ratta, A., 2001. *Urban agriculture: Food jobs and sustainable cities*. London: The Urban Agriculture Network, Inc.

Urban and Peri-Urban Agriculture as Green Infrastructure, 2020. *UPAGrI*. Available from www.upagri.net/

Emblematic fruit: Mapping aguaje palm fruit vendors during Covid-19 in Iquitos, Peru

Diana Tung

In Iquitos, the largest city in the Peruvian Amazon and the largest city in the world that cannot be reached by car, the aguaje (*Mauritia flexuosa*) palm fruit reigns supreme. Although the aguaje grows extensively throughout South America (Rull and Montoya, 2014), it is considered the emblematic fruit of the Peruvian Amazon and synonymous with Amazonian identity. In fact, "*si tú no comes aguaje, no eres amazónico* (if you don't eat aguaje, you're not Amazonian)" (Dennis del Castillo Torres, pers. comm., January 16, 2020).

The aguaje palm fruit

Estimates of aguaje consumption in Iquitos vary wildly from 5–50 metric tonnes daily (Virapongse *et al.*, 2017) and can take various forms: as the fruit itself after being matured in warm water (see fig. 1), as the popular *aguajina* drink (see fig. 2), as ice cream, jam, sweets, and more (Delgado, Couturier, and Mejia, 2007). In a city of over 413,000 people (Instituto Nacional de Estadística e Informática, 2018), utilising even a modest estimate of 25 metric tonnes a day translates into 29 kilograms of aguaje consumed per person each year in Iquitos.

A key feature of the aguaje is its mystical quality. The fruit is widely seen as women's food that possesses the power to turn straight men gay (Padoch, 1988). Some older men actively avoid consuming aguaje for this very reason, stating that *me va a malograr*, "it's going to ruin me" or more explicitly, "*me va a hacer chivo* (it's going to make me gay)". However, the largely

female street vendors (*aguajeras* for the fruit, and *aguajineras* for the beverage) are mostly dismissive of this myth. Many responded unequivocally that just as many men consume aguaje as women, while a more common acerbic response was that "*el aguaje se come por la boca no por el culo* (the aguaje is eaten through the mouth not through the ass)".

When Peruvian President Martín Vizcarra announced a national Covid-19 lockdown on March 16, 2020, for several months residents were allowed out only for emergencies. A curfew was instated, transportation was brought to a halt, and streets were patrolled by the military and police. With supplies cut off, a plethora of memes circulated on Facebook and Whatsapp to lament the dearth of aguaje. Commonly referred to as *el arbol de la vida* or "the tree of life" in the Peruvian Amazon, the socio-economic significance of the aguaje in this region cannot be overstated.

Ultimately, the goals of this chapter are twofold. Firstly, it seeks to demonstrate not only the ubiquity of aguaje street vendors in Iquitos, but to make explicit their outsized social and economic contributions to the life of the city through critical cartography. The practice of "testimony mapping" pays close attention to what is included and excluded, and provides a basis from which we may refocus on "overlooked phenomena" (Kim, 2015, 215), in this case, the undervalued labour and expertise of the mostly female aguaje street vendors. Secondly, this chapter demonstrates how even

DOI: 10.4324/9781003352280-22

Fig. 1: Semi-peeled aguaje fruit at a street stall

prior to the coronavirus pandemic, street vending was widely seen as indicative of "backwardness" and that which "harbours 'dirt'" (Roever and Skinner, 2016, p. 363). Aguaje street vendors' hypervisibility in urban spaces, in conjunction with the invisibility of their labour and expertise, made them an ideal target for post-Covid policy intervention.

Primary data were collected over a period of twenty months from 2020–2021, utilising an interdisciplinary mixed-methodology approach to conduct surveys, semi-structured interviews, as well as participant observation. Eighty-nine surveys were conducted with aguajeras and aguajineras largely concentrated in the municipality of Iquitos, which encompasses the city centre (see fig. 3). Given fluctuations in the fruit's seasonality throughout the year (Padoch, 1988), the surveys were conducted in July and August during high season to maintain consistency. Verbal consent was obtained prior to

conducting the surveys. Following the survey, participants who were particularly forthcoming with sharing their experiences were contacted for longer interviews as well as participant observation to allow for a better understanding of participants' everyday lived realities.

The anthropological research method of participant observation "is a form of production of knowledge through being and action . . . by which theory is dialectically produced and realized in action" (Shah, 2017, p. 45). As such, understanding by doing and by being present in the various spaces inhabited by participants is crucial to understanding how they themselves perceive and move through their social worlds. By privileging the experiences and knowledge of participants while simultaneously acknowledging the impact of the researcher's own positionality in shaping relationships and subsequently the data gathering process, academic research has the potential to counter "the

Fig. 2: Aguajinera Myriam Navarro Saldaña at her stall during Covid-19

construction of research participants as 'objects of study'" (Sundberg, 2003, p. 180).

In practice, this meant engaging in a "two-way process of exchange" (Shah, 2017, p. 47) and drawing on my own experiences of having grown up in my mother's Chinese takeaway shop (Tung, 2021) to relate to the aguaje street vendors who are engaged in their own small economic enterprises. I participated in activities such as accompanying vendors to the markets at dawn to negotiate the purchasing of aguaje, helped to *deschipar* or destem the aguaje in their homes, as well as assisted with small tasks around the stall such as washing used glassware, in addition to everyday and significant social activities such as birthday parties, baby showers, and Christmas dinners.

This project also draws on research conducted at public events such as the Regional Government of Loreto's (GOREL) launch of *Proyecto Aguaje* or "Aguaje Project", as well as interviews conducted with government officials and employees. With a budget of nearly 13 million Peruvian soles, *Proyecto Aguaje* aims to incorporate actors along the largely informal supply chain into an ambitious vision of industrialised transformation, which includes an aguaje oil, pulp, and flour manufacturing plant on the Iquitos-Nauta highway as well as the formalisation of aguaje street vendors in Iquitos.

Putting aguaje street vendors on the map

Almost 73 percent of the workforce in Peru is engaged in informal labour (Instituto Nacional de Estadística e Informática, 2020), one of the highest rates in Latin America. While informal labour for men in Iquitos is most closely associated with driving motorcars (Paris *et al*., 2001), for women it is to sell aguaje on the street. In Iquitos, the aguaje industry is largely informal, with only

5 percent estimated to be formalised (José Álvarez Alonso, pers. comm., August 22, 2022).

The aguaje street vendors form a very visible portion of the informal aguaje trade, yet are underrepresented in academic literature on aguaje. Fewer than ten peer-reviewed studies can be found containing the word *"aguajera"*, with the earliest article dating back to 1988 (Padoch, 1988). No academic texts could be found that contain *"aguajinera"*, the term referring to *aguajina* street vendors. Even state institutions such as GOREL conducted a city-wide survey of aguaje street vendors as recently as late 2020 but excluded aguajineras. As such, the decision to physically map aguajineras and to render them visible in academic literature demonstrates how "the practice of the cartographer is immediately political" (Rolnik, 1998 in Crampton and Krygier, 2006, p. 24).

During the first wave of Covid-19 in Peru, the situation in Iquitos was so dire it made international news (Collyns, 2020). During this time, it was reported that 99.6 percent of surveyed vendors in the renowned Belen markets of Iquitos tested positive for Covid-19 (Iglesias-Osores *et al.*, 2020), the highest rate in the nation. Despite protests from market vendors fearing economic insecurity, the markets were dismantled in May 2020 and vendors were forced to sell directly in front of their homes. In effect, Covid-19 propelled vendors to adapt and utilise public space in ways which aligned with that of aguaje street vendors, who have long utilised *las veredas* or sidewalks directly in front of their homes, or on nearby street corners. Due to their ubiquity as well as social and economic importance in Iquitos, aguaje street stalls arguably constitute a form of "social infrastructure" in the city (Ray, 2020, p. 4).

Even prior to the global coronavirus pandemic, the aguaje was widely seen as a vector for parasites and bacteria due to its handling and processing. The aguaje is often harvested and transported in unhygienic conditions, processed in water from questionable sources, and

then exposed to traffic and dust when being sold on the street (Nállarett Marina Dávila Cardozo, pers. comms., August 2, 2020).

When the national lockdown was put in place, mask-wearing became mandatory and enforced by police and military patrols. While some aguaje street vendors adopted additional measures such as wearing gloves and/or spraying money with alcohol, some of these actions became part of a collective Covid-19 "hygiene theatre" (Kemper, 2020), which included municipalities installing hand washing facilities at market entryways and then abandoning them soon after.

Aguaje sales were affected in part due to the public's heightened awareness of health and hygiene issues during the pandemic but additionally aguajina sales were affected because of the prevailing notion in Peru that cold drinks weaken the immune system. Hot drinks such as *emolientes* made out of aloe vera as well as teas made with ginger, lemon, garlic, and other plants (Reinders *et al.*, 2020) were preferred over iced beverages. Real or imagined, "[d]irt offends against order" (Douglas, 2001, p. 2) and the hygiene and public health issues surrounding aguaje street vending made it ripe for state intervention, particularly in the wake of the global pandemic.

Mapping aguaje street vendors

The map in figure 3 provides an aggregation of the various routes taken to conduct the surveys and shows the approximate location of streets vendors selling i) aguaje, ii) aguajina, iii) both, as well as iv) other products. This study distinguishes between aguaje and aguajina street vendors as the two products require differing expertise. Additionally, while there may be drastically fewer aguajineras than aguajeras, they are more likely to purchase more sacks of aguaje.

Of the eighty-nine participants surveyed, almost 95 percent were women. Not including children who were working the stands, the participants' ages ranged from 23 to 79 years old. Five vendors were over 70 years of age, with

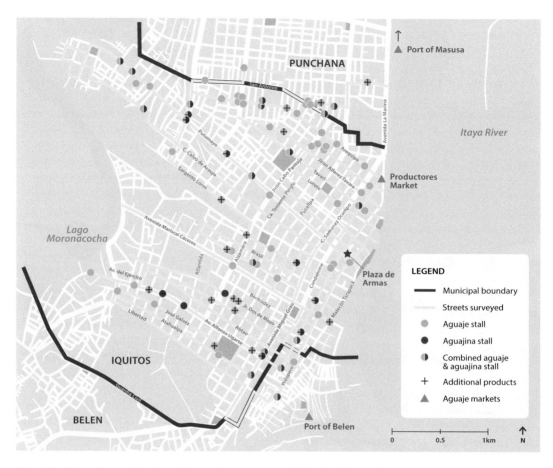

Fig. 3: Map of aguaje street vendors surveyed in Iquitos, Peru

one aguajera boasting over fifty years of experience. Twenty-seven aguaje vendors, or almost one in three respondents, had over twenty years of experience. The price of aguaje ranged from three to eight aguaje for 1 sol, depending on the size and quality of aguaje that day. Aguajina was sold at either 2 or 2.5 soles, with a few vendors selling it at 1.5 soles.

Despite the widespread consumption of aguaje in Iquitos, even regular consumers may not know how to mature the aguaje properly or how to choose the right ecotype of aguaje at the market. Aguajeras look for the *shambo* ecotype due to its prized mango-like flavour and attractive red colour, whereas aguajineras prefer the *amarillo* or "yellow" ecotype as it is less likely to oxidise and therefore is easier to work with for

aguajina beverage (Rojas-Ruiz *et al.*, 2006). The colour of the scales indicates the ripeness of the fruit, but a more accurate manner of checking this is to cut cross-sectionally into the fruit and slice into the seed. For those who do not know how to choose the right aguaje, buying large quantities of aguaje can be risky. The aguaje can fail to mature properly, leaving the street vendor to absorb the costs of the useless product.

Aguaje is difficult to work with also as it oxidises easily, and although it needs to be matured in water it can taste waterlogged if submerged for too long (see fig. 4). Its complicated processing requires expertise that is difficult to learn by oneself and street vendors have most commonly learned from female

Fig. 4: A tub of aguaje submerged in water left for maturing in the sun

Fig. 5: Aguaje for sale at the wholesale market of Puerto Masusa

family members, though some have learned from other street vendors.

One older respondent spoke about how when she initially came to Iquitos from Yurimaguas, "*yo no sabía vender* (I didn't know how to sell)", and wholesalers took advantage of her lack of knowledge. One day she took an aguajera out to breakfast and convinced the woman to teach her how to buy aguaje at the markets. However, learning to make the aguajina was another issue. The first time she made aguajina one of her customers laughed at her because she had cooked it, but "*el aguajina tiene sabor de maduro cuando lo haces hervir* (the aguajina has the taste of ripe plantain when you boil it)".

When speaking to local Iquiteños, those who are not involved in the aguaje business are more likely to consider this line of work a sort of economic safety net during hard times as opposed to it being a lifelong career. Some women did turn to selling aguaje as a way of making money during the national Covid-19 lockdown, but there were many others who for decades have chosen to exclusively sell aguaje and aguajina as their main economic livelihood. It is from selling aguaje that these women are able to be their own bosses, send their kids to school and university, construct their houses, and generate enough cash to support their families. Career aguaje street vendors referred

to newer sellers with unmasked disdain as "*aguajeras de ocasión, no de profesión* (occasional, not professional aguajeras)".

Seventy percent of vendors sold only aguaje. A quarter of respondents sold both aguaje and aguajina. Only three vendors sold only aguajina. One in four respondents sold additional products, including bakes, tamales, or regional foods such as *juanes*. During seasonal fluctuations when there is less aguaje arriving to the city, women are more likely to complement their sales with other economic activities such as sewing or selling additional food items. This included baked goods, produce, as well as cooked foods such as *pijuayo (Bactris gasipaes)*, another palm fruit.

In order to buy aguaje at the wholesale markets (see fig. 5), cash is needed upfront. Although a 40-kilogram sack of aguaje can cost as little as 15 soles, this represents half a day's wage in Iquitos and for some may be a barrier to entry into the aguaje economy. Those who were selling aguaje as an economic "band-aid" in response to Covid-19 were more likely to purchase only a *bandeja*, a plastic tub of aguaje to sell along with other produce. One woman who had come back home from Lima after the first Covid-19 lockdown was selling just one small *bandeja* or plastic bucket of aguaje along with some vegetables, saying that she was selling aguaje "*para sobrevivir, hasta que se arregla la situación* (to survive, until the situation gets better)". On the other hand, career aguajeras rarely buy just one sack at a time, with most women buying two or more sacks to last them a few days at a time. Aguajineras may buy up to four or five sacks at a time.

Vendors who used to be in other lines of work turned to aguaje because it is "*más rentable* (more profitable)". Some chose to sell aguaje over other jobs such as working at restaurants, where daily wages are 30 soles, or sewing clothes, which one aguajera said was tiring. Aguajeras highlighted the benefits of being their own boss, being able to manage their own time, and/or being able to take care of their children while working. As such, aguaje street vendors largely also assume the responsibilities of unpaid household labour.

Vendors tend to head to the markets alone in the early mornings while their children are still asleep, and usually manage the stalls from 10am to 6pm, or earlier if they sell out. At the same time, aguaje production is no solitary affair. The production process may involve extended family networks, be it directly in the production process (e.g., male family members *machacando* or smashing aguaje to remove the seeds for aguajina) or in more indirect forms such as childcare. Familial relations are also important in sales, with some individuals working with their immediate and extended family members to split the costs of aguaje, or to set up multiple stalls on the same street or on nearby blocks. Younger children are commonly roped into the business more in the form of ambulatory sales, and during the coronavirus pandemic when students couldn't study online due to poor internet connectivity in Iquitos, older children and teenagers could also be found helping out at the stalls.

When it came to earnings, many of the women were reluctant to discuss their profits. Many utilised the phrase, *mitad por mitad* or "fifty-fifty", as a generic response that didn't require them to disclose a number. Upon following up with a clarifying question, some women were still reluctant to provide a number.

One young woman gave her daily earnings as 150 soles, a considerably lower sum than what her mother had reported when surveyed earlier on the same street. Her mother had beamed with pride as she said that her daughter usually earned 500 soles a day, but sometimes earned up to 600–700 soles.

Post-Covid interventions

Numerous Peruvian exports such as chia seeds, quinoa, and maca have reached the global superfood market in the past few decades (Alandia *et al.*, 2020; Fonseca, 2016), but Amazonian products from Loreto in particular have not fared so well. More contemporary attempts to commercialise Amazonian products have followed a similar "boom and bust" cycle (Penn, 2006). These failed attempts at commercialisation included items such as the *sacha inchi* nut and *camu camu* fruit (Córdova, 2021; Penn, 2006).

In lowland Amazonia's long history of natural resource extraction, the singular focus on products such as rubber, gold, and oil has previously resulted in only short-lived and unsustainable economic booms. This cycle prompted one high-ranking official in Lima to refer to the region as "a cemetery of failed projects", an incident recounted to me separately by two interviewees who were on the call.

Nonetheless, the Loreto state government (Gobierno Regional de Loreto or GOREL) sees and portrays aguaje commercialisation as an economic miracle for the region, and given the cultural and economic significance of the local aguaje economy in Iquitos it is unsurprising that this sector and the vendors themselves have become a target of state intervention. In its promotional materials for *Proyecto Aguaje*, GOREL utilises the language of "economic reactivation" to position aguaje as a silver bullet for the post-pandemic economy (Gobierno Regional de Loreto, 2021). As its billboard states, the project promises to bring jobs to 10,000 beneficiaries in over three provinces in the state of Loreto and equates aguaje

Fig. 6: Billboard promoting GOREL's *Proyecto Aguaje*, located on Avenida La Marina, a main thoroughfare in Iquitos

Fig. 7: The public launch of GOREL's *Proyecto Aguaje* included the unveiling of a model cart for aguaje street vendors

industrialisation with "*la nueva economía de Loreto* (the new economy of Loreto)" (see fig. 6).

Given the ubiquity of aguaje street vending and its embeddedness in social and economic life, the rhetoric of *Proyecto Aguaje* as ushering in a distinctly new economy based on the aguaje inadvertently downplays the contributions of the mostly female aguaje street vendors. Rather, the aguaje is rendered ripe for policy intervention in the post-Covid era precisely because of the labour and expertise of street vendors in shaping and developing the aguaje economy into a sector that supports over five thousand families (Torres *et al.*, 2014).

As part of GOREL's plans to formalise aguaje street vending and to render vendors "legible" to the state (Scott, 1998), *Proyecto Aguaje* distributed eighty *carritos*, or food carts, to street vendors. The food cart was first revealed at the August 2020 launch event of Projecto Aguaje, where a model cart was placed prominently on display at the front of the auditorium (see fig. 7). Yet when showing photographs of the cart to survey participants, their responses were immediate and largely negative.

As some street vendors pointed out, the oversized carts would be difficult to maneuver in and out of the doorways of their homes, not to mention transport across the city. The

metal would overheat in the hot Iquitos sun. The shade wouldn't provide enough cover. The mouth of the aguajina jar was too small to allow for the paddle to mix the *crema* and sugar together. Furthermore, the cart did not address any underlying structural issues such as water supply. As quaint as the cart seemed to be at first glance, discussions with aguaje street vendors quickly revealed that it had not been designed in consultation with them.

GOREL also instituted a city-wide survey of aguajeras and later invited them to attend informational meetings, but as some survey respondents noted, they did not attend as they were not going to be compensated for the time, not to mention their loss of earnings. One aguajera said that it seemed like GOREL was trying to position themselves as the middleman and centralise the sale of aguaje, but was sceptical given the depth of knowledge needed to discern the quality and ecotypes of aguaje. Although difficult to verify, other aguajeras mentioned that the price of aguaje had skyrocketed and attributed these inflated prices to the artificial scarcity caused by GOREL purchasing aguaje in bulk.

Mapping as a tool to rectify missing information

Much has been written about the extraordinary characteristics of the aguaje and its promising economic potential as the next big super-food, but little information is available on the hundreds of mostly female street vendors who labour to meet the voracious appetite for aguaje in Iquitos. This research represents one attempt to rectify this dearth of information on aguaje street vendors.

Through an interdisciplinary mixed-method approach, critical cartography, surveys, interviews, and participant observation were employed to understand the day-to-day experiences of aguaje street vendors, the impacts of the global coronavirus pandemic, as well as the depth of the expertise and labour in one of the most significant local economies in Iquitos. The act of locating aguaje street vendors on a map allows for a visual representation of their ubiquity and distribution throughout the city, and as figure 3 shows, most residents of the city live within walking distance of an aguaje street vendor. Residents are also able to point out the cross streets where their favourite vendor is located, demonstrating how the aguaje mediates spatial relationality between residents and the city.

Just as the social significance of the aguaje cannot be overstated in this region, neither can the contributions of aguaje street vendors and their embeddedness in the social infrastructure and local landscape of Iquitos. Aguaje street vending is highly gendered, with over 90 percent of vendors being women. As such, this means that most vendors participate in overlapping social and economic worlds both inside and outside the home as they simultaneously inhabit the role of entrepreneur and primary caregiver for their families. Aguaje vending is not just a part of the urban food landscape, but a way of life for career aguaje street vendors. The aguaje economy also plays an important role for women who have limited economic opportunity in times of hardship, and as such serves as a kind of economic band-aid or safety net, provided cash can be obtained to purchase aguaje at the wholesale markets.

This research also examines how the hypervisibility of aguaje street vendors in the urban landscape occurs alongside the invisibility of their expertise and labour in being able to successfully commercialise a product that is notoriously difficult to handle. These concurrent dynamics, in addition to the highly gendered nature of the local aguaje economy, rendered aguaje street vendors an attractive target for the state government's post-Covid economic policies. Despite the state's attempts to formalise aguaje street vendors as part of the multi-million-soles *Proyecto Aguaje* scheme, much remains to be seen. What is clear, however, is that "street food is here to stay" (Ray, 2020, p. 10). Long after the remit of *Proyecto Aguaje*, aguaje street vendors will likely persist as the defining feature of the food landscape of Iquitos.

References

Alandia, G., Rodriguez, J.P., Jacobsen, S.-E., Bazile, D., and Condori, B., 2020. Global expansion of Quinoa and challenges for the Andean region. *Global Food Security*, 26, 100429. https://doi.org/10.1016/j.gfs.2020.100429.

Castillo, T., Dennis del, E.O.A., and Freitas Alvarado, L., 2014. *Aguaje: La Maravillosa Palmera de La Amazonía*. Iquitos: Instituto de Investigaciones de la Amazonía Peruana.

Collyns, D., 2020. 'We are living in a catastrophe': Peru's Jungle capital Choking for breath as Covid-19 hits. *The Guardian*, May 7. Available from www.theguardian.com/global-development/2020/may/07/peru-jungle-iquitos-coronavirus-covid-19.

Córdova, A., 2021. Buscan revertir fallos en la producción de sacha inchi. *Agrario.pe*, October 27. Available from https://agraria.pe/noticias/buscan-revertir-fallos-en-la-produccion-de-sacha-inchi-828.

Crampton, J.W., and Krygier, J., 2006. An introduction to critical cartography. *ACME: An International E-Journal for Critical Geographies*, 4 (1), 11–33.

Delgado, C., Couturier, G., and Mejia, K., 2007. *Mauritia Flexuosa* (Arecaceae: Calamoideae), an Amazonian palm with cultivation purposes in Peru. *Fruits*, 62 (3), 157–169. https://doi.org/10.1051/fruits:2007011.

Douglas, M., 2001. *Purity and danger: An analysis of the concepts of pollution and taboo*. London: Routledge.

Fonseca, V., 2016. Chia: From tribute to superfood. *In*: A. Lindgreen, M.K. Hingley, R.J. Angell, J. Memery and J. Vanhamme, eds. *A stakeholder approach to managing food: Local, national, and global issues*. London and New York: Routledge, Taylor & Francis Group, 55–67

Gobierno Regional de Loreto, 2021. Pro Aguaje, Reactivando la Economía de Loreto, April 19. Available from www.regionloreto.gob.pe/noticias/2021/04/19/pro-aguaje-reactivando-la-economia-de-loreto.

Iglesias-Osores, S., Saavedra Camacho, J.L., and Córdova Rojas, L.M., 2020. Mercados y estaciones de transporte como focos infecciosos de COVID-19. *Revista Experiencia en Medicina del Hospital Regional Lambayeque*, 6 (4), 120–22.

Instituto Nacional de Estadística e Informática, 2018. Loreto: Resultados Definitivos. *Tomo I. Lima, Perú*. Available from www.inei.gob.pe/media/MenuRecursivo/publicaciones_digitales/Est/Lib1561/.

Instituto Nacional de Estadística e Informática, 2020. *Producción y Empleo Informal En El Perú: Cuenta Satélite de La Economía Informal 2007–2019*. Lima. Available from www.inei.gob.pe/media/MenuRecursivo/publicaciones_digitales/Est/Lib1764/libro.pdf.

Kemper, C.A., 2020. Hygiene theater. *Internal Medicine Alert*, 42 (18).

Kim, A.M., 2015. Critical cartography 2.0: From 'participatory mapping' to authored visualizations of power and people. *Landscape and Urban Planning*, 142, 215–225.

Padoch, C., 1988. Aguaje (*Mauritia Flexuosa* L. f.) in the economy of Iquitos, Peru. *Advances in Economic Botany*, 6, 214–224.

Paris, M., Gotuzzo, E., Goyzueta, G., Aramburu, J., Caceres, C.F., Teudy Castellano, D.C., Vermund, S.H., and Hook, E.W., 2001. Motorcycle taxi drivers and sexually transmitted infections in a Peruvian Amazon city. *Sexually Transmitted Diseases*, 28 (1), 11–13. https://doi.org/10.1097/00007435-200101000-00004.

Penn, J.W., 2006. The cultivation of Camu Camu (*Myriciaria Dubia*): A tree planting program in the Peruvian Amazon. *Forests, Trees and Livelihoods*, 16 (1), 85–101. https://doi.org/10.1080/14728028.2006.9752547.

Ray, K., 2020. SOAS address: Rethinking street vending. *Gastronomica*, 20 (1), 1–15. https://doi.org/10.1525/gfc.2020.20.1.1.

Reinders, S., Alva, A., Huicho, L., and Blas, M.M., 2020. Indigenous communities' responses to the COVID-19 pandemic and consequences for maternal and neonatal health in remote Peruvian Amazon: A qualitative study based on routine programme supervision. *BMJ Open*, 10 (12), e044197. https://doi.org/10.1136/bmjopen-2020-044197.

Roever, S., and Skinner, C., 2016. Street vendors and cities. *Environment and Urbanization*, 28 (2), 359–374. https://doi.org/10.1177/0956247816653898.

Rojas-Ruiz, R., Ruíz-Panduro, G., Ramírez-Meléndez, P., Salazar-Jarama, C.F., Rengifo-Sias, C., Llerena-Flores, C., Marín-Ríos, C., et al., 2006. Comercialización de Masa y "Fruto Verde" de Aguaje *(Mauritia Flexuosa* L.F.) En Iquitos (Perú). *Folia Amazónica*, 12 (1–2), 15–38. https://doi.org/10.24841/fa.v12i1-2.123.

Rull, V., and Montoya, E., 2014. Mauritia Flexuosa palm swamp communities: Natural or human-made? A palynological study of the Gran Sabana Region (Northern South America) within a neotropical context. *Quaternary Science Reviews*, 99, 17–33. https://doi.org/10.1016/j.quascirev.2014.06.007.

Scott, J.C., 1998. *Seeing like a state: How certain schemes to improve the human condition have failed*. Yale Agrarian Studies. New Haven, CT: Yale University Press.

Shah, A., 2017. "Ethnography?: Participant observation, a potentially revolutionary praxis." *HAU: Journal of Ethnographic Theory*, 7 (1), 45–59. https://doi.org/10.14318/hau7.1.008.

Sundberg, J., 2003. Masculinist epistemologies and the politics of fieldwork in Latin Americanist geography. *The Professional Geographer*, 55 (2), 180–190. https://doi.org/10.1111/0033-0124.5502006.

Tung, D., 2021. What I learnt from My Mum's takeaway shop. *SBS*, January 27. Available from www.sbs.com.au/food/article/2021/01/27/what-i-learnt-my-mums-takeaway-shop.

Virapongse, A., Endress, B.A., Gilmore, M.P., Horn, C., and Romulo, C., 2017. Ecology, livelihoods, and management of the Mauritia Flexuosa palm in South America. *Global Ecology and Conservation*, 10, 70–92. https://doi.org/10.1016/j.gecco.2016.12.005.

Participative food culture mapping in polarised urban districts

Mila Brill

"I think everybody has his own identifiers, his own anchors . . . one person maybe attaches memories to people, another to stories, I don't know. And for me it is food. Because I always remember where something was tasty – there I want to go again – and where I didn't like something – there I don't need to go. It is like my own atlas. I also remember smells very clearly, they are anchors for me, too. Food is also connected to smells. So, in my head I am kind of just wired like this: I can recall pictures out of my memory immediately when I smell something." (Interview 01, line 526–530)

This is what one of my interviewees tells me about how she deals with changes in her former neighbourhood. We are sitting at a coffee table somewhere in the districts centre, just two bus stops away from where she was born. Some weeks before, she attended the final discussion of a public lecture series on food, materiality and migration at the university, as she had read about it in the local newspaper.[1] She described herself as a foodie and was born and raised in the district where I conducted my research, so we exchanged some e-mails, and she was keen to meet up for an interview. When we sit down at the table, I ask her to sketch the district and its food places, which doesn't seem to surprise her in the least. She starts drawing right away, explaining what she is sketching, without asking for further instructions (which happened frequently in other interviews). She draws places I know from previous fieldwork, and some I don't know. Soon I realise that she is representing different moments in time in her sketch map.

After talking about the district's characteristics and her personal connection to it for a while, she then explains why the initial sketching task seemed so natural to her. Her interest in the discussion at university stemmed from the fact that she connects most of the memories of her childhood and early adult life in the 1960s and '70s to food places in the district she later moved out of. She tells me she has never studied at university and isn't sure what sociology is about. However, connecting food, sketch mapping and an interest in the districts' history and future in a research project like mine is something she can relate to and that makes sense to her.

The quote from our interview points to some important aspects when examining food in the city from a sociological perspective. It illustrates that places of food consumption should not be considered solely through the lens of economics. Restaurants are more than places, where economic structures are generated, sustained or changed (cf. de Certeau, 1984; for a focus on economic structures see Yildiz, 2013; Möhring, 2014; Everts, 2008). When considering places of food consumption with regard to everyday practices (cf. Warde, 2016; de Certeau *et al.*, 1998), one should also focus on situations of individual or collective communication, classification, orientation and decisions of consumption (Parzer and Astleithner, 2018; Stock, 2013; Emmison, 2003). The interviewee calls food places "anchors" that help her connect personal memories to public space. She also notices that those anchors are subjective, and

DOI: 10.4324/9781003352280-23

Fig. 1: The inner city of Bad Godesberg

that different entities or types of impressions may play this role for different people. Consequently, some places, smells, buildings, restaurants, etc. that are important to her personally might not even be actively perceived by other users of the same neighbourhood. Sites of food consumption thus can serve to gain access to the different ways in which individuals perceive public space in the city.

Therefore, eating out does not only fulfil the function of nourishing the interviewee's body. When she visits a restaurant, she can later recall her opinion of the meal, the furniture, the interaction with the staff and the conversation with her companion – a lot of places she tells me about are for example connected to memories of her deceased mother, whom she used to motivate to try new and unknown dishes. She tells me that for every birthday she tries out a new restaurant: *"Because I think it is nice to try something new when a new year starts"*

(Interview 01, line 381). She lists an Ethiopian, a Tibetan and a Vietnamese restaurant as the places where she spent her last birthdays. That aspect of eating, especially outside of one's own home, depicts another basic, sociological assumption on food: Eating has a special relationship to place and place-making.

On the one hand, it is extremely personal and focused on the individual body. On the other hand, eating together plays an important role in group formation and is shaped by cultural norms. Georg Simmel (2001 [1910]) points out that, precisely because eating is such an individual practice, its cultural framing gets meaningful and is central in the organisation of groups. Because of the ambiguity of physical individuality and cultural commonality, eating practices and food in general is often viewed as having authentic qualities, "naturally" tied to distinct groups, places or regions. This kind of essentialising ascriptions of regional belonging, which are often "imaginative geographies" based on hasty culturalist assumptions (cf. May, 1996), can be very problematic when ascribed to groups of persons and their cultural practices.[2] Still, the regional references things, dishes and certain restaurants may carry, can also provide "*clear intimation of familiarity that one knows what to do with it, how to cook it, how to present it and how to eat it, thus promoting a multitude of homely practices*" (Hage, 1997, p. 8).

To explore this further, I will look at how this special relevance of regional references and ascriptions makes eating an aspect of everyday life, which helps to connect to places close to one's home, but also to those far away or imagined. That includes a sensitivity for the problematic consequences that ascriptions of authenticity can have in the context of conflicting perceptions of public space, urban places of consumption and regional belonging. Especially in a context of high mobility in one's own life or neighbourhood, this process of connecting people, food and memories to specific food places has a high relevance.

The introductive quote shows that on the one hand, eating out may create situations that help individuals to orientate in their local surroundings, tied to personal histories. On the other hand, eating practices, as well as dishes or food places, can also establish a connection to other regions, often including memories, as well as imaginations of the "other" (Spivak, 1988) or of place-bound authenticity. Both aspects of eating practices play a specific role in urban contexts, where many and highly heterogenous references to personal memories and imaginations of other places meet. Under such circumstances, a tension may emerge between diverse practices of homing in individuals' everyday lives and more general processes of city development (cf. Preissing, 2019; Blokland, 2017).

In this chapter, I will focus on this tension. It is visible in cases where the future trend of urban development measures is at stake, and

highly heterogenous actors have to be included and represented in the process. To make this point clear, I will first introduce the district of Bonn Bad-Godesberg as an ethnographic case, as well as my methodological approach to it via sketching interviews. I will then contrast my own research results with the outcomes of an urban regeneration programme run by the local administration in the district, to finally sum up my argument in a concluding section. The central question of the analysis will be how a mapping of gastronomic use preferences can help deepen public participation in inner city development processes, especially in the context of high polarisation.

City development in the context of discursive polarisation

Bad Godesberg is one of four districts of Bonn, the former capital of Germany. From 1949 until German reunification in 1990, Godesberg as a part of the capital was the site of many embassies and still holds several diplomatic offices, for example from Qatar, Tunisia or Russia. What is interesting about Godesberg is that for more than 200 years it has been a popular destination for wealthy visitors. First it was spa guests, then international diplomats and national politicians, and today it is again a health resort for tourists mainly from Qatar, Libya and the Emirates. Consequently, there is a well-developed touristic infrastructure for Arab speaking guests in the district. For example, you will frequently find labelling in Arab, English and German in shops, pharmacies, supermarkets or restaurants (see fig. 1).

Apart from the specific history, there is of course also the very normal district life, shaped by different groups of residents. Another consequence of the diplomatic background of the district is that those diverse groups are extremely heterogenous as measured by socio-structural criteria. Highest and lowest rental prices of the whole city are located right next to each other within the district; there is a big age gap between young and old residents;

there are three mosques and a lot of churches of different backgrounds. Besides, many residents have other than German citizenship. Also here, the backgrounds and legal statuses make up an extremely heterogenous mix, ranging from people within deportation proceedings living in a public accommodation, to families of former members of the embassies.

For my interests in homing processes in mobile contexts, Godesberg is thus a perfect example, because within the districts' sub centre you will meet people who have never left the city as well as residents with a hypermobile life. One more aspect that makes this situation so relevant is that communal politics and public discussions are very polarised. Criminality and security are the main issues of local politics, whereas mobility and homing are difficult and controversial topics to talk about directly in Godesberg. Asking inhabitants about eating out is a seemingly harmless entrance to those heated discussions. Here again, the ascription of authenticity to food and eating practices brings about an indirect negotiation of regional and national relations at a very ordinary and quotidian level. It didn't only help me to talk about emotionally charged topics in my interviews, but most notably it helps groups and individuals to talk and think about those topics in everyday life themselves.

This is a quality of everyday practices and especially of eating that could be used in city development programmes: Just as the interviewee mentioned earlier describes, mapping food places and one's own using preferences is a simple and accessible way for inhabitants to represent and reflect on their subjective ordering of urban spaces. Different perspectives and practices can thus be collected and brought into conversation. In the specific case of Bad Godesberg, the gastronomic range especially in the inner city is debated again and again. In the local discourse, one can find praise of the high diversity in regional references just as well as the thesis of "foreign infiltration". Some enjoy the changes in the highly dynamic

sector of gastronomic businesses and like to try new places, while others detect the downfall of the district, symbolised by the closure of high standard (and high-priced) restaurants with a history of prestigious guests from the era of diplomacy in the district.

Even though gastronomic places are so central in the discourse on district development, they played a minor role in a recent development process including civic participation and funding policy from the local government. As a result of a 2016 request from the local liberal party, between 2018 and 2020 a new guiding concept[3] for the district was developed by urban management and then enacted by the government. Several steps of civic participation were part of the process (see figs. 2 and 3), but as they were mainly directed to groups already actively engaged in local politics, the outcome was at best unidimensional. The final guiding concept was limited to general aims such as a "vivid nucleus", an "improvement of subjective perceptions of safety" or "respect and tolerance". Actual policies of the urban regeneration programme especially for the districts' centre didn't include the feedback of participating citizens, so that even the limited number of residents that knew details of the process still felt unrepresented in its outcomes in the end. In Bad Godesberg, the complexity of participation processes in a local context of high diversity, discursive polarisation and historically founded scepticism towards municipal authorities gets particularly evident.

Parallel to the development of the new guiding concept for Bad Godesberg I conducted my ethnographic research focused on diverse practices of eating out and an acknowledgement of belonging via food places. As described earlier, I found that eating in urban spaces is closely connected to orientation at a local level and beyond. My aim is now to show how future city development programmes and policies could apply food culture mapping as used in my research to better include diverse local residents.

Fig. 2a-b: Discussions on the city development, led by the local government, were conducted using aerial maps and Post-its (2018-2019)

Mapping preferences of eating out

Following a general approach of situational analysis (Clarke, 2005), to achieve a deep mapping (Roberts, 2016, 2015) of eating practices and food cultures in the district, in a first step in 2018 and 2019, I registered all places of non-domestic eating on a map. This mapping represented my academic perspective and helped me to derive a typology of eating out places for general orientation. In a second step and in contrast to this perspective, I conducted sketching interviews with residents of the district.

In the interviews, I collected information on specific food places as well as on their use by the interviewees themselves and by other groups they observed. Throughout the interview I asked the interviewees to sketch the district and mark gastronomic places they know or use. The sketching had very different outcomes (see fig. 4), fulfilling the "unique adequacy requirement" (Garfinkel, 1976, as cited in Bergmann, 1981, p. 16) of qualitative social research. Those sketches combined with the interview transcripts served as a basis for a way of grouping eating out preferences via several rounds of coding. The aim was to see which places are being used by rather homogenous groups, and others where

heterogenous groups meet and share their using preference.

I derived the characteristics that made up these groupings from the empirical data rather than from theory, to not transfer the problems of methodological nationalism on urban communities defined pre-empirically by religion, ethnicity or nationality (for a critique of the problematic implications of methodological nationalism see Çağlar and Glick Schiller, 2018; Amelina, 2017; Wimmer and Glick Schiller, 2002). In that respect my approach differs from research centred around "ethnic business", which in most cases essentialises ascriptions of ethnicity urban food places might be exposed to or deploy themselves for various (often marketing-based) reasons. I do take regional ascriptions of food places into account, but from a praxeological perspective, regional as well as ethnic, religious or similar referrals are seen as a part of everyday practices of local ordering and orientation rather than as indicators for essential differences between segregated groups of residents.

Contrasting outcomes and future prospects

During the public participation process in Bad Godesberg, certain groups of district residents expressed their critique of the districts' inner-city developments in the last years, which

Fig. 3a-b: People participating in the discussions on the city development events led by the local government (2018–2019)

they see as "foreign infiltration". Especially the rejection of food places labelled with Arab lettering clearly contained discriminatory tendencies, which defined discussions at the process meetings. Moreover, these groups didn't feel represented in the outcomes of the process (as described earlier). Consequently, the new guiding concept for the district fuelled the pre-existing polarisation among residents as well as their scepticism towards authorities. The development of the concept excluded many groups of residents and at the same time strengthened others. For example, assumptions of "foreign occupation" paralleled with ideas of segmentary "ethnic business" or "ethnic enclaves" in urban spaces. I will now contrast these outcomes with findings from the sketching interviews on food places. This demonstrates how eating, as an aspect of urban everyday life, can be helpful not only for individual orientation but also for collective participatory district development measures.

Revealed through the sketching and the interview process, I found that preferences of food places in the district are shaped more by age and especially by the duration of stay or residence within the district, than by a person's religion, nationality or "ethnicity". This directly connects to an individual's preferred level of mobility, and shows that residents who at first glance seem dissimilar (such as an employee working in the city centre but living outwards and a tourist from Qatar) do in fact share eating out preferences. For example, highly mobile residents need easily accessible food that allows fast orientation with a bit of variation. Taking this into account, a whole different map of food places and user groups comes to the fore.

From a mobility-centred perspective, residents of the district can be grouped into four categories: short-term, middle-term, long-term and non-residents. Each group has specific needs and wishes in how to organise urban spaces, including food places. Non-residents, as the two examples from earlier, use the inner-city areas

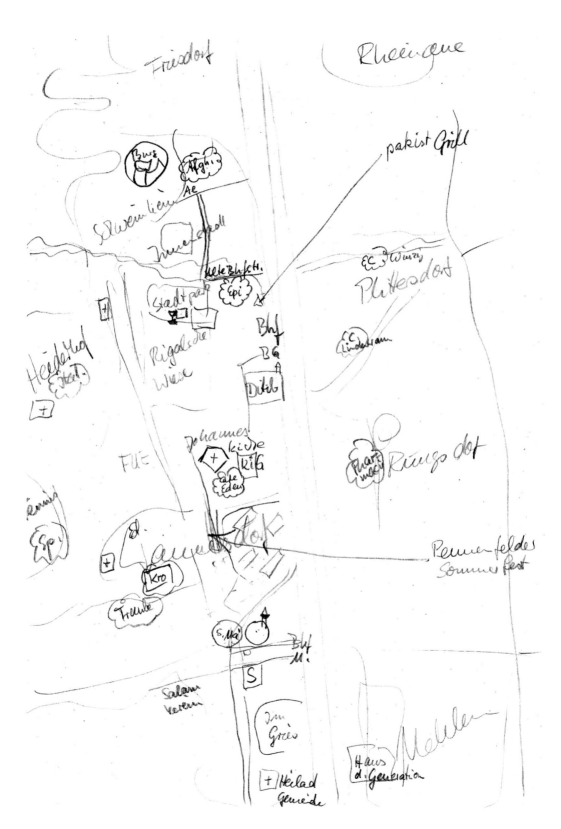

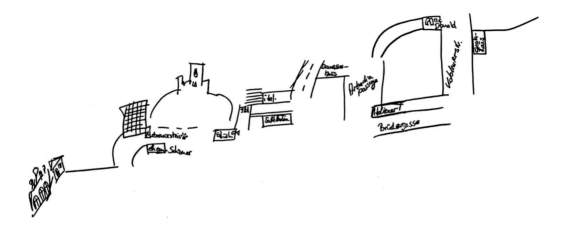

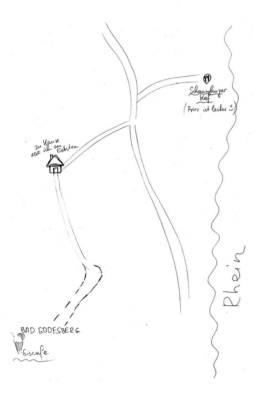

Fig. 4a-c: Sketch maps of food places
in Bad Godesberg drawn by interviewees
during the interview (Anonymous
interviewees, 2019-2020)

close to the train station, and rely on efficient, dependable but not necessarily personal culinary service. Likewise, short-term residents and especially young people have not as much close emotional attachment to specific places based

on personal memory as other groups. Affordable prices and tolerance regarding the length of stay in a commercial surrounding are central to this group's eating out preferences. Middle-term residents, mostly families, use the inner city less, and often prefer restaurants, snack bars or culinary events in their local neighbourhood, where the service is more personal and less focused on efficiency. Families can be seen in the inner city of Bad Godesberg mainly for special occasions like on village fairs, then preferring a reasonable level of prices. Many of the long-term residents of the district have more economic resources, as a lot of wealthy pensionaries live in the neighbourhoods at the riverside. They orient in the district not only by actual places, but also by memories, for example of old, now closed restaurants as in the interview quoted in the introduction. Their using preferences focus on high culinary quality and sophisticated service. For them, food places with a long and representative history have a special relevance (see fig. 5).

In comparing the use preferences of all four groups, one can see that most of the conflict potential in the district arises between young and old people or short-term and long-term residents. A very popular narrative in the district is that the boundary of segregation and thus polarisation is the train line parallel to the river, with the mansion district on the eastern and the city centre on the western side. But the most used places of young people are

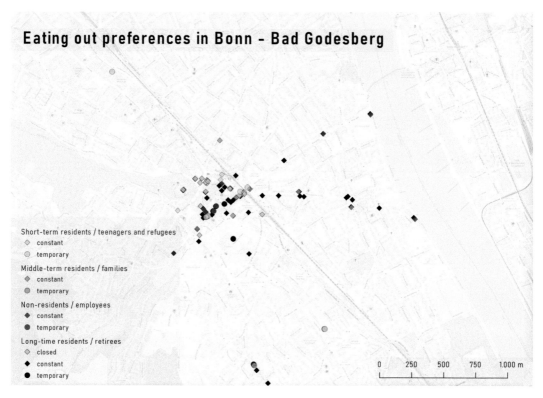

Eating out preferences in Bonn - Bad Godesberg

Short-term residents / teenagers and refugees
◇ constant
○ temporary

Middle-term residents / families
◆ constant
● temporary

Non-residents / employees
◆ constant
● temporary

Long-time residents / retirees
◇ closed
◆ constant
● temporary

0   250   500   750   1.000 m

Fig. 5: This map shows four different user groups and their use preferences of food places in Bad Godesberg (2020)

in the north, in direction of the city centre of Bonn, and the ones used most by older people are in the southern parts, which are the old, now incorporated villages. Both of them claim the district centre as a part of their preferred space: the older people as the traditional centre of the district and the surrounding villages, the younger people as a connecting point to the city centre of Bonn, as regional trains stop here and go to Bonn centre. So, their perspectives on the districts' centre differ – which doesn't mean that they can't come to a compromise. Similarly, the embedding of the centre within the surrounding neighbourhoods of the former villages is experienced in different ways by the different groups. Compromises can be found here if the diverse perspectives are given voice to and then compared.

Ethnic, national or regional references at eating out places do not on their own have the

potential to generate conflict as the differences described earlier. That also means that by focusing solely on these aspects in development discussions, the actual conflicts in using preferences of urban spaces and especially food places cannot be solved. Lack of sensitivity to this may fuel frustration and polarisation amongst participants.

In summary, it seems very instructive to look at how people use and feel about specific places, in this case local or district restaurants, especially when location, situation and their social context are considered. Even though global categories such as nationalities, ethnicities and religions are applied to describe the conflicts and processes in the district development, at a very local level other effects are at work, such as age and the duration of residence. At this level, the research can reveal how details of everyday practices are at play in ordinary places such as restaurants and how such practices are vital to how individuals build up relations to other people and other places. This realisation can be reflected in participatory district development programmes centred around community mapping workshops, etc., making use of the special qualities of food: Eating out connects personal memories to public space, and at the same time provides access to the reflection of ascriptions of belonging and authenticity on a quotidian level.

Notes

1   The lecture series was part of the project "Urban food cultures and integrative practices" (2018–2021, Bonn), funded by the German Federal Ministry of Education and Research and led by Prof. Dr. Clemens Albrecht. From 2018 on, I worked on my ethnographic PhD thesis about the district of Bonn-Bad Godesberg as a research assistant in the project.

2   I describe practices as cultural following Arjun Appadurais definition of "situated and embodied difference" (Appadurai, 1996, p. 13): "it is a useful heuristic that can highlight points of similarity and contrast between all sorts of categories: classes, genders, roles, groups, and nations. When we therefore point to a practice, a distinction, a conception, an object, or an ideology as having a cultural dimension (notice the adjectival use), we stress the idea of situated difference, that is, difference in relation to something local, embodied, and significant" (ibid., 12).

3   The original German term of a unitary guiding concept ("Leitbild") is closely connected to the debate around a national German guiding culture ("Leitkultur"), to which minorities have to adapt. For a critique of its nationalist notions see Mouritsen *et al.*, 2019.

Empirical data

Interview 01, 5th February 2020, conducted by Mila Brill in Bad Godesberg.

References

Amelina, A., 2017. After the reflexive turn in migration studies: Towards the doing migration approach. *Working Paper Series 'Gender, Diversity and Migration'*, 13.

Appadurai, A., 1996. *Modernity at large. Cultural dimensions of globalization*. Minneapolis: University of Minnesota Press.

Bergmann, J., 1981. Ethnomethodologische Konversationsanalyse. *In: Dialogforschung. Jahrbuch 1980 des Instituts für deutsche Sprache*. Düsseldorf: Schwann, 9–51.

Blokland, T., 2017. *Community as urban practice*. Cambridge: Polity Press.

Çağlar, A., and Glick Schiller, N., 2018. *Migrants and city-making. Dispossession, displacement and urban regeneration*. Durham, NC: London: Duke University Press.

Clarke, A., 2005. *Situational analysis. Grounded theory after the postmodern turn*. London: Sage Publications.

de Certeau, M., 1984. *The practice of everyday life*. Berkeley; Los Angeles: University of California Press.

de Certeau, M., Giard, L., and Mayol, P., 1998. *The practice of everyday life*, Vol. 2. Minneapolis: University of Minnesota Press.

Emmison, M., 2003. Social class and cultural mobility. Reconfiguring the cultural omnivore thesis. *Journal of Sociology*, 39 (3), 211–230.

Everts, J., 2008. *Konsum und Multikulturalität im Stadtteil. Eine sozialgeografische Analyse migrantengeführter Lebensmittelgeschäfte*. Bielefeld: Transcript Verlag.

Hage, G., 1997. At home in the entrails of the west: Multiculturalism, ethnic food and migrant home-building. *In*: H. Grace, G. Hage, L. Johnson, J. Langsworth, and M. Symonds, eds. *Home/world: Communality, identity and marginality in Sydney's west*. Sydney: Pluto Press, 99–153.

May, J., 1996. A little taste of something more exotic: The imaginative geographies of everyday life. *Geography*, 81 (1), 57–64.

Möhring, M., 2014. Food for thought: Rethinking the history of migration to West Germany through the migrant restaurant business. *Journal of Contemporary History*, 49 (1), 209–27.

Mouritsen, P., Faas, D., Meer, N., and de Witte, N., 2019. Leitkultur debates as civic integration in North-Western Europe: The nationalism of "values" and "good citizenship"'. *Ethnicities*, 19 (4), 632–653.

Parzer, M., and Astleithner, F., 2018. More than just shopping: Ethnic majority consumers and cosmopolitanism in immigrant grocery shops. *Journal of Ethnic and Migration Studies*, 44 (7), 1117–1135.

Preissing, S., 2019. *Jugend am Rande der Stadt. Eine vergleichende Studie zu Marginalisierung und Raumaneignung in Deutschland und Frankreich*. Wiesbaden: Springer VS.

Roberts, L., 2015. *Mapping cultures. Place, practice, performance*. Hampshire: Palgrave Macmillan.

Roberts, L., 2016. *Deep mapping*. Basel, Peking, Wuhan, Barcelona: MDIP.

Simmel, G., 2001. Soziologie Der Mahlzeit. *In*: O. Rammstedt, ed. *Georg Simmel Gesamtausgabe. Aufsätze und Abhandlungen 1909–1918. Band 1*, vol. 12. Berlin: Suhrkamp Verlag, 140–147.

Spivak, G.C., 1988. Can the subaltern speak? In C. Nelson and L. Grossberg, eds. *Marxism and the interpretation of culture*. Chicago: University of Illinois Press.

Stock, M., 2013. *Der Geschmack der Gentrifizierung. Arabische Imbisse in Berlin*. Bielefeld: Transcript Verlag.

Warde, A., 2016. *The practice of eating*. Cambridge: Polity Press.

Wimmer, A., and Glick Schiller, N., 2002. Methodological nationalism and beyond: Nation-State building, migration and the social sciences. *Global Networks*, 2 (4), 301–334.

Yildiz, E., 2013. *Die Weltoffene Stadt. Wie Migration Globalisierung zum urbanen Alltag macht*. Bielefeld: Transcript Verlag.

Reimagining the (agri)cultural city: Commoning and cultivating relationships in Utrecht, Holland

Merel Zwarts, Corelia Baibarac-Duignan and Asia Komarova

We are in the suburban area of Leidsche Rijn, a neighbourhood of Utrecht that has been built during the past 30 years on former prosperous farmlands. This is the territory in which the *Travelling Farm Museum of Forgotten Skills (TFM)* collects stories and forgotten past agricultural skills from farmers, neighbours, local resilience initiatives (e.g., food forest *Haarzuilens*, community garden *Johannitersveld*, microgreens company microrganics, eco-cultural centre *Metaal Kathedraal*, among others), schools and artists. The project was initiated by a group of artists, the Outsiders Union, together with Casco Art Institute – Working for the Commons. Initially, in 2018, it inhabited and animated one of the remaining farmhouses of the area, Farmhouse Terwijde (fig. 1). From seeding to harvest time, several activities unfolded to think about the agrarian past and future of Utrecht, all through the lens of food, ecology and heritage.

In our project, mapping is not about the creation of physical maps of the neighbourhood, but rather about the iterative formation of relations and collaborations between people (e.g., farmers, artists, residents, researchers, students) and with the land. By taking this relational approach, mapping becomes a form of commoning existing and emerging practices of resilience (Baibarac and Petrescu, 2017; Huybrechts *et al.*, 2020; Bresnihan, 2015). Building on Elinor Ostrom's original notion of the 'commons' (Ostrom, 1990), we focus on practices such as urban farming, community gardening, food forestry, strengthening

the local food economy or learning about (re) connecting to the land. The aim of this process of commoning is twofold. On the one hand, it is about 'scaling' such practices by forming networks around them, making visible the knowledge they generate and amplifying it as a critique and alternative to current unsustainable practices and development pathways. On the other hand, it is about participatory ways of reimagining sustainable urban futures by creating opportunities for encounter. In this sense, using Karen Barad's terminology, mapping can create "possibilities for worldly re-configurings" (Barad, 2012) – or transformation.

Mapping as a part of the *TFM* takes place in various ways. One way of mapping is on the move, through cycling tours. A second way of mapping is on location, through workshops and through direct interactions with the neighbourhood and its inhabitants. A third way of mapping is digital through a co-created website and podcast series. The cycling tours and workshops bring participants in proximity with the surrounding environment and existing resilience practices. This allows them to experience these practices and enhance awareness about them by listening and paying increased attention to existing knowledge that enables re-imagining other, more sustainable futures.

These forms of mapping the land and resilience practices allow for creative 'crossings' (Verhoeff and Dresscher, 2020) that support an enhanced awareness and alternative imaginaries of how food relationships in a sustainable

DOI: 10.4324/9781003352280-24

Fig. 1: Terwijde Farmhouse (Angela Tellier/Tellier Photography Concept & Design, 2018)

neighbourhood may look like. Crossings enable other ways of seeing and imagining that are not possible in isolation. For example, in our project, mapping enables exchanges – crossings – between different human and non-human participants, such as new residents, farmers, insects, birds and local crops. They connect different types of knowledge and practice, bringing together, among others, artists, farmers and academics. Furthermore, through interactions in the physical and digital spheres, they cross the past, present and future. Together, they support our commoning efforts.

How TFM came about

Originally, farmhouse Ter Weyde, owned by the family Van Vuuren, was part of a great agrarian landscape. This hinterland served the city and beyond, from the times of Roman occupation until 1980, when the city of

Utrecht started to expand by building the new vinex-neighbourhood, Leidsche Rijn. On our arrival in this neighbourhood, in 2018, the owner was leaving his farmhouse as he had lost his farmland in the complex process of redevelopment of the area, to make room for a shopping mall (fig. 2). The story we needed to tell was the untold one of the farmers from this area, but also from the soil and other non-human elements (e.g., seeds, objects from the area's past), in order not to forget the ecological value of the area. The project was embraced by the neighbouring schools, social organisations, art students within and passed the city, scientists, politicians, etc. One of the communication tools we created to communicate this story was a pamphlet: Words from the land (fig. 3). This pamphlet delves into the agrarian histories of Hof ter Weyde, how it has been the farmhouse of family Van Vuuren and how the landscape changed in recent decades.

1992   **2018**

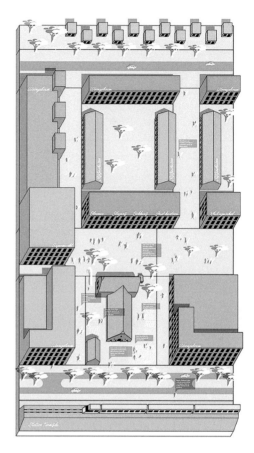

Fig. 2: Digital scale model of Terwijde Farmhouse in 1992 and 2018 (Txell Blanco Diaz, 2018)

Regardless of our efforts, in January 2019 the farmhouse was sold to a major developer for commercial purposes. Therefore, we needed to transform our practice to continue our conversation and expand our collective body of knowledge. With the shape of a farmhouse as the main inspiration, the project transformed into a mobile one: The *Travelling Farm Museum of Forgotten Skills*. This is a mobile adaptable structure, a nomadic installation that resembles the farmhouse, mirroring the surrounding landscape, preserving the stories, objects and produce we collect through mapping (fig. 4). It functions as a library, table, cabinet, showroom, market stand and even sound system. The farm

as a mobile installation and museum-in-the-making travels throughout the neighbourhood and listens to the stories of farmers, stories of eviction, survival and resilience.

Modes of mapping

Tours
In the summers of 2020, 2021 and 2022, every Saturday, the museum toured in a nearby rural area. We used the act of cycling to move around and engage with the local stories and skills of the previous farmlands now turned neighbourhood (fig. 5). Together with residents, we

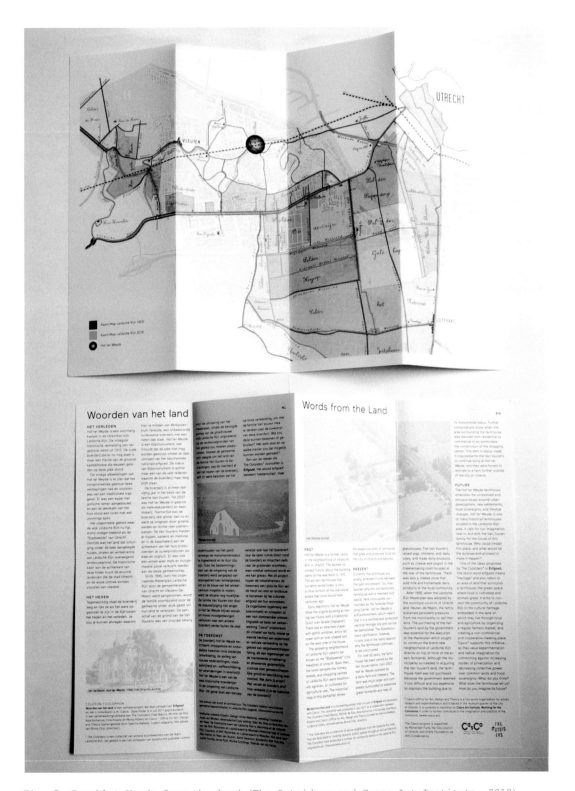

Fig. 3: Pamphlet Words from the land (The Outsiders and Casco Art Institute, 2018)

Fig. 4: The mobile installation in action (TFM, 2020)

cycled to farms and gardens, each time meeting new living beings and making them part of the process. Our aim was to stimulate a network of relationships. Those activities are not necessarily connected, but we used our museum as a platform for creating links as a form of commoning. For example, a vegetable farmer to a vegan chef, a potential consumer to a fruit farm, a farmer to a community gardener or a child to older generations. This is an illustration of how our take on food mapping fosters creative crossings between knowledges, practices, temporalities, through making visible different dimensions of food growing and transformation and building relationships. For instance, the vegan chef used her knowledge to transform, through fermentation, turnips produced by the vegetable farmer, while the resulting kimchi was eaten together with the residents. After that experience, the vegetable farmer became a supplier of the vegan restaurant.

In 2020, at the opening of our depot, we invited local residents and others from our network on a neighbourhood exploration, searching for traces from the past, ecological non-human neighbours, waterways and more through the method of 'deep mapping' (Mattern, 2015; Visser *et al.*, 2005). Participants created personal maps that express their relationship with the landscape, based on themes like flora, fauna, heritage and water from a subjective point of view (fig. 6). The maps represent personal experiences and relationships of humans with non-human or historical elements of the landscape, altogether initiating the first objects of the museum collection.

Digital elements

The opening of the physical depot coincided with the Corona virus outbreak, which meant that we had to reconsider our approach and combine digital and analogue forms of engaging with the neighbourhood. In collaboration with researchers from Utrecht University, we developed an open source, collectively designed website, which we use as the museum's digital depot and a way to continue the engagement with the residents at a time of social distancing (fig. 7). Being online, the website has the potential to invite contributions beyond a specific moment in time, which typically is the case in a physical workshop. Residents of Leidsche Rijn are continuously invited to reflect on questions such as: Which skills and stories are rooted in this land, its agricultural past and presence as a suburb? What can we learn from those skills and stories for our future? Furthermore, the website expands the possibilities for encounter and reconfiguration: it emerged through creative crossings between artistic practice and academic scholarship, while linking local issues with broader socio-technical sustainability challenges. The website was initially used as a research resource, while it started to be populated with content by the residents. For example, the Growing section contains an interactive map of places and crops that people grow in the area, from local farms to balconies.

Collected stories of farmers and residents are also brought together and shared through a

Fig. 5: Tour to Voedselbos Haarzuilens food forest (TFM, 2021)

Fig. 6: Collection of maps made by participants (Merel Zwarts, 2020)

series of podcasts allowing attentive listening to the sounds and voices of the area. This adds to the multiple ways of engaging with people by connecting, having conversations, and creating an actual soundscape. Offered on several podcast platforms, we invite people to join our audible journey of learning about the land, the forgotten skills, and the different perspectives.

We bring the recording equipment to almost every tour, and we go on the streets and talk to residents (fig. 8).

Workshops
Collective mapping also takes place through periodic workshops. For instance, in September 2020, we organised a small-scale workshop entitled *Sowing Sustainable Prospects: Explore the Landscape of Leidsche Rijn and imagine the future* (Baibarac-Duignan *et al.*, 2020). As suggested by its title, the main aim of the workshop was to enhance residents' awareness of their everyday environments and, together, start to imagine alternative neighbourhood futures. We developed our working method in collaboration with the researchers from Utrecht University with whom we collaborated on the website and who were interested in exploring issues around civic participation in datafied smart cities. The method included a broader and shared interest in sustainability and built on ideas that emerged during the co-design of the website.

Fig. 7: Screenshot of the digital depot website (TFM and UU, 2020)

Fig. 8: Recording podcasts of talking to people we encounter (Merel Zwarts, 2021)

The questions from which we started were: *What is 'data'?* and *How can it be meaningful for the future of your neighbourhood?* Departing from these two questions, we organised a first experimental low(no)-tech walk-shop to explore the landscape of Leidsche Rijn and imagine potential futures together with a group of residents.

Rather than looking for 'data' understood in a technological sense (which is typically the case in ethnographic critical data studies, e.g., Powell (2018), we invited the participants, organised in small groups, to explore the landscape of the neighbourhood. We proposed the themes of sustainability, nature and food, and asked them to take (instant) photos and collect any fragments of the landscape that made them think about these themes (e.g., objects from nature, stories from people they met). After this 'data walk', we analysed the physical materials and mapped them onto a large tablecloth in our physical depot.

The participants mapped the data – or objects collected – by making associations between the various items and grouping them into themes, which became co-created bottom-up categories (fig. 9). The relationships between the items were marked with tape and annotated with a brief explanation. At the end of the mapping, a constellation was formed, involving the data (objects, photos) and links between them (tape). The 'map' emerged spontaneously, through creating spaces for encounter and negotiation between participants.

Fig. 9: Mapping 'data' (Merel Zwarts, 2020)

Fig. 10: Collecting future stories (Asia Komarova, 2020)

Subsequently, we used the constellation as a prompt to re-imagine futures for the neighbourhood in the form of writing speculative postcards from the future to the present (fig. 10). This way of 'making' the future through experiencing the present and creating artefacts together can make possible futures tangible and concrete (Pelzer and Versteeg, 2019). From this perspective, mapping as a participatory, experiential and performative activity offers potential for transformation.

Harvesting the commons

What we harvest from our hybrid encounters are relationships, imagination and knowledge. Through the various approaches within our

fieldwork, such as workshops, tours and podcasts, we create and initiate relationships and collaborations. The outcomes of our mapping activities, which derive from experimental art practices, are not exactly measurable or resulting in physical maps. They generate relationships and actions that help reshape food imaginaries about the neighbourhood. To preserve these imaginaries and support further encounters and actions, we create objects for our museum. In this way, we make space for historical objects and heritage as well. Every story, collected through a podcast, workshop or tour, adds to the collection. Both the museum collection and the relationships function as a form of commoning.

What emerges is a commons of social relations that we build together: between residents, farmers, soil, digital tools and artefacts in the museum, while also connecting with wider socio-technical discourses around sustainability. By speculative storytelling, non-humans and other entities are given a voice through collective artistic exploration. We look at how we can establish a sense or relationality, in search for how we can create meaning and acts of listening as a *we* (Vazquez, 2012). It is therefore important for us to work non-hierarchically as a group with different beings. Every story is equally valuable to our collection, and everyone is welcome to participate, collaborate or only listen. Inspired by institutional critique and social practice (Jackson, 2011), TFM questions how art could look like, its role in society and within the broader sustainability discourses. We therefore look beyond the creation of mere aesthetical objects, focusing on establishing meaningful and actual relationships that can change how we perceive agricultural practices in urban environments.

Overall, we hope to create a humble connection to the land, to the beings that feed us, so we can co-exist together in a world where local traditions, soil and nourishing food are accessible to everyone in our communities. To achieve that, acts of collective mapping and commoning are crucial.

References

Baibarac, C., and Petrescu, D., 2017. Co-design and urban resilience: Visioning tools for commoning resilience practices. *CoDesign*, 15 (2), 91–109.

Baibarac-Duignan, C., Zwart, M., and Kumar, A., 2020. *Sowing sustainable prospects: Explore the landscape of Leidsche Rijn and imagine the future*. Available from https://tfmde-pot.hotglue.me/?workshop [Accessed 7 Nov 2022].

Barad, K., 2012. Interview with Karen Barad. *In*: R. Dolphijn and I. van der Tuin, eds. *New materialism: Interviews & cartographies*. Michigan: Open Humanities Press, 48–70.

Bresnihan, P., 2015. The more than human commons: From commons to commoning. *In*: S. Kirwan, L. Dawney and J. Brigstocke, eds. *Space, power and the commons: The struggle for alternative futures*. New York: Routledge, 93–112.

Huybrechts, L., Teli, M., Zuljevic, M., et al., 2020. Visions that change. Articulating the politics of participatory design. *CoDesign*, 16 (1), 3–16.

Jackson, S., 2011. *Social works: Performing art, supporting publics*. London: Routledge.

Mattern, S., 2015. *Deep mapping the media city* (Forerunners: Ideas First). Minneapolis: University of Minnesota Press.

Ostrom, E., 1990. *Governing the commons: The evolution of institutions for collective action* (Political Economy of Institutions and Decisions). Cambridge: Cambridge University Press.

Pelzer, P., and Versteeg, W., 2019. Imagination for change: The post-fossil city contest. *Futures*, 108, 12–26.

Powell, A., 2018. The data walkshop and radical bottom-up data knowledge. *In*: H. Knox and D. Nafus, eds. *Ethnography for a data-saturated world*. Manchester: Manchester University Press.

Vazquez, R., 2012. Towards a decolonial critique of modernity. Buen Vivir, relationality and the task of listening. *In*: R. Fornet-Betancourt, ed. *Capital, poverty, development*. Aachen: Wissenschaftsverlag Mainz, 241–252.

Verhoeff, N., and Dresscher, P., 2020. XR: Crossing and interfering artistic media spaces. *In*: L. Hjorth, A. de Souza e Silva and K. Lanson, eds. *The Routledge companion to mobile media art*. London: Routledge, 482–492.

Visser, F.S., Stappers, P.J., van der Lugt, R., et al., 2005. Contextmapping: Experiences from practice. *CoDesign*, 1 (2), 119–149.

A fairy tale of a place: Depictions of 21st century London as a fantasy foodscape in contemporary food writing

Silvia Rosivalová Baučeková

Writing about food is nothing new: cookbooks were already produced in Ancient Greece and Rome (Albala, 2012, p. 228), and authors such as the Frenchman Jean Anthelme Brillat-Savarin or the 19th century journalist George Dodd had been documenting eating practices and tastes long before the recent boom of culinary literature. However, since the beginning of the new millennium, writing about food has transformed from a niche endeavour of a few gourmands into a successful literary field. Contemporary food writers, such as Nigel Slater or Madhur Jaffrey, or chefs-turned-authors, like Anthony Bourdain or Antonio Carluccio, have earned celebrity status both in literary and gastronomic circles. Mirroring popular interest, literary scholars and other academics have also turned their attention to culinary literature. Nicola Humble maintains that "we should take cookbooks and other practical food writings seriously as objects worthy of detailed textual analysis" (Humble, 2020, p. 2). Humble's recent book *The Literature of Food: An Introduction from 1830 to Present* (2020), Janet Theophano's *Eat My Words: Reading Women's Lives Through the Cookbooks They Wrote* (2002), or Arlene Voski Avakian's anthology of female food writing titled *Through the Kitchen Window* (2005) are just a few examples of academic engagement with culinary texts.

I aim to contribute to this emerging debate[1] by conducting an analysis of four texts: *Eating for Britain* (2011) by Simon Majumdar, *Eat London 3* (2017) by Peter Prescott and Terence Conran, *Infused: Adventures in Tea* (2019) by Henrietta

Lovell, and *Towpath: Recipes and Stories* (2020) by Lori de Mori and Laura Jackson (see fig. 1). These books reflect the variety of literary genres within food writing, while dealing in one way or another with the foodscape of postmillennial London.[2]

They are, however, by no means unique in the themes they present. On the contrary, they serve as examples of a broader narrative running through contemporary food writing. Either consciously or unconsciously, this narrative engages with hypermodernity. I argue that in reaction to the anxieties caused by hypermodernity, the four analysed books offer their readers a romanticised portrayal of an imagined foodscape of London, where eating can provide satisfaction, happiness, or even a renewed sense of belonging. I further claim that although the four texts are steeped with notions of community and openness, the escapist fantasy they offer is not accessible to all. Instead, participation in the idealised forms of food consumption is reserved for those on the winning side of contemporary British society.

Hypermodernity and hyperconsumption in the 21st century

As a result of a number of social processes including globalisation, the expansion of neoliberal ideas into all spheres of life, and the digital revolution, we have entered a new epoch in the history of humanity. Gilles Lipovetsky refers to this period as 'hypermodernity' and claims that its chief characteristic

DOI: 10.4324/9781003352280-25

Fig. 1: Eating for Britain, Eat London 3, Towpath: Recipes and Stories, and Infused: Adventures in Tea

is paradoxicality, or a coexistence of contradictory behaviours and values: a hedonistic ethos accompanied by a focus on self-regulation, postmodern cynicism and a simultaneous strife for earnestness, proliferation of consumption alongside growing fascination with restriction (2005, pp. 32–33). Ronnie Lippens describes hypermodernity as "a thoroughly globalized modernity" (1998, p. 17) in which "ambivalence and paradox gradually penetrate, in Deleuzean fashion, *nomadic*, unfixed, borderless, beaconless, *desert-like* everyday experiences" (p. 18, emphasis in the original).

Zygmunt Bauman claims that contemporary life is characterised by increased precarity and social atomisation. It seems that "it is now each of us, individually, that is the 'longest living' of all the bonds and institutions we have met: and the only entity whose life-expectation is steadily rising rather than shrinking" (Bauman, 2001, p. 21). This isolation and uncertainty provide fertile ground for a proliferation of consumerism and individualism. Hypermodern individuals are not inclined to plan or create permanent interpersonal bonds: these seem to be meaningless in a world where it is impossible to predict the future with at least a modicum of

certainty. Instead, focus is shifted to the present moment. As a result of hyperindividualism, the breakdown of family and class allegiances, and a dissolution of "all previous geographical and time constraints on consumerism" (Lipovetsky, 2010, p. 25), the contemporary consumer is "liberated from the weight of convention, ethos and class traditions. From that, the profile of this new style of consumer can be described as erratic, nomadic, volatile, fragmented and deregulated" (p. 27). Consumption has become an end in itself. Lipovetsky observes that "what is important . . . is that something new is happening at the core of our daily lives. Somewhat like when going on a journey or on holiday: what counts is not so much the place visited as the journey itself" (p. 29).

Eating as salvation: The role of food in the global metropolis

The global metropolis represents the nexus of various forces shaping hypermodern society. Consequently, "cities are dumping grounds for globally produced troubles" (Bauman, 2007, p. 92). Cities are also increasingly construed as sites of danger, where one is surrounded by possibly hostile strangers in an anonymous environment. Paradoxically, the metropolis seems to attract as much as it repels. "The bigger and more heterogeneous a city, the more attractions it may support and offer. The massive concentration of strangers is, simultaneously, a repellent and a most powerful magnet, drawing to the city ever new cohorts of men and women" (p. 89) searching for a better life. Thus, global cities are ever expanding, promising to provide a home to a multitude of diverse inhabitants.

Naturally, in such densely populated places, food is of central importance. Taking London as my example, Caroline Steel notes that "every day for a city the size of London, enough food for thirty million meals must be produced, imported, sold, cooked, eaten and disposed of again" (2013, p. ix). However, in a hypermodern metropolis, food consumption is by no means limited to fulfilling citizens' nutritional needs. Instead, food becomes the ultimate consumer product: perfectly suited to satisfy hyperconsumers' desire for limitless consumption. Food can be – indeed, it must be – consumed repeatedly, multiple times a day, every day of the week. Thanks to global supply chains, we have access to a seemingly inexhaustible variety of foodstuffs. Supermarkets and restaurants are often open twenty-four hours a day, seven days a week. Together with online retailers and delivery services, they make it possible for consumers to enact their shopping fantasies irrespective of time and place.

While food shopping gratifies the desire for consumption and variety, eating out responds to another desire of the hyperindividual: it transforms consumption into experience. In the introduction to *Eat London 3*, London is called "the dining-out capital of the world" (2017, p. 7), and Londoners are referred to as "a populace that is willing to endure anything from queueing . . . or an arduous booking process, or sky-high prices to down-at-heel locations, just to sate their desire for a tasty morsel" (ibid.). It seems that contemporary Londoners are model hyperconsumers, craving the escapism and pleasure of eating as a cure for the anxieties of hypermodern urban life.

However, there is more to the burgeoning of interest in food than a simple desire for oblivion. The community-building potential of eating is often construed as a possible solution to hyperindividualism, urban isolation, and uprootedness. It is widely accepted that eating is a social act and that sharing food is crucial in creating and maintaining community ties. In the contemporary city, it is food markets, restaurants, and other public food spaces where it might be possible to engage in communal eating and in the construction of relationships. In this context, Carolyn Steel points out the growing popularity of London's Borough Market – a space where hypermodern individuals can enact fantasies of communal living:

What Borough offers is an experience; an echo, for those who can afford it, of the excitement that food markets once brought to cities. . . . The people who come here, although plainly enjoying themselves, seem to be searching for something more: for roots, for meaning, for salvation, even.

(2013, p. 107)

This search for "something more" is a running thread in the books I analysed. The authors imbue foodstuffs and foodscapes with a sense of nostalgia that helps construct a fantasy dreamland in which the paradoxes and plight of the hypermodern condition cease to exist. In this sense, food writing must be understood as a hybrid, semi-fictional genre.

Ostensibly, food writing is non-fiction. The books are set in real places, the characters are real people, and the events portrayed have really happened. The realistic setting in particular is emphasised in all four books. Thanks to numerous verbal descriptions, readers can easily locate the settings on a map, follow the trajectories of characters' journeys, and imagine the appearance and ambiance of the places described. Realism is heightened by the inclusion of photographs, and in case of *Infused* and *Eat London 3* also by maps that form an integral part of the texts. *Infused* starts with a page titled "Map of locations" (see fig. 2), while

Fig. 2: The map of the world featured at the beginning of Henrietta Lovell's *Infused*

the cover of *Eat London 3* is illustrated with a hand-drawn map of Battersea and Clapham (see fig. 3) and each section of the book begins with a similar map of the boroughs described.

By emphasising real-world settings, the authors seek to lend their ideas a semblance of truth. However, as Barbara Piatti and colleagues observe, "[a] specific feature of a literary space is its numerous gaps – all you can detect on the spatial level is reduced, incomplete information" (2009, p. 185). In fiction and non-fiction alike, real places are fictionalised to fit the narrative and advance the argument presented by the author. The map at the beginning of Lovell's book is a blind map of the world with only a few dots indicating the places where the narrator sources and sells her teas: the rest is deemed unimportant or uninteresting.

Similarly, in *Eat London 3* the maps only depict segments of London chosen by the editors as

noteworthy, hip, or exclusive enough to be included. Most of the streets in the maps are not labelled. Instead, the maps feature what the two authors consider to be the most prestigious eateries in the area. The same is true for the photographs and verbal descriptions of settings: although the places depicted are undoubtedly real, the purpose of the depictions is to produce a fiction. As I argue in the following section, these settings are designed to evoke feelings of contentment, security, and community.

Hypermodernity and culinary nostalgia

In his last book titled *Retrotopia* (2017), Zygmunt Bauman suggested that contemporary society struggles with a loss of belief in the possibility of a better future. Instead, the hypermodern individual fixates on a fabricated version of the past to find comfort. Svetlana Boym defined nostalgia

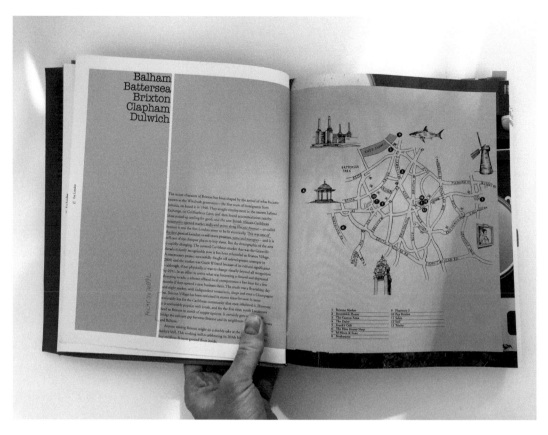

Fig. 3: A hand-drawn map highlighting selected eateries and sights in a particular area is featured at the beginning of each section of *Eat London 3*

as "a sentiment of loss and displacement, but . . . also a romance with one's own fantasy" (2001, p. xiii). Just like Bauman, Boym noted a gradual turn from the utopian spirit of modernity to a postmodern or hypermodern sense of nostalgia (p. xiv). A nostalgic tone pervades contemporary discourse on food as well. The negative aspects of contemporary food production and consumption, such as industrial farming, reliance on processed and convenience foods, or lack of domestic cooking skills, are frequently contrasted with an allegedly superior past when food was wholesome and tasty and consumers and producers alike had an intimate relationship with what they grew, cooked, and ate.[3]

Nostalgia emerges as a dominant theme in the four books analysed in this chapter. In the first chapter of *Infused*, Henrietta Lovell reminisces about her childhood visits to Scotland, where she was treated to posh afternoon teas by her great-aunt. Lovell juxtaposes the "scruffy, terraced streets of south London" (2019, p. 2) with the village of Beeswing where her great-aunt lived, which is referred to as "a fairy tale of a place" complete with "rough-tongued calves with velvet creases behind their ears, and woods thick with wet bracken" (ibid.). This idyllic setting serves as a backdrop to the magical tea rituals taking place in her great-aunt's drawing room. The memory of these afternoon teas functions as a frame for the remainder of the book. Today, Lovell's company supplies loose leaf teas to various upscale venues in central London. What she wishes to provide for her customers, she suggests, is a sensory experience as unadulterated and satisfying as those she once used to enjoy.

Simon Majumdar's travel stories are equally steeped in nostalgia. He fondly reminisces about the cheap eatery on Walworth Road where he used to have breakfast as a university student (2011, p. 21) and about the builder's tea he used to drink with it (p. 23). However, Majumdar does not only express nostalgia for remembered meals. His book is an exercise in nostalgia for an imagined period in British food history, when Britain allegedly boasted excellent, high-quality, local foods. Majumdar posits that food culture in Britain has deteriorated due to a loss of tradition and a resultant decline in cooking and food production skills. His book, he claims, aims to reacquaint readers with Britain's lost foods and with the artisans who still produce them today (pp. 1, 3, 9, etc.).

While nostalgia can be defined in temporal terms, as "a yearning for a different time – the time of our childhood, the slower rhythms of our dreams" (Boym, 2001, p. xv), it is often specific places that trigger nostalgic feelings. In fact, place and memory are inextricably linked. Some neuroscientists even claim that the hippocampus works as "a 'memory map' – at once a map of space, a map of the brain and a register of the links between these" (Jeffery, 2018, p. 66). Thus, memory is understood not only as embodied, but also as "emplaced", that is "lived somewhere" and tied to a specific location (Farrar, 2011, p. 725). Nostalgia, too, has a strong spatial element. In fact, the condition was originally described as melancholia caused by being far away from home (p. 727).

Spatiality is emphasised in all four analysed books. As shown earlier, nostalgic foods are tied to specific locations, and it is this locatedness that distinguishes good and authentic foods from those that are framed as fake and inferior. In Majumdar's book, the gin produced in the Beefeater distillery in Kennington, or the tea served at Brown's Hotel are presented as valuable not only due to their taste and quality, but also because they are connected to a particular place. Maps, photographs of streets and restaurants, travel itineraries, and copious other geographical detail help create a nostalgic tone that simultaneously evokes a sense of longing and of

Fig. 4: Photographs depicting idyllic scenes at the bank of Regent's Canal help create the nostalgic tone of *Towpath: Recipes and Stories*

possibility. The authors seem to suggest that readers themselves could visit the places mentioned and experience first-hand the pleasures and emotions described.

The association of a specific location with nostalgic feelings is probably most prominent in *Towpath*. This book is set in and around a café of the same name located on the bank of Regent's Canal. The book is liberally illustrated with photographs of the canal featuring Londoners engaging in pleasant activities: joggers (de Mori and Jackson, 2020, p. 69), gossiping children (p. 86), or residents walking their dogs (p. 147). The book is divided into nine sections, each representing one month of the year, and the pictures in each section reflect changing weather and flora around the canal. All of this serves to create a romantic, pastoral ambiance (see fig. 4). Towpath's owners purposefully nurture this fantasy by banning electronic devices, not providing Wi-Fi access, and not operating a website for the café (p. 40). They say their aim is to

create a place with a small-town sense of friendliness, but also a vibrancy – a bit like a schoolyard at lunchtime, where you could just turn up and know that, at least until the bell rang, there would be an escape from the tedium of being pinned to a desk with a pencil in your hand trying to learn long divisions. (ibid.)

Although Towpath's customers are not schoolchildren stuck in a boring class, they, too, crave momentary respite from the stresses of the hypermodern metropolis. A neighbourhood café straight from an imagined past, when mobile phones and other distractions of contemporary life did not yet exist, seems to offer just that.

In *Eat London 3* the overall tone is more restrained, but the photographs that illustrate the volume make it obvious that nostalgia is a prominent theme in London's upscale restaurants, too. Many of the spaces depicted are designed to evoke a nostalgic feeling: some are decorated in a rustic style and outfitted with reclaimed furniture, while others allude to Victorian tearooms or gentlemen's clubs with dainty china and patterned wallpapers. The interior of Casse-Croûte bistro at 109 Bermondsey Street in Southwark is described as follows:

It's a tiny room but it just oozes a certain Frenchness. There are red leather banquettes, a black-and-white tiled floor, old French posters and copper pans on the wall, red-and-white gingham undercloths and paper table tops. . . . Nothing new or innovative, nothing challenging or quirky, just well-known classics. Thankfully, there are no attempts to modernize.
(Prescott and Conran, 2017, p. 287)

Casse-Croûte is a carefully constructed stage on which diners can act out a fantasy of being transported to a mythical place in France, where food is prepared from simple ingredients based on age-old recipes, and one can partake in it peacefully, without worrying about carbon footprints, caloric intake, harmful pesticides, or the myriad of other anxieties that plague the hypermodern eater. Just like Lovell's rose-tinted memory of the tea parties at her aunt's or de Mori's pastoral reimagining of Regent's Canal, the French bistro experience at Casse-Croûte is crafted to offer an escape from contemporary life. But while such fantasies

can provide temporary relief to those who can afford to indulge in them, they are not available to everyone equally.

Distinction and privilege in a hyperconsumer society

In the third chapter of her book, Lovell describes her first visit to Claridge's Hotel:

The first time I ever ventured inside Claridge's, the doorman opened the door for me and smiled warmly, greeting me with a 'Good afternoon, madam' as if it was the most normal thing in the world that I should be there. That's the genius of the place. No one looks you up and down or judges you by your shoes. They truly understand gracious hospitality.
(2019, p. 22)

Of course, the warm welcome and "gracious hospitality" come at a price. At the time of writing, the standard afternoon tea menu in the tearooms of Claridge's, featuring teas supplied by Lovell's Rare Tea Company, starts at a whopping 75 pounds, which is more than the entire weekly food budget of the average Briton.[4] Indeed, as Lovell laconically observes, she has "come a long way from St John's Wood" (p. 109).

While Lipovetsky notes that in a hyperconsumer society traditional class cultural models have become destabilised (2010, p. 27) and individuals are free to purchase a variety of products irrespective of their cultural status, this freedom of choice is not unlimited. Obviously, only those who have the dispensable income can choose what they will spend it on. Moreover, even those who are in theory free to buy whatever they desire do not actually do so. Instead, there are complex processes at play in the creation of class distinction in hypermodern societies. Johnston and Baumann refer to the phenomenon as cultural omnivorousness, wherein "high status is signaled by selectively drawing from multiple cultural forms from across the cultural hierarchy" (Johnston and Baumann, 2007, p. 167).

Having analysed a large corpus of American food writing, Johnston and Baumann conclude that "food is legitimized for omnivores when it can be framed as *authentic* or *exotic*" (p. 169, emphasis added). The analysis of the books discussed in this chapter corroborates their findings. While the books present as desirable both builder's teabags and expensive loose-leaf teas, and almost any foods from chicken soup with noodles to oysters and truffles, for each of these foods to qualify as such they need to be framed as authentic, exotic, or both.

The concept of authenticity is central to the narratives of all four books. If we are to believe the authors of *Eat London 3*, London offers "authentic" food and drink of any possible kind: "strictly authentic dim sum" (Prescott and Conran, 2017, p. 50), authentic Vietnamese coffee (p. 121), authentic Spanish food (p. 301), authentic Beijing cuisine (p. 66) – the list goes on. A connection to a specific location is of central importance here. Majumdar and Lovell also stress the geographic origin of the products promoted. Majumdar travels to Dufftown, Scotland to drink whiskey, and back to London to have a glass of gin. He sings odes to the salmon smoked in the former Jewish district in East London, but also to the Arbroath smokie produced solely in the town of Arbroath, Scotland. Lovell details her travels around the world in search of rare local varieties of tea: from the Chinese province of Fujian to the Cederberg Mountains in South Africa where she sources the rooibos herb endemic to the region (2019, p. 64).

The obsession with geographic origin is also connected to the second quality that has the potential to signal distinction: exoticism. According to Lisa Heldke, a food or drink are understood as exotic either if they come from a far-away location, or if they seem extremely unusual or striking compared to more mainstream fare (2003, p. 18). Similarly, Johnston and Baumann differentiate between geographically and socially exotic foodstuffs. For a person living in a contemporary metropolis like London, the category of geographically exotic is rapidly shrinking. As a result of globalisation and mass migration, large cities now offer a wide variety of 'ethnic' restaurants and markets, and formerly exotic foodstuffs have become mainstream. The focus is thus shifting towards the socially exotic, that is to food that is "distant from the lives of gourmet food writers" (Johnston and Baumann, 2007, p. 189) in terms of class, or that which "flagrantly violates social or culinary conventions" (p. 194). The first type of socially exotic can be exemplified by the peasant food of Tuscany celebrated by the authors of *Towpath*, or by the builder's tea so fondly drunk by Simon Majumdar. The second type is often represented by consuming tabooed foods (Johnston and Baumann, 2007, p. 192). For a contemporary Westerner this typically includes certain parts of animal bodies (offal, blood, feet), or consuming animals one has killed oneself. Majumdar partakes in these types of food on multiple occasions. His trip to the Berkshire restaurant run by the famous London chef Mike Robinson (see fig. 5) is particularly noteworthy in this context. He narrates the experience as follows:

Mike dragged the carcass on to the nearby field, then produced a large hunting knife from his trouser pocket. He began the operation of gralloching or field dressing the animal, slitting it along the belly from tail to throat and pulling out the intestines and the rest of the innards, checking for signs of reportable disease as he went. He discarded most of the guts of the catch but pulled aside the kidneys, heart and liver. 'This,' he said, waving them at me, 'is what we want for breakfast'.

(2011, p. 53)

Clearly, the two men are taking part in a staged experience. The event provides a boost of adrenaline, a suitable amount of excitement or even danger, and enough outrageous taboo-breaking to allow the actors, as well as readers, to momentarily "escape the tedium of everyday life" (Lipovetsky, 2010, p. 29). It also aims to set Majumdar and Robinson apart from

Fig. 5: Chef Mike Robinson and his dog
Sassy wait for their prey

the mainstream eater who might be hesitant to partake in a dish of freshly killed deer liver. By not exhibiting such qualms themselves, the pair assert their superior expertise and taste.

The dreams and reality of hypermodern urban eating

Just like the hypermodern world, hypermodern food discourse is paradoxical in its nature. On the one hand, it is ostensibly non-fictional, recounting the experiences of real people in real settings, giving instructions for food preparation, or promoting restaurants and businesses. On the other hand, it is purposely fictional, creating nostalgic fantasies designed to allow readers to escape the anxieties of their everyday lives. In the books discussed in this chapter, the nostalgic tone was invoked through spatial elements: descriptions of localities in London and beyond, maps, photographs of places and of the foods eaten in them, and retellings of journeys. The focus on place helped blend the non-fictional with the fictional, as real locations were imbued with symbolic significance and transformed into sites of fantasy.

These places were paradoxical in another way, too: while presented as open, welcoming, and communal, they were in fact meant to appeal

to a privileged clientele: they were – consciously or unconsciously – designed to create "a symbolic boundary" (Concha, 2019, p. 72). While *Eat London 3* celebrates the gentrification of London, its authors admit that the cost of restaurant meals in the up-and-coming neighbourhoods is prohibitive to most. In *Infused*, Henrietta Lovell argues that all Britons should drink and appreciate rare, organically grown loose-leaf teas. In the same book, she explains how tea consumption on a mass scale was only made possible thanks to the proliferation of cheap, industrially produced teabags. *Eating for Britain* promotes artisanal foods which often used to be staples of the working-class diet, but today are inaccessible to urban working classes, who must rely on the vilified supermarket food instead. Finally, in *Towpath* de Mori and Jackson describe their ideal customer as someone who has enough spare time to queue for a table and sit at a café all day, making it obvious that Towpath is intended to cater to middle class creatives and independent professionals residing in the fast-gentrifying Dalston. Clearly, the nostalgic escape from the hypermodern condition promised by the authors of the books, as well as by the proprietors of the restaurants described in them, is merely a pleasant fantasy. Unfortunately, for many even such escapism remains inaccessible.

Notes

1 This work was realised with financial support of the MS SR VEGA project titled *The Global and the Local in Postmillennial Anglophone Literatures, Cultures and Media* (project number: 1/0447/20).

2 While *Eat London 3* and *Towpath: Recipes and Stories* are set (almost) exclusively in London, *Eating for Britain* and *Infused: Adventures in Tea* represent the genre of culinary memoir/travelogue, and as such depict multiple settings. However, they both contain numerous sections devoted to the foodscape of London and explore many of the same themes as the two purely London-based books.

3 I discuss the use of the nostalgic tone in British cookbooks in an earlier paper titled "Indulgent, wholesome, authentic: 21st-century cookbooks as hypermodern artefacts" (in S. Šnircová and S. Tomaščíková (Eds.), *Postmillennial Trends in Anglophone Literatures,*

Cultures and Media (Newcastle upon Tyne: Cambridge Scholars Publishing, 2019).

4   According to the Office for National Statistics, in 2020 the average weekly household expenditure on food and drink in the UK was £63.70 pounds. In addition, an average household spent £52.90 a week at restaurants and hotels (Kidd, 2021, *Family spending workbook 1: Detailed expenditure and trends*). In the same year, the average number of members in a UK household was 2.4 (Sharfman and Cobb, 2021, *Families and households in the UK: 2020*).

References

Albala, K., 2012. Cookbooks as historical documents. *In*: J.M. Pilcher, ed. *The Oxford handbook of food history*. Oxford: Oxford University Press, 227–240.

Avakian, A.V. (ed.), 2005. *Through the kitchen window: Women explore the intimate meanings of food and cooking*. Oxford: Berg.

Bauman, Z., 2001. Consuming life. *Journal of Consumer Culture*, 1 (3), 9–29. https://doi.org/10.1177/146954050100100102

Bauman, Z., 2007. *Liquid times: Living in an age of uncertainty*. Cambridge: Polity.

Bauman, Z., 2017. *Retrotopia*. Cambridge: Polity.

Boym, S., 2001. *The future of nostalgia*. New York: Basic Books.

Concha, P., 2019. Curators of markets, designers of place: The case of the street food scene in London. *Design Issues*, 35 (4), 69–78. https://doi.org/10.1162/desi_a_00566

de Mori, L., and Jackson, L., 2020. *Towpath: Recipes and stories*. White River Junction: Chelsea Green Publishing.

Farrar, M.E., 2011. Amnesia, nostalgia, and the politics of place memory. *Political Research Quarterly*, 64 (4), 723–735. https://doi.org/10.1177/1065912910373553

Heldke, L.M., 2003. *Exotic appetites: Ruminations of a food adventurer*. New York and London: Routledge.

Humble, N., 2020. *The literature of food: An introduction from 1830 to present*. London: Bloomsbury Academic.

Jeffery, K., 2018. The hippocampus: From memory, to map, to memory map. *Trends in Neurosciences*, 41 (2), 64–66. https://doi.org/10.1016/j.tins.2017.12.004

Johnston, J., and Baumann, S., 2007. Democracy versus distinction: A study of omnivorousness in gourmet food writing. *American Journal of Sociology*, 113 (1), 165–204. https://doi.org/10.1086/518923

Kidd, C., 2021. Family spending workbook 1: Detailed expenditure and trends. [Data set]. *Office for National Statistics*, March 16. Available from www.ons.gov.uk/peoplepopulationandcommunity/personalandhouseholdfinances/expenditure/datasets/familyspendingworkbook1detailedexpenditureandtrends

Lipovetsky, G., 2004/2005. *Hypermodern times*. Translated by A. Brown. Cambridge: Polity Press.

Lipovetsky, G., 2010. The hyperconsumption society. *In*: K.M. Ekström and K. Glans, eds. *Beyond the consumption bubble*. London: Routledge. ProQuest Ebook Central, 37–48.

Lippens, R., 1998. Hypermodernity, nomadic subjectivities, and radical democracy: Roads through ambivalent clews. *Social Justice*, 25 (2 (72)), 6–43.

Lovell, H., 2019. *Infused: Adventures in tea*. London: Faber and Faber.

Majumdar, S., 2011. *Eating for Britain: A journey into the heart (and belly) of the nation*. London: John Murrat

Piatti, B., Bär, H.R., Reuschel, A.K., Hurni, L., and Cartwright, W., 2009. Mapping literature: Towards a geography of fiction. *In*: W. Cartwright, G. Gartner and A. Lehn, eds. *Cartography and art: Lecture notes in geoinformation and cartography*. Berlin: Springer, 177–192. https://doi.org/10.1007/978-3-540-68569-2_15

Prescott, P., and Conran, T., 2017. *Eat London 3: All about food*. London: Conran Octopus.

Sharfman, A., and Cobb, P., 2021. Families and households in the UK: 2020. [Data set]. *Office for National Statistics*, 2 March. Available from www.ons.gov.uk/peoplepopulationandcommunity/birthsdeathsandmarriages/families/bulletins/familiesandhouseholds/2020

Steel, C., 2008/2013. *Hungry city: How food shapes our lives*. London: Vintage.

Theophano, J., 2002. *Eat my words: Reading women's lives through the cookbooks they wrote*. New York: Palgrave.

FOOD NETWORKS AND RESOURCES: Connecting people and places

Chapters in this section highlight **maps and mapping as registers of the complex, often hidden linkages and interdependencies** between stakeholders, space, produce and resources **in urban food systems**. Whilst covering inner-city and peri-urban places geographically, urban food maps are often employed by various urban agents to capture the need for food practices to be rescaled across and between all food system aspects and to be integrated into local, regional, national and global networks.

Benefiting from a range of mapping methods, including participatory, co-design and artistic, as well as techniques, such as GIS, photography, plan drawing and installation, urban food maps can demonstrate the potential, nature and urgency of change within current urban food systems. They aim **for a better understanding of network-based food spaces and practices** and how these can be safeguarded and developed to secure regenerative urban ecologies in the future.

DOI: 10.4324/9781003352280-26

Daniel Löschenbrand et al. develop their Food Atlas of Vienna to question the discipline of urban planning in terms of food systems and regional cycles seeking to provide **a fundamental reflection on how food metabolism has the power to shape urban areas** – and vice versa. Using cross-media mapping, they present methods and synchronous visualisations to make the connections between food and urban morphology more evident.

Raphaella Mascia and Daina Cheyenne Harvey reveal future alternatives for what our food systems could look like. Centred on the apple, they set out to find and map "lost" orchards in Worcester, Massachusetts, USA, which experienced rapid suburbanisation beginning in the 1980s. The goal is to create **a database for foragers** interested in these apples and to collect grafts of wild and abandoned (but cultivated) apple trees so that those species could be propagated in the future.

Mariana Sanchez Salvador uses the power of remapping to combine different data sources such as cartography, statistical data, archive documents, photographs and literary descriptions in an attempt **to understand the historical foodscapes of Lisbon**,

Portugal, in dialogue with the present, thereby making visible possible future developments. Such understanding, she argues, is the basis for any re-localising of urban food systems.

Jessica Ann Diehl reminds us that in much of the world food procurement takes informal forms. She provides **a geonarrative approach to interrogate formal and informal representations of assets and gaps in the foodscape** of Hebbal, an unplanned settlement in north Bangalore, India, where informal practices include kitchen gardens and roaming food carts. Her work expands urban food distribution and retail networks to acknowledge their alternative economic diversity.

Gundula Proksch and George Lee investigate the location and potential of different urban agriculture resources from community gardens to commercial controlled-environment operations in the metropolitan foodshed of Chicago, Illinois. The combination of GIS-based urban data and aerial photography at various scales allows for the **spatial, structural, economic and social analysis of the diverse opportunities within urban agricultural networks**.

Food networks & resources

	Purpose WHY?	Citizen WHO?
	recording *counting* *comparing* *uncovering* *responding* *proposing*	*urban farmers* *food system activists* *food initiatives* *consumers* *local communities* *public institutions*
Löschenbrand et al. Food Atlas Vienna: A collective cartography of the urban food landscape	counting food activities recording land uses  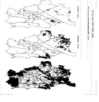	urban farmers food system stakeholders 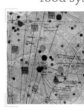
Mascia et al. Mapping Malus in Massachusetts: Creating a system for apple foraging	making visible a food product recording change 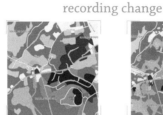 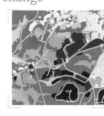	local communities  
Salvador The historic foodscapes of Lisbon: Mapping for a sustainable future	recording food culture comparing food activities  	food system stakeholders public institutions 
Diehl A food security geonarrative: Mapping in/formal foodscapes in Bangalore, India	making visible food system practices and spaces  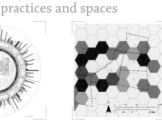	local communities food system stakeholders  
Proksch et al. Chicago's urban food networks: Mapping the future of a thriving metropolitan foodshed	recording food spaces proposing change  	urban farmers food system stakeholders 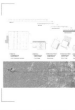

Place **WHERE?**	Time **WHEN?**	Methods **HOW?**
the peri-urban *city* *borough* *neighbourhood* *building* *open space*	*historical* *begin UA movement* *recent past* *present* *near future* *future*	*Mapping methods practices and products*
city	recent past / present	**Drawing Collaging**

the peri-urban / neighbourhood	history / begin UA movement recent past	**Drawing Photographing**

city	history / present	**Drawing Listing**

neighbourhood	recent past / present	**Photographing Drawing**

city / the peri-urban	begin UA movement present / future	**Drawing Collaging**
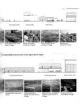 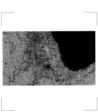	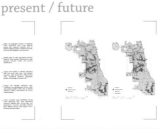	

Food Atlas Vienna:
A collective cartography of the urban food landscape

Daniel Löschenbrand, Vanessa Giolai and Angelika Psenner

The research project *Food Atlas Vienna* addresses the detachment industrialisation and globalisation have brought to food production and our urban food system where collective knowledge about our nutrition has been lost, especially in recent decades. The project seeks to provide a fundamental reflection on how the food cycle had and still has the power to shape urban areas – and vice versa: how our producing, eating and throwaway habits are indeed related to the city and its urban characteristics. Thus, this chapter offers an invitation to travel through Vienna and understand and experience food in connection with space from an urban planning perspective. The text approaches the subject on two levels: on the one hand, at a thematically general level and on the other hand, as a subjective travelogue through the Viennese food landscape (fig. 1).

Mapping concept

We share the view that,

"in Western culture, it is in fact not uncommon to feel, in the face of major changes and transformations in the surrounding world, a need to step outside of libraries in order to experience forms of knowledge that lie not in books but elsewhere" (Blumenberg, 1989, cited in: Grulois *et al.*, 2018, p. 105).

Accordingly, we conceived an interactive project: three open studios took place at different locations in the city as part of various art events of the "*studio mobil*" (a mobile city lab) initiated by Hubert Klumpner *et al.* (URL 3, n.d.). The three studios aimed to address the

Viennese residents directly, to get in touch with them and to involve them in the project (figs. 2 and 3). Each open studio was organised with a focus theme along the food cycle: production, consumption and waste/recycling.

An in-depth research phase preceded each event to provide content, facts and graphics as a basis for discussion with visitors and guests, both lay people and experts. Using targeted public events around the *studio mobil*, various approaches to topic-related data production in the Viennese context were also shown to the public. For the interactive approach, specially designed maps and visual tools like information maps, statistics visualisation, axonometric representations of spatial typologies, area comparisons and, for example, the representation of human land consumption for food were prepared in a layman-friendly way and used as further instruments for knowledge and data production. We chose cross-media mapping as the primary method for data collection.

The first open studio took place during the *Vienna Biennale 2021* where the collective mapping process of the existing food landscape was launched. The mapping was done analogue in the city lab and digitally via our website with an online mapping tool. In both scenarios, citizen science represented a key aspect of the project. In addition to the researched content, the goal was to (re)activate, collect public knowledge about food and share it with the inhabitants. Specific maps and visualisations were created based on the three focus themes. Since the beginning of the project, the maps

DOI: 10.4324/9781003352280-27

Fig. 1: Food cycle overview: Approaching the food cycle from production to consumption to disposal and recycling in the Viennese context

have constantly been growing and developing. We see the project as a baseline study with the aim of compiling the available data, facts and figures and of collecting missing data on which to build further work. As Grulois *et al.* state:

Comparing territories through mapmaking – juxtaposing and examining their differences or similarities and for establishing their side by side –

has proven useful for considering their differences or similarities and for establishing a mutual relationship between territories that allows for them to be evaluated. (Grulois *et al.*, 2018, p. 106)

Journey
It is 25 June 2021, a sunny warm day. Since 6 am, the Viktor-Adler-Markt, one of Vienna's food markets, has been filled with hustle and bustle. Market

Fig. 2: Viktor-Adler-Markt: The food map as part of the "studio mobil/think tank station" (Christoph Kleinsasser)

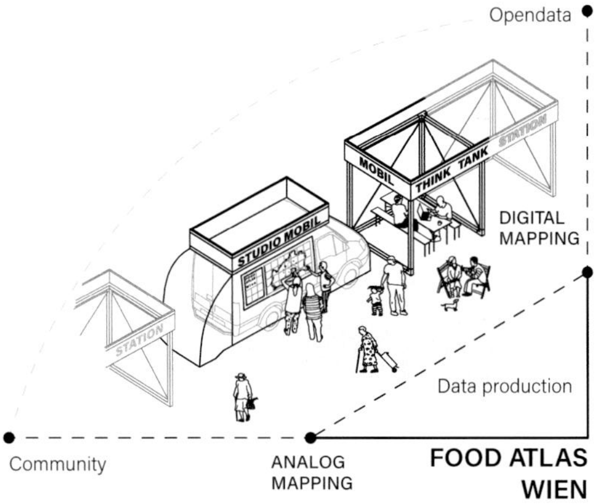

Opendata

MOBIL THINK TANK STATION

STUDIO MOBIL

STATION

DIGITAL MAPPING

Data production

Community ANALOG MAPPING

FOOD ATLAS WIEN

Fig. 3: Concept graphic Food Atlas: Process and elements of the interactive research

criers roar across the square where food has been sold and consumed every day since 1877. At the end of the square, between fruit stands and falafel sellers, space has been transformed into a city laboratory. A cluster of people starts to form in front of the lab, alternately looking at their shopping bags, and a meter-long map of Vienna and surrounding areas. Can we link the food we eat with the city we live in? How are people, place and food connected?

For over 10,000 years, food supply and food trade have been an essential part of Austria's economic, cultural and social life. Vienna was a highly productive region that not only consumed food, but also produced a considerable amount. For Vienna, as for many cities, self-supply in pre-industrial society has been an essential component and determined its size and shape (Steel, 2020). Still today, vineyards and orchards characterise the outskirts of the city. In his essay *Stadtentwicklung mit dem Gartenspaten [Urban development with the garden spade]*, Philipp Stierand argues that food supply was a local task in European history due to transportation and conservation issues. Food production was inevitably urban and included, unimaginably nowadays, animal husbandry. Today, with the reliance on cheap food from elsewhere, produced at scale,

Viennese food systems are becoming increasingly non-transparent and incomprehensible. Large, anonymous supply chains have replaced the former direct relationship between producer and consumer and the specialised food trade. As a result, supply chains have changed due to industrialisation, economic growth and production, which is now detached from the local context. In the current urban food system, food production spaces are interchangeable and replaceable. Space no longer influences the characteristics of products (Wiskerke, 2009, pp. 370–371).

Nowadays, most of Austria's food supply depends on internationally imported products (Küntzle, 2020). The country's supposedly secure food supply is romanticised, whereas Austrian agriculture, in reality, is internationally interconnected, and we are dependent on it (fig. 4). Even though the city of Vienna signed the *Milan Urban Food Policy Pact* in 2015 (Schwarzl *et al.*, 2017), it seems that food policy is considered a task of global entities. The *Common Agricultural Policy (CAP)* at the European level follows contradictory goals: on the one hand, the policy aims to support farmers, improve agricultural productivity and ensure a stable supply of affordable food (URL 1, n.d.),

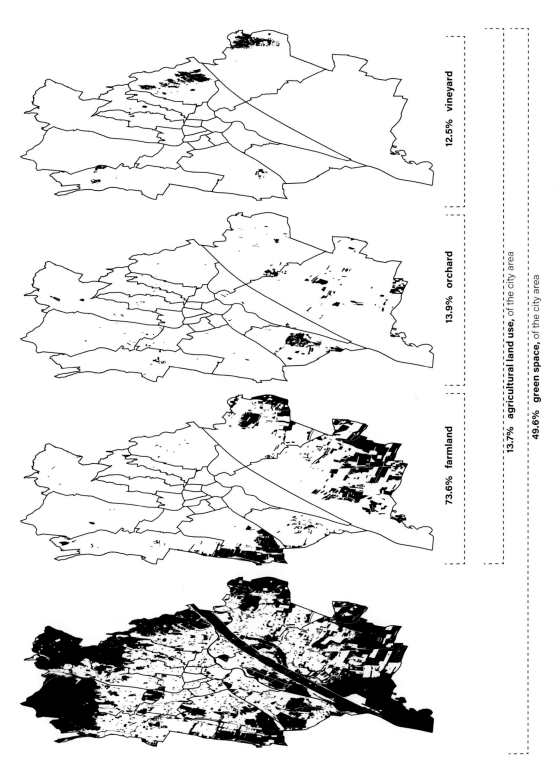

Fig. 4: Agricultural land use in Vienna: For a European metropolis, Vienna still maintains relatively large agricultural areas within the city border, with 14% arable land (City of Vienna, 2018)

Fig. 5: Knowledge sharing and mapping by citizens in an interplay of analogue and digital data (Christoph Kleinsasser)

and on the other hand, paradoxically, it has been promoting large-scale, monoculture agriculture for years. Seen in this light, the *CAP* can also be described as a cause of an aberration of capital, as it has triggered a wave of land acquisitions that give power to agribusiness and financial investors (Bartz/Stockmar, 2019).

Journey

The Viktor-Adler-Markt in Vienna reaches its most turbulent peak time. The weather is still warm, but strong winds blow clouds across the blue summer sky. But neither wind nor sun can harm our PVC map. The prepared mapping cards flutter, and the markers hang ready for use on the map. An elderly lady with slightly greying hair breaks away from the group and tells her story of former food markets that were much more central than the Viktor-Adler-Markt. She starts looking for the places and runs her finger over the map. The large map completely fulfils its role as a work surface but also as an attractor in the public space. In the early evening, the market hustle and bustle calms down and the nocturnal activities slowly awaken. The map is filled with the first stickers, sketches and snapshots from the discussions, conversations, chance encounters and collaborative mapping workshops that took place throughout the day (see fig. 5).

How can we orient ourselves in a world dominated by food, yet our modern diet being so detached from the local context? We live in a world shaped by food, but today we can hardly make a connection between space and food. It is surprising that maps can be created with all kinds of content, but there is nothing coherent and complete about food, excluding gastronomy and the mere consumption of meals. "Mapping is rooted in wayfinding. We begin by making sense of our surroundings so that we can go somewhere" (O'Rourke, 2016, p. 101).

Since 1990, the internet has been used to display maps and with the possibilities of *Google Maps* and *Google Earth* so-called web mapping has become a mass phenomenon (cf. Gartner and Schmidt, 2012). Our everyday life is no longer imaginable without maps that we can display on mobile devices. For planning institutions in Vienna, the platform *ViennaGIS*, an online city map, has been available since 1995 where address search and map display based on urban municipal data is possible (cf. Gartner and Schmidt, 2012). There is a wealth of data available to the public, but there is little information on food, its production, distribution and disposal. When analysing spatial data about food, it is equally important to consider the role of citizens as map makers. How do the Viennese themselves perceive their city related to food? Our continuously growing map presents a snapshot, an imaginary image of the city by its inhabitants (fig. 6). At this point, the map reveals the level of snippets of conversations and sketches that capture everyday life in the city. It also makes visible a second layer, that of food points in the urban fabric linking city dwellers to food in the city.

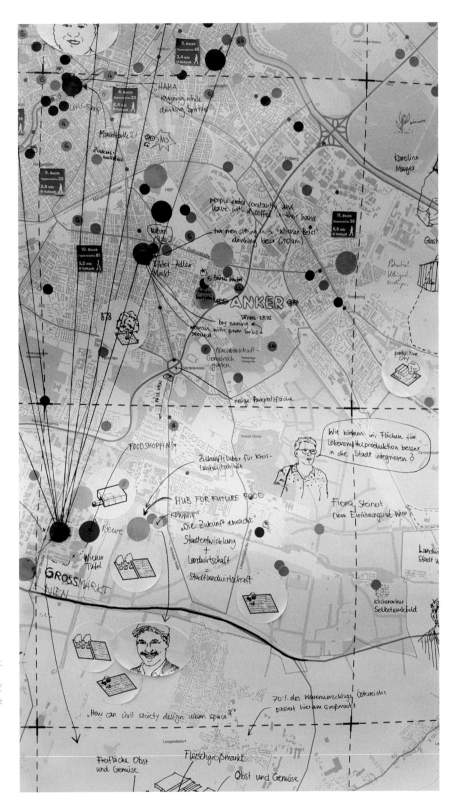

Fig. 6:
Detailed view
of the food
map: different
coloured dots
mark places of
the food cycle
in Vienna.
Sketches and
documented
comments
capture the
life of the
city

17 Permanent Food Markets
with walking radius 5min, 10min

Wholesale market

(source: City of Vienna)

Green spaces secured by dedication

(source: City of Vienna)

1 km

Fig. 7: Permanent food markets in Vienna: These markets are closely linked to the
wholesale market in the south of the city

Journey

*On his way north-east towards the Donaukanal
[Danube Canal], the Vienna River loops lazily back
and forth until it vanishes under layers of earth and
city. A few metres further along, the meandering
street that accompanies the canal and connects
the city with the western hinterland is the Naschmarkt. In the 19th century, this was a vibrant place
for supplying Vienna with food, since all fruit and
vegetables imported on wagons had to be sold at
this market (URL 2, n.d.). Where the city lab is set
up today, 31 July 2021, fresh produce used to be
delivered and sold in wholesale quantities. But now,
with the wholesale market being relocated to the
outskirts of the city, the market has shrunk by more
than half (City of Vienna MA59, 2021). The Food*

*Atlas Vienna map faces an endless, heated concrete
surface where flea market vendors set up their stalls
and prepare for the tourists eager to buy. Shoppers
emerge from the impenetrable density of market
stalls and move lethargically across the square.
Further back is the actual market, formerly known
for its sweets and fish. Small groups keep forming in
front of the city map, interested in the multitude of
marked points and connecting lines to a point south,
where the "belly of the city" is now located (fig. 7).*

*This vital organ of Vienna's urban body today provides
supermarkets, gastronomy and the food markets.
More than 70% of the fruit and vegetables sold come
from foreign trade (cf. Schwarzl et al., 2017). The
example of the Naschmarkt clearly shows the shift in*

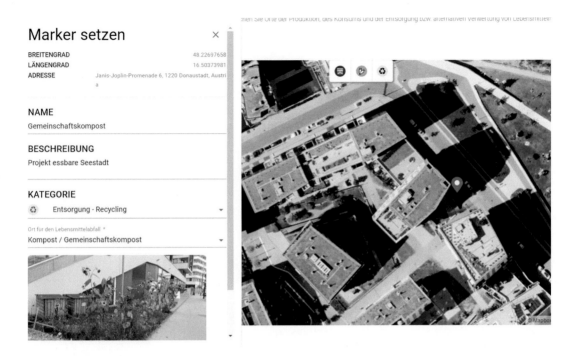

Fig. 8: Screenshot from the online food map on the Food Atlas website: Example of how to participate in mapping online in parallel to the analogue process. Both processes overlap and benefit from each other

scale in the modern food system: The small-structured, specialised retail trade tied to local conditions – once characteristic of Vienna – has completely disappeared over the years. At the beginning of the 19th century, four farmers fed one additional person; today, over a hundred people are being feed by one farmer (cf. Stierand, 2012). A parallel phenomenon is the decreasing financial outlay we have to make for our diet (cf. Stierand, 2012). The remarkably high density of supermarkets in Vienna shows the effects of a gigantic oligopoly of three large market-dominating companies. The market's value as a daily local supplier has almost disappeared. Do we want three profit-oriented corporations to determine our future? An unpleasant feeling spreads when asking: Who is responsible for our food?

As the number of points and comments mapped by residents grows, our map becomes a living sign of civic expression. We distinguish between the mapping process itself as a tool for visualising subjective perceptions and our physical map as the result of accumulated knowledge and as a medium of communication to the outside world. During the process-integrated data collection, a web-based mapping tool was developed in parallel to the analogue events. This digital mapping tool served on the one hand for precise documentation and on the other hand, offered the possibility of accessing citizens' knowledge online. In this sense, continuous manual synchronisation of the analogue data took place to obtain evaluable data sets for further processing. After the workshops, all analogue mapping points were inserted into the digital tool (fig. 8). Relating the data collected in the project back to official data and planning bases of the city of Vienna will therefore allow interesting conclusions to be drawn about the connection between food, the city and its inhabitants (fig. 9).

Journey
Arriving at a point where the analogue map can speak for itself, can tell stories and impressions

- ● Producing
- ○ Processing

(source: Food Atlas food mapping workshop)

- ▨ Agricultural use
- ▨ Green spaces secured by dedication

(source: City of Vienna)

1 km

Fig. 9: Exemplary workshop result: Map with publicly available data concerning land use overlaid with collected points of a workshop day

of food, space and people, we slowly begin to grasp the complexity of food related to space and yearn for the reality of the potentials that already/still exist. Collaborative map-making allows cross-cutting perspectives from competing actors and stakeholders at multiple social levels. The challenges and tasks involved concern both the individual city dweller and the higher-level administration and urban policy. Having toured Vienna over the past months, interacting with people, linking food and urban space, exploring food flows and tracing boundaries has given us a tool for gaining knowledge that goes beyond a general consideration of food and the city. This work must be continued, so to provide an elaborated instrument; as for the moment, the spatial

implications of food are far from being sufficiently understood and researched. We thoroughly believe that mapping and visualising food locations in a collective process is the first and fundamental step towards addressing local and global challenges in the food system.

References

Bartz, D., Stockmar, E., CC BY 4.0, H., 2019. *Agrar-Atlas: Daten und Fakten zur EU-Landwirtschaft*. 2nd ed. Available from https://www.global2000.at/sites/global/files/Agrar-Atlas-2019.pdf [Accessed 28 Aug 2022]
City of Vienna, CC BY 4.0, 2018. *Katalog Realnutzungskartierung*. Available from www.data.gv.at/katalog/dataset/stadt-wien_realnutzungskartierungab200708wien [Accessed 30 Sep 2021].

Gartner, G., and Schmidt, M., 2012. Moderne Kartographie – Technologische Entwicklungen und Implikationen. *Vermessung Und Geoinformation 1/2012*, 53–60.

Grulois, G., Tosi, M.C., and Crosas, C., 2018. *Designing territorial metabolism: Metropolitan studio on Brussels, Barcelona, and Veneto*. Berlin: Jovis.

Küntzle, T., 2020. Die Illusion von der Selbstversorgung. *Addendum*. Available from www.addendum.org/coronavirus/selbstversorgung-oesterreich/ [Accessed 24 Aug 2021].

O'Rourke, K., 2016. *Walking and mapping: Artists as cartographers* [(Leonardo), Reprint]. Cambridge: The MIT Press.

Schwarzl, B., Weiß, M., and Umweltbundesamt, 2017. *SUM-FOOD Regionale Lebensmittelpfade am Beispiel der Stadt Wien für die Produktgruppe Gemüse*. Vienna: Umweltbundesamt GmbH. Available from https://www.umweltbundesamt.at/fileadmin/site/publikationen/rep0621.pdf [Accessed 28 Aug 2022].

Steel, C., 2020. *Sitopia – How food can save the world*. London: Penguin Random House.

Stierand, P., 2012. Stadtentwicklung mit dem Gartenspaten – Umrisse einer Stadternährungsplanung. *CC3.0* [online]. Available from https://speiseraeume.de/stadternaehrungsplanung/ [Accessed 15 Jan 2022].

URL 1: European Commission, n.d. CAP at a glance. *Agriculture and Rural Development*. Available from https://agriculture.ec.europa.eu/common-agricultural-policy/cap-overview/cap-glance_en [Accessed 25 Aug 2021].

URL 2: City of Vienna 2, n.d. *Naschmarkt*. Naschmarkt Wien Geschichtewiki. Available from www.geschichtewiki.wien.gv.at/Naschmarkt [Accessed 28 Aug 2022].

URL 3: Klumpner, H., and Walczak, M., *Urban think tank next*. Available from https://uttnext.com/?gclid=Cj0KCQiA6NOPBhCPARIsAHAy2zDAePRGMgNTiK-a6uUUPsnL-4Ne7KsTGmK8fkvFCEHdj2dtMXXk-D5caAlvREALw_wcB

Wiskerke, J.S.C., 2009. On places lost and places regained. Reflections on the alternative food geography and sustainable regional development. *International Planning Studies*, 14 (4), 369–387.

Mapping Malus in Massachusetts: Creating a system for apple foraging

Raphaella Mascia and Daina Cheyenne Harvey

In fall of 2020, students from an environmental studies capstone course set out to map urban apple orchards in Worcester, Massachusetts (MA). The mapping was part of a multi-year project to find "lost" orchards. While we were interested in pippins[1], we expected to mainly find Malus domestica (domesticated or planted/cultivated apple trees). Worcester, unlike many industrialised cities in the United States, experienced rapid residential development and suburbanisation beginning in the 1980s. The expansion of the city often took place in semi-urban areas, where old farmlands and orchards dating back to the late nineteenth and early twentieth centuries had existed. Worcester's airport, for instance, sits atop what was once the oldest orchard in the city. Many of the apple orchards in Worcester and surrounding towns were destroyed during this period. These developments are now marked by subdivisions with names like "Apple Farms" or neighbourhoods consisting of streets dedicated to what came before, for example, "Orchard Lane" or "Apple Tree Road."

Additionally, we set out to map a number of urban orchards that were maintained by various non-profit organisations over the last decade. Most of these orchards were planted by the community partner we worked with, the Worcester Tree Initiative. Some of these orchards were continuously managed by other nonprofits, while others had been abandoned. In most instances, the state of the orchard and the variety of apples planted were unknown. The goal of the course was to create a database for foragers interested in these apples and in collecting grafts of wild and abandoned (but cultivated) apple trees so that those trees could be propagated in the future[2].

Apples were of specific interest to us as they have a particular mnemonic resonance to most New Englanders, being a key component of the mythos of New England's foodways. Most New Englanders from first grade on can proudly tell the story of Johnny Appleseed and show you on a map where his hometown of Leominster, MA, is located. Second, the industrialisation of our food system has dramatically reduced the variety of foodways, and perhaps nowhere else is this as apparent than with apples. A hundred years ago, there were thousands of varieties of apples, while today only a handful dominate the market in the US and elsewhere. Finally, climate change has prompted concern regarding the diversity of apples. Most of the apples we have today have been selected for colour, i.e. redness, durability rather than taste, and certainly not sustainability or resistance to climate change. In *Walden Warming*, Richard Primack (2014) notes that wild apples now flower two to four weeks earlier than they did when Henry David Thoreau wrote about them in the 1850s.

Concerns about climate change and apple diversity have prompted two burgeoning movements. The first takes place in the lab where scientists are engineering climate resistant apples. The second takes place in fields and farms, especially where development has occurred and trees have been "lost," and where foragers are looking for apples that have successfully grown for years without human intervention.

DOI: 10.4324/9781003352280-28

Fig. 1: Apple tree location using Map Plus

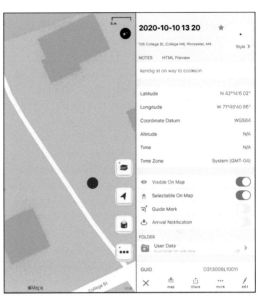

Fig. 2: Detailed information from tree location using Map Plus

Through our work, we seek to expand upon the latter of these two movements. We employed a land use mapping system available through the Bureau of Geographic Information in Massachusetts (MassGIS), which allows us to locate apple orchards existing in 1985 – the peak of development in Worcester County. Using the same system, we created maps to identify locations today (2020) where orchards have been dramatically reduced or altogether disappeared as a result of development. We then physically visited those spaces to visually inspect the landscape for wild or abandoned trees, and if found, mapped them using *Map Plus* – a smartphone app – to create a database of wild and abandoned apple trees. Included in the database are other "found" trees, located in both public and private spaces. In this chapter, we focus on both the ethics and process of mapping wild and abandoned apple trees in Worcester County, MA, particularly as it regards foraging.

Foraging complications

Much of foraging is viewed as *present work*. It immediately helps to satisfy food insecurity (Phillips *et al.*, 2014) and to provide access to culturally appropriate foods (Tsing, 2015), build social capital (Colinas *et al.*, 2019), obtain medicine (McLain *et al.*, 2014; Poe *et al.*, 2013) and generate income (Tsing, 2015), but there are other temporal dimensions to foraging. It has also become an important way to manage urban ecosystems for future generations (Lin *et al.*, 2015) and an in-situ experiment for climate resilient foodstuffs. Grasses, fungi, nuts, herbs and fruits that have been able to survive and flourish without human intervention (in many cases in spite of it), could make for good candidates for future cultivation in the Anthropocene. In other words, foraging should also be seen as *future work*.

While we are beginning to see green planning initiatives include urban agriculture and food production (McLain *et al.*, 2014; Viljoen and Bohn, 2014), foraging is often perceived as a pejorative activity. First and foremost, contemporary foraging maintains its historical association with gleaning, poverty and food insecurity, and as such is seen as tantamount to dumpster diving or soliciting for handouts. Despite it being a popular activity among elite chefs and other foodies (i.e. Dan Barber at *Stone Barns*, Chris Erasmus at *Foliage*, René Redzepi at *Noma* or Doug McMaster at *Silo*, to name just a few), it is usually a discouraged activity, especially in urban areas (McLain *et al.*, 2014). It can also be a dangerous activity. Foragers in urban areas, especially cities that have a history of industrialisation like Worcester, run the risk of making themselves ill by consuming foods contaminated with heavy chemicals. Surface runoff from parking lots and streets after a rainstorm can also leach chemicals into fields and meadows. Finally, foraging can act as a contested claims-making activity. In Anna Tsing's (2015) work on mushroom foraging in California, she shows how immigrants, back-to-the-landers and middle-men selling to high-end businesses and restaurants all stake claims on the matsutake mushroom and thus the land where it grows. These claims likewise become even more contentious when loggers, developers and others make claims on the commons where foraging might occur. As Melissa Poe *et al.* (2013) note, foraging can be an unsettling activity as it complicates long held social and ecological demarcations. It is this last issue with urban foraging, coupled with the desire to find "lost" apple trees, that led us to develop a quasi-open-access mapping tool.

Mapping Malus

With the projected increase of urban populations globally, numerous research approaches utilise technological advancements to address urban environmental issues such as attaining sustainable urban food systems (Silva de Amorim *et al.*, 2019). In these efforts to effectively assess urban environmental concerns, mobile apps have quickly become a significant part of the conversation (Desouza and Bhagwatwar, 2012; Gebresselassie and Sanchez, 2018). As urban environmental issues are wide-ranging and variable, so too are the apps created to evaluate and assess them; moreover, these apps often serve manifold purposes and are user malleable

in their applications (Desouza and Bhagwatwar, 2012). For instance, geographic information apps (GIS) mobile apps such as *ArcGIS*'s suite of apps have been utilised to cover issues ranging from urban ecology research to understanding rural-urban food environments (Carolan, 2020).

Amongst the diversity of mapping-related apps to choose from, we selected a mapping mobile app that enabled us to record, locate and describe "lost" apple trees while also allowing us to share this information easily. In our search for mobile mapping apps, we considered both general GIS mapping apps in addition to more specialised apps geared toward fields such as botany or foraging. We first reviewed various types of mobile apps that we considered in our efforts to map urban orchards. Then we delved into our reasoning behind selecting the app *Map Plus* in our project.

Upon examining the range of mobile apps applied within the context of urban environmental issues or urban food systems, we roughly find two distinct categories: GIS-only mobile apps and identification apps with mapping capabilities. GIS-only mobile apps feature general location and description capabilities for broad subject matters while identification mobile apps specifically identify and locate plants and other living things and largely feature crowdsourced information (Baumbach *et al.*, 2019).

This latter field of mobile apps, linked to current trends in community-based monitoring techniques and citizen science projects involving plant identification and foraging (Baumbach *et al.*, 2019; Conrad and Daoust, 2007), differs from the GIS-only mapping mobile apps in that they collect specific, crowdsourced data that largely aims at identifying plants or other species (Arrington, 2017). One of the most popular and reputable nature apps to appear in recent years is *iNaturalist*. *iNaturalist* aims to foster a community who contributes to scientific research, crowdsourced data and citizen science projects (Aristeidou *et al.*, 2021; iNaturalist, n.d.). The

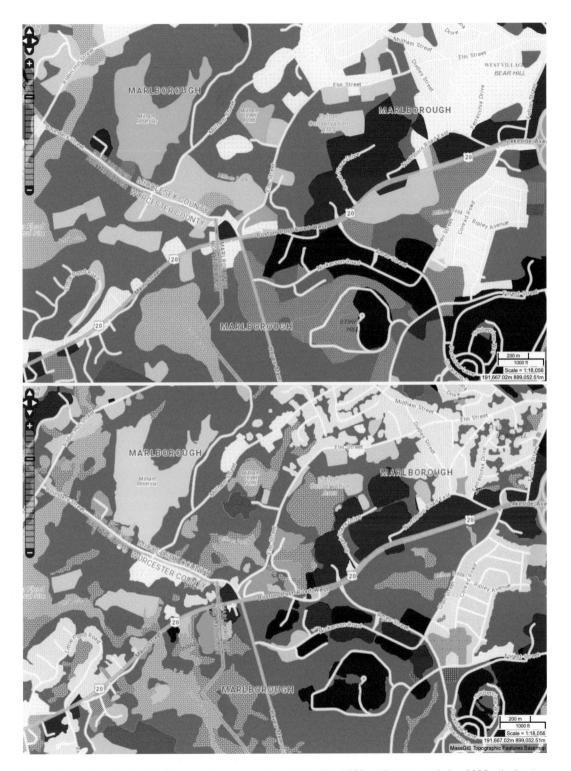

Fig. 3: Orchards in Marlborough, Massachusetts, in 1985 (above) and in 2005 (below) using Oliver. Orchards are symbolised by orange fractals with a red nucleus. In the map from 2005, there are two small orchards remaining in the area—towards the bottom along Forest Street.

app is used to identify and record locations or sightings of plants, animals, insects and fungi around the world (Aristeidou *et al.*, 2021; Arrington *et al.*, 2017). *Plant Snap* is another app dedicated to identification, akin to *iNaturalist*, which seeks, using snapchat, to map every plant species on earth by 2022 (Plantsnap, n.d.). Additionally, there is an entire subset of identification apps specifically devoted to foraging or identifying edible plants. Two notable apps in this field are *Wild Edibles Forage* and *Falling Fruit*. Of the two, *Falling Fruit* has been involved in previous research regarding urban foraging trends (Arrington *et al.*, 2017).

While crowdsourcing has major advantages, such as establishing large databases in a short period of time and allowing for the mapping of large areas, it often results in contradictory identifications. Likewise, many users do not provide exact longitudinal and latitudinal coordinates, perhaps for fear of over-harvesting or to limit other negative ecosystems effects from foraging in particular areas (Arrington *et al.*, 2017). Anna Davies (2019) has also noted data sharing issues in other app-based food sharing initiatives.

Some sites only focus on specific kingdoms or species, use automated identifiers based on user-taken photographs, are prone to misidentification, are not user-friendly, or function at a very basic level and require subscriptions to actually map or share maps.

Specifically, for our purposes, *Wild Edibles Forage* solely allows users to identify common backyard foraged plants thus acting as a mobile field guide of sorts but does not have any GIS functionality and thus was not selected (Brill, n.d.; McLain *et al.*, 2014). The set-up of *Falling Fruit* is highly akin to *iNaturalist* in that it is a crowdsourced platform, however *Falling Fruit* specifically gathers data on foraged plants, such as fruit trees (McLain *et al.*, 2014). The cost of both apps factored into rejecting these apps as options for the project. Moreover, the *Falling Fruit* app was more widely accessible than we intended for this data collection where we were

looking to limit access to folks who were interested in both foraging and future use of the foraged materials (for example grafts).

In regard to common GIS mapping software, a primary concern in selecting a mapping system is the capability to be accessible across various mobile operating systems. Using proprietary software systems presents issues for shareability. This issue can be mitigated, especially if point data or layer data can be sent via email. For example, different operating systems could use a centralised web application that has numerous versions across operating systems, such as *QGIS*, as a space to combine data from the different mobile apps, but this can create numerous issues for users. Closed-source GIS mobile apps such as the ESRI *ArcGIS* products which are commonly used in field mapping and surveying (Lerner, 2017) are likewise more costly than the identification apps mentioned earlier. While they are highly versatile, users must acquire a license to use *ArcGIS* mobile and web applications which impedes widespread availability and usage of the app (Lerner, 2017).

In our endeavors to establish an accessible project to share locations of "lost" apples trees and "lost" orchards, we eliminated the *ArcGIS* mobile apps for their more limited accessibility. However, *ArcGIS* may still be valuable in that users can capture geographic data and then relay that data, for example geographic coordinate points of apple trees, via a free platform that may be more accessible. Free GIS mobile applications include *Input* and *Map Plus* (Input, n.d.; Map Plus, n.d.) which offer the opportunity to easily transfer data including points and layers from their mobile apps to notable open-source GIS web apps like *QGIS* for free (Input, n.d.; Map Plus, n.d.). Both *Input* and *Map Plus* provide the necessary tools to map and locate apple trees and orchards at no cost.

Ultimately, the app *Map Plus* was chosen for this project for a few reasons. First, as mentioned earlier, many apps do not allow users to provide the exact location of the tree, but with *Map Plus* pins could be placed to locate distinct

Fig. 4: Image of Marlborough, Massachusetts, using Oliver's Orthoimagery

apple trees. Likewise, the coordinates for each tree could be easily extracted and shared via email, iCloud and, perhaps more impressively, QR codes. Finally, the app was free to use. While apps such as *iNaturalist* and *Falling Fruit* provide a wider audience with which to share information about the project, these apps did not meet all of the previous criteria. Moreover, the level of sharing data, such as tree coordinates, should be considered thoroughly, and some sense of foraging ethics should be applied to prevent exploitation. In figures 1 and 2, you can see that, in addition to mapping *Malus*, we can also provide longitudinal and latitudinal coordinates and make notes (the type of apple, if identified) and/or take images of the tree.

On the front end of the mapping process, we use *Oliver* which is an open-access mapping tool offered by the Bureau of Geographic Information in Massachusetts (MassGIS). *Oliver* allows the user to create maps using dozens of data layers. For the purposes of this project, we were interested in locating orchards in 1985, which is the earliest date for which orchards were digitally mapped. This proved, however, to be a useful period due to the development of mixed-use land in urban areas and agricultural areas on the urban periphery. We thus selected "Land Use 1985" and located orchards through the legend (see fig. 3).

The orchards are the orange fractal images (as opposed to solid orange). We then selected "Land Use 2005," which was the most recent year for which data was included (see fig. 3). By comparing the two images, it is noticeable that the orchards (orange fractals) have been primarily replaced by industrial (red areas) and commercial (purple areas) land use areas. This development has occurred off highway U.S.-20, which goes from Boston to Oregon – the longest road in the US at 3,365 miles. It is located in the city of Marlborough, MA, which in 2020 had a population of close to 42,000. Marlborough was an industrialised town that experienced a large technology boom after the turnpike was built.

Next, we used another data layer, "2015 WorldView Orthoimagery," which provides aerial photographs from 2015. Here, we can see if there are trees left from the development that occurred between 1985 and 2005 (see fig. 4). While we cannot usually tell if the trees are apple trees, if there are trees, we make a site visit to record existing apple trees.

What is also useful about *Oliver* is that, if queried, it supplies parcel data, including address, size and ownership. In this particular case, we found that the main parcel of interest, where we see the biggest change from orchard to developed land, is owned by the Shipley Company LLC, and a secondary address lists Dow Chemical Tax Department and provides an address in Michigan. From experience, there is a good chance that some apple trees will have been left during the removal of the orchards. In this case, there was one remaining apple tree (fig. 5). Apples were collected – here quite easy because of the number of drops – and saved for identification.

Analysing eighty-four trees

Over the course of the semester, we mapped approximately eighty-four apple trees in the Worcester metro-area. Most of these were cultivars, planted by nonprofits in community gardens, parks or publicly accessible greenspaces. Some were cultivars that were abandoned due to the rapid development of the area over the last forty years. A few of the trees we found were most likely pippins or wild trees but would need to be analysed by genomic sequencing to confirm their heritage. This mapping produced twenty-four unique sites that were shared with the Worcester Tree Initiative.

The system that we developed allowed us to tag and provide notes regarding the social and environmental contexts in which the trees could be found. For instance, in one case, a student

noted that one site was adjacent to and possibly on the property of a public school and as such permission should be obtained before foraging. In another case, we noted that the trees were in an enclosed fence and were maintained by a nonprofit which preferred local residents (defined by people living on that particular street) have first access to the fruit. As such, and with permission, we included the contact information for the nonprofit. Because the motivations of foragers widely differ (Arrington *et al.*, 2017) and most mapping platforms are not sufficiently disseminated or engaged with to be user-friendly (Davies, 2019), we felt that our system served the purpose of allowing interested nonprofits and local foragers and members of the pomological community, with similar goals of both identifying and cultivating apples for increasing diversity and sustainability, the opportunity to share information. In this sense, we both limit the possibility of over-harvesting and of other sustainability issues sometimes associated with urban foraging. Future iterations of the course will work with the chemistry and biology departments at the college to analyse soil samples from the mapped trees in order to include potential toxins in our database.

As our mapping process involved looking for wild and abandoned trees and thus used maps from 1985 and 2005 to inspect areas where trees were "missing," we expected to still find a few trees. We, however, surprised that recent urban and semi-urban development had completely removed entire, often large, orchards. While we found a few areas where trees had been saved, the majority of the sites we visited were void of any remnant of the original orchard. This suggests a need to incorporate foraging sites into future developed areas.

Our mapping also revealed a dearth of wild trees. Several trees that we originally thought were pippins were in fact well known varietals such as *Baldwin* or *Roxbury Russet*. Because the trees were not cared for and it was late in the season, many of the fruits were misshapen

Fig. 5: Apple tree in Marlborough, Massachusetts, after industrial development
(Finch Harvey)

and diseased, making them more difficult to identify. The lack of wild trees, while not as surprising as the lack of cultivated trees, shows the need to rewild urban areas and for further mapping of wild *Malus* trees.

Both the creation of the database as well as the activity of identifying and mapping apple trees provided students (as foragers) with an understanding of the "future" work of foraging as a type of meaning-making in the food system (Nyman, 2019). Here, foraging is future work that aids in the identification of members of the *Malus* species that might be prime candidates for grafting, and thus reproduction, in a changing climate. Students, a portion of the population that typically does not engage in foraging, were excited to find wild apple trees as possible solutions to pests and blight that are currently wrecking New England's orchards. They understood that we were engaged in an

attempt to find food in places where others were not looking.

Wild apple and seedling salons are beginning to pop up in various places. In October 2021, the *Wild and Seedling Show* and *Taste Trials* at Kestle Barton in the UK featured close to fifty wild apples (@someinterestingapples). In the US, in 2020 and 2021, as part of *Franklin County Cider Days*, Matt Kaminsky gathered and later documented hundreds of wild apples (Kaminsky, 2020). These kinds of efforts from foragers to establish foraged apples as potential cultivars provide both a present and future orientation to foraging.

While a number of the trees we mapped showed various signs of having already been foraged (few drops under trees or few apples remaining on the trees for the varietal and time of the season), most of the trees were full of apples. This suggests a hesitancy to forage from trees and thus to engage with both present and missing trees. For the most part. we were allowed to freely forage and walk around the city's greenspaces, but on a couple of occasions, out of curiosity, passersby would ask what we were doing. In some cases, they were surprised the apples were available to take. Some would ask if they tasted like apples – apparently not knowing that non-market apples can taste dramatically different or thinking that urban apples must not taste good. In cases where trees were gone, residents were not aware that they were living in what used to be an apple orchard. Our work thus suggests a need for not only mapping, but signage that encourages urban foraging.

Foraging apples and the future

Worcester and its surrounding environs have seen a drastic decline in their orchards over the last forty years. While most of this is due to development, a number of orchardists have described how increasing spring temperatures are encouraging blight and pests that are usually only seen much farther south. Entire orchards have been decimated. The community partner for our course, the Worcester Tree Initiative, which had recently become part of a larger nonprofit, Tower Hill Botanic Garden, was forced to remove all 250 of its apple trees due to fire blight just a few years ago, a condition that was incredibly uncommon in New England a few decades ago. Foraging for wild apples allows us to map trees, create databases and take scion wood for grafting trees that might be better suited to a warming climate.

In this chapter, we looked to establish a new mapping system for *Malus*. With considerations regarding making it open access for nonprofits, other foragers and orchardists, we chose a system that was open source and easy to use, could be shareable with anyone and yet still used GIS and could work on different mobile platforms. We coupled this with a state-sourced GIS mapping tool that makes it easy to look for "lost" apple trees. In this way, almost anyone

can look for trees to forage from and write up notes regarding the condition of the tree, the type of apple, etc. for fellow foragers. While more complex than other freeware or low-cost apps, our mapping process limits claims making to others who will use the fruit, but also learn and teach from it. In doing so, ultimately, we hope to make foraging for *Malus* an important part of the conversation regarding food system sustainability.

Notes

1 Foragers and orchardists denote "pippins" as apple trees planted as seed, usually by animals, versus "cultivars" that are planted by humans, usually by grafting scion wood to rootstocks (see Kaminsky, 2016).
2 The students in the course were also charged with assisting in the replanting of 250 apple trees at Tower Hill Botanic Garden in Boylston, MA (US), and in designing an orchard for the college that could be used to graft scions from pippins to observe how different trees do in the changing climate.

References

Aristeidou, M., Herodotou, C., Ballard, H.L., Young, A.N., Miller, A.E., Higgins, L., and Johnson, R.F., 2021. Exploring the participation of young citizen scientists in scientific research: The case of iNaturalist. *PLoS One*, 16 (1), 1–13.
Arrington, A.B., Diemont, S.A.W., Phillips, C.T., and Welty, Z., 2017. Demographic and landscape-level urban foraging trends in the USA derived from web and mobile app usage. *Journal of Urban Ecology*, 3 (1), 1–9.
Baumbach, D.S., Anger, E.C., Collado, N.A., and Dunbar, S.G., 2019. Identifying sea turtle home ranges utilizing citizen-science data from novel web-based and smartphone GIS applications. *Chelonian Conservation and Biology*, 18 (2), 133–144.
Brill, S., n.d. *Wild edibles apps: Wildman Steve Brill*. Wild Edibles Apps | Wildman Steve Brill. Available from bwww.wildmanstevebrill.com/mobile-app.
Carolan, M., 2020. Putting food access in its topological place: Thinking in terms of relational becomings when mapping space. *Agriculture and Human Values*, 38 (1), 243–256.
Colinas, J., Bush, P., and Manaugh, K., 2019. The socio-environmental impacts of public urban fruit trees: A Montreal case-study. *Urban Forestry and Urban Greening*, 45.
Conrad, C. T., and Daoust, T., 2007. Community-based monitoring frameworks: Increasing the effectiveness of environmental stewardship. *Environmental Management*, 41 (3), 358–366.
Davies, A.R., 2019. *Urban food sharing: Rules, tools, and networks*. Bristol: Policy Press.

Desouza, K.C., and Bhagwatwar, A., 2012. Citizen apps to solve complex urban problems. *Journal of Urban Technology*, 19 (3), 107–136.

Gebresselassie, M., and Sanchez, T.W., 2018. Smart' tools for socially sustainable transport: A review of mobility apps. *Urban Science*, 2 (2), 45.

iNaturalist, n.d. Available from www.inaturalist.org/.

Input, n.d. Available from https://inputapp.io/en/.

Kaminsky, M., 2016. *The wild apple forager's guide: Teachings, anecdotes and waxings on malus in America*. MA: Matt Kaminsky.

Kaminsky, M., 2020. *Proceedings from the first annual wild and seedling pomological exhibition*. Colorado: Matt Kaminsky.

Lerner, J., 2017. Sustainability planning just got more accessible with a free suite of GIS apps and datasets from Esri. *Planning*, 83 (5), 23–27.

Lin, B.B., Philpott, S.M., and Jha, S., 2015. The future of urban agriculture and biodiversity-ecosystem services: Challenges and next steps. *Basic and Applied Ecology*, 16, 189–201.

Map Plus., n.d. *Map Plus*. Available from https://duweis.com/en/mapplus.html.

McLain, R.J., Hurley, P.T., Emery, M.R., and Poe, M.R., 2014. Gathering wild food in the city: Rethinking the role of foraging in urban ecosystem planning and management. *Local Environment*, 19 (2), 220–240.

Nyman, M., 2019. Food, meaning-making and ontological uncertainty: Exploring 'urban foraging' and productive landscapes in London. *Geofourm*, 99, 170–180.

Phillips, K.M., Pehrsson, P.R., Agnew, W., Scheett, A.J., Follett, J.R., Lukaski, H.C., and Patterson, K.Y., 2014. Nutrient composition of selected traditional United States northern plains native American plant foods. *Journal of Food Composition and Analysis*, 34 (2), 136–152.

Plantsnap, n.d. Available from www.plantsnap.com/.

Primack, R., 2014. *Walden warming: Climate change comes to Thoreau's woods*. Chicago: University of Chicago Press.

Poe, M.R., McLain, R.J., Emery, M., and Hurley, P.T., 2013. Urban forest justice and the rights to wild foods, medicines, and materials in the city. *Human Ecology*, 41, 409–422.

Silva de Amorim, W., Borchardt Deggau, A., do Livramento Gonçalves, G., da Silva Neiva, S., Prasath, A.R., and Osório de Andrade Guerra, J.B.S., 2019. Urban challenges and opportunities to promote sustainable food security through smart cities and the 4th industrial revolution. *Land Use Policy*, 87.

Tsing, A.L., 2015. *The mushroom at the end of the world: On the possibility of life in capitalist ruins*. Princeton, NJ: Princeton University Press.

Viljoen, A., and Bohn, K., 2014. *Second Nature Urban Agriculture: designing productive cities*. New York: Routledge.

The historic foodscapes of Lisbon: Mapping for a sustainable future

Mariana Sanchez Salvador

Urban settlements raise specific issues regarding the intensification of consumption, particularly food, while also holding tremendous potential to address these same issues. This potential lies in the way cities concentrate resources, economic activities, knowledge and innovation. They are therefore specially equipped to tackle complex issues that interconnect society, environment and economy (FAO, 2019, p. 7), becoming living laboratories where to explore more sustainable solutions, specifically around food which can hold the biggest share of urban footprints (Baabou et al., 2017, p. 99).

Currently, urban nutrient and energy flows are organised as open systems where resources flow in and waste flows out. There is a growing argument that cities should shift towards a circular model with more local, resilient food systems. Closing cycles (circular metabolism) may carry an enhancement of urban agriculture and shorter food supply chains, while promoting greater resilience. Since food has always been intrinsic to urban spaces and social practices, re-localising urban food systems implies understanding each *historic urban foodscape*, so as to grasp its *food assets*, constraints and potential, to support successful interventions.

Mapping foodscapes and food assets

Food activities can be matched to specific spaces – fields, roads, harbours, markets or kitchens – which concentrate particularly within cities, configuring (urban) foodscapes. Lauren Baker defined them as *food assets*:

Food assets include . . . farms, processing and distribution capacity, food enterprises, markets, retailers, community gardens, urban farms, community gardens, community kitchens, student nutrition programmes, emergency food distribution and community food organisations and centres.

(Baker, 2018, p. 266)

Characterising foodscapes – a crucial step before their redesign – often requires data from multiple sources: statistics, photographs, literature and especially cartography. Besides being a valuable primary source, cartography provides a spatial setting for other data, making patterns visible (Atkins, 2005, p. 267). Maps that describe food flows (*food cartography*) can encompass different activities:

Food cartography falls into the category of special purpose mapping that first arose in the nineteenth century for the portrayal of themes such as agriculture, the transport of foodstuffs to market, the sale of food in restaurants and retail shops, and also cuisines and diets.

(Atkins, 2005, p. 267)

Mapping such *food assets* may contribute to improve foodscapes, correct problems with assets' distribution, find locations for urban agriculture, community programmes and other activities, clarify interconnections, expose the role of food in the city's infrastructure, engage planners, etc. (Baker, 2018) – thus, unveiling solutions.

But foodscapes also possess an inherent historical quality: as in a palimpsest, food spaces overlap in time. Vegetable gardens persist, food

DOI: 10.4324/9781003352280-29

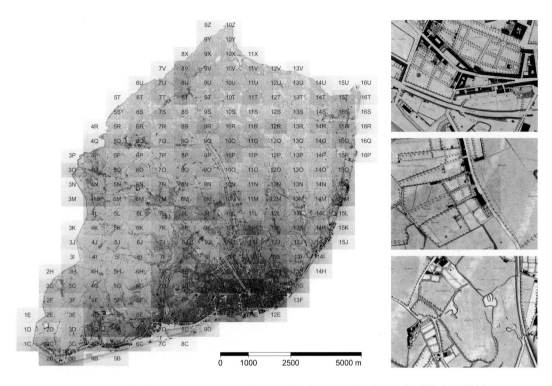

Fig. 1: *Survey of Lisbon*: Overview and details (maps 2B, 9M and 13K) by Júlio António Vieira da Silva Pinto and Alberto Sá Correia, 1904–1911 (Câmara Municipal de Lisboa, source: Lisboa Aberta)

routes endure in streets' layout, while markets display longevity. Through food, the contemporary city inextricably connects to its heritage, shaping *historic urban foodscapes*. Thus, the combined study of past and present realities is argued to provide a more comprehensive portrait of each *historic urban foodscape*, allowing the identification of food assets to be explored (or protected) for more sustainable cities.

The historic foodscapes of Lisbon

Considering this background, extensive research was conducted on the *historic foodscape* of Lisbon (Portugal). Food production spaces, distribution routes, and food retailing spaces, existing in early 20th and 21st centuries, were mapped and described, by withdrawing data from cartography, literature, newspapers, databases, statistics, historical and current photographs, etc. The city's current vectorial map

was also complemented by open-source GIS information (https://geodados-cml.hub.arcgis.com/), and by a photographic survey of existing markets and horticultural parks, conducted between 2021 and 2022.

Mapping Lisbon's foodscapes of early 20th century

For the past foodscape, the *Survey of Lisbon* (1904–1911) was the primary source used (see fig. 1). With 249 water-coloured charts (930 × 640 mm each), at the scale of 1:1000, it was the first comprehensive survey of Lisbon, after several perimeter changes in the decades before.

Food production spaces
Although the 'representation of crops' was required by contract, no legend to this *Survey* is known to date, preventing in-depth studies on its land use. Recently, however, Marat-Mendes *et al.*

265

LEGEND

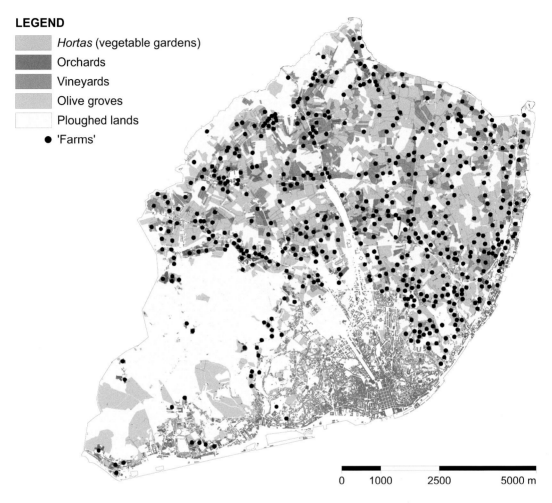

Fig. 2a: Lisbon's food production: Crops and 'farms' existing in Lisbon in the early 20th century

(2014) were able to propose one, by comparison with another contemporary map, which finally allowed the identification of its crops (see fig. 2a).

Hortas [vegetable gardens] covered 751 ha (8.6% of the municipality), mainly near houses and along streets (see figs. 2a and 2b). Some *hortas* were represented as light-yellow polygons, while others possessed trees around the edges (see fig. 1), maybe indicating orchards – a theory supported by descriptions of several authors (e.g., Caldas, 1999; Carapinha, 1995). These occupied around 253 ha (2.9%), while vineyards, light-purple

polygons (see fig. 1), amounted to 606 ha, or 6.9% (see fig. 2a).

Ploughed lands added 2499 ha (28.5% of the municipality), the largest area taken by a crop, while olive groves were found in 1991 ha (22.7%) (see fig. 2a). However, doubts arose regarding the representation of ploughed lands (beige polygons and green outline, which, in the reference map, matched both cultivated fields and empty plots) and the olive groves (similar representation, with trees along some edges) (see fig. 1). Thus, the true land use of these plots can be questioned.

Fig. 2b: Overview of Lisbon's vegetable gardens (Eduardo Portugal © Arquivo Municipal de Lisboa)

Altogether, at least 15.5% (1357 ha of 8770 ha) of the city was cultivated as *hortas* and vineyards – or 38.2%, if olive groves are added (3348 ha). If *all* ploughed lands were cultivated, up to 67.7% would have been productive (5938 ha). Since, however, this is unlikely, probably 54.7% was cultivated (4795 ha), if the results of Marat-Mendes *et al.* (2014) are combined with the ones mapped here. Therefore, a significant portion of Lisbon was devoted to food production – contrasting with the built area (530 ha, just over 6%). Plus, 529 place-names of *quintas* ('farms') were identified in the *Survey* (see fig. 2a), further attesting Lisbon's productive character.

Despite the city's exceptional fertility, Lisbon was never self-sufficient, resorting to imports from its hinterland, the rest of Portugal and overseas to feed the country's largest urban population.

Food distribution
Historically, four land routes connected Lisbon to its fertile outskirts, often described as

constant flows of fresh produce and other food products (see fig. 3a). Two followed the riverfront, towards the east (*Road of Enxobregas*) and the west (*Road of Alcântara*), while the other two converged at the city centre, from the north (*Roads of Arroios* and *Andaluz*).

Most supply, however, arrived via the river Tagus, even from nearby towns. Products were unloaded at specific docks, according to type or provenance, an organisation that prevails in place names (see fig. 3a): *Campo das Cebolas* ('Onion Field') and *Cais do Trigo* ('Wheat Wharf'), or *Cais de Santarém* and *Praia dos Algarves* (wharfs for products coming from those regions).

Food retailing
Land and river routes were closely linked with the location of the city's markets (see fig. 3a): Market of Ribeira Nova, Market of Alcântara (see fig. 3b), Praça da Figueira Market (see fig. 3c), Market of Belém, Market of São Bento,

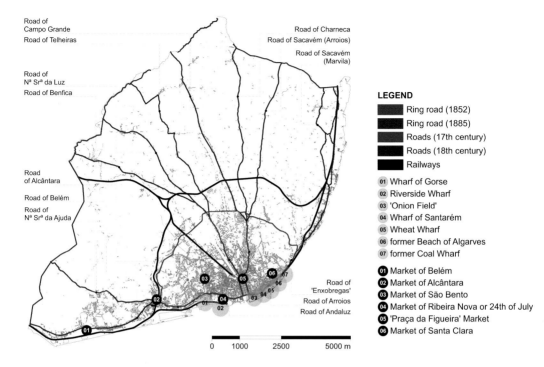

LEGEND

- Ring road (1852)
- Ring road (1885)
- Roads (17th century)
- Roads (18th century)
- Railways

01 Wharf of Gorse
02 Riverside Wharf
03 'Onion Field'
04 Wharf of Santarém
05 Wheat Wharf
06 former Beach of Algarves
07 former Coal Wharf

01 Market of Belém
02 Market of Alcântara
03 Market of São Bento
04 Market of Ribeira Nova or 24th of July
05 'Praça da Figueira' Market
06 Market of Santa Clara

Road of Campo Grande
Road of Telheiras
Road of Charneca
Road of Sacavém (Arroios)
Road of Sacavém (Marvila)
Road of Nª Srª da Luz
Road of Benfica
Road of Alcântara
Road of Belém
Road of Nª Srª da Ajuda
Road of 'Enxobregas'
Road of Arroios
Road of Andaluz

0   1000   2500   5000 m

Fig. 3a: Lisbon's food distribution (main land routes, railways and unloading docks by River Tagus) and connection to the markets existing in the early 20th century

Fig. 3b: Market of Alcântara (Eduardo Portugal © Arquivo Municipal de Lisboa)

and Market of Santa Clara. Previously, food trade mainly occurred in two open-air markets (Figueira, where the northern roads converged, and Ribeira, by the Tagus), which were replaced by modern glass and steel buildings in the 1880s. As the city developed, other markets settled along the food routes – the exceptions being São Bento and Santa Clara, which quickly shifted towards antiques trade. Lisbon's noisy and lively markets provided colourful sights, described by writers and travellers (e.g., Castilho, 1893).

There were also numerous food stores. In fact, food products were the most commonly sold items, amounting to almost half of all commercial licenses – 47.6% in 1900, 45.4% in 1915 (Alves, 2010, p. 89). In 1910, Lisbon's food stores included 1460 grocery stores, 553 vegetable and fruits stores, 324 bakeries, 58 olive oil stores and a striking 1986 wine stores (see fig. 4).

Meat and milk trade

Meat and milk trade configured specific networks. Cattle walked into the city to be inspected at the General Cattle Market (see fig. 5a, no. 1), before moving to the Municipal Slaughterhouse (see fig. 5a, no. 2) or to licensed butchers. In 1910, 260 commercial licenses included fresh/dried pork, sausages and other meat products (see fig. 5a). Meat was also sold by itinerant butchers or street sales (e.g., Christmas turkeys, see fig. 5c).

Freshly milked milk was sold by the glass at the 122 *vacarias* (see fig. 5a) or on the streets (see fig. 5b).

Fig. 3c: Praça da Figueira Market (Eduardo Portugal © Arquivo Municipal de Lisboa)

LEGEND

- Grocery stores (1910)
- Vegetable & Fruit stores (1910)
- Bread & Cereals stores (1910)
- Olive oil stores (1910)
- Wine stores (1910)

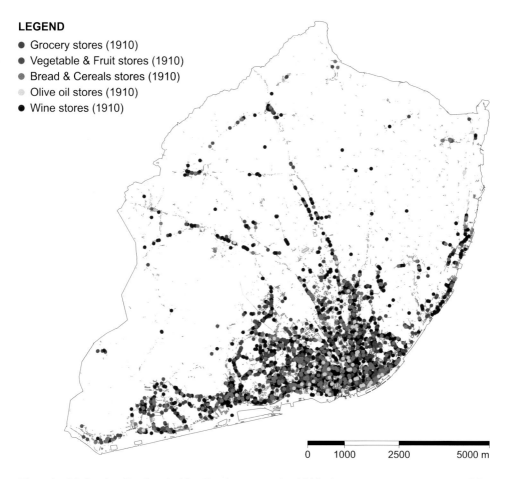

0   1000   2500   5000 m

Fig. 4: Lisbon's food retail: Food stores in 1910 (grocery stores, vegetables and fruits, bread and grains, olive oil and wine)

Fig. 5b: Milk street sale (Paulo Guedes © Arquivo Municipal de Lisboa)

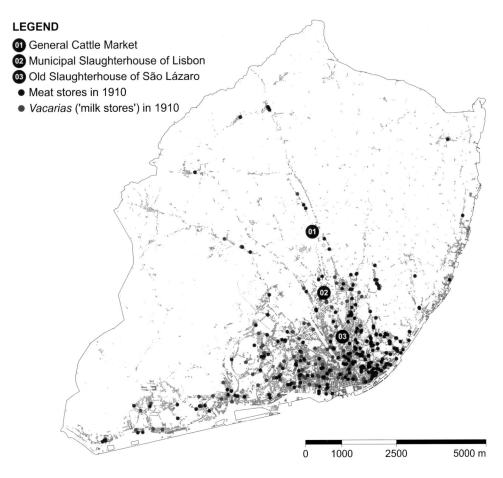

LEGEND

- **01** General Cattle Market
- **02** Municipal Slaughterhouse of Lisbon
- **03** Old Slaughterhouse of São Lázaro
- ● Meat stores in 1910
- ● *Vacarias* ('milk stores') in 1910

0   1000   2500   5000 m

Fig. 5a: Meat and milk in Lisbon in the early 20th century: General Cattle Market, Municipal Slaughterhouse, meat stores and 'vacarias'

Fig. 5c: Turkeys street sale during Christmas (Paulo Guedes © Arquivo Municipal de Lisboa)

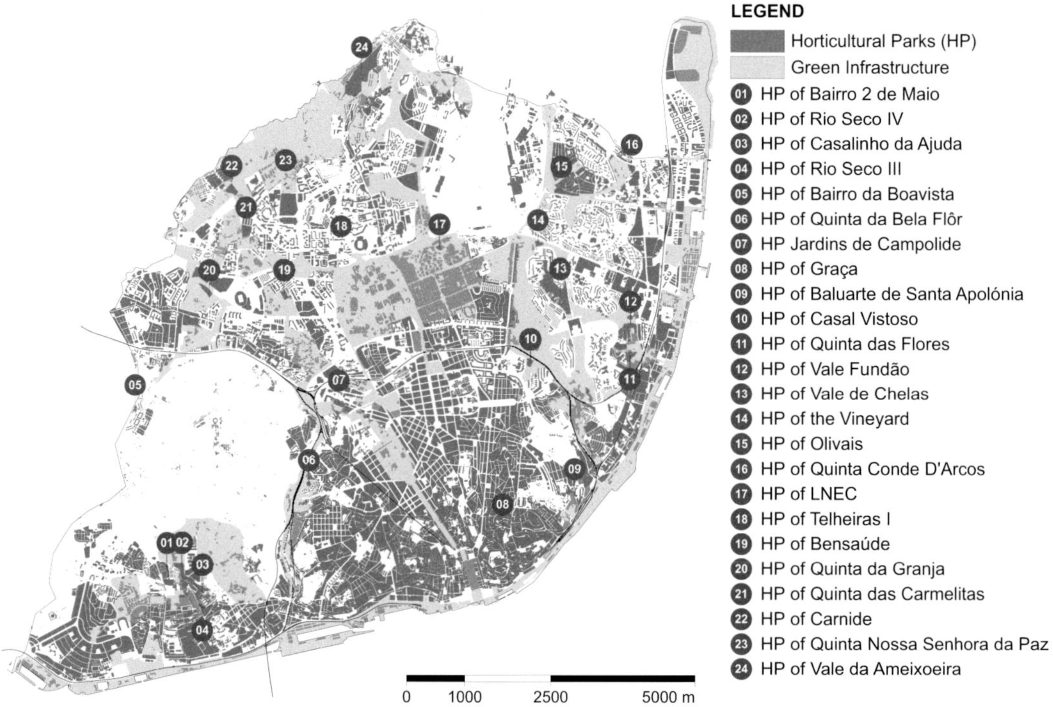
LEGEND
Horticultural Parks (HP)
Green Infrastructure
01 HP of Bairro 2 de Maio
02 HP of Rio Seco IV
03 HP of Casalinho da Ajuda
04 HP of Rio Seco III
05 HP of Bairro da Boavista
06 HP of Quinta da Bela Flôr
07 HP Jardins de Campolide
08 HP of Graça
09 HP of Baluarte de Santa Apolónia
10 HP of Casal Vistoso
11 HP of Quinta das Flores
12 HP of Vale Fundão
13 HP of Vale de Chelas
14 HP of the Vineyard
15 HP of Olivais
16 HP of Quinta Conde D'Arcos
17 HP of LNEC
18 HP of Telheiras I
19 HP of Bensaúde
20 HP of Quinta da Granja
21 HP of Quinta das Carmelitas
22 HP of Carnide
23 HP of Quinta Nossa Senhora da Paz
24 HP of Vale da Ameixoeira
0
1000
2500
5000 m

Fig. 6: Lisbon's food production: Municipal Horticultural Parks and green infrastructure in 2022

Indeed, Lisbon overflowed with street sellers, trading vegetables, fruit, cooked meals, pastries, nuts, fish, etc.

In early 20th century, Lisbon's foodscape thus consisted of multi-scale, interconnected networks of food flows and food spaces. Food was present everywhere in the city – in farms, fields, orchards, vegetable gardens, roads, wharfs, streets, squares and buildings – a true food infrastructure, interwoven with the built fabric.

Mapping Lisbon's foodscapes of the 21st century

Lisbon's foodscape coevolved with the city. With modernity and hygiene prevailing over urban planning, agriculture began to be perceived as a backwards, dirty activity, unsuited to a European capital. It survived mostly as a residual land use, close to social housing. Other activities, such as animal rearing, slaughterhouses and wholesale markets, were progressively pushed out. Today, apart from retail and consumption, food activities have virtually disappeared.

Food production spaces

Recently, however, urban agriculture was integrated into Lisbon's strategy for a multifunctional green infrastructure, the *Municipal Director Plan*. Thus, since 2011, 24 Horticultural Parks with over 800 *hortas* have been created (see fig. 6), predominantly in areas planned as 'green and productive spaces'. With peripheral locations mostly, there's no connection with former agricultural sites.

Also, private and informal *hortas* subsist, but their location and size are difficult to assess due to insufficient data.

Despite the ongoing relevance of metropolitan supply (fresh produce), Lisbon increasingly relies on global food systems. Thus, its own production is largely irrelevant, a residual land use (slightly over 1% of the municipality) and almost exclusively devoted to leisure and education.

Food distribution and retailing
Lisbon's food distribution currently includes a complex set of transportation networks and locations, such as the airport, extensive docks and cargo ships, freight trains, speedways in and around the city, and countless trucks. Food is transported enclosed, refrigerated and invisible into supermarkets, grocery stores and other retailing spaces. Tracing these food routes is difficult, since most food distributors are unwilling to share this data.

From the 1930s on, new markets were built as centres of the emerging modern neighbourhoods. Nowadays, Lisbon possesses 26 evenly distributed markets (see fig. 7), recently subjected to a Municipal Plan (2016–2020), so to address their insufficiencies for today's customers, such as opening hours. In 2000, food wholesaling, previously housed at Market of Ribeira Nova, was moved to the neighbouring municipality of Loures.

In 2010, the city possessed 1823 food stores (see fig. 8), including 492 grocery stores, 257 mini-markets, 54 supermarkets and five hypermarkets, besides numerous specialised food stores, such as bakeries (204), butchers (263), fruit stores (68), beverages (46), fish (66) and vegetables (38). Thus, even under supermarket dominance, small neighbourhood shops remain relevant in Lisbon's foodscape.

The significance of mapping the historic foodscapes of Lisbon

Food cartographies expose the complexity of networks, spatial overlapping, proximities, and gaps between food spaces, a knowledge that can be further enriched by an historical perspective, which frames the evolution of these foodscapes. But not without challenges.

Historical maps raise specific difficulties, requiring creative combinations of sources, data, and pairing with up-to-date mapping tools. Simultaneously, and despite the technological ease of contemporary maps, different challenges arise, since some information (e.g., land use, distribution routes) is no longer collected or made public. Nevertheless, comparisons between both moments can be established.

There was a striking reduction of cultivated spaces in Lisbon, with the current Horticultural Parks covering a merely residual area (11 ha). Even though a significant part of the municipality is unbuilt, its agricultural potential remains unexplored, even in previously farmed sites. Retrofitting agriculture into these areas could be further explored, holding the potential of closing metabolic loops and reconnecting people to food.

Although there are more municipal markets in the city (6 vs 26), their central role in food trading was lost, with most acquisitions now being made in supermarket chains. Plus, there are fewer food stores per inhabitant, but they are more evenly dispersed, again blurring the perception of centrality.

If we are to pursue more resilient food systems in Lisbon, these activities have to be planned as a whole, considering resources, flows, people, and their interconnections. By exploring their spatiality, maps can, thus, become a key tool to (re)design a livelier and more resilient city for the future.

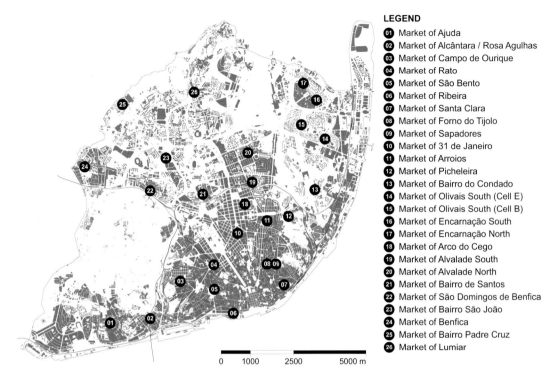

LEGEND
01 Market of Ajuda
02 Market of Alcântara / Rosa Agulhas
03 Market of Campo de Ourique
04 Market of Rato
05 Market of São Bento
06 Market of Ribeira
07 Market of Santa Clara
08 Market of Forno do Tijolo
09 Market of Sapadores
10 Market of 31 de Janeiro
11 Market of Arroios
12 Market of Picheleira
13 Market of Bairro do Condado
14 Market of Olivais South (Cell E)
15 Market of Olivais South (Cell B)
16 Market of Encarnação South
17 Market of Encarnação North
18 Market of Arco do Cego
19 Market of Alvalade South
20 Market of Alvalade North
21 Market of Bairro de Santos
22 Market of São Domingos de Benfica
23 Market of Bairro São João
24 Market of Benfica
25 Market of Bairro Padre Cruz
26 Market of Lumiar

Fig. 7: Lisbon's food retail: Municipal markets in 2022

LEGEND
● Butcher
● Charcuterie store
● Vegetable & Fruit store
● Fruit store
● Bakery
● Pastry & Confectionery store
● Drinks' store
○ Fishmonger
○ Frozen products store
● Coffee & Tea store
● Preserves, Nuts & Appetizers store
● Bonbons & Chocolate store
○ Organic products
○ Natural products
○ Other specialised food stores
● Grocery store
● Mini-market
● Supermarket
● Hypermarket
○ Convenience store
● Other non-specialised food stores

Fig. 8: Lisbon's food retail: Food stores in 2010

References

Alves, D., 2010. *A república atrás do balcão: os lojistas de Lisboa na fase final da monarquia (1870–1910)*. Contemporary Economical and Social History (PhD). Lisbon: FCSH-UNL. Available from https://run.unl.pt/handle/10362/4658

Atkins, P.J., 2005. Mapping foodscapes. *Food & History*, 3 (1), 267–280 [online]. Available from www.academia.edu/3165048/Mapping_Foodscapes

Baabou, W., Grunewald, N., Ouellet-Plamondon, C., Gressot, M., and Galli, A., 2017. The Ecological Footprint of Mediterranean cities: Awareness creation and policy implications. *Environmental Science & Policy*, 69, 94–104. Available from www.sciencedirect.com/science/article/pii/S1462901116303987

Baker, L., 2018. Food asset mapping in Toronto and Greater Golden Horseshoe region. *In*: Y. Cabannes and C. Marocchino, eds. *Integrating food into urban planning*. London: UCL Press, 264–275. Available from http://discovery.ucl.ac.uk/10061454/1/Integrating-Food-into-Urban-Planning.pdf

Caldas, J.V., 1999. *A Casa Rural dos Arredores de Lisboa no Século XVIII*. Oporto: FAUP.

Carapinha, A., 1995. *Da Essência do Jardim Português*. Landscape Architecture (PhD). Évora: Universidade de Évora. Available from https://dspace.uevora.pt/rdpc/handle/10174/11178

Castilho, J., 1893. *A Ribeira de Lisboa*. Lisboa: Imprensa Nacional.

FAO, 2019. *FAO framework for the Urban Food Agenda* [online]. Available from www.fao.org/3/CA3151EN/ca3151en.pdf

Marat-Mendes, T., Bento D'Almeida, P., Mourão, J., Niza, S., and Ferreira, D., 2014. Mapping Lisbon agriculture (1898–1911). *EUAH Conference* [online]. Available from https://memoproject.files.wordpress.com/2014/12/mapping-lisbon-agriculture_23_07_2014.pdf

A food security geonarrative: Mapping in/formal foodscapes in Bangalore, India

Jessica Ann Diehl

Community food security has complex environmental, economic, and social dimensions that require both formal and informal spaces to be acknowledged. A holistic understanding is particularly relevant in places that face rapid urbanisation, population growth, rising prices, and increased food transport distances. This chapter interrogates how such complex food environments can be assessed. It goes beyond conceptualising the food environment as a "food desert" discourse that focuses on gaps in access, providing a partial story. Criticisms of food desert maps include overlooking the presence of community assets and utilising decontextualised and overdetermined indicators, such as proximity to supermarkets and transportation access (De Master and Daniels, 2019). This deficit-orientation illuminates various forms of injustice (such as deprivation and exclusion), while often omitting insightful qualitative and temporal data with the result a biased representation of reality.

The use of geographic information systems (GIS) to map food environments has advanced our knowledge and understanding of urban procurement. However, discrepancies arise between the *objective* knowledge provided by GIS data and people's *partial* knowledge revealed through qualitative oral histories and participant observation. Critical cartography has emerged in response to this gap heralding the *geonarrative*: a method for integrating GIS with ethnography and grounded theory by intersecting qualitative GIS, narrative analysis, 3D GIS-based time-geographic methods,

and computer-aided qualitative data analysis. A geonarrative approach acknowledges quantitative, spatial, and qualitative formal and informal aspects of food security (Kwan and Ding, 2008).

This chapter interrogates the state of food security in Hebbal, Bangalore through a foodscape geonarrative. Situated in the agricultural state of Karnataka, the "Garden City" Bangalore, with approximately 11 million people, is considered the Silicon Valley of India. It is rapidly urbanising beyond its peri-urban edge, threatening urban food security. Despite economic growth, most residents continue to purchase food from informal vendors (see fig. 1) (Ali, Kapoor and Moorthy, 2010). Located in north Bangalore, Hebbal is an unplanned formal settlement representing a typical residential and mixed-use neighbourhood with a diverse population in terms of income, education, and religion.

This geonarrative was inspired by a Master of Landscape Architecture community design studio conducted at the National University of Singapore. A group of 13 students and one professor travelled to India in February 2018 to conduct fieldwork for nine days in a one-half square kilometre site in Hebbal. Satellite imagery and on-site observations were used to map food outlets (such as restaurants, cafes, markets, and food carts), as well as kitchen gardens, small farms, and edible container gardens. Surveys were conducted through convenience sampling to understand the residents' food

 DOI: 10.4324/9781003352280-30

Fig. 1: Informal vendors (left) and local produce stall (right)

provisioning habits and preferences. Findings were compared to the macroscale context comprising food markets, farmland, transportation, and other characteristics. Data collected by the students were combined with additional spatial data created by the professor for analysis. All the maps in this chapter were created using *ArcGIS Pro Version 2.0* (ESRI, 2018).

The objective was to provide a more complete understanding of the foodscape in Hebbal by interrogating formal and informal spaces and practices. Charreire *et al.* (2010) suggested conceptualising food access dimensions by adapting a model of healthcare access proposed by Penchansky and Thomas (1981) comprising availability, accessibility, affordability, acceptability, and accommodation (Caspi *et al.*, 2012). In this chapter, I add dimensions of stability, utilisation, environmental conditions, and behaviour.

A geonarrative of Hebbal's foodscape

The analysis began with an orthophoto that provided information on density and spatial organisation of the urban environment, e.g., roads, buildings (see fig. 2, left). An orthophoto is a photographic map that serves as a basemap on which other information can be overlaid. It was complemented by an informal photonarrative with photographs showing building heights, design complexity and texture, viewsheds, and maintenance (see fig. 2, right).

Availability refers to the adequate supply of healthy food, measured as presence of food outlets and supply of healthy food at outlets. A proportional symbol map (see fig. 3, top left) shows availability using Google maps data (hereafter, formal data). Food outlets were categorised by supply of healthy food (larger circles represent higher availability). Formal food

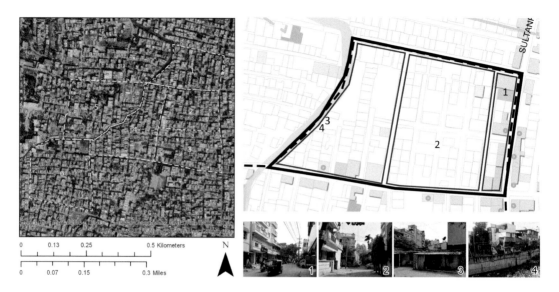

Fig. 2: Context: Formal ortho-map (left) and informal photonarrative (right) (1–3 Fan Lei, 4 Liu Xiaolei)

outlets (see fig. 3, top right) were compared with informal on-the-ground documentation of food outlets (see fig. 3, bottom) to make the availability map more complete.

A hexabin analysis of utilisation (see fig. 4, top left) reveals the ability of the local food market to meet dietary demand in variety, quantity, and nutrition. Formal food outlets were aggregated in 100-metre hexabins. Dark red indicates higher utilisation. In contrast, a kernel density map (see fig. 4, top right) shows informal vegetable sellers. Comparing the two maps, a dark purple cluster in the centre of the map corresponds with a dark red hexabin meaning high utilisation of formal and informal outlets at this location. However, another purple cluster, towards the east, corresponds with low formal utilisation. Here, informal food outlets fill a gap in formal outlets.

Food security depends on the availability of food outlets selling healthy food, but outlets must also be accessible to the public. Point buffer analysis (see fig. 4, bottom left) shows formal food outlet walking distances of 50 and 100 metres. Due to carrying purchases, food shopping walking distances are shorter than recreational distances,

usually set at 500 to 1,000 metres. Distance was compared with pedestrian quality of streets (informal walking environment or walkability; see fig. 4, bottom right). Using survey data collected during fieldwork based on Cook et al. (2013), red and orange show low walkability, light and dark green indicate high walkability, and red stars show areas of high traffic congestion.

Affordability relates to food prices and perceptions of worth relative to cost. The choropleth map in figure 5 shows deprivation across Bangalore based on 2001 data. In the map, the deprivation index is overlaid with proportional symbols showing slum populations, illustrating Hebbal's relatively low deprivation index and small population of slum dwellers.

Affordable and safe food is crucial for people to survive on limited incomes. Household income directly relates to foodscape affordability. Household dwellings in Hebbal were grouped into three categories as a proxy of income (see fig. 5, bottom). Low-income households spend 70% of monthly income on food, highlighting their precarity as compared to middle- and high-income households that spend 40% (Roy et al., 2018).

Fig. 3:
Availability:
formal food
outlets
(top left);
comparison of
formal and
informal food
outlets (top
right). Formal
provision shop
(bottom left)
and informal
food stall
(bottom right)

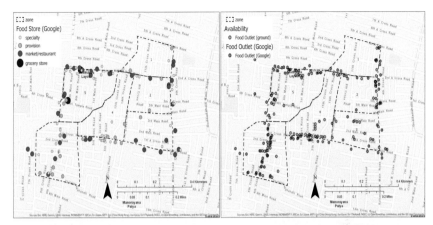

Fig. 4:
Utilisation:
hexabin map
of formal
food outlets
(top left) and
kernel density
of informal
food outlets
(top right).
Accessibility:
formal food
outlet walking
distance
(bottom
left) and
street-level
walkability
(bottom right)

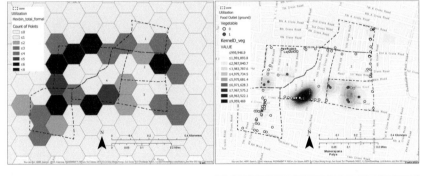

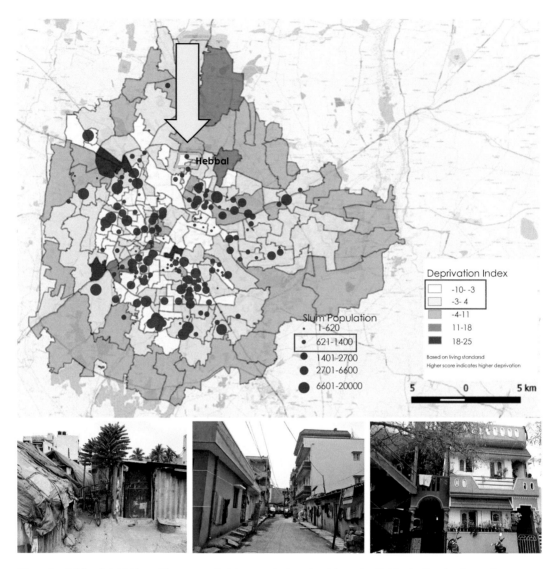

Fig. 5: Affordability: Slum population and deprivation in Hebbal (top) (based on map from Census of India, 2011; Worldbank). Low, middle, and high income dwellings (bottom) (left, middle: Nur Azilla Bte Nazli; right: Liu Xiaolei)

Informal settlements, often referred to as slums, are interspersed across Bangalore among middle class neighbourhoods where the dwellers work. Fourteen informal settlements were documented in Hebbal (see fig. 6), including one large community with a few dozen households. Residents in these places have low incomes and face challenges in foodscape affordability.

Natural and human-made environmental conditions also impact food security. Bangalore's annual monsoons, coupled with under-developed stormwater infrastructure, cause flooding. Informally planned streets cause traffic congestion. Both cause pollution. Figure 7 shows topography as a formal indicator of flood risk (left) and observed street-level sources of pollution including vehicular emissions, water pollution, and trash (right).

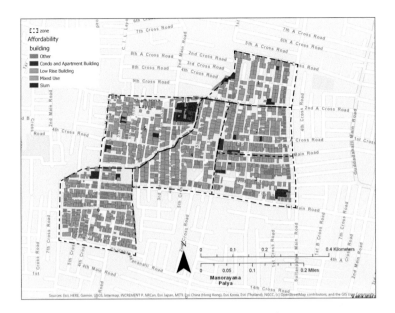

Fig. 6: Affordability: Ground-sleuthed map of housing types

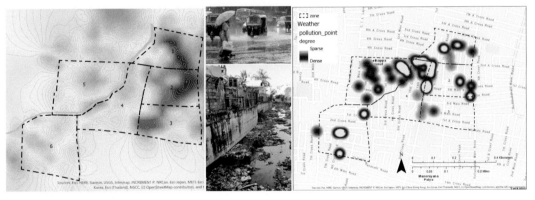

Fig. 7: Environmental conditions: Isoline map of low areas prone to flooding (in blue; left); monsoon flooding canal during dry season (filled with household waste) (centre; top: Skymet Weather Team, 2014; bottom: Fan Lei); and point density map of pollution as severe (yellow), medium (maroon), and sparse (blue) (right)

Accommodation, defined as how well local food sources accept and adapt to local residents' needs, is rarely measured. For this dimension, the availability map of informal food outlets was overlaid on a kernel density map of formal outlets (see fig. 8a, left) and re-interpreted through the lens of accommodation. Some informal food outlets clustered in the same places formal outlets were denser, but there were also informal outlet clusters where formal outlets were sparser. Accommodation, like

affordability, varies by social group. Residents had different dietary needs: the map (fig. 8a, right) shows many vegetarian outlets (red), fewer and scattered butchers (yellow), and a 100-metre service area where food carts might roam (blue).

The residents of Hebbal were predominantly Hindu and Muslim (see fig. 8b). This was important to understand because, culturally, Hindus do not eat beef, Muslims and high caste

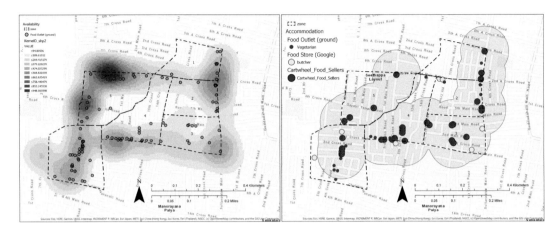

Fig. 8a: Accommodation: Kernal density of formal food outlets overlaid with informal outlets (left). Formal and informal food outlets categorised as vegetarian, butcher, and food carts with 100-metre buffer (right)

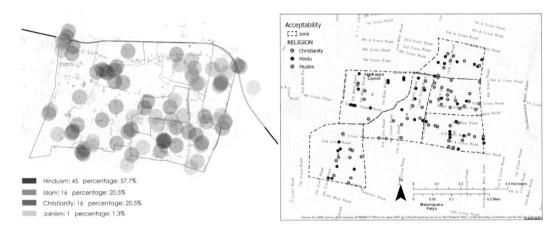

Fig. 8b: Accommodation: Distribution of religious places of worship around Hebbal with 100-metre buffers (left) (Wang Hanfeng). Distribution of survey participants by religious affiliation (right)

Hindus do not eat pork, devout Hindus and Buddhists are vegetarian, and Jains are strict vegetarians and do not eat eggs.

Complementing accommodation (supply-side) is the dimension of acceptability (demand-side). A survey conducted with Hebbal residents (n = 111) to understand their food habits and preferences is shown in figure 9. People usually shopped for food one to three times per day, matching the high quantity of food outlets.

Most residents, when asked if they grew their own food, responded that they did not have a garden but grew herbs and vegetables in small pots. They were also asked what their preferred type of garden would be if given space to grow food. The most common response was a community garden – a typical intervention in food-deprived places. Growing food locally could improve food security, but land availability was recognised as a major barrier by respondents. It was estimated that Hebbal residents

Fig. 10: Behaviour mapped in a food photo diary (Yong Keng-Whye, Raymond)

would require 6.6 square miles (4,242 acres or 0.44 acres per person) for 100% self-sufficiency in vegetables based on a daily recommended 3 cups of vegetables (Indian Council of Medical Research). The site was one half square mile (320 acres) with almost no vacant land.

Acceptability acknowledges that food security goes beyond meeting nutritional requirements – it also encompasses economic, social, and environmental conditions. To reference some of those conditions, this geonarrative concludes with a photo diary of observed behaviours and the many ways food manifests and intersects with Hebbal residents' daily lives (see fig. 10).

I offer several final thoughts. First is the issue of wicked problems where a geonarrative approach relies on triangulation of multiple types and sources of partial data, integrated analysis, and ground-sleuthing; there is no clear stopping point of saturation. There is the related issue of ecological fallacy in which aggregated data should not be interpreted as representative of individuals and specific places. This is why ground-sleuthing should be ongoing to verify and validate analysis and conclusions. With these in mind, the geonarrative is a promising method for investigating foodscapes – limited only by the expertise, critical thinking, and novel research methods.

A tool to visualise food security

The geonarrative approach in this chapter demonstrates the complex foodscape of Hebbal, an unplanned formal settlement in Bangalore, India. Presence of grocery stores is only one dimension of food security. Food security can be spatially analysed through dimensions of availability, accessibility, affordability, acceptability, accommodation, stability, utilisation, environmental conditions, and behaviour. By interrogating formal to informal spaces and practices there is evidence that the informal foodscape – including roaming food carts and kitchen gardens – fills gaps in food availability and affordability. However, according to the community surveys, residents still desired formal public spaces for community gardens.

Overall findings present a food secure Hebbal, yet poverty, pollution, and dependency on external supplies also suggest precarity. This case study is indicative, rather than conclusive. A critical cartography approach that bridges *objective* knowledge from GIS and *partial* knowledge from ethnography can lead to practical plans for social change that are grounded in a more complete understanding of environmental, policy, social, and infrastructure conditions.

Geonarrative approaches offer a useful holistic approach for understanding increasingly complex and pressured urban foodscapes. By using maps to increase the dimensions of food security beyond capitalist retail approaches, stakeholders can become empowered to make counterclaims that express diverse interests around food and make visible otherwise marginalised experiences.

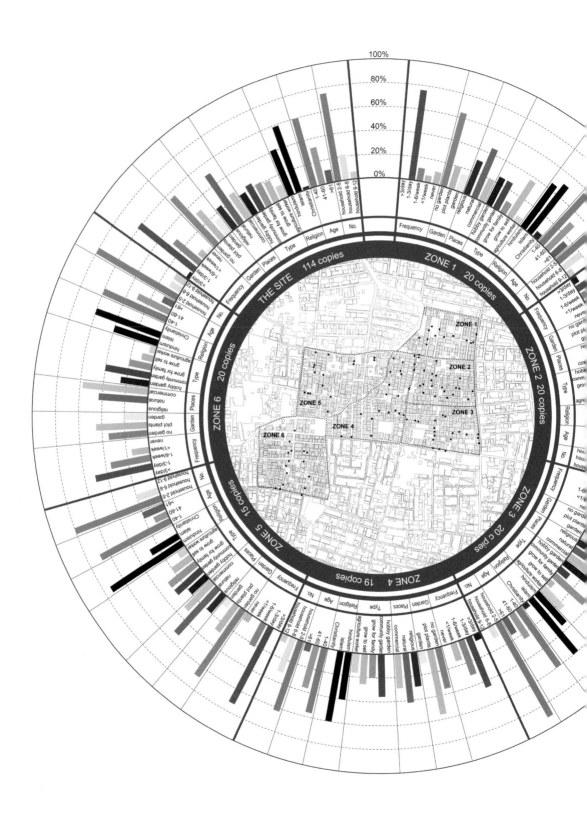

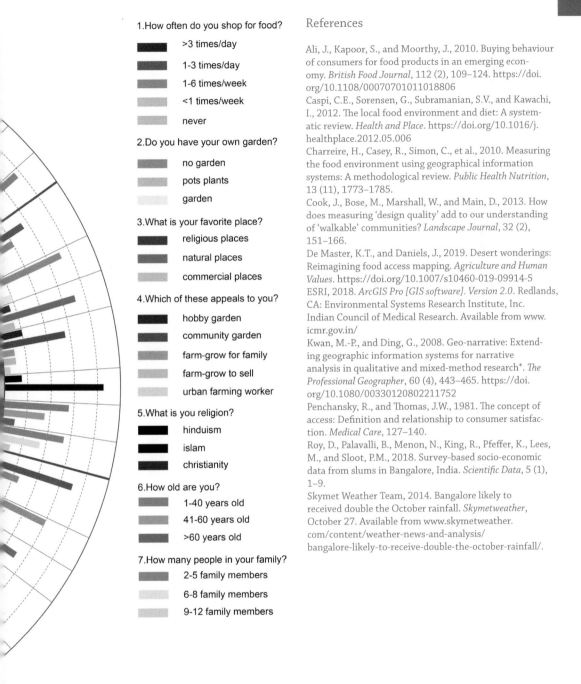

1.How often do you shop for food?

- >3 times/day
- 1-3 times/day
- 1-6 times/week
- <1 times/week
- never

2.Do you have your own garden?

- no garden
- pots plants
- garden

3.What is your favorite place?

- religious places
- natural places
- commercial places

4.Which of these appeals to you?

- hobby garden
- community garden
- farm-grow for family
- farm-grow to sell
- urban farming worker

5.What is you religion?

- hinduism
- islam
- christianity

6.How old are you?

- 1-40 years old
- 41-60 years old
- >60 years old

7.How many people in your family?

- 2-5 family members
- 6-8 family members
- 9-12 family members

References

Ali, J., Kapoor, S., and Moorthy, J., 2010. Buying behaviour of consumers for food products in an emerging economy. *British Food Journal*, 112 (2), 109–124. https://doi.org/10.1108/00070701011018806

Caspi, C.E., Sorensen, G., Subramanian, S.V., and Kawachi, I., 2012. The local food environment and diet: A systematic review. *Health and Place*. https://doi.org/10.1016/j.healthplace.2012.05.006

Charreire, H., Casey, R., Simon, C., et al., 2010. Measuring the food environment using geographical information systems: A methodological review. *Public Health Nutrition*, 13 (11), 1773–1785.

Cook, J., Bose, M., Marshall, W., and Main, D., 2013. How does measuring 'design quality' add to our understanding of 'walkable' communities? *Landscape Journal*, 32 (2), 151–166.

De Master, K.T., and Daniels, J., 2019. Desert wonderings: Reimagining food access mapping. *Agriculture and Human Values*. https://doi.org/10.1007/s10460-019-09914-5

ESRI, 2018. *ArcGIS Pro [GIS software]. Version 2.0*. Redlands, CA: Environmental Systems Research Institute, Inc.

Indian Council of Medical Research. Available from www.icmr.gov.in/

Kwan, M.-P., and Ding, G., 2008. Geo-narrative: Extending geographic information systems for narrative analysis in qualitative and mixed-method research*. *The Professional Geographer*, 60 (4), 443–465. https://doi.org/10.1080/00330120802211752

Penchansky, R., and Thomas, J.W., 1981. The concept of access: Definition and relationship to consumer satisfaction. *Medical Care*, 127–140.

Roy, D., Palavalli, B., Menon, N., King, R., Pfeffer, K., Lees, M., and Sloot, P.M., 2018. Survey-based socio-economic data from slums in Bangalore, India. *Scientific Data*, 5 (1), 1–9.

Skymet Weather Team, 2014. Bangalore likely to received double the October rainfall. *Skymetweather*, October 27. Available from www.skymetweather.com/content/weather-news-and-analysis/bangalore-likely-to-receive-double-the-october-rainfall/.

Fig. 9: Acceptability: Community survey results and survey questions (Wang Hanfeng)

Chicago's urban food networks: Mapping the future of a thriving metropolitan foodshed

Gundula Proksch and George Lee

The history and development of Chicago, Illinois, have been connected to the production and processing of agricultural products and the advancement of technological innovations in the food industry. Due to its geographic location, evolving rail networks, and industrialization in the mid-1800s, Chicago emerged as a central agricultural food hub in the Midwest, providing the growing urban centers along the east coast with food (Block and Rosing, 2015).

Chicago as regional food hub

In the 1970s, the city started to redefine its relation to agriculture through community gardening and urban agriculture (Haddix *et al.*, 2017), in which locals began to grow food in their house gardens and neighborhoods (Taylor and Lovell, 2012). Today, the city is known for its strong networks of urban agriculture operations, such as community gardens and urban farms with educational and job training programs. Over the last decade, the city has also attracted various entrepreneurial urban farms that honed their production methods and economic models, such as hydroponic greenhouses, rooftop greenhouses, and vertical indoor farms. These innovative, multi-layered farm operations have solid commercial objectives and impactful social missions that contribute to community empowerment and urban revitalization. The combination of various types of urban agriculture practices that intersect within the metro area makes Chicago a noteworthy case study of a localized, regional food system within a thriving foodshed (Horst and Gaolach, 2015), which produces food in the city and for the city.

This chapter summarizes urban food mapping conducted at various scales in a three-part mixed-method investigation of Chicago's existing urban agriculture networks, their urban indicators, organizational structures, built environment manifestations, and future development opportunities (Proksch *et al.*, 2023). It is part of the Belmont Forum and Urban Europe initiated, US National Science Foundation (NSF) funded CITYFOOD project, which examines the potential for urban integration and scaling up of sustainable food production systems (Proksch and Baganz, 2020). This chapter focuses on place-based and purpose-based food maps; it uses various mapping methods, such as diagramming, creating an inventory of sites, and opportunity mapping, as described in the Urban Food Mapping Matrix (see introduction chapter). A set of maps introduces the metropolitan foodshed, its physical configuration, and its demographic background. Building on data collected by the Chicago Urban Agriculture Mapping Project (CUAMP, n.d.), previous research, and the authors, the study identifies urban agriculture types – community-based and commercial – and their built environment-related infrastructure. Geographic information systems (GIS)-based mappings investigate the distribution of these different urban agriculture types across the city and on an urban-rural gradient. Furthermore, it examines how their locations relate to existing zoning, urban equity indicators, and future development potential within the metropolitan area of Chicago.

Through urban food mapping, the study aims to document the current state of urban

DOI: 10.4324/9781003352280-31

Mapping Process

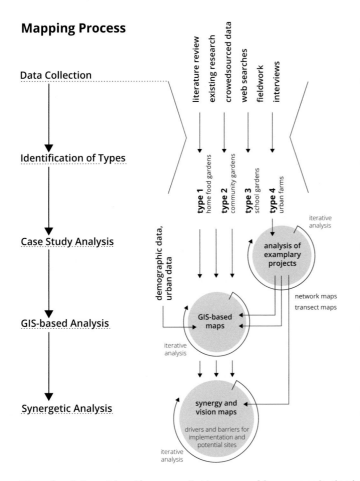

Data Collection
- literature review
- existing research
- crowdsourced data
- web searches
- fieldwork
- interviews

Collect the geographic location of individual urban agricultural sites using different sources and collection methods, such as satellite imagery analysis, crowdsourced data, web searches, fieldwork, and interviews.

Identification of Types
- **type 1** home food gardens
- **type 2** community gardens
- **type 3** school gardens
- **type 4** urban farms

Identify types of urban agricultural activities based on their location, infrastructure, main purpose, business model, and primary stakeholders.

Case Study Analysis

demographic data, urban data

analysis of examplary projects

iterative analysis

Analyze case studies to identify exemplary sites and study their farm and business operation, built environment infrastructure used, operational networks, geographic location, and zoning of the farm site.

network maps
transect maps

GIS-based Analysis

GIS-based maps

iterative analysis

Analyze and visualize GIS-based data, complemen- tary demographic (Census) data, and publicly available urban data to identify indicators, drivers, and barriers for future implementation.

Synergetic Analysis

synergy and vision maps

drivers and barriers for implementation and potential sites

iterative analysis

Create composite maps identifying existing urban agriculture sites, their operational networks, available sites, zoning maps, and development incentives. Synergies between these different factors may support future (commercial) urban farms.

Fig. 1: Schematic diagram of the overall research design, data collection, and mapping process

agricultural conditions in Chicago by revealing where various urban agriculture types are located within the metropolitan foodshed. It determines which factors and sites different types need to thrive and how various operations are connected. Finally, it identifies opportunities for successfully implementing future urban farms to create a thriving urban foodshed.

Mapping types and methods

This mixed-methods, interdisciplinary research and mapping project combines urban studies, social science, urban agriculture research, and urban design approaches at multiple scales.

The digital visualizations include GIS-based maps, vector-based diagrams, and photographic (pixel-based) material and often combine various representational strategies into one coherent mapping.

The study starts with a comprehensive collection of urban agriculture sites in Chicago. The sources include existing literature, crowdsourced datasets, and data collected by the authors in web searches, fieldwork, and interviews (fig. 1). Based on the empirical data collected, types of existing practices and associated stakeholders – home gardens, community gardens, school gardens, and diverse kinds of urban farms – are identified in an inductive

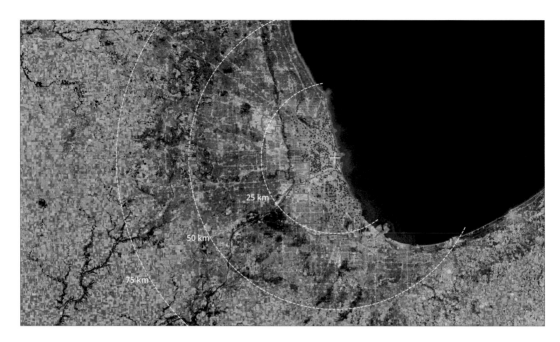

Fig. 2: Chicago's foodshed expands from the city of Chicago with numerous urban agriculture sites into the surrounding croplands

study. As part of an in-depth case study analysis, exemplary urban farm operations are investigated to map operational networks and their infrastructure. The study maps the geographic locations of all urban agriculture sites and businesses (with QGIS). It correlates them with publicly available urban data, such as demographic (Census) data, urban zoning maps, and planning data, to assess which factors indicate the locations of the urban agriculture sites. All datasets used are documented in a data directory (Proksch *et al.*, 2023). The mappings also reveal potential geographic intersections between urban agriculture practices in residential neighborhoods, industrial corridors, and the larger peri-urban foodshed.

In a final step, the findings are interrelated to identify potential urban development patterns and future sites for urban farms to foster the implementation of commercial urban farms on a larger scale in Chicago. The documentation of the current situation is used to project future developments in this multi-scaler study

spanning from the individual sites and understanding of operation types to neighborhoods, networks of operations, and Chicago's metropolitan foodshed.

The mapping process

Chicago, a city of 2.6 million, radiates from the edge of Lake Michigan to encompass a metro population of almost 7 million. The Chicago region is relatively flat and located on a fertile prairie of former swampland. These fertile soils are used for croplands at the periphery of the metro area stretching far into the American Midwest, producing corn (maize) and soybeans at scale. They are also the base for many community-based urban agriculture sites throughout the city (fig. 2). Connecting GIS-based data with satellite aerial imagery emphasizes the contrast between urban and agricultural land uses in this overview map. The satellite view captures additional physical details and land cover qualities that convey scale by, for

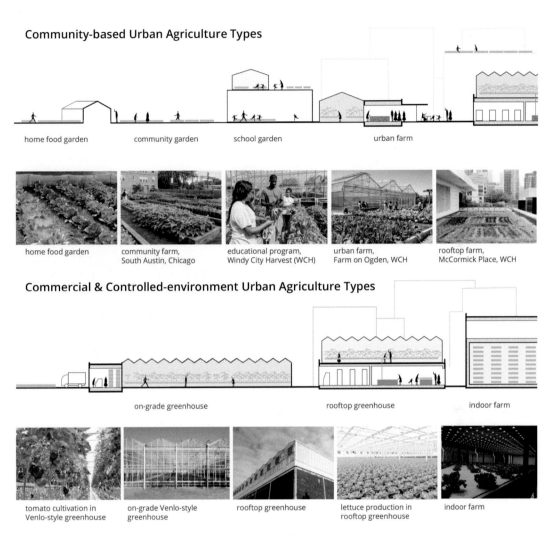

Community-based Urban Agriculture Types

home food garden   community garden   school garden   urban farm

home food garden

community farm,
South Austin, Chicago

educational program,
Windy City Harvest (WCH)

urban farm,
Farm on Ogden, WCH

rooftop farm,
McCormick Place, WCH

Commercial & Controlled-environment Urban Agriculture Types

on-grade greenhouse   rooftop greenhouse   indoor farm

tomato cultivation in
Venlo-style greenhouse

on-grade Venlo-style
greenhouse

rooftop greenhouse

lettuce production in
rooftop greenhouse

indoor farm

Fig. 3: a) Community-based urban agriculture types and exemplary sites; b) commercial urban agriculture types using controlled-environment urban agricultural systems and exemplary operations (photos 2–5 Chicago Botanic Garden, photos 8+9, Lufa Farms)

example, juxtaposing the block structure of the urban fabric and the parcels of agricultural land. It also captures the radial infrastructure of railyards, industrial corridors, and highways connecting the city center and massive agrarian hinterland.

The urban agriculture movement reconnects city dwellers and especially underserved communities with agricultural activities and food production through four different types of

urban agriculture: home food gardens (Taylor and Lovell, 2012), community gardens (which include allotment-type site allocations), school gardens (CUAMP, n.d.), and urban farms (Proksch et al., 2023). The latter often combine production and social missions, such as educational and job training programs and community-building efforts (fig. 3a). In addition to soil-based farming, several commercial urban farms operate Controlled-Environment Agriculture (CEA) (fig. 3b).

Fig. 4: Mappings of urban agriculture sites in Chicago: a) community gardens color-coded median household income (MHI) from black = highest MHI to yellow = lowest MHI; b) school gardens (small circles) and urban farms (large circles)

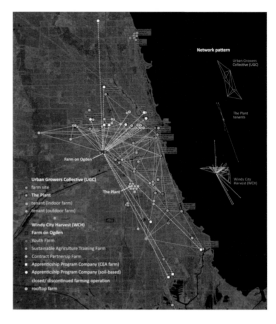

Fig. 5: Urban farm networks provide food production at scale, various educational and job training programs, and community support (Proksch, 2023)

The longstanding interest in documenting these grassroots and entrepreneurial activities is well represented in two mapping projects: Taylor and Lovell's identification of private home food gardens (2012) based on the analysis of satellite images and the CUAMP project. The latter is a crowdsourced, collaboratively generated data collection and mapping project that makes street addresses of urban agriculture locations available (CUAMP, n.d.); the project's database currently includes over 800 entries. The datasets are organized based on the earlier-identified types and are shown in urban agriculture maps (fig. 4).

Plotting the locations of different types of urban agriculture in conjunction with socio-economic, demographic, and publicly available urban data allows pinpointing indicators for the placement of specific types. More home gardens can be found in census tracts with a lower population density. Such neighborhoods often have more single-family

dwellings, which allow for food cultivation on private properties. Community gardens are primarily located in census tracts with low median household incomes (fig. 4a). A significantly higher concentration of this type can be found on Chicago's West Side. School gardens are more evenly distributed between census tracts regardless of income level. In contrast to the community and school gardens, which are primarily situated in residential areas, urban farms are often located on or close to commercially and industrially zoned properties (fig. 4b). A comparative view shows that high densities of urban agricultural activities are located on Chicago's West Side and in the Back of the Yards neighborhood.

In-depth research of the organizational strategies of urban farms reveals that they are often embedded into collaborative networks to provide community support and ensure business success (fig. 5). Three outstanding examples are: (1) the Urban Growers Collective, which operates

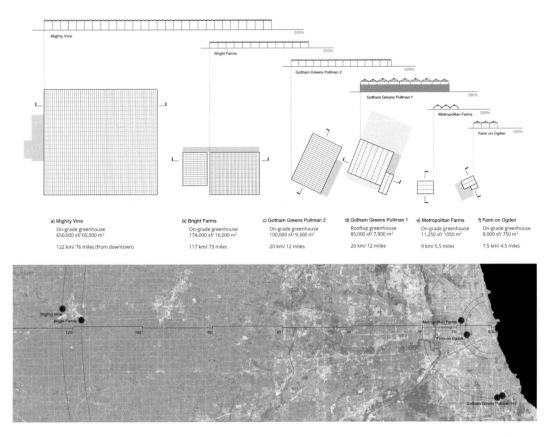

a) Mighty Vine

On-grade greenhouse
650,000 sf/ 60,000 m²

122 km/ 76 miles (from downtown)

b) Bright Farms

On-grade greenhouse
174,000 sf/ 16,000 m²

117 km/ 73 miles

c) Gotham Greens Pullman 2

On-grade greenhouse
100,000 sf/ 9,300 m²

20 km/ 12 miles

d) Gotham Greens Pullman 1

Rooftop greenhouse
85,000 sf/ 7,900 m²

20 km/ 12 miles

e) Metropolitan Farms

On-grade greenhouse
11,250 sf/ 1050 m²

9 km/ 5.5 miles

f) Farm on Ogden

On-grade greenhouse
8,000 sf/ 750 m²

7.5 km/ 4.5 miles

Fig. 6: Urban-rural transect with a selection of existing commercial CEA operations and greenhouse infrastructure

eight farm sites primarily located on Chicago's South Side that grow produce with and for local communities (UGC, n.d.); (2) *The Plant*, a food business incubator that generates among others urban agriculture start-ups (The Plant, n.d.); and (3) *Windy City Harvest*, the most extensive network of urban farm sites which offers several educational programs, job training, and an apprenticeship program in collaboration with other commercial urban farms (WCH, n.d.).

Commercial urban farms utilizing capital-intensive CEA systems can achieve a consistent year-round production of high-value crops (usually lettuce, leafy greens, and tomatoes), including during the winter months, generating premium prices. An assessment of an urban-rural-transect shows that the size of the CEA greenhouses

increases the farther away from downtown they are located (fig. 6). Greenhouses in exurban and rural communities on the outskirts of the metropolitan foodshed are the largest. Gotham Greens' greenhouses Pullman 1 and 2 are located at the former site of the Ryerson Steel factory where Pullman rail cars were built. The project received about a quarter of its total cost through the city's tax increment financing plan (Gallun, 2018). Could more urban farms benefit from such incentives and locate larger CEA greenhouses within the city limits?

The city of Chicago actively promotes the reactivation of industrial areas within the city proper with enticements for redevelopment projects in empowerment zones and specific industrial corridors (City of Chicago, 2013).

Fig. 7: Diagrammatic drawing of a) industrial corridors and urban farms (including CEA operations) and b) location of existing food industry. Maps adapted from Chicago Sustainable Industries (CSI), City of Chicago

Fig. 8: Overlay of existing urban agriculture activity and industrial corridors described in the Chicago Sustainable Industries (CIS) program

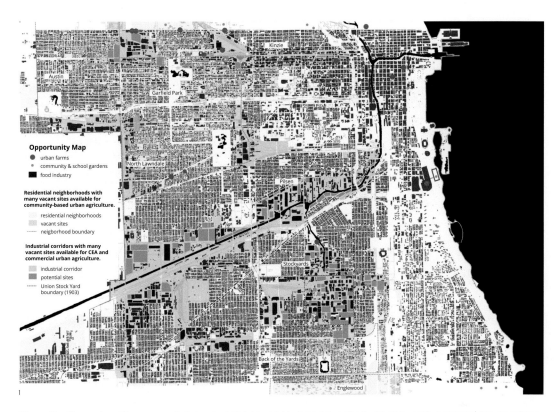

Fig. 9: Opportunity map of how existing soil-based urban farms and community gardens can expand while innovative production facilities can be located in industrial corridors connecting social and economic benefits

Urban farms and industrial corridors are concentrated on the West Side and around the former stockyards. This area also houses a large number of existing food industries (fig. 7). The confluence of existing urban agriculture activity and policy incentives on Chicago's West Side and the northern part of the South Side makes them an ideal study area. A synergy map juxtaposes existing sites of urban agriculture operations and industrial corridors eligible for incentives (fig. 8). The opportunity map demonstrates how existing soil-based urban farms can further expand, and CEA operations may use the vacant sites and existing infrastructure to locate innovative production facilities within the historic center of Chicago's food industry (fig. 9). Refocusing the view on the metropolitan foodshed shows that it offers a myriad of similar industrial and commercially zoned sites (fig. 10). Utilizing industrial

corridors and former railyards for intensifying urban agriculture brings food production full circle. This intermix of existing and new food industries allows for exchanging resources between different operations to apply circular city principles and create new bioeconomic urban networks (Nehls *et al.*, 2016). Locations used in the past for storage, exchange, and processing of food from the hinterland have the potential to become the sites for new green industries and grow local, sustainable, healthy food in the city, for the city.

Food mapping as research and planning tool

This study of urban agricultural practices in Chicago reveals unseen connections and opportunities between social, commercial, and urban development potentials. This multilayered aim is reflected in the mapping themes and types

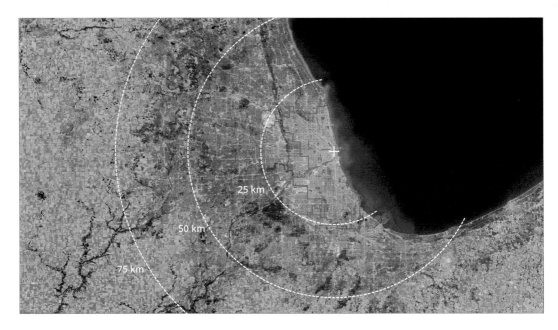

Fig. 10: Future sites for urban farms in the industrial and commercial corridors connecting downtown and peri-urban croplands

of the *Urban Food Mapping Matrix* (see fig. 1, introduction chapter).

Urban agriculture data are not yet collected in one central place, and due to the differences in operation type, size, and economic capacity, partial datasets cannot be easily combined. The aggregation of data and the research on how these operations build supportive networks of geographic locations, educational support, job training, resource inventories, and collaborations are essential. It allows stakeholders to assess urban agriculture in the context of significant development goals for the city and region. Cities need to collect data on existing urban agriculture sites or support nonprofits such as CUAMP to continue and expand their work. Correlating these datasets with demographic and urban data generates a potent planning tool for communities. Based on this regional understanding, cities can shape their incentives, policies, and legislation to advance the further integration of urban farms (Goodman and Minner, 2019).

Urban food mapping manifests itself in various shapes and forms, as this edited volume impressively documents. As an interdisciplinary field, urban food mapping thrives in collaboration with other disciplines from art and architecture to social science, urban studies, and planning. This study highlights the importance of utilizing the intersection with planning, urban development, and economic incentives. Methodologically, it demonstrates how assembling and integrating datasets effectively at multiple scales with other urban data helps document and assess formally unseen connections, networks, capacity, and future opportunities. With such mapping tools, communities, cities, and researchers can successfully determine approaches to scaling up the integration of urban agricultural operations to meet social and economic development goals.

References

Block, D.R., and Rosing, H., 2015. *Chicago: A food biography*. London: Rowman & Littlefield.

Chicago Urban Agriculture Mapping Project (CUAMP), n.d. Available from https://cuamp.org/ [Accessed 3 August 2022].

City of Chicago, 2013. *Chicago Sustainable Industries (CSI)*.
Available from www.chicago.gov/city/en/depts/dcd/supp_
info/chicago_sustainableindustries.html [Accessed
3 Aug 2022]

Gallun, A., 2018. *Rail cars to lettuce: Second big greenhouse
coming to Pullman*. Available from www.chicagobusiness.
com/article/20180207/CRED0701/180209903/gotham-
greens-plans-second-big-greenhouse-in-pullman [Accessed
3 Aug 2022].

Goodman, W., and Minner. J., 2019. Will the urban agricultural revolution be vertical and soilless? A case study
of controlled environment agriculture in New York City.
Land Use Policy, 83, 160–173. https://doi.org/10.1016/j.
landusepol.2018.12.038.

Haddix, C.M., et al., 2017. *The Chicago food encyclopedia*.
Chicago, IL: The University of Illinois Press.

Horst, M., and Gaolach, B., 2015. The potential of local food
systems in North America: A review of foodshed analyses.
Renewable Agriculture and Food Systems, 30 (5), 399–407.
https://doi.org/10.1017/S1742170514000271

Nehls, T., et al., 2016. From waste to value: Urban agriculture enables cycling of resources in cities. *In*: F. Lohrberg,
et al., eds. *Urban agriculture Europe*. London: Jovis.

Proksch, G., 2023. Architectural nodes in Chicago's urban
agricultural food networks. *In*: *Commons: 111th annual
meeting*. London: Association of Collegiate Schools of
Architecture, ACSA.

Proksch, G., and Baganz, D., 2020. CITYFOOD: Research
design for an international, transdisciplinary collaboration.
Technology| Architecture + Design, 4 (1), 35–43. https://doi.
org/10.1080/24751448.2020.1705714

Proksch, G., et al., Forthcoming. Expanding Chicago's urban
agriculture networks: Revitalizing neighborhoods through
innovative production. *Land Use Policy.*

Taylor, J.R., and Lovell, S.T., 2012. Mapping public and
private spaces of urban agriculture in Chicago through the
analysis of high-resolution aerial images in Google Earth.
Landscape and Urban Planning, 108 (1), 57–70. https://doi.
org/10.1016/j.landurbplan.2012.08.001.

The Plant, n.d. Available from www.insidetheplant.com/
about-the-plant [Accessed 3 Aug 2022].

Urban Growers Collective (UGC), n.d. *Farmers fostering
pathways to freedom*. Available from https://urbangrower-
scollective.org/ [Accessed 3 Aug 2022].

Windy City Harvest (WCH), n.d. *Chicago Botanic Garden*.
Available from www.chicagobotanic.org/urbanagriculture
[Accessed 3 Aug 2022].

Glossary

Agropolitan. Areas characterised by agricultural activity and urban development, often specialised in different production systems, in the presence of a strong use of the territory by infrastructure, residential and industry. Agropolitan also defines the concept of regional development where agricultural production and distribution take place within the context of a decision making appropriately sized to the local community.

Aguaje. *Mauritia flexuosa* palm found commonly throughout tropical regions of South America.

Aguajera. Mostly female street vendors who sell aguaje fruit.

Aguajina. Beverage made of aguaje fruit. Sellers of aguajina are called aguajineras.

Alternative Food Networks (AFNs). Comprehensive body of practices related to food provisioning which are different from the mainstream food systems and often began as informal social practices unsanctioned by municipal codes.

Biodiversity. The diversity of all living organisms and ecological systems on our planet, including genetic diversity.

Cartography. The study and practice of making and using maps. Combining science, aesthetics and technique, cartography builds on the premise that reality (or an imagined reality) can be modelled in ways that communicate spatial information effectively.

Circular system. A closed dynamic system. Substances needed to produce a product can – after the product's use – be recycled (including waste) for the production of a new product.

Citizen-based urban food maps focus on visualising food issues in relation to people in the city. Typical citizen-based urban food maps depict urban farmers, food system activists and initiatives, consumers and local communities as well as public institutions (Bohn and Tomkins).

Citizen-led mapping = community-based mapping. A collaborative process in which individuals, often members of a local community or the general public, actively participate in creating maps or geospatial data.

Commoning. Social practices of governing a resource which does not involve state or market actors, but a community of users that self-governs the resource (i.e. the commons) through the institutions that it creates.

Commons. Cultural and natural resources, which may be tangible or intangible, and that are held in common even when privately or publicly used, including air, water, soil and academic knowledge.

Continuous Productive Urban Landscape (CPUL). "An urban green infrastructure linking food-producing sites of varying scales and operating types with other (green) open spaces through and across towns or cities, connecting those parcels of land to the citizens as well as to other food system activities and ultimately to the rural landscape" (Bohn&Viljoen).

Controlled-Environment Agriculture (CEA). An advanced and intensive form of soilless agriculture where plants grow within an environment that controls nutrient and energy flows to optimise horticultural practices (Cornell CALS).

Counter-mapping. Mapping that begins with alternative forms of knowledge and experience and that questions and explores alternatives to dominant land use categories rather than employing the totalising view of conventional cartography.

CPUL Opportunity Mapping Method. A participatory urban design and planning tool aimed at the integration of urban agriculture and food system activities into cities. Outcomes of these processes are food maps that record/count/order and opportunity maps that explore/propose/envision (Viljoen and Bohn).

Critical cartography. A set of mapping practices and methods of analysis grounded in critical theory, specifically the thesis that maps reflect and perpetuate relations of power, typically in favour of a society's dominant group.

(Critical) food literacy. A relatively new and fluid term involving contested debates about individual responsibility, information, knowledge and issues of power surrounding food (Sumner).

Crossings. Creative encounters and intersections between usually separate domains, such as academic theory and artistic practice, physical and virtual environments.

Data-led spatial analysis. A set of techniques designed to find pattern, detect anomalies or test hypotheses and theories, based on spatial data.

Datafication [as in datafied cities]. Technological trend centred on turning many aspects of our lives into digital data, which, coupled with the computational power of predictive analytics, can be transformed into information creating new forms of value and consequent social implications.

Design research "charts the paths from research methods to research findings to design principles to design results and demonstrates the transformation of theory into a richly satisfying and more reliably successful practice" (Laurel).

Ecological literacy. An educational approach aimed at teaching responsibility for the environment and natural resources. It does not only focus on ecology but also incorporates social, economic, political and cultural elements.

Edible Map. Map that has a distinct food focus (Tomkins).

Follow-the-things. A method that traces commodities through diverse locations to expose the connections between the production, trade, retail, consumption and disposal of goods. This mode of researching and telling stories with commodities was initially characterised by ethnographic analysis but has evolved into an approach that is methodologically open and benefits from a variety of creative formats (Cook).

Food geographies. The study of foodscapes which examine the cultural, spatial, economic, political and material connections between people and the places where food is produced, processed and consumed around the world. Food geographies also link aspects of human experience, such as health, gender and race, as well as environmental aspects with a heterogeneous range of sites and fields of research (Flowers and Swan; Ermann; Goodman; Cook et al.).

Food growing sites. One of the five key themes in urban food mapping (Bohn and Tomkins).

Food map. An urban food map helps to 1) capture all relevant aspects of the existing local food system; 2) visualise the complexity of the given site in planning terms; and 3) enable viewers to see spatial connections between local food actors and activities that previously remained hidden (Bohn).

Food networks and resources. One of the five key themes in urban food mapping (Bohn and Tomkins).

Food produce and cultures. One of the five key themes in urban food mapping (Bohn and Tomkins).

Food security. Based on the 1996 World Food Summit, food security is achieved when all people, at all times, have physical and economic access to sufficient safe and nutritious food that meets their dietary needs and food preferences for an active and healthy life.

Food sovereignty. Defined as "the right of people to healthy and culturally appropriate food, produced through ecologically sound and sustainable methods, and their right to define their own food and agriculture systems" (Vía Campesina).

Food stakeholders. One of the five key themes in urban food mapping (Bohn and Tomkins).

Food system activities. One of the five key themes in urban food mapping (Bohn and Tomkins).

Geographic information system (GIS). A computer system that analyses and displays geographically referenced information.

Geonarrative is a web application that combines interactive web maps with narrative text, images and multimedia content.

Household Food Insecurity Access Scale (HFIAS). A survey tool designed to collect information on household-level food security through nine core questions. The survey collects data on anxieties around food, access to food and sufficient food quantity.

Hyperconsumption. A term used by the French philosopher Gilles Lipovetsky to refer to the "new stage of consumer capitalism" we have entered at the beginning of the 21st century in which consumption is "expanding at a hyperbolic rate" and permeating life of individuals at all times and in all places.

Incredible Edible Network. A federation of independent groups worldwide that promotes the rights of people to grow food on suitable public sector land (Incredible Edible).

Infrastructural ecology. A reimagining of infrastructure as interlinked, synergistic systems operating as ecological fabric at a landscape scale.

Infrastructural inversion. A term coined by Pierre Bélanger referring to when large-scale, mechanical, engineered infrastructures open to multiple trajectories and indeterminate form.

KmZero describes a short supply chain in the agri-food system where the products are cultivated, transformed, distributed and consumed at local scale. Generally, the products are distributed without intermediaries, often in urban markets or directly in the farm. KmZero, especially in the Italian context, also became a branding strategy.

Low-cost supermarket. Budget-friendly variants of larger supermarkets in some countries that focus on selling cheaper food items. These supermarkets have a smaller physical footprint than typical supermarkets and are usually found in low-income areas.

Opportunity maps. Food-focused opportunity maps "visualise food system activities from a spatial perspective and can serve as cross-disciplinary links and communication tools between professional designers and planners, food system actors, local authorities and lay audiences. Such maps are not masterplans in the traditional planning sense but act as strategic, conceptual steps ahead of them. They capture ideas, desires and possibilities and make them accessible to diverse audiences" (Bohn).

Paca Digestora Silva (PDS). A device developed by Guillermo Silva, in Medellín, Colombia, to manage organic waste by compacting leaves and kitchen waste layers.

Participation. In participatory processes, individuals and organisations (so-called stakeholders) are tied into decision-making processes.

Participatory mapping. A group-based qualitative research method that gives participants freedom to shape discussion on a given topic with minimal intervention from researchers (NJTPA).

Place-based urban food maps focus on visualising food issues in relation to one or several distinct urban spaces. Typical place-based urban food maps deal with food in or on buildings, in open space, in a neighbourhood, borough or city and in the peri-urban realm (Bohn and Tomkins).

Purpose-based urban food maps focus on visualising a particular concern that the mappers have in relation to food. Typical purpose-based urban food maps deal with uncovering, recording, counting, comparing and responding to food issues as well as with proposing change (Bohn and Tomkins).

Red de Huerteros Medellín (RHM). A collective organisation based in Medellín, Colombia, which questions the origin of agricultural products that feed cities, reflects on practices in place to produce them, supports those practices that maintain life and makes alliances with other collectives to support the establishment of vibrant towns.

Right to the city. Henri Lefebvre coined the concept of the right to the city arguing that cities are unfair and unequal places and said that cities' inhabitants were the ones called to fight against such a situation. This fight is against capitalist urbanisation and the mode of production to which it contributes.

Seed guardians. People who protect seeds with the intention of benefiting humanity instead of them becoming private propriety of multinational corporations.

Space production describes that the making of urban space can, will and needs to happen again and again. This is due to constantly changing social, cultural or political local needs of the users of that space.

Sustainability. A concept originally developed in silviculture to ascertain the careful use of natural resources. Today, the United Nations' definition describes sustainable development as "development that meets the needs of the present without compromising the ability of future generations to meet their own needs".

Time-based urban food maps focus on visualising food aspects over time and in relation to processes. Typical time-based urban food maps deal with urban food issues of the recent past, the present and the near future. They range from historical maps to those imagining a future far away (Bohn and Tomkins).

Tuck shops (also known as spaza shops) are small-scale, informal convenience shops that are operated from homes or informal structures such as repurposed shipping containers or trailers.

Urban agriculture. "An industry that produces and markets food and fuel, largely in response to the daily demand of consumers within a town, city or metropolis; on land and water dispersed throughout the urban and peri-urban metropolis. Applying intensive production methods, using and reusing natural resources and urban waste, to yield a diversity of crops and livestock" (Smit *et al.*).

Urban ecology. The approaches and methods of the academic discipline of Ecology used to explore urban habitats.

Urban farming. *See urban agriculture*

Urban food mapping tackles a diverse range of food-focused data related to specific urban situations that makes visible issues about the feeding of cities or proposes solutions for their inclusive and sustainable development.

Urban Food Mapping Matrix. A diagram developed by Katrin Bohn and Mikey Tomkins to visualise their systematisation of important and common urban food mapping themes, types and methods.

Urban food system. "All the interdependent parts of the system that provides food to a [city]. This includes the growing, harvesting, storing, transporting, processing, packaging, marketing, retailing and consuming of the product" (Wilkins and Eames-Sheavly). It also includes the disposal of food waste and food packages.

Urban morphology. A study of urban forms and physical elements and of the processes responsible for their transformation over time with the aim to create design solutions for sustainable urban development.

Contributors

Katrin Bohn

is an architect and urban practitioner and a principal lecturer at the University of Brighton, UK. Previously, she was a guest professor at the Technical University of Berlin, Germany, where she set up and ran the Department of City & Food. Since the 2000s, she has taught, talked and lectured to many audiences in Europe and worldwide. Together with André Viljoen, she forms Bohn&Viljoen Architects and has worked intensely on their food-focused urban design concept *CPUL (Continuous Productive Urban Landscape)* which, in 2015, won the international RIBA President's "Award for outstanding university-located research".

Bohn&Viljoen's work has been published widely and translated into several languages, including German, Arabic, Chinese, Dutch, French, Persian, Russian and Spanish. In the complex subject areas of urban agriculture and green infrastructure, Katrin has been conducting, participating in or advising on national and international design and research, urban planning and policy as well as pioneering food projects.

Mikey Tomkins

is an independent researcher and artist. He holds a PhD from the University of Brighton, UK, where he researched the contribution of everyday community gardening to urban agriculture. Since 2004, he has extensively used mapping with urban agriculture research to answer questions on land availability and potential yields and the more qualitative exploration of the everyday experience of food gardening in cities. The map work is encapsulated in the *Edible Mapping Project*, initiated in 2009. It is a participatory mapping practice that has run in multiple cities and engages communities in revisioning urban space for food production through walking, mapping and growing. Since 2014, he has also been working with forced migrant communities and refugees in the US and Iraq. This work necessitates in depth community engagement often under difficult situations, involving mapping constantly evolving spaces and implementing urban agriculture both in camps and cities.

Jacques Abelman

is a landscape architect, educator and researcher based in Amsterdam, the Netherlands. He examines notions of human and ecosystem health through the lens of infrastructure and public space design. His built work seeks to bring ecological cycles and food systems to life through aesthetic, tactile and educational interventions, such as *The Landscape Table* (Brussels, 2014) and *Prairie Futures* (Joes, Colorado, 2020). He has taught at the Amsterdam and Rotterdam Academies of Architecture, the European Master's in Landscape Architecture programme and the University of Oregon. His writing has been published in *Flourishing Foodscapes, The Routledge Handbook of Food and Landscape* and *Future of Food Journal*.

Amélie André

worked for ten years as an architect and urban planner before starting a PhD at the University of Hertfordshire, UK, in 2018. This background influenced the research design of her doctoral project, using visual tools as methods combined with an ethnographical approach to highlight how the shape of a city can suggest an efficient use of the land. Her interest in food, city and the edible landscape includes individual practices and local governance that shape resilient foodscapes while interrogating wider food trade impacts on decision making at different levels.

Corelia Baibarac-Duignan

is an assistant professor in the Faculty of Behavioural, Management and Social Sciences and a founding member of the RUrban Futures Collective, at the University of Twente, the Netherlands. Originally trained as an architect, she has research expertise in the fields of urban sustainability, community-led urban resilience and smart cities. She conducted research in various European contexts, including Dublin, London, Paris, Bucharest and Utrecht. Her current work involves transdisciplinary collaborations aimed at co-creating context-appropriate methods and tools for widening civic engagement in inclusive transformations towards sustainable futures.

Silvia Rosivalová Baučeková

is an assistant professor at Pavol Jozef Šafárik University in Košice, Slovakia. In her book *Dining Room Detectives: Analysing Food in the Novels of Agatha Christie* (2015), she discussed the symbolic role of food in detective fiction. In 2020, she spent six months at the Food Studies Program of the University of Oregon as a Fulbright visiting scholar. Currently, her research focuses on fictional and non-fictional representations of food as a force that helps construct locality in globalised spaces. She is a member of the Association for the Study of Food and Society.

Janie Bickersteth

has been a director of *Incredible Edible Lambeth*,

UK, since 2017, being chair and co-ordinator from 2019 to 2022. She has recently contributed to *Framework for Community Growing*, a collaborative project between *Incredible Edible Lambeth* and Arup, UK. With the *Urban Agriculture Consortium*, she has been convening a UK-wide group of land mappers. With *Incredible Edible*, she has worked on the national 'Right to Grow' campaign. She moved to Oxford in 2020, where she now works with *Good Food Oxfordshire*, establishing short food supply chains, linking local producers with local institutions.

Mila Brill

works at the Center for Academic Development of the University of Applied Sciences in Cologne, Germany. Before, she was a research assistant in the project *Urban food cultures and integrative practices* at the Institute for Political Sciences and Sociology, Bonn, Germany. She has recently published an ethnographic case study of gastronomic places and their role in home- and place-making processes in polarised urban districts. Her areas of interest are theories of everyday practices, urban food cultures, diverse neighbourhoods and mapping methods in qualitative social research.

Fabrizio D'Angelo

is a PhD candidate in urbanism at Università Iuav di Venezia, Italy, graduate in architecture (Iuav 2016) and teaching assistant in geography (Iuav, since 2017). His current research area is energy transition through a spatial perspective. He has also followed research activities in the field of agricultural landscapes and renewable energy development. As a member of ISOIPS Egroup, he develops projects and activities in the Dolomites area on rural architecture and landscape, environmental education and sustainable tourism.

Marthe Derkzen

is a researcher at Wageningen University & Research in the Netherlands. She holds a PhD in environmental geography from Vrije Universiteit Amsterdam, the Netherlands. Her research on green cities, climate adaptation and social justice has been published in books (*Mapping Ecosystem Services*, *Routledge Handbook of Urban Ecology*) and journals, such as *Landscape and Urban Planning*, *Journal of Applied Ecology* and *COSUST*. She conducts participatory action research on green citizen initiatives and a healthy living environment. Marthe also grows food in her local community garden.

Jessica Ann Diehl

is an assistant professor in the Department of Architecture at the National University of Singapore where she teaches geodesign as well as a community design studio addressing issues of urban food security in the Master of Landscape Architecture

programme. Research interests include place-based investigation of social networks, health equity and alternative food systems. She holds a PhD in health and behavioural sciences from the University of Colorado Denver, USA, where she was a National Science Foundation (NSF) IGERT PhD fellow in sustainable urban infrastructure systems, and a BLA/MLA in landscape architecture from the Pennsylvania State University.

Ferne Edwards

has conducted research on just and sustainable cities across Australia, Venezuela, Ireland, Spain, Norway and the UK. Her books include, *Food for Degrowth: Perspectives and Practices* (with Nelson, Routledge, 2021) and *Food, Senses and the City* (with Gerritsen and Wesser, Routledge, 2021), *Food Resistance Movements: A Journey into Alternative Food Networks* (Palgrave, 2023) and *Urban Natures: Living the More-than-Human City* (with Popartan and Petersen, Berghan 2023). She has worked on the international just and sustainable urban food projects SHARECITY, EdiCitNet and FoodCLIC.

Viviana Ferrario

holds a PhD in urbanism and is a professor of landscape geography at the Università Iuav di Venezia, Italy. She is a member of the scientific board of the PhD program in Historical, Geographical and Anthropological Studies at

the University of Padova. She researches landscape studies, especially driving forces of landscape change, such as urbanisation, agricultural policies, heritage protection and renewable energy development. She coordinated several research projects and participates in national and international research networks, among which are the *Alpine Network* and *Eucaland*. She is a member of the scientific committee of the International Agricultural Library *La Vigna* and President of the Comelico-Dolomiti Foundation.

Joana Ferro

is a London-based landscape architect at global multidisciplinary engineering and design firm Arup and cofounder of the Humanitarian Landscape Collective nonprofit. She has experience in developing landscape and urban concepts, strategies and designs with work that ranges from city-wide masterplans and green infrastructure projects to urban realm improvements, regeneration and placemaking projects. She has an interest in facilitating community-led design projects using action-based design research towards shaping resilient, imaginative, equitable and sensitive places for both people and the planet. Joana kickstarted a partnership with Incredible Edible Lambeth after meeting on an emergency mutual aid call as a volunteer during the first UK Covid-19 national lockdown in 2020.

Patrick S. Ford

currently lives and works in the UK after having previously taught within the School of Communication & Design at RMIT University, Vietnam. He has had papers presented at various conferences, participated in international performance art festivals and has had articles published in magazines and journals, including the *Living Maps Review*. Originally trained in sculpture, Patrick is currently pursuing projects involving the development of an approach to drawing methodology and performance, especially related to walking art. His practice seeks to take art-making out into the environment to encourage observation and response and often focuses on the border between disciplines.

Vanessa Giolai

studied architecture at the Technical University of Vienna, Austria, and at the L'ENSA Paris Val de Seine, France. Next to her research work on the interactions between cities, food supply and circularity, she works as an architect and urban planner in a Viennese office with a focus on participation. Furthermore, she is also teaching at the TU Vienna.

Natacha Quintero González

is a lecturer at the Department of Urban Planning at BTU Cottbus-Senftenberg, Germany, and a doctoral candidate at the Technical University of Berlin. She received training as an architect at the Universidad Central de Venezuela (UCV) and holds a MSc in urban development from the TU Berlin. Her PhD research focuses on human-nature relations within marginalised urban spaces in Latin America and the Caribbean. She is particularly interested in how storytelling and relational perspectives can contribute to social-ecological knowledge co-production.

Anke Hagemann

is an urban and architectural researcher based in Berlin, Germany. She studied architecture, co-founded the journal *AnArchitektur*, worked as a research associate in the project *Shrinking Cities* and taught at various universities (ETH Zurich, HCU Hamburg, Uni Stuttgart, TU Berlin). In the research project *Transnational Production Spaces* (2016–2019), she has investigated the mutual impact of global commodity production and urban transformation (together with Elke Beyer, TU Berlin). From 2020–2021, she was interim professor of urban planning at BTU Cottbus-Senftenberg, and since 2021 she is guest professor of international urbanism at TU Berlin.

Daina Cheyenne Harvey

is an associate professor of sociology at the College of the Holy Cross, USA. He is the co-editor of *Beer Places* (University of Arkansas Press) and finishing up a book on the long-term aftermath of Hurricane Katrina (Bristol University Press), tentatively titled *Black Ecologies*. He is the author of over twenty-five articles and chapters. His current research project looks at how orchardists and cideries are dealing with climate change.

Will Hughes

is an experienced programme leader and lecturer who started working at Hadlow College, UK, in 2012, shortly after completing his BSc (Hons) and MRes at the University of London in physical geography. He has previous field experience working in Iceland, Sweden and the Norwegian Arctic and a particular interest in how technology can be used in conservation science as an engagement tool. He is proficient in ArcGIS and other digital mapping tools.

Maitreyi Koduganti

works as an researcher at the Indian Institute for Human Settlements. She has earned a second master's degree in water management and governance from UNESCO-IHE Institute for Water Education, the Netherlands. Her work is focused on urban sustainability, climate sciences, vulnerability studies, resource management and gender studies. Her current research looks at the impacts of urban agriculture on sustainability and wellbeing in cities.

Asia Komarova

completed the Liceo Artistico di Brera of Milan, Italy, specialising in architecture and obtained a degree in spatial design at the Escola Massana, Spain. She upgraded to a Bachelor of Arts in the Gerrit Rietveld Academie in Amsterdam, the Netherlands, and a Master of Arts at the UFF, Rio de Janeiro, Brazil. In 2013, she founded the organisation *The Outsiders*, headquartered in Utrecht, together with Txell Blanco, the Netherlands. Asia collaborates with the institution *Casco*, working for the Commons. She teaches at the Rietveld Academie in Amsterdam.

Marjorie Landels

has been a director of *Incredible Edible Lambeth*, UK, since the start and is part of its collaboration with engineering firm Arup. She is also chair of Myatts Fields Park, a pioneer park in Lambeth, where she helps run the horticulture program. She has experienced first-hand the impact of work done in the park by providing plants to the local population (last year, over 40,000 plants). Marjorie sees what can be done on a small scale and by locals and would like to take this knowledge to a wider audience.

George Lee

received a BA in architecture and sustainable design from the University of California, Berkeley, and a Master of Architecture from the University of Washington, USA. He practices architecture in Seattle, WA, and is a research asso-

ciate at the Circular City and Living Systems Lab (CCLS), focusing on GIS-based food system mapping, integrated ecology, regenerative practices and social equity in the built environment.

Howard Lee

is a lecturer in sustainable agriculture at Hadlow College (University of Greenwich). He has a history of work for applied agricultural development (e.g. plant breeding) and of field research on aspects of sustainable crop production. He is currently committed to mapping urban horticultural agroecosystems, which contribute to greater food security and enhanced wellbeing.

Nina Yiu Lai Lei

is currently living and working in the UK after managing the fashion program at the School of Communication and Design at RMIT University, Vietnam. She holds a doctorate in education (educational psychology) from the Chinese University of Hong Kong, a master's in business administration (fashion business) from the Hong Kong Polytechnic University and a BA (Hons) degree in fashion textile/design from Manchester Metropolitan University, UK. Her research interests include fashion sustainability, craftsmanship, fashion technology and flipped classroom pedagogy. Her creative design research investigates the integration between art and slow fashion as a mixed medium.

Daniel Löschenbrand

was born in Zell am See, Austria. After finishing his Master's in Architecture in 2021 at the Technical University of Vienna, he is now a PhD student researching on the *Urban Parterre*. He has study experience in Vienna, Weimar, Germany, and Paris, France, and works, in parallel to his PhD, in an architecture office.

Raphaella Mascia

holds a Master's degree in biodiversity, conservation and management from the University of Oxford and is a graduate of the College of the Holy Cross, USA. She is currently a data scientist at the Leverhulme Centre for Nature Recovery, University of Oxford, where she supports UK nature recovery efforts across agricultural landscapes. She has previously published on the topics of urban forestry & ecology and climate change discourse.

Anna-Lisa Müller

holds a PhD in human geography and is affiliated with Osnabrück University, Germany, and its Institute for Geography. She has recently published in *Cities* and is author of several monographs, including, in 2020, of *Migration, Materialität und Identität: Verortungen zwischen Hier und Dort* (Steiner).

Sheetal Patil

is a senior researcher at the Indian Institute for Human

Settlements, Bengaluru, India. Using the lens of sustainability in her research, she focuses on agrarian and related issues that range from natural resource management to food security, livelihood sustenance and institutional and policy influence. Her current research involves sustainability of urban and peri-urban agriculture, food system transformation and social innovation.

Adrian Paulsen

holds a master's degree in geography and environmental studies from the University of the Western Cape, South Africa, specialising in food security and GIS. He is also an alumni of the prestigious Mandela-Rhodes Foundation which recognises and provides resources to academically gifted leaders in Africa. He is passionate about investigating maps and people, the intersections between both and how they create new meanings. His most recent research output has focused on the lived realities of people who are classified as food insecure in the Delft area of Cape Town, South Africa.

Matthew Potteiger

is a professor of landscape architecture at the College of Environmental Science and Forestry, SUNY, Syracuse, USA. His teaching, research and community engagement is on the intersection of food and landscape – how the food we eat shapes the ecology,

public spaces and social life of our landscapes. He has worked with local farmers, market managers and other stakeholders in the food system. Currently, he is working on a community-based project for an edible ecology along a nine-mile riparian corridor in Syracuse, New York. He has studied food systems in cities in North America, Japan, Brazil, Italy and the Czech Republic.

Gundula Proksch

is a scholar, licensed architect and associate professor of architecture at the University of Washington in Seattle, USA. She is the founding director of the Circular City and Living Systems Lab, an interdisciplinary research group investigating transformative strategies for sustainable urban futures. Gundula is a principal investigator of the National Science Foundation-funded project *CITYFOOD* with partners in Germany, Sweden, Norway, the Netherlands and Brazil. Her book *Creating Urban Agricultural Systems: An Integrated Approach to Design* approaches urban agriculture from a systems perspective.

Angelika Psenner

is a professor of urban structure studies at the Institute of Urban Design and Landscape Architecture, TU Wien, Austria. Her research and teaching cover topics such as urban structures studies, urban planning, develop-

ment & design, theories on the city, urban parterre (Stadtparterre), resilience, use-neutral building structures, mobility, perception of urban space and architecture as well as 3D-modelling on an urban scale. Her work has been awarded with several academic prizes, amongst those the Hochschuljubiläumsstiftungs-Preis by the City of Vienna, a research fellowship by the International Research Center for Cultural Studies and the Dr. Maria Schaumayer research funding prize.

Paula Restrepo

is a tenured professor at the Research Group *Comunicación, periodismo y sociedad*, Faculty of Communications and Philology, Universidad de Antioquia (UdeA), Medellín, Colombia. She is an anthropologist and doctor in philosophy and also part of the urban collective Red de Huerteros Medellín (RHM). Her latest projects, in alliance with RHM, are *Prácticas comunicativas de la agricultura urbana en Medellín*, *Saberes y sabores de las semillas criollas, nativas y diversas* and the book *Prácticas sociales de la agricultura urbana en Colombia* (2022).

Bradley Rink

is a human geographer and associate professor in the Department of Geography, Environmental Studies & Tourism at the University of the Western Cape (UWC), South Africa. His research and teaching focus on a range of issues related to lives and livelihoods in cities of the Global South. His recent outputs have been published in edited collections and journals within this field, including *Geoforum*, *Mobilities*, *Transfers*, *Cities & Health* and *Contemporary Social Science*.

Stephanie Robson
is a senior consultant at global multidisciplinary engineering and design firm Arup, UK, working on climate change and resilience. She has a particular interest in shaping sustainable food systems and the role of communities in addressing the social and environmental challenges we are facing. Stephanie is continuing to work with *Incredible Edible Lambeth*, UK, on a further exploration of how to accelerate urban food growing and ensure it benefits those most in need.

Tim Rodber
is a designer and strategic thinker with a background in architecture and urban planning. Having worked in a range of award-winning architectural studios in London, he is now helping to establish a newly forming practice. He enjoys thinking, writing and eating.

Parama Roy
is a lead researcher at Okapi Research & Advisory and Adjunct Faculty at IIT-Madras, Chennai, India. She has a PhD in human geography from University of Wisconsin–Milwaukee, USA. Her research on urban transformations through community-based greening/gardening and collaborative planning processes has been published in international peer-reviewed journals like *Urban Affairs Review*, *City* and *Geoforum*. In 2019, she published the book chapter *Community gardening for integrated urban renewal in Copenhagen: Securing or denying minorities' right to the city?* in *Urban gardening and the struggles of social and spatial justice*, edited by Certoma, Noori and Sondermann.

Mariana Sanchez Salvador
is an architect and foodscape researcher from Lisbon, Portugal. Her research focuses on how spaces, from the house to the city, are transformed by food and food-related activities. Her master's thesis *Architecture and Commensality: A history of the house through foodways* (Architect Quelhas dos Santos Prize, 2015) was published in Portuguese by *Caleidoscópio* (2016), and will soon have an English version. She wrote several articles related to her PhD research on the foodscape of Lisbon and was awarded a PhD fellowship by the Foundation for Science and Technology. She currently teaches food systems at the Master's in Food Design at ESHTE Estoril (Portugal).

Gesine Tuitjer
works as a postdoc at the Thünen Institute of Rural Studies, Braunschweig, Germany. Her work focuses on questions of regional development and planning, rural economies and entrepreneurship, and female participation in the labour market. She has recently published in *Journal of Rural Studies* and *Journal of Innovation Economics & Management*.

Leonie Tuitjer
works as an assistant professor at the Research Center for Sustainability at the University of Bremen, Germany. Her work as a social geographer focuses on topics such as urban infrastructures, environmental change, mobility and refuge as well as on urban life in periods of crisis. She has recently published in *Mobilities*, *Area*, *Geography Compass* and *Social and Cultural Geography*.

Diana Tung
is a doctoral student in social anthropology at the Australian National University. She has contributed writing on her fieldwork experiences in the Peruvian Amazon to *Antipode* and *SBS Australia*. She serves as the visual editor of the *Journal of Latin American Geography* where she advises authors on visual submissions such as maps, photographs and infographics. Her research interests include interactions between society and environment, culture and place, gender, as well as economic anthropology.

André Viljoen

is a professor of architecture at the University of Brighton, UK. Since the 1990s, he has been researching the role that urban agriculture can play in shaping cities to be more sustainable and resilient. Significant publications include Bohn&Viljoen's book *CPULs Continuous Productive Urban Landscapes: Designing Urban Agriculture for Sustainable Cities* (2005) and its sequel, *Second Nature Urban Agriculture: Designing Productive Cities* (2014). André has been chair of the Association of European Schools of Planning (AESOP) Food Planning Group, and in 2015, with Katrin Bohn, won the RIBA president's "award for outstanding university-located research".

Dominic Walker

is an architect. He graduated top of class at University College London, UK (2019), and was the recipient of the Sir Banister Fletcher Medal. He has presented his research at the annual British Archaeology Conference (2019) and exhibited works at the Royal Academy (2020, 2021). He is the 2023 Rome Scholar in Architecture at the British School at Rome.

Ivonne Weichold

is an architect, lecturer and researcher at the Luxembourg Institute of Socio-Economic Research, LU. She is currently an affiliated guest lecturer at the KU Leuven, Belgium, where she is teaching design studios at master's level. In her research, she works at the intersection of urbanisation, design and geospatial analysis, focusing on the dialogue of soil fertility in spatial planning. Ivonne holds a PhD in Architecture from the University of Luxembourg and a MA in Architecture and BA in Art History from the Technical University of Berlin, Germany.

Merel Zwarts

is an artist living and working in Utrecht, the Netherlands. In her artistic practice she explores collective creation and exchange through different forms of pedagogical experiments and object making. In response to and in collaboration with different environments and communities, she creates interventions in public spaces and during performative field trips or workshops. She invites people to collectively imagine new structures and relations around ecology, agriculture and resilient living. Together with Asia Komarova and Txell Blanco, she forms artist collective *The Outsiders*. She collaborated with Casco Art Institute: Working for the Commons, BAK, Jan van Eyck Academie, Marres and Oerol Festival, among others.

Acknowledgements

Katrin Bohn and Mikey Tomkins would like, first of all, to thank our editorial board members Howard Lee, Gundula Proksch, André Viljoen, Ivonne Weichold, Ferne Edwards and Mila Brill for many enjoyable and inspiring meetings over the last two years as well as your hands-on editing contributions without which this book project would not have happened.

Thank you too to all our contributors for your invaluable contributions and the fruitful exchanges, when we asked (and reasked) for maps and texts until everything made sense and fitted the *Urban Food Mapping* story on just over 300 pages.

Thank you to Kevin Morgan who, at the very beginning, supported the conference panel *Mapping the Edible City: Making visible communities and food in the city* that Ferne Edwards and Katrin convened with André Viljoen, as well as to the conference organisers and all our panel contributors because this is where the book project started: at the 2020 RGS/RAI conference *Anthropology and Geography: Dialogues Past, Present and Future*.

We would also like to thank our production team at Routledge, especially our editors, Megha Patel and Nick Craggs, as well as producer Denise File, for their support in navigating so many chapters and images through the production process.

Thank you to Alma Bohn for rising to the challenge of helping produce an incredible draft layout that enabled us to "play" with our 225 map images, searching for their best positions and sizes.

We would also like to thank our families for their patience, especially during the time-intensive manuscript preparation months in 2022. Thank you, Lilo, Bertie, Alma, André and Hermann. Thank you, Jules, Cassia and Fabian.

We do look forward to many more urban food mapping adventures with all of you.

Janie Bickersteth and Marjorie Landels would like to thank the 800 plus members of *Incredible Edible Lambeth* for their contribution to making Lambeth a better place to live and for going some way towards making the borough more food resilient. We would also like to thank Lis Watkins for her illustrations of our walking trails and Michelle Shackleford (a fellow director of IEL) for her research.

Stephanie Robson and Joana Ferro were supported by a wider Arup team including Dima Zogheib and Niki Apostolopoulou-Maniati.

Katrin Bohn would like to acknowledge that parts of the design research for my chapter received funding from the European Union's Horizon 2020 research program under grant agreement n° 776665 (*EdiCitNet* project). Thank you to Boubaker Houman, Hayet Bayoudh, Latifa Bousselmi, Lamia Bouziri, Hanen Sbei, Karim Malki, Max Manderscheid and Milena Klimek for enriching the *CPUL Opportunity Mapping Method* with your invaluable insights, just when this chapter was written.

Marthe Derkzen, Sheetal Patil, Maitreyi Koduganti and Parama Roy's chapter benefitted from the following support: The findings narrated in story 1 are derived from the project *TURAS: Transitioning to Urban Resilience and Sustainability*, funded by the European Union's Seventh Framework Programme (FP7) under grant agreement no. 282834, and an USAID PEER grant to ATREE (Ashoka Trust for Research in Ecology and the Environment). The findings narrated in stories 2–4 are derived from the project titled *Urban and Peri-urban Agriculture as Green Infrastructure: Implications on Wellbeing and Sustainability in the Global South (Tanzania and India)*, funded by British Academy, grant no. UWB190091.

Jessica Ann Diehl's chapter is based on a Master's in Landscape Architecture community design studio conducted through the National University of Singapore in Bangalore, India. It was presented in an early format as a paper in Helsinki, Finland: Diehl, J.A., 2019. *A foodscape geo-narrative in an unplanned settlement in Bangalore, India: spatial visualization of in/formal spaces and habits*. Thanks also to the students who participated in the NUS LA4702 Studio *City*, Jan-Apr 2018: Nur Azilla Bte Nazli, Gao Chenchen, Wang Hanfeng, Fan Lei Helen, Kong Lingchang Charlie, Xu Linxin, Yong Keng-Whye Raymond, Yao Haomu Ryan, Lam Si Yun Swan, Kuan Wai Tuck Victor, Liu Xiaolei Carrie, Xu Yuexin and Wang Zhe Zoe. A special thanks to knowledgeable local English-Canadian translators David and Sumitra Bodapati, who made it possible for us to engage the residents of Hebbal, and to the residents of Hebbal, who welcomed us into their community and let us be part of their lives and daily routines for a brief five days.

Viviana Ferrario and Fabrizio D'Angelo want to thank Angelica Dal Pozzo for her valuable contribution to the research; and Pietro Caltarossa, Stefano Dissette, Marianna Fabbrizioli and Leonardo Rossi for their collaboration in the fieldwork and photo-interpretation. This research has been funded by the Università Iuav di Venezia and by the Municipality of Padua within the framework of the *Municipal Plan for Green Spaces*.

Adrian Paulsen and Bradley Rink acknowledge that the research upon which their chapter is based would not have been possible without the support of the South African National Research Foundation (NRF) and the Mandela-Rhodes Foundation. Adrian dedicates this work to his late mother, Sunette Paulsen: "*I can never thank you enough for everything you've done for me*".

Diana Tung would like to thank first and foremost the participants in the study that forms the basis for her chapter, in particular Doña Myriam Navarro Saldaña, without whom this project would not have been possible. Additional support from Francesca Merlan, Tim Denham, Caroline Schuster, Rosario Garcia, José Tumulco and Carlos Paxitao was much appreciated. This research was conducted as part of a doctoral project on the commercialisation of the aguaje and was supported by the Australian National University,

the Australian Government Research Training Program and the Australian National Center for Latin American Studies.

André Viljoen would like to acknowledge the support received from Professor Makoto Yokohari and his team at the University of Tokyo, in particular Akane Bessho who arranged a number of field trips to urban agriculture sites in Tokyo. Also the support for two field trips to Tokyo funded by Nerima City's Mayor's office, and staff in the city's urban agriculture division, and farmer Mr. Shiraishi who made the mapping described in his chapter possible.

Ivonne Weichold acknowledges that the work in her chapter formed part of her PhD study *Agroecologics. Towards a territorial, integrative agri-urban design. Luxembourg as a case study* conducted at the University of Luxembourg, Department Geography and Spatial Planning during 2017–2021.

MAPPING CONTENT

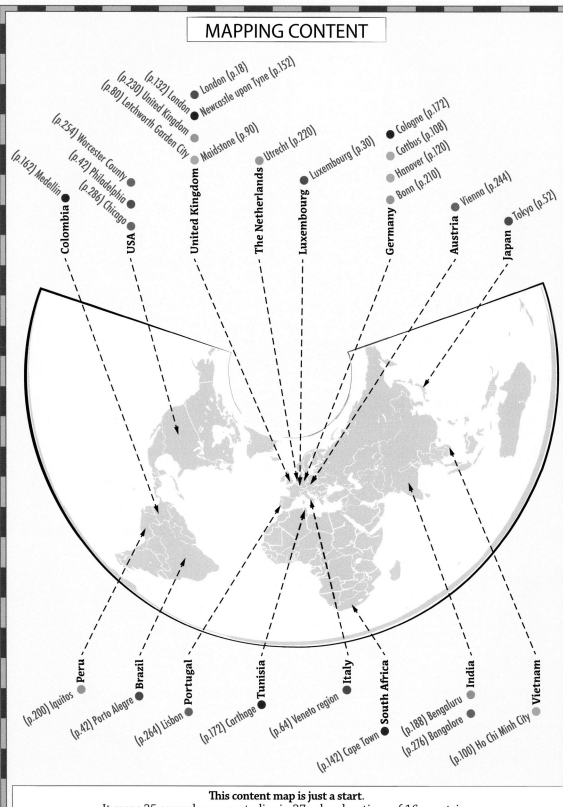

This content map is just a start.
It maps 25 exemplary case studies in 27 urban locations of 16 countries.
This first book on **Urban Food Mapping** captures a "growing movement".
Please contact us with similar projects to contribute to the growth of the subject area.

Index

Note: Page locators in *italics* indicate a figure on the corresponding page.